Children's
Literature
Review

Guide to Gale Literary Criticism Series

For criticism on	Consult these Gale series
Authors now living or who died after December 31, 1959	*CONTEMPORARY LITERARY CRITICISM (CLC)*
Authors who died between 1900 and 1959	*TWENTIETH-CENTURY LITERARY CRITICISM (TCLC)*
Authors who died between 1800 and 1899	*NINETEENTH-CENTURY LITERATURE CRITICISM (NCLC)*
Authors who died between 1400 and 1799	*LITERATURE CRITICISM FROM 1400 TO 1800 (LC)* *SHAKESPEAREAN CRITICISM (SC)*
Authors who died before 1400	*CLASSICAL AND MEDIEVAL LITERATURE CRITICISM (CMLC)*
Black writers of the past two hundred years	*BLACK LITERATURE CRITICISM (BLC) AND BLACK LITERATURE CRITICISM SUPPLEMENT (BLCS)*
Authors of books for children and young adults	*CHILDREN'S LITERATURE REVIEW (CLR)*
Dramatists	*DRAMA CRITICISM (DC)*
Hispanic writers of the late nineteenth and twentieth centuries	*HISPANIC LITERATURE CRITICISM (HLC)*
Native North American writers and orators of the eighteenth, nineteenth, and twentieth centuries	*NATIVE NORTH AMERICAN LITERATURE (NNAL)*
Poets	*POETRY CRITICISM (PC)*
Short story writers	*SHORT STORY CRITICISM (SSC)*
Major authors from the Renaissance to the present	*WORLD LITERATURE CRITICISM, 1500 TO THE PRESENT (WLC)*
Major authors and works from the Bible to the present	*WORLD LITERATURE CRITICISM SUPPLEMENT (WLCS)*

ISSN 0362-4145

volume 61

Children's Literature Review

Excerpts from Reviews,
Criticism, and Commentary
on Books for Children
and Young People

Deborah J. Morad
Michelle Lee
Editors

GALE GROUP

Detroit
New York
San Francisco
London
Boston
Woodbridge, CT

STAFF

Deborah J. Morad and Michelle Lee, *Editors*

Elisabeth Gellert and Arlene M. Johnson, *Associate Editors*

Sara Constantakis, Motoko Fujishiro Huthwaite, Tom Schoenberg, Erin E. White, *Contributing Editors*

Tim White, *Technical Training Specialist*

Joyce Nakamura, *Managing Editor*

Maria Franklin, *Permissions Manager*
Sarah Tomasek, Edna Hedblad, *Permissions Associates*

Victoria B. Cariappa, *Research Manager*
Corrine A. Boland, *Project Coordinator*
Andrew Guy Malonis, Gary J. Oudersluys, Cheryl D. Warnock, *Research Specialists*
Tamara C. Nott, Tracie A. Richardson, *Research Associates*
Phyllis J. Blackman, Tim Lehnerer, *Research Assistants*

Mary Beth Trimper, *Production Director*
Stacy Melson, *Production Assistant*

Michael Logusz, *Graphic Artist*
Randy Bassett, *Image Database Supervisor*
Robert Duncan, *Imaging Specialists*
Pamela A. Reed, *Imaging Coordinator*

The paper used in this publication meets the minimum requirements of the American National Standard for Information Sciences—Permanence Paper for Printed Library Materials, ANSI Z39.48-1984.

Library of Congress Catalog Card Number 76-643301
ISBN 0-7876-3226-0
ISSN 0362-4145
Printed in the United States of America

10   9   8   7   6   5   4   3   2   1

Contents

Preface   vii
Acknowledgments   xi

Preface

Literature for children and young adults has evolved into both a respected branch of creative writing and a successful industry. Currently, books for young readers are considered among the most popular segments of publishing. Criticism of juvenile literature is instrumental in recording the literary or artistic development of the creators of children's books as well as the trends and controversies that result from changing values or attitudes about young people and their literature. Designed to provide a permanent, accessible record of this ongoing scholarship, *Children's Literature Review (CLR)* presents parents, teachers, and librarians—those responsible for bringing children and books together—with the opportunity to make informed choices when selecting reading materials for the young. In addition, *CLR* provides researchers of children's literature with easy access to a wide variety of critical information from English-language sources in the field. Users will find balanced overviews of the careers of the authors and illustrators of the books that children and young adults are reading; these entries, which contain excerpts from published criticism in books and periodicals, assist users by sparking ideas for papers and assignments and suggesting supplementary and classroom reading. Ann L. Kalkhoff, president and editor of *Children's Book Review Service Inc.,* writes that "CLR has filled a gap in the field of children's books, and it is one series that will never lose its validity or importance."

Scope of the Series

Each volume of *CLR* profiles the careers of a selection of authors and illustrators of books for children and young adults from preschool through high school. Author lists in each volume reflect:

- an international scope.

- representation of authors of all eras.

- the variety of genres covered by children's and/or YA literature: picture books, fiction, nonfiction, poetry, folklore, and drama.

Although the focus of the series is on authors new to *CLR*, entries will be updated as the need arises.

Organization of This Book

An entry consists of the following elements: author heading, author portrait, author introduction, excerpts of criticism (each preceded by a bibliographical citation), and illustrations, when available.

- The **Author Heading** consists of the author's name followed by birth and death dates. The portion of the name outside the parentheses denotes the form under which the author is most frequently published. If the majority of the author's works for children were written under a pseudonym, the pseudonym will be listed in the author heading and the real name given on the first line of the author introduction. Also located at the beginning of the introduction are any other pseudonyms used by the author in writing for children and any name variations, including transliterated forms for authors whose languages use nonroman alphabets. Uncertainty as to a birth or death date is indicated by question marks.

- An **Author Portrait** is included when available.

- The **Author Introduction** contains information designed to introduce an author to *CLR* users by presenting an overview of the author's themes and styles, biographical facts that relate to the author's literary career or critical responses to the author's works, and information about major awards and prizes the author has received. The introduction begins by identifying the nationality of the author and by listing the genres in which s/he has written for children and young adults. Introductions also list a group of representative titles for which the author or illustrator being profiled is best known; this section, which begins with the words "major works include," follows the genre line of the introduction. For seminal figures, a listing of major works about the author follows when appropriate, highlighting important biographies about the author or illustrator that are not excerpted in the entry. The centered heading "Introduction" announces the body of the text.

- **Criticism** is located in three sections: **Author's Commentary** (when available), **General Commentary** (when available), and **Title Commentary** (commentary on specific titles).

    - The **Author's Commentary** presents background material written by the author or by an interviewer. This commentary may cover a specific work or several works. Author's commentary on more than one work appears after the author introduction, while commentary on an individual book follows the title entry heading.

    - The **General Commentary** consists of critical excerpts that consider more than one work by the author or illustrator being profiled. General commentary is preceded by the critic's name in boldface type or, in the case of unsigned criticism, by the title of the journal. *CLR* also features entries that emphasize general criticism on the oeuvre of an author or illustrator. When appropriate, a selection of reviews is included to supplement the general commentary.

    - The **Title Commentary** begins with the title entry headings, which precede the criticism on a title and cite publication information on the work being reviewed. Title headings list the title of the work as it appeared in its first English-language edition. The first English-language publication date of each work (unless otherwise noted) is listed in parentheses following the title. Differing U.S. and British titles follow the publication date within the parentheses. When a work is written by an individual other than the one being profiled, as is the case when illustrators are featured, the parenthetical material following the title cites the author of the work before listing its publication date.

      Entries in each title commentary section consist of critical excerpts on the author's individual works, arranged chronologically by publication date. The entries generally contain two to seven reviews per title, depending on the stature of the book and the amount of criticism it has generated. The editors select titles that reflect the entire scope of the author's literary contribution, covering each genre and subject. An effort is made to reprint criticism that represents the full range of each title's reception, from the year of its initial publication to current assessments. Thus, the reader is provided with a record of the author's critical history. Publication information (such as publisher names and book prices) and parenthetical numerical references (such as footnotes or page and line references to specific editions of works) have been deleted at the discretion of the editors to provide smoother reading of the text.

- Centered headings introduce each section, in which criticism is arranged chronologically; beginning with Volume 35, each excerpt is preceded by a boldface source heading for easier access by readers. Within the text, titles by authors being profiled are also highlighted in boldface type.

- Selected excerpts are preceded by **Explanatory Annotations**, which provide information on the critic or work of criticism to enhance the reader's understanding of the excerpt.

- A complete **Bibliographical Citation** designed to facilitate the location of the original book or article precedes each piece of criticism.

- Numerous **Illustrations** are featured in *CLR*. For entries on illustrators, an effort has been made to include illustrations that reflect the characteristics discussed in the criticism. Entries on authors who do not illustrate their own works may also include photographs and other illustrative material pertinent to their careers.

Special Features: Entries on Illustrators

Entries on authors who are also illustrators will occasionally feature commentary on selected works illustrated but not written by the author being profiled. These works are strongly associated with the illustrator and have received critical acclaim for their art. By including critical comment on works of this type, the editors wish to provide a more complete representation of the artist's career. Criticism on these works has been chosen to stress artistic, rather than literary, contributions. Title entry headings for works illustrated by the author being profiled are arranged chronologically within the entry by date of publication and include notes identifying the author of the illustrated work. In order to provide easier access for users, all titles illustrated by the subject of the entry are boldfaced.

CLR also includes entries on prominent illustrators who have contributed to the field of children's literature. These entries are designed to represent the development of the illustrator as an artist rather than as a literary stylist. The illustrator's section is organized like that of an author, with two exceptions: the introduction presents an overview of the illustrator's styles and techniques rather than outlining his or her literary background, and the commentary written by the illustrator on his or her works is called "illustrator's commentary" rather than "author's commentary." All titles of books containing illustrations by the artist being profiled are highlighted in boldface type.

Other Features: Acknowledgments, Indexes

■ The **Acknowledgments** section, which immediately follows the preface, lists the sources from which material has been reprinted in the volume. It does not, however, list every book or periodical consulted for the volume.

■ The **Cumulative Index to Authors** lists all of the authors who have appeared in *CLR* with cross-references to the biographical, autobiographical, and literary criticism series published by The Gale Group. A full listing of the series titles appears before the first page of the indexes of this volume.

■ The **Cumulative Index to Nationalities** lists authors alphabetically under their respective nationalities. Author names are followed by the volume number(s) in which they appear.

■ The **Cumulative Index to Titles** lists titles covered in *CLR* followed by the volume and page number where criticism begins.

A Note to the Reader

CLR is one of several critical references sources in the Literature Criticism Series published by The Gale Group. When writing papers, students who quote directly from any volume in the Literature Criticism Series may use the following general forms to footnote reprinted criticism. The first example pertains to material drawn from periodicals, the second to material reprinted from books.

¹T. S. Eliot, "John Donne," *The Nation and the Athenaeum*, 33 (9 June 1923), 321-32; excerpted and reprinted in *Literature Criticism from 1400 to 1800*, Vol. 10, ed. James E. Person, Jr. (Detroit: Gale Research, 1989), pp. 28-9.

¹Henry Brooke, *Leslie Brooke and Johnny Crow* (Frederick Warne, 1982); excerpted and reprinted in *Children's Literature Review*, Vol. 20, ed. Gerard J. Senick (Detroit: Gale Research, 1990), p. 47.

Suggestions Are Welcome

In response to various suggestions, several features have been added to *CLR* since the beginning of the series, including author entries on retellers of traditional literature as well as those who have been the first to record oral tales and other folklore; entries on prominent illustrators featuring commentary on their styles and techniques; entries on authors whose works are considered controversial; occasional entries devoted to criticism on a single work or a series of works; sections in author introductions that list major works by and about the author or illustrator being profiled; explanatory notes that provide information on the critic or work of criticism to enhance the usefulness of the excerpt; more extensive illustrative material, such as holographs of manuscript pages and photographs of people and places pertinent to the careers of the authors and artists; a cumulative nationality index for easy access to authors by nationality; and occasional guest essays written specifically for *CLR* by prominent critics on subjects of their choice.

Readers who wish to suggest authors to appear in future volumes, or who have other suggestions, are cordially invited to contact the editor. By mail: Editor, *Children's Literature Review,* The Gale Group, 27500 Drake Road, Farmington Hills, MI 48331-3535; by telephone: (800) 347-GALE, (248) 699-4253; by fax: (248) 699-8065.

Acknowledgments

The editors wish to thank the copyright holders of the excerpted criticism included in this volume and the permissions managers of many book and magazine publishing companies for assisting us in securing reproduction rights. We are also grateful to the staffs of the Detroit Public Library, the Library of Congress, the University of Detroit Mercy Library, Wayne State University Purdy/Kresge Library Complex, and the University of Michigan Libraries for making their resources available to us. Following is a list of the copyright holders who have granted us permission to reproduce material in this volume of *CLR*. Every effort has been made to trace copyright, but if omissions have been made, please let us know.

Appraisal: Science Books for Young People, v. 14, Winter, 1981; v. 15, Spring-Summer, 1982; v. 16, Fall, 1983; v. 17, Winter, 1984; v. 18, Summer, 1985; v. 18, Autumn, 1985; v. 20, Spring, 1987; v. 20, Winter, 1987; v. 21, Spring, 1988; v. 21, Winter, 1988; v. 22, Autumn, 1989; v. 22, Summer, 1989; v. 22, Winter & Spring, 1989; v. 23, Summer, 1990; v. 23, Winter, 1990; v. 24, Spring-Summer, 1991; v. 24, Autumn, 1991; v. 24, Winter, 1991; v. 25, Spring, 1992; v. 28, Spring-Summer, 1995; v. 28, Winter, 1995. Copyright © 1981, 1982, 1983, 1984, 1985, 1987, 1988, 1989, 1990, 1991, 1992, 1995 by the Children's Science Book Review Committee. All reproduced by permission.—*The Antioch Review,* v. XVIII, March 1958 for *"Robinson Crusoe:* The Man Alone" by Harvey Swados. Copyright © 1958 by the Antioch Review Inc. Reproduced by permission of the author.—*Armchair Detective,* v. 15, 1982. Copyright © 1982 by The Armchair Detective. Reproduced by permission.—*The Atlantic,* v. 267, June, 1991 for "Starting Over: The Same Old Stories" by Cullen Murphy. Reproduced by permission.—*Australian Book Review,* January, 1995; June, 1995; August, 1995; April, 1998. All reproduced by permission.—*Black Enterprise,* v. 23, June, 1993. Copyright June, 1993, by Earl G. Graves Publishing Co. Inc., New York, NY. All rights reserved. Reprinted by permission of the publisher.—*Bookbird,* 1981. Reproduced by permission of the publisher.—*The Book Report,* v. 6, January-February, 1988; v. 9, March-April, 1991; v. 10, September-October, 1991. © copyright 1988, 1991 by Linworth Publishing, Inc., Worthington, Ohio. All reproduced by permission.—*Booklist,* v. 76, February 15, 1980; v. 77, January 1, 1981; v. 77, May 15, 1981; v. 78, February 15, 1982; v. 79, December 1, 1982; v. 79, January 15, 1983; v. 84, April 15, 1984; v. 80, August, 1984; v. 81, April 1, 1985; v. 81, November 1, 1985; v. 82, November 1, 1985; v. 82, December 15, 1985; v. 83, December 15, 1986; v. 83, January 15, 1987; v. 83, February 11, 1987; v. 84, July, 1988; v. 85, November 1, 1988; v. 85, May 15, 1989; v. 85, June 15, 1989; v. 86, September 1, 1989; v. 86, March 15, 1990; v. 86, April 15, 1990; v. 87, November 15, 1990; v. 87, January 15, 1991; v. 87, February 1, 1991; v. 87, April 15, 1991; v. 87, August, 1991; v. 88, October 1, 1991; v. 88, January 1, 1992; v. 88, May 1, 1992; v. 89, October 1, 1992; v. 89, December 15, 1992; v. 89, April 15, 1993; v. 89, July, 1993; v. 91, December 15, 1994; v. 92, September 15, 1995; v. 92, February 15, 1996; v. 92, July, 1996; v. 93, March 15, 1997; v. 93, June 1 & 15, 1997; v. 94, September 15, 1997; v. 95, September 15, 1998; v. 95, October 1, 1998; v. 95, March 1, 1999. Copyright © 1980, 1981, 1982, 1983, 1984, 1985, 1986, 1987, 1988, 1989, 1990, 1991, 1992, 1993, 1994, 1995, 1996, 1997, 1998, 1999 by the American Library Association. All reproduced by permission.—*Books for Keeps,* January, 1991; March, 1993. © School Bookshop Association 1991, 1993. Both reproduced by permission.—*Books for Your Children,* v. 21, Summer, 1986. © *Books for Your Children* 1986. Reproduced by permission.—*Books in Canada,* v. XXIII, February, 1994 for "Portraits of the Past" by Frieda Wishinsky. Reproduced by permission of the author.—*Bulletin for the Center of Children's Books,* v. 34, January, 1981; v. 35, September, 1981; v. 37, June, 1984; v. 38, March, 1985; v. 40, November, 1986; v. 40, March, 1987; v. 40, June, 1987; v. 42, October, 1988; v. 43, December, 1989; v. 43, May, 1990; v. 43, June, 1990; v. 43, July-August, 1990; v. 44, January, 1991. Copyright © 1981, 1984, 1985, 1986, 1987, 1988, 1989, 1990, 1991 by The University of Chicago. / v. 46, January, 1993; v. 46, April, 1993; v. 47, February, 1994; v. 48, December, 1994; v. 49, January, 1996; v. 49, May, 1996; v. 50, April, 1997. Copyright © 1993, 1994, 1996, 1997 by The Board of Trustees of the University of Illinois. All reproduced by permission.—*Canadian Book Review Annual,* 1996, 1997. Both reproduced by permission.—*Canadian Children's Literature,* 1980, 1992, 1995, 1997. Copyright © 1980, 1992, 1995, 1997 Canadian Children's Press. All reproduced by permission.—*Canadian Materials,* v. XX, May, 1992 for a review of *Prince Ivan and the Firebird* by Marion Scott / v. XXII, May, 1994 for a review of *East of the Sun and West of the Moon* by Gillian Martin Noonan. Both reproduced by permission of the author.—*Catholic Library World,* v. 41, January, 1970; v. 59, September-October, 1987. Both reproduced by permission.—*Children's Book Review Service,* v. 15, Spring, 1987; v. 15, July, 1987. Copyright 1987 Children's Book Review Service Inc. Both reproduced by permission.—*Children's Literature Association Quarterly,* v. 18, Spring, 1993. Reproduced by permission.—*Children's Literature in Education,* v. 8, Spring, 1977 for *Robinson Crusoe* by Barbara Hardy. © 1977, Agathon Press, Inc. Reproduced by permission of the publisher and the author.—*Christian Science Monitor,* v. 74, November 17, 1982. © 1982 The Christian Science Publishing Society. All rights reserved. Reproduced by permission from *The Christian Science Monitor;* v. 82, February 21, 1990 for a review of *Justin and the Best Biscuits in the World* by Heather Vogel Frederick. © 1990 The Christian Science Publishing Society. All rights reserved. Reproduced by permission of the author.—*Emergency Librarian,* v. 19, March-April, 1992. Reproduced by permission.—*Esquire,* v. 105, June, 1986 for "Hale and Hardy" by Jonathon Cott. Copyright

COPYRIGHTED MATERIAL IN *CLR,* VOLUME 61, WERE REPRODUCED FROM THE FOLLOWING BOOKS:

Company. Reproduced by permission.—Sutherland, Zena. From *Children & Books, Ninth Edition.* Longman, 1997. Copyright © 1997 Addison-Wesley Educational Publishers Inc. Reproduced by permission of Addison Wesley Longman, Inc.—Watt, Ian. From *The Rise of the Novel: Studies in Defoe, Richardson and Fielding.* University of California Press, 1967. Reproduced by permission.

PHOTOGRAPHS AND ILLUSTRATIONS APPEARING IN *CLR,* VOLUME 61, WERE RECEIVED FROM THE FOLLOWING SOURCES:

Children's
Literature
Review

Caroline Arnold

1944-

American author and illustrator of nonfiction and fiction.

Major works include *Saving the Peregrine Falcon* (1985), *Koala* (1987), *Trapped in Tar: Fossils from the Ice Age* (1987), *A Walk on the Great Barrier Reef* (1987), *The Ancient Cliff Dwellers of Mesa Verde* (1992).

INTRODUCTION

The author of more than one hundred titles, Arnold is best known for her books on science and nature for primary and middle graders. Her books about natural environments have encouraged young readers to imagine visiting such places as the desert, the woods, the seashore, and a coral reef. She also has discussed medical issues, such as heart disease and weight control, for slightly older readers. Arnold's own interests in archaeology and paleontology are evident in her books about dinosaur discoveries, ice age animals, and ancient settlements in Mexico, Scotland, and the United States. Additionally, she has collaborated with photographer Richard Hewett on more than twenty portraits of animals, tracing their history and noting their place within the environment, including ways the animals are threatened by humans. The author has been praised for her straightforward style in presenting complicated materials to children, and for keeping her style simple while providing accurate information. "Lucid, concise, and helpful," is how Elaine Goldberg describes Arnold's work, and Nancy Palmer calls the author's writing "cohesive, interesting, lucid." Arnold has used this clarity of prose to explain such complicated subjects as genetics, the El Niño weather pattern, and pain. She is also known for her honest treatment of potentially disturbing or sentimental subjects. *Pets without Homes* (1983), for example, takes readers inside an animal shelter and sensitively but directly acknowledges that animals must routinely be killed; *What We Do When Someone Dies* (1987) describes embalming, burial, and cremation practices.

Critics have noted Arnold's excitement about her subjects; Richard C. Riis called *Trapped in Tar: Fossils from the Ice Age* "a clear, enthusiastic text." She has been praised for her innovative approaches to her subjects, transforming dry scientific facts into topics children can become engaged in and excited by. In a review of *Who Keeps Us Healthy?* (1982), Diane Holzheimer wrote, "Ms. Arnold has approached her topic with imagination and sensitivity, and has turned what could have been a merely utilitarian item into a book which can stretch the minds of its readers. . . . " Arnold's books on dinosaurs, for example, introduce their subjects by presenting a picture of the scientists who study the prehistoric creatures, the

tools used in unearthing the fossils, and the sites where remains have been found. The "Animal Favorites" series, too, shows an innovative streak: the books examine individual animals in zoos or wildlife parks, follow the activities of the animals in captivity, and explain what life is like in the wild. Arnold also has been commended for her environmentalist stance, with books about recovering California condors from near-extinction, and the delicate balance of the Great Barrier Reef.

Biographical Information

Arnold grew up in Minneapolis, Minnesota, with a love for both reading and nature. She fondly remembers trips to the library and long afternoons of reading at nearby lakes. Her family spent part of each summer vacationing at a camp in northern Wisconsin. Arnold wrote in *Something about the Author (SATA)*, "It was at Camp Bovey that I first began to love the outdoors, and my experiences there are probably among the most important early influences on my writing." The author's early exploration and discoveries in those northern woods also influenced her books for children, promoting a sense of adventure and discovery. She told *SATA* that she remembers the "sense of excitement that we shared when we spied a deer or uncovered a fossil of an ancient sea creature. . . . As I write about animals, dinosaur bones and other scientific subjects, my goal is to convey that same sense of discovery."

Another experience that shaped Arnold's writing was the four months she spent living in Uganda in 1971. While her husband, Art Arnold, conducted a research experiment, she spent time traveling and keeping house in the students' rough quarters. It was there that Arnold was first able to closely observe wild animals in their natural habitat, experiences she would later reproduce in books such as the "Animal Favorites" series.

Though a lifelong reader, Arnold did not consider becoming a writer until she had completed her education as an art student. She studied art and literature at Grinnell College in Iowa, and received a master's degree in art from the University of Iowa. Arnold taught art to children and worked as a substitute teacher and secretary for a number of years before illustrating books for children. She began writing stories to accompany her drawings, and eventually realized her keen interest in writing nonfiction. Arnold then began to write in earnest, focusing on nature and science subjects. Her first book, *Five Nests* (1980), was inspired by conversations the author had with her husband, whose research frequently involved the study of bird behavior.

Major Works

In *Koala*, the first book in Morrow's "Animal Favorites" series, Arnold focuses on Frangipani, a female koala living in the Lone Pine Koala Sanctuary in Australia. Arnold follows the life of Frangipani and her newborn daughter Karen, describing the life cycles of the animals, including what they eat and where they live. She also describes the obstacles that the koalas face, and presents information on the efforts of the sanctuary to protect the animals and their environment. The rest of the more than twenty books in this series—including *Kangaroo* (1987), *Cheetah* (1989), *Camel* (1992), and *Bat* (1996)—follow a similar format. Another of Arnold's series, "Nature Watch," is published by Carolrhoda. Her book *A Walk on the Great Barrier Reef*, with photographs by her husband Art Arnold, illustrates the very delicate balance needed for a coral reef to survive. The unique creatures of the reef are introduced through the photographs and text, and scientific facts about the formation and development of the reef are woven throughout the book. Other books in this series include *Watching Desert Wildlife* (1994) and *Ostriches and Other Flightless Birds* (1990).

In books such as *Saving the Peregrine Falcon* and *On the Brink of Extinction: The California Condor* (1993), Arnold describes the work of conservationists in keeping endangered birds from disappearing from the earth. *Saving the Peregrine Falcon*, with photographs by Richard Hewett, describes the Santa Cruz Predatory Bird Re-

search Group's efforts to rebuild the peregrine population in the United States. The book shows scientists hatching peregrine eggs, caring for the chicks, and releasing the birds to the wild, while explaining the environmental problem that endangered the birds in the first place. *On the Brink of Extinction* also traces the comeback of a threatened species, the California condor. In 1986 there were only two known condors left in the world. Arnold's book—photographed by Michael Wallace, founder of the California condor release program—provides an up-close look at the birds, their thousands of years of natural history, and their slow recovery. Arnold highlights the work of scientists in other books as well, such as *Trapped in Tar: Fossils from the Ice Age*. This book describes the discovery of the La Brea tar pits in Southern California, and the work of the George C. Page Museum in recovering and analyzing the animal remains found in the pits. In *Dinosaur Mountain: Graveyard of the Past* (1989) Arnold describes the work of the scientists at the Dinosaur National Monument in Jensen, Utah, the tools they use, and the techniques they have developed to discover and preserve dinosaur bones. Readers also learn about the ten kinds of dinosaurs found at the site, and are informed that children can participate in the hunt: young people are issued dinosaur hunting licenses and are encouraged to join in the search.

Another topic Arnold has written about is archaeology. She invites the reader to come with her on excursions of discovery, exploring the ruins of past civilizations, the techniques used to link the clues together, and theories about the people who once inhabited the places she visits. *The Ancient Cliff Dwellers of Mesa Verde* is about the Anasazi, a group of people who once lived in the pueblos that still stand in the southwestern corner of Colorado. Arnold explores theories about what may have happened to this ancient people, and the tools used by the archaeologists to study the artifacts they left behind. Similarly, *City of the Gods: Mexico's Ancient City of Teotihuacán* (1994) speculates on the purpose of the spectacular buildings erected before the Aztecs arrived; *Stone Age Farmers beside the Sea: Scotland's Prehistoric Village of Skara Brae* (1997) is a study of the village of Skara Brae, a farming community in Scotland that was abandoned in 2500 B.C., buried by sand, and rediscovered after a storm in 1850.

Awards

Arnold has been the recipient of many awards and citations. *Saving the Peregrine Falcon* was named the Children's Editors' Choice by *Booklist*, the Best Book Selection by *School Library Journal*, and a Notable Book selection by the American Library Association, all in 1985. In 1994 *Koala* won the Best Children's Books and Films selection by the American Academy of Arts and Sciences and Favorite Paperbacks selection by IRA/CBC. *Trapped in Tar: Fossils from the Ice Age* received a Children's Science Book Award Honorable Mention from the New York Academy of Science, a Best Children's Books and Films selection from the American Academy of Arts and

Sciences, and a *Junior Library Guild* Book selection, all in 1987. Arnold received a John Burroughs Nature Book Award, and the Best Children's Books and Films selection by the American Academy of Arts and Sciences, both for *A Walk on the Great Barrier Reef. The Ancient Cliff Dwellers of Mesa Verde* won a Best Book Selection by *School Library Journal* and a *Junior Library Guild* Book selection in 1992. More than twenty of Arnold's books have been awarded Outstanding Science Trade Book citations by the National Science Teachers Association–Children's Book Council Joint Committee, including *Rhino* in 1996, *Bat* in 1997, and *Hawk Highway in the Sky: Watching Raptor Migration* in 1998.

GENERAL COMMENTARY

Karen Jameyson

SOURCE: A review of *Kangaroo* and *Koala,* in *The Horn Book Magazine,* Vol. LXIII, No. 3, May-June, 1987, pp. 354-55.

Among the titles in the recent ripple of books concerning the Land Down Under are two attractive new volumes by the author and photographer team that produced **Saving the Peregrine Falcon** and **Pets without Homes.** Both **Kangaroo** and **Koala** concentrate on one specific animal, using it to make generalizations about the diet, reproduction, locomotion, and physical characteristics of the species. Able to leap "forty-four feet in a single bound," capable of moving forty miles per hour on its own two feet—the kangaroo has always been a subject of endless fascination. Vivid descriptions, such as "when entering the pouch, a joey dives in headfirst and then somersaults to turn itself around," enhance the writing, as do the copious photographs. They range from action shots of leaping kangaroos to an impressive closeup of a tiny, glistening joey newly arrived in its mother's pouch. In the second volume koalas, looking "more like stuffed toys than live animals," receive an equally thorough treatment. Whether they're moving "nimbly among the branches" or munching contentedly on their favorite snack of eucalyptus leaves, these endangered animals manage to look absolutely captivating. Informative, handsome treatments of two perennially popular marsupials.

Miriam Schlein

SOURCE: A review of *Zebra* and *Giraffe,* in *Appraisal: Science Books for Young People,* Vol. 21, No. 2, Spring, 1988, pp. 7-9.

SPECIALIST: Two new books by writer/photographer team Arnold and Hewett; their generic titles tell us their subjects. (I like generic titles.) Most of the full-color photographs for both books are taken at Six Flags Great

Adventure Safari Park in Jackson, New Jersey. In *Zebra* we follow the growth of Punda, a new baby zebra at the animal park. *Giraffe* is more giraffe-generalized; at the end of the book a baby giraffe is born. In both, the text is precise and workmanlike, weaving in and out between life at the animal park and pertinent facts-of-zebra-and-giraffe-life in the wild.

Nancy R. Spence

SOURCE: A review of *Zebra* and *Giraffe,* in *Appraisal: Science Books for Young People,* Vol. 21, No. 2, Spring, 1988, pp. 7-9.

LIBRARIAN: Author Caroline Arnold and photographer Richard Hewett have collaborated once again, this time offering the reader two excellent books on animals native to the African plains. *Zebra* and *Giraffe* join previously published photo-essays: *Koala* and *Kangaroo.* Each book is a close-up look at the life and behavior of a particular animal species in captivity and in the wild. The focus is on an individual born in the Six Flags Great Adventure Safari Park in Jackson, New Jersey with similarities and differences noted with regard to its relatives living in Africa. The text in each book is interesting, reads well, and is appropriate for this age group. . . . [The] beautiful pictures creatively complement and extend the text. Each book has an easy to use index with photographs listed in boldface.

There has always been a fascination with zebras—striped horses. Are they white animals with black stripes or black animals with white stripes? *Zebra* answers this question while offering possible reasons for the stripes and the marked variation in the striping. A zebra is as identifiable by its markings as is a human by his fingerprints. These differentiations are clearly and imaginatively illustrated by Richard Hewett's photographs. Caroline Arnold chronicles the life of Punda, the new born zebra in the Safari Park by including the routines of daily living, growth, play, availability of food and water, predators, protection of the young and mating. She also discusses the historical interest in the zebra and notes the three extant species, including the several subspecies of one. She also cautions the reader on the necessity of protection of the zebra and its land.

As in *Zebra,* the giraffe of *Giraffe* on the title page seems to be inviting the reader into his world. In fact he almost seems to be verbally asking. This time we follow the activities of Easter, a giraffe calf, so named because he was born on Easter morning. Again there is the perfect combination of text and photographs. Giraffes, too, are identifiable by their markings. . . .

Dawn Amsberry

A review of *Sleepytime for Zoo Animals* and *Splashtime for Zoo Animals*, in *School Library Journal*, Vol. 45, No. 8, August, 1999, p. 143.

With appealing covers, large type, and bright photographs of adorable animals, these books are bound to please. On each left-hand page, a short sentence describes a zoo animal's sleeping or water-related behavior, which is then illustrated in the photo on the right. Children will recognize many of the animals, though a few may be unfamiliar (crested crane, ibex). *Sleepytime* captures the quieter side of zoo life with pictures of a koala sleeping on its mother's back and flamingos dozing standing up, while *Splashtime* captures animals in their more playful moments, showing tigers playing ball and polar bears boxing. The books will be a hit with the preschool storytime crowd, who will enjoy guessing the names of the animals pictured. Although the texts include some difficult words (orangutan, rhinoceros), most of the vocabulary is simple enough for beginning readers. Primarily enjoyable for their beautiful photographs, these books also provide basic information on animal behavior and help fill the need for easy nonfiction.

TITLE COMMENTARY

📖 *FIVE NESTS* (1980)

Kirkus Reviews

SOURCE: A review of *Five Nests,* in *Kirkus Reviews,* Vol. XLVIII, No. 13, July 1, 1980, p. 835.

The pictures [by Ruth Sanderson] are black and white with a little green for the background foliage, and that's unfortunate to start with, considering that the opening double pages show the nests and then the females ("The mother bird is called a female") and males ("The father bird is called a male") of five different species: robin, cowbird, Mexican jay, rhea, and redwing blackbird. The writing proves as colorless, though the lesson, in the common needs of baby birds and the diversity of parenting patterns that meet them, is a good one. With robins, readers learn, both parents care for the young; the father blackbird does not help at all but does protect his many nests; the father rhea makes the nest and hatches the eggs that his herd of females lays there; the older young help Mexican jay parents care for their babies; and the cowbird dumps her eggs on other parent birds. ("The other birds do a good job.") The message is clear, the points worth making. If only it didn't seem so dull.

Karen Ritter

SOURCE: A review of *Five Nests,* in *School Library Journal,* Vol. 27, No. 1, September, 1980, p. 56.

Once eggs are laid, the manner in which they are hatched and the baby birds cared for and raised varies from one species to another. Sometimes, both the male and female take care of the young, sometimes only the female or the male, and occasionally neither male nor female will take the responsibility—cowbirds, for example. In choppy primerese, the differences in parenting among five birds—robin, red-wing blackbird, Mexican jay, rhea, and cowbird—who represent as many different styles of raising young, are described. The male rhea (a South American ostrich-like bird) incubates and hatches all the eggs from his herd of females, hardly a familiar sight in the average child's backyard. The sentences are not only choppy but repetitious, lacking the smooth flow that characterizes *A Nest of Wood Ducks* by Evelyn Shaw, which demonstrates that factual information can be put into easy-reader format with some grace and style. At least one major omission is the fact that the cowbird nestling almost always kills its host's young in the fierce competition for food—an example of the author's euphemistic (and often anthropomorphic) approach.

Yvonne H. Burry

SOURCE: A review of *Five Nests,* in *Science Books & Films,* Vol. 16, No. 3, January-February, 1981, p. 155.

Arnold describes how different species of birds have adapted to fostering their young. From robin to rhea, carefully presented drawings illustrate such topics as nest configuration, and number and size of eggs. Physical differences in the male and female birds are also nicely differentiated. Although most youngsters have had the opportunity to observe nesting birds, few realize that egg tending and education of the baby birds is an activity not exclusively relegated to the mother bird. In this book, they will discover that the protocol of nesting habits varies greatly. Certainly a new level of awareness of bird habits will result from reading this book. The book's only drawback is that some species are discussed more fully than others, thus leaving the reader waiting for just a bit more information about some of the inhabitants of the *Five Nests.*

📖 *ELECTRIC FISH* (1980)

Lee Jeffers

SOURCE: A review of *Electric Fish,* in *Appraisal: Science Books for Young People,* Vol. 14, No. 1, Winter, 1981, pp. 10-11.

LIBRARIAN: Electricity as a sixth sense in fish such as the electric eel and catfish, the Nile fish and the snout fish, is the subject of Caroline Arnold's fascinating book. This ability to transmit and receive electric signals is unique in the animal world, manifested differently in different fish: some, like the eel, have large electric organs used mainly for predation; others, like the paddlefish, have electric receptors with which to navigate and locate food, as well as for defense; still others, like the Nile fish, have weak electric organs which are never turned off, and are used for electrolocation and communication.

In addition to being logically organized according to these categories, the book contains a table of contents and a comprehensive index. Arnold's lucid, succinct prose is enhanced by George Gershowitz's clear, pleasing black and white illustrations and diagrams, both of which are well placed in relation to the text.

Several "fish books" have touched upon electric fish within a larger context, such as Braz Walker's *Oddball Fishes and Other Strange Creatures of the Deep,* and Maurice Burton's *The Life of Fishes.* And there are books such as John F. Water's *The Mysterious Eel,* devoted to a single electric fish. Arnold's book, however, offers an excellent overview of the entire spectrum of these remarkable fish. It's a subject that should prove as interesting as the perennially popular sharks, whales and dolphins.

Norma Bagnall

SOURCE: A review of *Electric Fish,* in *Appraisal: Science Books for Young People,* Vol. 14, No. 1, Winter, 1981, pp. 10-11.

SPECIALIST: This is going to provide little satisfaction for readers because information is inadequately presented. For example, diagrams and drawings are not always clear. Arnold says of one diagram that it "shows how an object can change the shape of an electrical field." The diagram in question shows (I suppose) two fish, two objects, and two electrical fields, but no other information is given, and it is not clear to me what is happening.

At least one pronoun reference makes understanding difficult. In explaining superstitions, Arnold says "They also believe . . . "; the "they" refers to people of South America mentioned above three sentences earlier. In yet another instance, Arnold says that the largest "electric ray can grow to be five feet long and two hundred pounds." The omission of "weigh" in that sentence is unnecessarily jarring.

The intrusion of the author "Can you imagine . . . " like a condescending pat on the head, along with words like *Scyliorhinus canicula* and *Raja clavata* without pronouncing guides is indicative of the uneven tone of the entire book. Arnold does discuss various kinds of electric fish and includes information about their discovery and history. However, teachers wanting to use this in the classroom would also need a good encyclopedia or other reference to fill in the gaps.

Judith Goldberger

SOURCE: A review of *Electric Fish,* in *Booklist,* Vol. 77, No. 9, January 1, 1981, p. 622.

There is more to electric fish than the stinging effect of an eel, as the author makes clear. Not only are there a number of species of high- and low-voltage fish, but also many weak-sighted varieties, such as sharks, which use receptors of electricity to gather information. According to some researchers, senders may also use their electric powers to communicate with members of their own species. Although a more detailed explanation of the physics of electricity and the mechanics of its use as an information-gathering device would have been useful, the material included on scientific work and on variations among species is quite adequate.

Margaret Bush

SOURCE: A review of *Electric Fish,* in *School Library Journal,* Vol. 27, No. 7, March, 1981, p. 140.

Arnold discusses how fish use electricity to locate and kill prey, to defend themselves, or to communicate. She describes the general principles and processes by which familiar and less familiar species such as rays, skates, stargazers, snout fish and knife fish send out and receive electrical impulses. Her explanations are clear and not technical, but the text becomes repetitive and wanders as she describes several fish, separately, in unspecific terms, only to conclude each time that scientists know little about the animal. Brief descriptions of experiments are used to demonstrate points, but the overall effect is a wooden narrative constructed to fill out the four chapters.

MY FRIEND FROM OUTER SPACE (1981)

Barbara Elleman

SOURCE: A review of *My Friend from Outer Space,* in *Booklist,* Vol. 77, No. 18, May 15, 1981, p. 1258.

Claiming she is from outer space, Sherry invites her friend on a rocket-ship ride to her home planet. The launching pad, however, looks surprisingly like a garage, and the spaceship like a cardboard box. The friend remains skeptical until Sherry takes off her "earth disguise" and reveals an astonishing—and very convincing—space face. Humor emanates through the story and three-color, cartoon-style pictures [by Carol Nicklaus] and culminates in a sly bluff, leaving readers to draw their own conclusions.

Zena Sutherland

SOURCE: A review of *My Friend from Outer Space,* in *Bulletin of the Center for Children's Books,* Vol. 35, No. 1, September, 1981, p. 3.

Almost in strip format and style (framed pictures have the illustrations in a top box, with text printed against a yellow background in the bottom box) the casual drawings give the only clue to the other-world appearance of Sherry when she casts off (or so she claims) her Earth-disguise. Her nameless best friend, who tells the story, is not convinced by any of Sherry's plausible answers that she's really from outer space. They go into Sherry's dark garage, crawl into an even darker box, and go "a million miles an hour," says Sherry. When they get there it still looks like Sherry's garage. Sherry explains that, too. She had picked a place on earth that looked like home so she wouldn't get homesick. She disappears briefly, returning in hideous guise and convincing her friend it's true; the guise is shed, they get back into the box. "Now do you believe I come from outer space?" "Yes." A brisk and amusing story, very nicely told in simple dialogue, will have primary-grade readers feeling that they're in on a good scam; this should also appeal to the read-aloud audience.

SUN FUN (1981)

Nancy Palmer

SOURCE: A review of *Sun Fun,* in *School Library Journal,* Vol. 28, No. 4, December, 1981, p. 79.

The *Sun Fun* in Caroline Arnold's title includes an ice-cube race experiment, making shadow puppets, baking apples in a simple foil cooker, making a sun clock and six other simple but intriguing activities. It's a good introduction to the sun's uses, and solar information included relates directly to the experiment or project outlined. The instructions and illustrations are clear, and information on where to get any special materials (e.g., studio-proof paper for sun prints) is included. In short, cohesive, interesting, lucid material unavailable elsewhere at this level.

John Pancella

SOURCE: A review of *Sun Fun,* in *Science Books & Films,* Vol. 17, No. 4, March-April, 1982, p. 214.

Ten solar projects are described in *Sun Fun.* These include melting ice cubes; making a sun clock, shadow puppets, sun visor, sun prints, solar cooker, and sun reflector; comparing heating of light and dark rocks; observing plants bending toward sunlight; and observing the shadow of a solar eclipse. An eye-safety note is made about the latter but not strongly enough. The instructions, list of materials, and drawings are clear and useful. Each project includes an introduction with information; however, the results of the projects are open-ended and encourage critical thinking. Some of the concepts may be too ambitious for the intended readers.

Margaret Bush

SOURCE: A review of *Sun Fun,* in *Appraisal: Science Books for Young People,* Vol. 15, No. 2, Spring-Summer, 1982, pp. 19-20.

LIBRARIAN: Simple text and pictures provide directions for activities which demonstrate the effects of the heat and light of the sun and the movement of the planets. Projects include a paper plate sun dial, shadow puppets, sun prints on studio proof paper, cooking with the sun (iced tea and baked apple), sun reflectors, and watching a solar eclipse. Although each section begins with a brief statement about the principle which is to be demonstrated by the particular activity, there is actually a very modest amount of information provided and explanation of terms is not entirely adequate (i.e. 'reflect' and 'solar' are not defined, and no term is provided for the tendency of plants to move towards the sun). However, the book is an attractive introduction, and the activities can generally be done without adult supervision—though they would also be useful in the classroom or for young scout groups.

Norman F. Smith

SOURCE: A review of *Sun Fun,* in *Appraisal: Science Books for Young People,* Vol. 15, No. 2, Spring-Summer, 1982, pp. 19-20.

SPECIALIST: This "easy-read activity book" presents in simple language a dozen simple activities dealing with the sun or solar energy: a sun clock, cooking with the sun, heat absorption, reflection, etc. Illustrations are very attractive and instructions clear. All activities are on a very elementary level suited for beginning readers and the very first exposure to science.

SEX HORMONES: WHY MALES AND FEMALES ARE DIFFERENT (1981)

Kirkus Reviews

SOURCE: A review of *Sex Hormones: Why Males and Females Are Different,* in *Kirkus Reviews,* Vol. L, No. 1, January 1, 1982, p. 8.

Arnold, who has written for younger readers on electric fish and bird parenting, seems to be a little out of her depth in this complex and touchy subject. She plods through the basic facts and definitions with explanations that do not explain and historical and other material that dampens reader interest because it is not ordered along any route of natural curiosity or rational inquiry. Later, in the tricky areas of how sex hormones affect behavior, she cites a number of interesting experiments on animals. However, they appear here as in isolation, without the considered context that would be provided, say, by the Silversteins; and Arnold carelessly makes too much of them. For example, she jumps from "In most cases, female [animals] develop faster and live longer than males" to "currently in the United States the life expectancy for men is 68.7 years, and for women it is 76.5 years." This is poor logic, poor science, and abysmal pedagogy. Arnold's generalizations about the differences between men's and women's brains and areas of intelligence also present controversial assumptions (based on performance), as known fact. All in all, though this might be welcomed for its coverage, it is more likely to muddle than clarify the issues.

Denise M. Wilms

SOURCE: A review of *Sex Hormones: Why Males and Females Are Different,* in *Booklist,* Vol. 78, No. 12, February 15, 1982, p. 755.

Research has turned up some fascinating disclosures on the role of hormones, specifically sex hormones, in matters of body function and behavior. Arnold's introduction to this complex topic sticks to mostly neutral ground, explaining what androgens, estrogens, and progestins are and looking at some of the ways they influence both reproductive functions and body development. Studies with rats, doves, and monkeys are the focus for much of her explanation. The role of hormones in human behavior is left largely unexamined: "In all these studies, it is difficult to know which findings to attribute to hormones and which ones to experience, heredity, and other factors." One flaw of note: birth control pills (which employ hormones to suppress ovulation) are labeled the "most effective way to prevent pregnancy," but there is no note of their potential dangers. Nonetheless, this is an accessible introduction to an often-encountered scientific topic.

Roberta J. Navickis

SOURCE: A review of *Sex Hormones: Why Males and Females Are Different,* in *Science Books & Films,* Vol. 18, No. 1, September-October, 1982, p. 18.

Arnold generally accomplishes her ambitious goal of explaining how the sex hormones make for differences between males and females. She draws on the great number of animal studies in this area, and entertains the reader with a stable of interesting anecdotes, particularly about birds. The first chapters describe the nature of hormones, the reproductive cycle in animals, sex differences—including genetic and environmental effects—sex horomones' role in aggression, and sexual and parental behavior. Humans are not the book's central focus, but human puberty, pregnancy, birth control, and hormonal-influenced behavior are covered in the final chapter. Although Arnold is a lucid writer, she has covered sophisticated ground, and junior high and beginning high school students will find the book challenging. Not only are complex scientific principles covered, but the vocabulary is advanced. The glossary helps, but Arnold does routinely use scientific, uncommon words. One nice touch is that the etymology of many of these words is given; the illustrations [by Jean Zallinger] are also exceptionally pleasing. The descriptions of early endocrinology sometimes seemed superfluous, but, on balance, the book is well-written and accurate.

ANIMALS THAT MIGRATE (1982)

Sonia W. Thomas

SOURCE: A review of *Animals That Migrate,* in *The Christian Science Monitor,* November 17, 1982, p. 15.

Animals That Migrate, with text by Caroline Arnold and pictures by Michele Zylman, should delight beginning readers who want to try their new skills on a science book. The migrating habits of seven animals are described in a fairly interesting way, even though the vocabulary is limited to words an early reader can recognize and understand. As author Arnold explores the reasons for migration—extremes of heat and cold, the need for food, and for a safe place for babies to be born—she spotlights arctic terns, which fly 11,000 miles each way from pole to pole; South American green turtles; and Lapland reindeer.

Denise M. Wilms

SOURCE: A review of *Animals That Migrate,* in *Booklist,* Vol. 79, No. 10, January 15, 1983, p. 681.

The concept of animal migration is effectively reduced to its simplest elements for presentation in this easy-to-read format. Arnold explains that "some animals have two homes" and might have to travel long distances to get from one to the other. She explores some of the reasons why (food, a suitable place to bear and rear young, a more temperate climate) and looks at the distances that could be involved. Then come brief looks at a number of species for whom migration is an important fact of life: chinook salmon, eels, green turtles, whales, and reindeer.

Judy Diamond

SOURCE: A review of *Animals That Migrate,* in *Science Books & Films,* Vol. 18, No. 5, May-June, 1983, p. 274.

Animals That Migrate is an introduction for young readers to the animals that have what she describes as "two homes." The book acquaints readers with an impressive diversity of species. Up-to-date information on animals' migration routes and their probable reasons for migrating are given for arctic terns, deer, monarch butterflies, Chinook salmon, eels, green sea turtles, gray whales, and reindeer. We learn that eels will travel over land from ponds to the streams that they will use to migrate to the ocean. We are introduced to the Samit people who migrate with the reindeer. Maps and black-and-white illustrations are provided along with information about each species. The book's strengths lie in its well-chosen examples; its weaknesses are the sometimes uneven vocabulary and in the generally poor illustrations. The term "mammal," for example, is introduced without definition, and the illustration of the arctic terns is incorrect because it omits their forked tails.

WHO KEEPS US HEALTHY? ("Community" series, 1982)

Margretta R. Seashore

SOURCE: A review of *Who Keeps Us Healthy?*, in *Science Books & Films*, Vol. 19, No. 1, September-October, 1983, p. 35.

This book tries to describe different members of the health care team in a manner that children can understand. The black-and-white photographs [by Carole Bertol] are evocative and nicely framed. The descriptions are accurate. In the effort to give equal consideration to all races and both sexes, the book becomes a bit bland. The characterization of the different professionals lacks detail or distinguishing features, and although accurate, it is not very imaginative. Children who can read the book will not gain much, if any, new information. For the child to whom it is read, it may stimulate further discussion. Therefore, it may be useful in a nursery or kindergarten classroom as a starting point, but it does not have as much information as other books on this subject.

Diane A. Holzheimer

SOURCE: A review of *Who Keeps Us Healthy?*, in *Appraisal: Science Books for Young People*, Vol. 16, No. 3, Fall, 1983, pp. 11-12.

LIBRARIAN: This is an excellent example of what can be done with a standard, (usually) pedestrian category like "community helper" books. Ms. Arnold has approached her topic with imagination and sensitivity, and has turned what could have been a merely utilitarian item into a book which can stretch the minds of its readers, adults as well as children. She does not keep to the ordinary limits of doctors, nurses, dentists, hospital workers, and paramedics, but includes workers with the elderly and handicapped, counselors for mental, emotional, and family problems, pharmacists, support groups such as AA, educational and funding groups such as the March of Dimes, restaurant inspectors, garbage collectors, pollution monitors, and others, including veterinarians (because "animals need to stay healthy just as people do."). Women and minority races are well represented in positions of authority as well as the more stereotypical nurse-technician-patient roles. It's almost a shame that the simple text limits this to the primary school level, as it's the sort of mind-opener that should be more common at all reading levels; this contents itself pretty much with a catalogue of jobs and very minimal explanation. Not to complain, however, because this text and the sharp black-and white photographs outclass many more "thorough" books on the subject; no index, and none needed.

Evelyn E. Ames

SOURCE: A review of *Who Keeps Us Healthy?*, in *Appraisal: Science Books for Young People*, Vol. 16, No. 3, Fall, 1983, pp. 11-12.

SPECIALIST: The common theme in this Easy-Read Community Book is who are the providers and what are the services that are available to help people and communities stay healthy, overcome illness, or prevent diseases. Having divided the book into sections titled "Health Care People," "Places Where Health Care People Work," and "Communities Help People Stay Healthy," the author briefly mentions the work that various traditional health care professionals do and the services that communities provide to promote public health. This is not a science book; it would be more appropriate to classify it as a community resource booklet. One wonders why the author omitted the mention of dental hygienists and flossing on the page pertaining to the dentist.

PETS WITHOUT HOMES (1983)

Kirkus Reviews

SOURCE: A review of *Pets without Homes*, in *Kirkus Reviews*, Vol. LI, No. 17, September 1, 1983, p. 167.

Simple, direct, and very effectively pictured: the story of a stray puppy, taken to the (Santa Monica) animal shelter—and what happens there as the animals wait to be adopted or (unflinchingly) "killed." ("No one at a shelter likes to do it, but when it is necessary, it is done quickly and painlessly.") The point, made apropos of the shelter's functions and then emphasized at the close, is that people should learn "to spay or neuter their pets." ("Then shelters won't have too many animals to care for, and fewer animals will have to be killed.") The text is helpfully explanatory throughout: why it's all right for Officer Terrie Lee, and her colleagues, to approach and handle strays—but other people shouldn't; how the cages are kept clean, how the animals get exercise; what else the animal pet control officers do—in Officer Lee's city, they patrol pet stores. The material is relevant, but it also fills out the time as we wait to see, first, if Buffy's owner will claim him and, then, if someone will adopt him. To Arnold and [Richard] Hewett's credit, this bit isn't overplayed. Buffy has the personality to pretty much assure him of a home, but it's the bent head of the not-so-little girl carrying him out that speaks volumes.

Jacqueline Elsner

SOURCE: A review of *Pets without Homes*, in *School Library Journal*, Vol. 30, No. 5, January, 1984, p. 61.

The workings of a big-city animal shelter are explained through this black-and-white photographic essay. Arnold's carefully developed text follows the fortunes of Buffy, an appealing stray puppy and Max, a grown cat whose owner puts him up for adoption. Police Officer Terrie Lee of the Santa Monica Animal Shelter patrols the city enforcing laws pertaining to animals and picking up strays. Her duties are clearly explained and photographed: both on the street talking to owners of pet shops and un-leashed dogs and at the shelter. Her job takes her and selected animals to schools for sessions with children to teach proper care of pets, both domestic and wild. Compassion and consideration combine with compliance with the animal laws. Max and Buffy are eventually adopted, but the consequences of neglect and the fact that the animals sometimes must be killed are also explained. . . . Throughout, the text and illustrations form a harmonious unity of compassion and care beyond the lucid, informative focus of the book. This is the only book for a young audience on the subject. A distinguished, superlative job.

Sarah S. Gagné

SOURCE: A review of *Pets without Homes,* in *The Horn Book Magazine,* Vol. LX, No. 1, February, 1984, p. 88.

An engaging account tells what an animal shelter officer does to assist lost and unwanted pets. Its opening phrase sets the tone: "Buffy was a lost, lonely, and hungry puppy." Buffy is the winsome terrier who stars on the book jacket, and Officer Lee the attractive, determined-looking woman who takes Buffy to the city shelter. While Buffy waits for possible adoption, Officer Lee goes on outdoor jobs, checking that owners have their dogs leashed and wearing license tags; inspecting pet shops; and watching for strays. In time, of course, Buffy is adopted. The problem of having too many unwanted pets is addressed, but gently; nothing in the book will unnerve young children. It is especially fine for its beautiful photographs, its easy-to-read text, and its presentation of a subject with automatic appeal to young children. The author does not preach by asking whether the reader's local animal laws and animal shelters are as good as those indicated for the city of Santa Monica, California; but one hopes that an adult would be knowledgeable enough to discuss the subject with children after they read the book.

Eleanor Wenger

SOURCE: A review of *Pets without Homes,* in *Science Books & Films,* Vol. 19, No. 5, May-June, 1984, p. 295.

Pets without Homes is a charming book. The message it presents is excellent, including the author's final gentle statements about the value of neutering pets and preventing the destruction of unwanted animals. The black-and-white photographs are excellent and complement the text; there is not one I would delete. Terrie Lee is the animal control officer featured in the book—an idealist, perhaps, who enjoys her work and who would surely inspire children (would that other animal control officers were like her). I would not be surprised if children insisted on visiting the animal control shelters in their communities after reading about her and her

work. In short, I highly recommend this book to children through grades three or four. Younger children could certainly benefit from seeing the pictures and will enjoy having the book read to them.

THE BIGGEST LIVING THING (1983)

Nancy Palmer

SOURCE: A review of *The Biggest Living Thing,* in *School Library Journal,* Vol. 30, No. 4, December, 1983, p. 78.

"Question: What plant is taller than the Statute of Liberty? weighs more than a big ship? is bigger than any other living thing?" Nothing fishy about this riddle; the giant sequoia tree is the straight (about 272 feet worth) answer, and while other trees may be taller, none is weightier. How these giants are measured, how they were found and named, how they grow, how fire helps them and various other facts about these California mountain behemoths are related here. The language is a straightforward string of declaratives, but works well for the subject, only occasionally lock-stepping into stilt-edness.

Ruth S. Beebe

SOURCE: A review of *The Biggest Living Thing,* in *Appraisal: Science Books for Young People,* Vol. 17, No. 1, Winter, 1984, pp. 6-7.

LIBRARIAN: Here is another to join the ranks of the easy-to-read science books. The child who prefers non-fiction even in his/her earliest reading experiences will find these well-selected, well-presented facts about the giant sequoia trees very readable. Of particular interest is the role forest fires play in helping these huge trees to attain their growth.

R. Gregory Belcher

SOURCE: A review of *The Biggest Living Thing,* in *Appraisal: Science Books for Young People,* Vol. 17, No. 1, Winter, 1984, pp. 6-7.

SPECIALIST: This otherwise delightful book contains two minor flaws. On page 32: "At first it (the sequoia seedling) looks like other pine trees. . . ." Sequoia is *not* a pine, but a member of the family *Pinaceae,* which contains, among others, the pines, cedars, larches and many other *genera.* Then, on page 40: "Fires add minerals to the soil too." Actually fire liberates minerals from the organic matter, and makes it available to the growing tree. Decay accomplishes the same act, but not as quickly or dramatically. In general, *The Biggest Living Thing* is well worth its price. It is a fine introduction to one of Nature's greatest wonders.

Jane H. Bock

SOURCE: A review of *The Biggest Living Thing,* in *Science Books & Films,* Vol. 19, No. 4, March-April, 1984, p. 217.

Ask small children, or many adults for that matter, what the "biggest living thing" is, and they might answer "the whale" or "the elephant." But this dear little book is about the giant sequoia, and it is particularly well suited to small children. It may be best suited to those to whom it must be read, rather than to those who can read it themselves. The scientific information is accurate and efficiently presented. Most of the facts that would be presented in a popular lecture to a college audience are included.

THE SUMMER OLYMPICS (1983; revised edition, 1988)

Phillis Wilson

SOURCE: A review of *The Summer Olympics,* in *Booklist,* Vol. 84, No. 16, April 15, 1988, p. 1425.

This timely update to the 1983 edition is newly illustrated with 23 photos taken at the 1984 Los Angeles games. Nearly 3,000 years ago athletes in Greece competed in much the same way as the best amateur athletes in the world do today. The first modern Olympics in 1896 hosted 285 people from 13 countries; today 151 countries are represented by more than 10,000 citizens. The summer games include track and field, water and ball sports, gymnastics, sports of strength and defense, shooting and riding sports, and the modern pentathlon. Arnold gives a clear brief description of the individual events in each of the eight major categories with an abundance of current and historic photos. Succinct and serviceable.

Tom S. Hurlburt

SOURCE: A review of *The Summer Olympics,* in *School Library Journal,* Vol. 35, No. 8, May, 1988, p. 91.

An updated version of a 1983 title, **The Summer Olympics** attempts to explain the games to young children. Beginning with a brief description of the first Olympiad and a short chapter on how the games are organized, the main thrust of the book is to explain the numerous events that are contested every four years. Arnold divides the sporting events into eight categories, such as water sports, track and field, and ball sports, and then gives a brief description of the rules and format of the events that are grouped under the various headings. Some of the events are summarized in as few as three short sentences. While this is a limiting factor, children will still be able to familiarize themselves with each sport and glean a fact or two,

such as why staggered starts are used in sprints. This version contains new black-and-white photographs, many from the 1984 Games in Los Angeles, and includes descriptions of some of the new events such as rhythmic gymnastics. Arnold does not state that Seoul will be the sight of the 1988 Summer Games. There are also no appendixes of past gold medal winners or event records. The book's main value is as an introduction to the various Olympic sports, rather than as a history or reference source of the Summer Games.

TOO FAT? TOO THIN? DO YOU HAVE A CHOICE? (1984)

Zena Sutherland

SOURCE: A review of *Too Fat? Too Thin? Do You Have a Choice?,* in *Bulletin of the Center for Children's Books,* Vol. 37, No. 10, June, 1984, pp. 179-80.

While discussing the usual weight control factors like a well-balanced diet, exercise, and the need to distinguish between hunger and the social or psychological reasons for eating, Arnold also emphasizes what cannot be done about altering body size. Starting with a clear chapter on physiology, she then presents recent research; her special focus is on the set-point theory, that each person's weight may be controlled by a sort of weight thermostat which changes the body's metabolic rate so as always to keep fat stores at a set level. On the whole Arnold is careful to show how much is still not proven, for example, the influence of hormones on body fat and on the disease of anorexia; but her discussion of environment and inherited body types is questionable, and some awkard style mars the text. Charts show calorie and nutritional content of common foods, daily nutritional needs, and calories used during exercise; and an annotated bibliography pays attention to both boys and girls.

Denise M. Wilms

SOURCE: A review of *Too Fat? Too Thin? Do You Have a Choice?,* in *Booklist,* Vol. 80, No. 22, August, 1984, pp. 1622-23.

As Arnold's subtitle implies, there is more to the question of weight than calories. Her survey of the weight-watch problem shows that an individual's weight is determined by a combination of genetics, nutrition, and exercise. A discussion of the role of fat in body health gets things under way. Readers are told the body needs a certain amount of fat to stay healthy, and fat storage is explained. The complexities of changing your weight come next. Research indicates that radically altering weight up or down is not easy and that the body will resist it. Arnold looks at current theories that each body has a "set point" that regulates weight and adjusts metabolism to maintain that weight within narrow variations no matter what. As for setting reasonable weight goals, Arnold suggests seeing a doctor for an assessment of what's right for you and then following a sound nutrition and exercise program—while keeping in mind that "few people choose whether to be fat or thin."

Elaine Goldberg

SOURCE: A review of *Too Fat? Too Thin? Do You Have a Choice?*, in *Kliatt,* Vol. 18, No. 6, Fall, 1984, pp. 43-44.

This is in no sense of the word a diet book, nor is it the usual diatribe and/or "how-to" sort of book. It is an intelligent, instructive, factual presentation of the basic knowledge necessary to a better understanding of nutrition, body shape, hunger and the like. Whether the problem is obesity or being too thin, many of the questions and answers to the problem and its resolution are similar. The important thing underlined by Arnold is what can and cannot be accomplished. If a dieter understands these limits, life will be easier. Arnold interestingly discusses the "set-point" theory, the role of hormones, of one's metabolism, of one's genes, the importance of baby fat, and much more. This is a book written for adolescents that will be very accessible to them and will also be found to be interesting by their elders. Lucid, concise, and helpful are only a few of the appropriately laudatory words that could be used for this work.

John D. Chilgren

SOURCE: A review of *Too Fat? Too Thin? Do You Have a Choice?*, in *Science Books & Films,* Vol. 20, No. 5, May-June, 1985, pp. 299-300.

Obesity is generally considered an adult problem, but its roots are often in youth, where overeating and inactivity provide the foundation for future obesity-related diseases. The cultural norms of the day picture thinness alongside self-discipline, fashion, and health. For self-conscious teen-agers unaware of their choices, this book will be illuminating. However, the author breaks no new ground in this short, simple essay. It's not a "how to" book but a collection of current ideas and "fat" facts, highlighting what teen-agers can and cannot do about their size and how to accept what cannot be changed. Being as objective as possible, Arnold avoids controversy, but the result is somewhat bland reading. Her strongest statements are never admonitions and are buried in the text. However, she accurately depicts the information gap regarding obesity, its development and resolution, and identifies the major issues of weight control: why diets don't work, attitudes toward eating, cultural norms, the role of genetics, the set-point hypothesis, and the recurring theme of the value of daily exercise. Anorexia and bulimia are superficially treated, and a useful ten-item supplemental reading list and index complete the book.

 MEASUREMENTS: FUN, FACTS, AND ACTIVITIES ("Easy-Read Geography Activity Book Series," 1984)

Zena Sutherland

SOURCE: A review of *Measurements: Fun, Facts, and Activities,* in *Bulletin of the Center for Children's Books,* Vol. 38, No. 7, March, 1985, p. 119.

Arnold uses home experiments to help clarify concepts of measurement. The writing is direct and simple; occasionally it moves abruptly from one topic to another ("The tallest building in the world is in the city of Chicago. How tall are you?") but for the most part, the text uses an approach that should be both comprehensible and interesting to the primary grades reader. A series of brief statements and questions, addressed to a particular kind of measurement (speed, time, weight, and so on) is followed by a list of supplies needed and then step-by-step directions for a demonstration of measuring a particular attribute of an object.

Sallie Hope Erhard

SOURCE: A review of *Measurements: Fun, Facts, and Activities,* in *Appraisal: Science Books for Young People,* Vol. 18, No. 3, Summer, 1985, p. 11.

LIBRARIAN: This is a book for young children to demonstrate how they can measure some simple phenomenon, and according to the sub-title with "Fun, Facts and Activities." There are a few facts, but not much substantive information. Each chapter on how to measure such things as height, weight, distance, speed, time, temperature, wind, and area is accompanied by an activity that can be done by children, but I am not sure how much fun is involved. I found certain flaws in the text and the illustrations [by Pam Johnson] to give me pause. The first activity gives elaborate directions for making four digit "counting sticks" but doesn't explain how they work. The directions on page 18 for making a sand-clock timer were unclear enough that I could not understand them, and the illustrations were no help either. And finally I think the statement on page 20 concerning measuring time that states: "Each time the earth turns around is a new day. We measure the days of the year with a calendar." could have added one more sentence to the effect that each turn around the sun is a year. Perhaps some children can have some amusement with some of the experiments, but I'm not sure how much scientific knowledge they will gain.

Clarence C. Truesdell

SOURCE: A review of *Measurements: Fun, Facts, and Activities,* in *Appraisal: Science Books for Young People,* Vol. 18, No. 3, Summer, 1985, p. 11.

SPECIALIST: Another addition to the series "An Easy Read Geography Activity Book," which perpetuates the notion that short, choppy sentences can somehow facilitate comprehension. Since you may not agree that chopping up text until it yields: "R. L. 2.5 Spache Revised Formula" is the way to write a book on measurements, I recommend that you preview this book before buying. Some of the activities have a great deal of merit, yet this does not seem to me to be a science book because so little effort is made to understand the activities.

ANTI-SEMITISM: A MODERN PERSPECTIVE (with Herma Silverstein, 1985)

Stephanie Zvirin

SOURCE: A review of *Anti-Semitism: A Modern Perspective*, in *Booklist*, Vol. 81, No. 5, November 1, 1984, p. 358.

A frightening catalog of examples demonstrating that discrimination against Jews still exists all over the world. Some background and a discussion of the Holocaust lead into a roughly geographic overview of anti-Semitism that examines its various manifestations in Eastern bloc countries (particularly the USSR), Western Europe, the Middle East, Latin America, and the U.S. Along the way, the authors discuss negative stereotypes and myths that have resulted in the Jews' being blamed over the centuries for everything from the death of Christ to bubonic plague and the collapse of the German economy. The authors' decision to narrow their scope by focusing mainly on anti-Semitism in Hitler's Germany and after the war has resulted in a somewhat diluted view of the religious roots of the problem, and their consideration of anti-Semitism in the Middle East skims over the subject as it is related to political events during the last few years. Yet specific examples are vivid and disturbing, and the book has a good deal to contribute toward the identification of anti-Jewish prejudice (and its perpetrators) in both its blatant and more subtle forms.

Ruth Levien

SOURCE: A review of *Anti-Semitism: A Modern Perspective*, in *School Library Journal*, Vol. 31, No. 8, April, 1985, p. 95.

Indeed, a modern perspective; far less a history than an accounting of anti-Semitism in modern times. The authors begin briefly with general background and a chapter on the Holocaust and then deal with the subject in specific world areas such as the United States, the Soviet Union, the Middle East and Latin America. The section dealing with anti-Semitism in this country is especially well done. The authors believe that world-wide anti-Semitism in its various guises is as virulent as ever, and that Jews everywhere must always be on the alert. Competently written but presented in an uninspired textbook format, the book includes numerous well-chosen and extremely graphic photographs which complement the text, but unfortunately the quality of many of the historic photographs is poor. The net effect is to add to the chilling quality of the text. Charles Patterson's recent book *Anti-Semitism: The Road to the Holocaust & Beyond* is better written and has more of an emotional impact than this, but still, with its slightly different focus, this is an adequate if pessimistic presentation of an important subject which is rarely dealt with in children's books.

Albert V. Schwartz

SOURCE: A review of *Anti-Semitism: A Modern Perspective*, in *Interracial Books for Children Bulletin*, Vol. 17, No. 2, 1986, pp. 18-19.

Here is a text for children on an important topic. It is a pity that the book's "modern perspective" seems to be based upon the authors' own prejudices.

The authors seem to feel that merely presenting one terrible incident after another is sufficient to enlist the reader against anti-Semitism; they state: "An awareness of its many faces will help more people to recognize anti-Semitism, and then to stamp it out before it has a chance to grow." Reading about anti-Semitic acts is important, but not enough. Neither is learning of major organizations that fight anti-Semitism. A section on what children can do in their own schools and communities—and more information about what adults are doing—would have improved this book considerably.

The text itself, in addition to being poorly written, is flawed. Some explanations are outrageously misleading; for example, among the reasons given for an increase in anti-Semitic incidents in 1982 in Los Angeles, a city with a large Jewish population, is that "the depressed economy, scapegoating, and the *prevalence of black, Jewish and Hispanic public officials whose new position of authority pose a perceived threat to much of the lower economic Anglo population contributed to the increase*" (emphasis added). In addition to blaming the victim, this suggests that we fuel anti-Semitism by electing candidates of color!

And then there is the misinformation. I groaned, for example, when I read, "Livingston also succeeded in getting the Associated Press to cease its custom of identifying Jews—and only Jews—when reporting crimes." People of color, Italians, and others (as well as Jews) have long complained of such reporting.

And again: "German soldiers had fought against the Bolsheviks in the Russian Revolution of 1917 and absorbed some of the Russian brand of Jew-hatred." The German soldiers had nothing to learn about anti-Semitism, especially from the Bolsheviks, whose constitution outlawed this form of bias. (And the term "Jew-hatred" only repeats the oppressor's terminology.)

The book's discussion of the Middle East is seriously limited by a superficial discussion that ignores the plight of the Palestinian people. Moreover, the anti-Arab racism of Meir Kahane, who is mentioned in passing early in the book, is glossed over as "incitement" and "disturbing the peace."

The authors appear to be documenting anti-Semitism around the world, country by country. This goal is worthwhile, but, why are African and Asian nations totally omitted? Are they considered less important than European nations? If research had revealed that there are fewer incidents of anti-Semitism in these nations, that would be good to know.

Fuller and more balanced treatments of anti-Semitism are needed so that this limited volume may be replaced quickly.

SAVING THE PEREGRINE FALCON ("Nature Watch" series, 1985)

Ellen Fader

SOURCE: A review of *Saving the Peregrine Falcon,* in *School Library Journal,* Vol. 31, No. 7, March, 1985, p. 160.

The same human intervention that caused peregrine falcons to become endangered is now helping to save the peregrine. In this lucid, straightforward text, Arnold relates a brief natural history of this species and describes the efforts of West Coast scientists who hatch eggs taken from wild falcons, rear the chicks and then release the birds back into the wild. Spectacular color photographs [by Richard R. Hewett], many full page, show the scientists at work and the eggs from the time they hatch until the birds are given their permanent freedom. These arresting photographs are so well integrated with the text that labeling them is unnecessary. Alice Schick's *The Peregrine Falcons, Falcons Return* by John Kaufmann and Heinz Meng and *Saving America's Birds* by Paula Hendrich are for older readers and describe only the preservation efforts of the Peregrine Fund at Cornell University. Due to the book's brevity, the lack of a table of contents and an index is not a serious omission. This is an excellent introduction to the peregrine falcon for younger readers or newcomers to the subject. It updates reports on current research, and it is the only book available that describes the activities of the Santa Cruz Predatory Bird Research Group.

Denise M. Wilms

SOURCE: A review of *Saving the Peregrine Falcon,* in *Booklist,* Vol. 81, No. 15, April 1, 1985, pp. 1116-17.

In a few cities, Los Angeles among them, peregrine falcons can be seen soaring between high buildings. The sight is a startling one, especially since it is a species that has been threatened for some time. A concerted effort to save these birds, whose eggs are weakened by DDT, is in progress, and Arnold reports on what scientists are doing to insure that falcons will keep up their numbers in the wild. With sharp color photographs backing up the text, Arnold explains how scientists remove thin-shelled eggs from wild nests, watch them in the laboratory, and, when the chicks are off to a healthy start, return them to their original nest. While bird numbers are up, the pesticide problem won't go away anytime soon, because the birds on which peregrine falcons prey winter in Central and South American areas where DDT is still in use. "The more birds the peregrines eat, the more DDT they store." Still, it's nice to know these handsome birds are multiplying; this crystal-clear exposition makes you hope the numbers keep growing.

Appraisal: Science Books for Young People

SOURCE: A review of *Saving the Peregrine Falcon,* in *Appraisal: Science Books for Young People,* Vol. 18, No. 4, Autumn, 1985, p. 10.

SPECIALIST: **Saving the Peregrine Falcon** chronicles the tremendous effort being made by scientists to save this endangered falcon from extinction. The book focuses on the Santa Cruz Predatory Bird Research Group (SCPBRG) which collects and releases bird eggs for the western United States. To understand the detailed process of egg collection and redistribution into the wild, the reader journeys from rocky cliffs to the SCPBRG center where the hatching of eggs and brooding and feeding of the young chicks takes place. The challenge of human efforts to duplicate a wild "upbringing" is readily apparent in the book. For example, scientists peep to encourage chicks to hatch, use puppets to prevent imprinting on humans, and provide prairie falcons as substitute parents. Author Caroline Arnold skillfully integrates a vast amount of scientific information into the story of the effort to increase the Peregrine falcon population. Abundant photographs clearly and beautifully illustrate the text. The reader sees how scientists candle eggs, band birds, and provide man made nests atop skyscrapers. A glossary provides definitions of the scientific terms used within the book.

This book would be an excellent resource for the science classroom and for independent science reading as it inspires an appreciation for both bird and scientist.

Sallie Hope Erhard

SOURCE: A review of *Saving the Peregrine Falcon,* in *Appraisal: Science Books for Young People,* Vol. 18, No. 4, Autumn, 1985, p. 10.

LIBRARIAN: This Carolrhoda Nature Watch Book is truly outstanding. The text is well organized and very interesting with special words that appear in the glossary at the end printed in bold letters. The author starts with a general description of the peregrine falcon and explains why the species has become endangered. The second half of the book is devoted to a detailed explanation of the work being done to hatch eggs in captivity and train the young birds so they can be released again to the wild. Did you know that some peregrines feel at home amongst high-rise buildings in modern cities which in many ways resemble cliffs and mountains where they usually live? . . . After this book was read to a group of eight year olds, they were asked "What did you like about it"? Their response was, "Everything!", and I agree.

MUSIC LESSONS FOR ALEX (1985)

Denise M. Wilms

SOURCE: A review of *Music Lessons for Alex,* in *Booklist,* Vol. 82, No. 5, November 1, 1985, pp. 398, 400.

After attending a concert, young Alex decides that the violin is the instrument for her. This engaging photo essay records her path as a novice student: going to a violin shop to find an instrument that fits her small stature, taking her first lesson with Mrs. Weisner, and practicing at home. There are also group lessons with other beginners and music reading sessions too. Alex's progress is slow and steady; by the end of a year, she manages her first successful recital performance. A good deal of music information is woven through the description of Alex's activities. For those interested, it's the Suzuki method that's unveiled here. Well photographed [by Richard Hewett] and written in a lively manner, this should whet the appetite of many an aspiring musician.

Amanda J. Williams

SOURCE: A review of *Music Lessons for Alex,* in *School Library Journal,* Vol. 32, No. 6, February, 1986, p. 70.

A thoughtful and informative story of a young girl's first year of violin lessons. After attending a concert with her family, Alex wishes she could play the violin. Hewett's numerous, excellent black-and-white photographs and Arnold's informative well-written text describe the basic concepts of beginning violin. Through Alex's eyes, readers learn how to choose, tune and handle a violin and the importance of lessons and practicing. At first Alex has private lessons, then she joins a group of other beginning violinists. Eventually Alex has her own music books and learns her first piece. The final page of the book shows a happy and confident Alex playing her violin. Basic concepts of dedication, friendship and confidence are felt throughout Arnold's book. An exceptional story in a well-crafted book.

Elizabeth S. Watson

SOURCE: A review of *Music Lessons for Alex,* in *The Horn Book Magazine,* Vol. LXII, No. 2, March-April, 1986, p. 215.

A young violin student's first year of study is chronicled in this fine introduction to the world of music lessons. In photo essay style the book follows Alex, an appealing nine- or ten-year-old, from the concert that offers her inspiration, through the several stages of choosing an instrument, attending lessons, and practicing, to the displaying of accomplishment at the year-end recital. Alex is shown participating in group lessons as well as private ones, learning to read music as well as violin technique. The method of instruction described was developed by Japanese educator and violin teacher, Dr. Shinichi Suzuki, for the teaching of young children. The book clearly portrays moments of frustration, concentration, and enjoyment as the lessons progress. The black-and-white photographs are well composed and effectively placed throughout the book, varying in size and shape as appropriate to content and text. This is an attractive and informative book, made to inspire the fledgling musician.

NATURAL RESOURCES: FUN, FACTS, AND ACTIVITIES ("Easy-Read Geography Activity Book" series, 1985)

Joanne D. Denko

SOURCE: A review of *Natural Resources: Fun, Facts, and Activities,* in *Science Books & Films,* Vol. 21, No. 2, November-December, 1985, p. 66.

The simple projects described in this book for observing grass, wind, rocks, and so on should help upper-elementary children start thinking about their surroundings as resources. Only the advanced students—in terms of intelligence and motivation—will be likely to do the projects alone. Therefore, and because several projects require more than one child (fish pond game, resources parade), I see the book as a supplement for certain upper-elementary nature units. The children's understanding of such words as "water," "wood," and "land" will be broadened by the book's glossary, which contains resource-oriented definitions. While the technical vocabulary in this sense is simple, the nontechnical vocabulary is sometimes a bit abstract and difficult ("construction," "horizontal," "community").

Kathleen Bogan Miksis

SOURCE: A review of *Natural Resources: Fun, Facts, and Activities,* in *School Library Journal,* Vol. 32, No. 4, December, 1985, p. 66.

Combining geography facts and experiments, Arnold offers 12 activities associated with natural resources.

The suggested activities range from having a parade in which children dress as natural resources to building a toothpick log cabin. They show little imagination, and most of the experiments would need additional interpretation to make sense to children. For example, the process of making a compost heap is shown without explaining what it is and why anyone would want one. Other activities include making a jar butter churn, a solar water heater, a wind machine and a magnet/paper clip fishing game. The book itself is attractive with colorful illustrations and photographs [by Penny Carter], and the combination of activities with geography could be a welcome addition, but there just aren't enough original projects offered here. Almost everyone has already planted grass seed in egg cartons.

📖 *PAIN: WHAT IS IT? HOW DO WE DEAL WITH IT?* (1986)

Kirkus Reviews

SOURCE: A review of *Pain: What Is It? How Do We Deal With It?*, in *Kirkus Reviews*, Vol. LIV, No. 13, July 1, 1986, p. 1025.

A concise overview of the warning system we call pain that includes the different types (acute, chronic, phantom, and referred), how we differ in our feelings about pain, how it's measured, how the nervous system sends us pain messages, and how we can effectively block those messages. There is also an up-to-date discussion of drugs, from aspirin to narcotics.

Arnold's vocabulary occasionally turns overly technical for the targeted age group. Syllable sneezes are showered onto the pages—words like enkephalin, prostaglandins, and bradykinin. Readers *will* find some of their questions answered: Why injuries swell and how aspirin affects the system, for example. What they *won't* find is a drama that reaches out to grab them. A phenomenon such as the human capacity to turn off pain with acupuncture, hypnotism, and other means should be fascinating, almost miraculous. This is nearly lost in the scientific discussion.

Still, a useful addition to a reference shelf.

Kathryn M. Weisman

SOURCE: A review of *Pain: What Is It? How Do We Deal With It?*, in *School Library Journal*, Vol. 33, No. 1, September, 1986, p. 130.

Arnold has done a commendable job of introducing a difficult topic in a clear and succinct manner. She describes what pain is (both in terms of the sensation itself and the physiological changes which occur in the body during pain), types of pain (chronic, acute, referred, etc.), and how pain is measured. Also included are sections on common types of pain (headaches, stomach and muscle aches, etc.) as well as a thorough section on the nervous system itself. The last section deals with a variety of pain-killing remedies—from ancient folk medicines such as willow-bark tea and linaments to nonprescription remedies such as aspirin and heat or cold to more extreme methods such as narcotics, anesthesia, and acupuncture. (An interesting part of this section describes the body's own natural narcotics which are manufactured in the brain.) More often than not, the illustrations [by Frank Schwartz] do not add any new information to the text, but the book is clearly written and covers material not generally available for this age group.

Rene Blumenkrantz

SOURCE: A review of *Pain: What Is It? How Do We Deal With It?*, in *Appraisal: Science Books for Young People*, Vol. 20, No. 1, Winter, 1987, p. 12.

LIBRARIAN: The author begins her discussion by reminding us that pain is a normal part of life. It is a warning system that helps us to adapt to the environment. The type, measurement, and tolerance of pain are discussed. How pain messages are relayed, methods of pain relief, and methods of pain reduction are also discussed.

The text has many strengths. It is thorough and current. In its chapter Using Medication to Relieve Pain, it discusses aspirin, acetaminophen, ibuprofen, morphine, codeine, heroin, and finally the body's own pain relievers, enkephalins and endorphins. Other methods of pain relief explored include heat, cold, massage, bio-feedback, acupuncture, and hypnotism. Historical background as well as current research are discussed. Terms are defined within the text and their etymologies are explained. There are also a good introduction and many excellent graphic comparisons. A nerve cell is compared to a flower, with the axion as its stem.

There are also weaknesses. A pronunciation guide is absent, and many of the highlighted text terms are not in the glossary. The index has few cross-references, there are no further readings or bibliography, and there are few illustrations. "Stomachache" is used instead of "stomach ache." Although the thalamus, midbrain, brainstem and medulla are discussed, there is no corresponding diagram. The diagram of the reflex arc is not labeled. It is also confusing to discuss painless surgery in one section (page 4) and then discuss the extreme pain of surgery (page 13). The final chapter should be called Minimizing Pain instead of Pain Prevention, for anesthetics block pain but are included here. The text at times can be very technical; further illustrations are needed to clarify terms and concepts. There also appears to be a conflict concerning the target audience. The introduction, many of the illustrations, and the type size address 4th or 5th graders. But the text, because it becomes very technical at times, is geared to 8th graders to adults. This later group would be put off by the introduction, type size, and some of the illustrations.

I feel that this text is a good overview of the subject but I'd recommend waiting for a revised edition.

Bertrand Gary Hoyle

SOURCE: A review of *Pain: What Is It? How Do We Deal With It?*, in *Appraisal: Science Books for Young People*, Vol. 20, No. 1, Winter, 1987, p. 12.

SPECIALIST: This book describes the types and perceptions of pain and the importance of the pain response in our lives. Pain relief is explored from massage, hypnosis, and acupuncture through various classes of chemicals, culminating at the body's own pain-killers. An extensive glossary accompanies the text.

GENETICS: FROM MENDEL TO GENE SPLICING (1986)

Zena Sutherland

SOURCE: A review of *Genetics: From Mendel to Gene Splicing*, in *Bulletin of the Center for Children's Books*, Vol. 40, No. 3, November, 1986, pp. 41-2.

Usually a capable science writer, Arnold does only an adequate job of describing the history of the science of genetics, the contributions of individual workers whose theories and/or research contributed to present knowledge, and those recent discoveries that have made possible—for good or ill—genetic engineering. The text is competently organized and is written with clarity and directness; it is weakened, unfortunately, by gaps in information (not by erroneous information), a fault echoed by the inadequacy of the illustrative material (no diagram of flower parts to clarify the discussion of fertilization, for example, and no schematic drawing of DNA structure).

Carolyn Phelan

SOURCE: A review of *Genetics: From Mendel to Gene Splicing*, in *Booklist*, Vol. 83, No. 10, January 15, 1987, p. 779.

The historical development of genetics is Arnold's main topic. Clearly written, the text traces the story through false starts, rediscovered treatises, and breakthroughs, identifying the imaginative and methodical men and women who have influenced genetics' coming of age. Don't look here for a discussion of the moral and ecological dilemmas raised by the new capabilities of controlled genetic mutation; Arnold raises that question briefly, only to dismiss it as a thing of the past. This narrative stresses the benefits to humans, its tone reflecting a march-of-progress view of science, with mod-

ern genetics providing hope for an end to world hunger and genetically transmitted diseases. A few diagrams and several full-page, black-and-white photographs, mainly of significant genetic scientists, add visual interest. Valuable chiefly for its cogent overview of the subject.

Martha T. Kane

SOURCE: A review of *Genetics: From Mendel to Gene Splicing*, in *Appraisal: Science Books for Young People*, Vol. 20, No. 2, Spring, 1987, pp. 10-11.

SPECIALIST: ***Genetics: From Mendel to Gene Splicing*** is a well-written, historical survey of the science of genetics, from Mendel through Watson and Crick on to Paul Berg and other current-day researchers. The author includes many interesting topics of concern today such as gene splicing, genetic counseling, and cloning. Applications are given for producing better food crops as well as for preventing and treating human genetic diseases.

The author states the facts about current scientific techniques clearly and accurately, yet also identifies issues or controversies surrounding these techniques. For example, in discussing recombinant DNA (gene splicing) research, she recognizes the fears regarding the dangers of using this technique, from both inside and outside the scientific community. She also reports on new discoveries that have greatly reduced these fears. In describing genetic counseling, the author is careful to point out that many ethical questions exist which must be answered by the parents of the unborn child, and perhaps by society in general. The counselor's role is merely to help the parents understand the risks involved and the future impacts on their lives. Although the author does not avoid the issues, she is clearly coming from a scientific perspective and emphasizes the many benefits received from modern genetic technologies.

Christopher B. Lindsay

SOURCE: A review of *Genetics: From Mendel to Gene Splicing*, in *Appraisal: Science Books for Young People*, Vol. 20, No. 2, Spring, 1987, pp. 10-11.

LIBRARIAN: Arnold has taken a complex subject and made it accessible, in places even exciting, for the young reader. Explanations of heredity and the people who made major contributions to our knowledge of genetics are presented in a highly readable fashion without stinting on either terminology or necessary detail.

Discussion of genetic disorders is slightly less helpful. In an entry on Genetic Counseling, for instance, she discusses the benefits of chorionic villi sampling over amniocentesis, stating that "because the sample can be taken earlier in the pregnancy and because it can be analyzed more quickly, it allows people to make an earlier decision." The nature of the decision is not mentioned. And while cloning is a hot topic about which young readers might turn to this book for information, there is only a brief mention of the subject in reference to the production of dwarf fruit trees.

The index could be more accessible to the young reader. (The only reference in the index to mental retardation is under "mongoloidism", a word few children will think to check). Despite small flaws, however, librarians serving students in intermediate and middle school grades will find this a helpful volume.

THE GOLDEN GATE BRIDGE (1986)

Mary Lathrope

SOURCE: A review of *The Golden Gate Bridge,* in *Booklist,* Vol. 83, No. 8, December 15, 1986, pp. 642-43.

Arnold's account of the history of this dramatically beautiful suspension bridge begins with an Indian legend concerning the formation of San Francisco Bay and continues with its discovery by Spanish explorers and the ensuing rapid settlement of the Bay Area, with its transportation problems due to topographical peculiarities. From there, the author launches into comments about the pressure by local citizens who foresaw what a bridge could mean and the vision and skill of bridge maker Joseph Strauss, who designed the bridge. The actual construction is detailed with numerous black-and-white photographs showing each stage of the difficult and dangerous operation. Arnold describes the elaborate opening celebration and concludes with an explanation of what is involved in maintaining the bridge today. Two pages of "Bridge Facts" are appended, but unfortunately there is no map of the Bay Area. Students seeking information on bridges of San Francisco will find this volume useful, while Californians and tourists will welcome the background information.

Rosie Peasley

SOURCE: A review of *The Golden Gate Bridge,* in *School Library Journal,* Vol. 33, No. 5, January, 1987, p. 70.

Arnold discusses the early discovery of the Golden Gate, the legend about its creation, and a brief geological explanation of its formation. The following chapters offer an explanation of why a bridge was needed; a brief biography of Joseph Strauss (the bridge's engineer); the construction of the bridge; opening ceremonies; maintenance and repair; and changes that have occurred over the years. The 20 black-and-white photographs are of generally good quality; however, there are no maps and only one diagram to clarify difficult concepts on the formation of the bay and the construction of the bridge. A final chapter discusses changes which have taken place on the bridge over the years—toll booths, tolls, and

traffic patterns. A table of "Bridge Facts" is included. Overall, Arnold does an excellent job of explaining the whys and hows of the "number one man-made attraction in the United States." If young readers were not already enamored of the bridge, they should be after reading this lucid, well organized account.

Leslie Chamberlin

SOURCE: A review of *The Golden Gate Bridge,* in *Voice of Youth Advocates,* Vol. 10, No.1, April, 1987, p. 42.

The subject of this slim book limits its appeal nationwide. It covers its purpose carefully and well though perhaps it is better suited to a somewhat younger audience. It is more than adequate in describing political history, brief but understandable engineering details, current policy changes and the need for constant repair, earthquake safety considerations, and the hooplah surrounding the opening. Like many San Francisco events, the first official cars to cross the bridge were treated to spectacular fanfare: log-sawing contests; torching apart a silver, gold, and copper chain; beauty queens; prizes for the first pedestrians in bizarre categories, and more. Profusely illustrated with photos and drawings. Very suitable for reports. The most outstanding aspect of this book is the exploration of Strauss's motivation in conceiving and executing the design of the bridge. He was viewed as an exceptional blend of the poet and the scientist, able himself to bridge the worlds of fact and dreamy imagination.

WHAT WE DO WHEN SOMEONE DIES ("Ceremonies and Celebrations" series, 1987)

Emily Holchin McCarty

SOURCE: A review of *What We Do When Someone Dies,* in *Children's Book Review Service,* Vol. 15, No. 12, Spring, 1987, p. 132.

Using full-color illustrations and a simple, straightforward text, the rites and customs of death are dealt with in an honest manner with just the right combination of facts and feelings. Such subject areas as funerals, cremation, mourning, wills, memorials and remembrance are covered to express the concerns of death in a realistic fashion.

Ruth Amernick

SOURCE: A review of *What We Do When Someone Dies,* in *School Library Journal,* Vol. 33, No. 10, June-July, 1987, p. 76.

In clear language Arnold defines traditional Western death customs, such as funerals, autopsies, embalming, and death notices. Young children will find honest information about the rituals surrounding the death of a friend or relative. The italicized words and index ensure that children can find quickly the context meaning of each key word. Arnold's succinct discussion is complemented by [Helen] Davie's contemporary watercolor illustrations. Parents, teachers, librarians, and children will be pleased to have an accessible, non-judgmental book on a topic that has seemed so difficult to explain.

TRAPPED IN TAR: FOSSILS FROM THE ICE AGE (1987)

Betsy Hearne

SOURCE: A review of *Trapped in Tar: Fossils from the Ice Age,* in *Bulletin of the Center for Children's Books,* Vol. 40, No. 10, June, 1987, p. 181.

Along with black-and-white photographs [by Richard Hewett] of models and reconstructed skeletons from the George C. Page Museum of La Brea Discoveries, an enthusiastic text describes the kinds of fossils found in southern California tar pits. The processes of recovery and paleontologic research are the real emphasis here, but these reveal more than a glimpse of animal and plant life in the Ice Age. In addition to the inherent child appeal of the subject and the clear explanations, the book has a lively format, with pictures dramatically featuring young museum visitors in involved inspection or even hands-on experience of the displays. Closeups of scientists working with bones in excavation pits and laboratories lend a sense of excitement that will inspire students working on prehistoric units and time lines.

Robert M. Schoch

SOURCE: A review of *Trapped in Tar: Fossils from the Ice Age,* in *Science Books & Films,* Vol. 23, No. 2, November-December, 1987, p. 103.

Trapped in Tar is a black-and-white photographic essay with accompanying text focusing on the exhibits and research of the George C. Page Museum of the Rancho La Brea tar pits discoveries in Los Angeles. The book opens by briefly delineating how, 15,000 years ago, animals became trapped in the tar and fossilized. Approximately one-third of the book is devoted to the history of the discovery of fossil bones in the La Brea tar pits and the techniques used to excavate, prepare, and study the fossils. Another third of the book describes some of the organisms that have been found—mammoths, sloths, bison, dire wolves, sabertooth cats, bears, birds, snails, pine cones, seeds, pollen, and a single human skull. The book concludes with speculations on why the large ice-age mammals became extinct. Although appropriate for elementary school students, this book contains a wealth of information on the methods used by paleontologists to learn about ancient life. However, most youngsters will probably find the book a little dull. It will probably have the greatest impact if read in conjunction with a trip to the Page Museum.

Richard C. Riis

SOURCE: A review of *Trapped in Tar: Fossils from the Ice Age,* in *Appraisal: Science Books for Young People,* Vol. 21, No. 1, Winter, 1988, pp. 12-13.

LIBRARIAN: Fascinating black-and-white photographs and a clear, enthusiastic text examine the kind of fossils found in the tar pits of southern California, as excavated and reconstructed by the paleontologists at the George C. Page Museum of La Brea Discoveries in Los Angeles. While the emphasis is on the actual process of fossil recovery and research, there is a great deal of information to be found here about Ice Age plant and animal life, always a popular topic with young readers. Many of the photographs feature scientists at work in laboratories and in the field, as well as young museum visitors in close-up inspection of the displays, making an already appealing subject appear all the more exciting. This is an engaging, engrossing book that should whet the appetite of many a young paleontologist.

Kristiana Gregory

SOURCE: A review of *Trapped in Tar: Fossils from the Ice Age,* in *Los Angeles Times Book Review,* February 7, 1988, p. 10.

During the Ice Age, Southern California was home to more than 400 types of creatures, many of them preserved by the goo of what is now known as the La Brea Tar Pits. The wonderful George C. Page Museum of La Brea Discoveries next to the pits is a surreal oasis where life-size models of prehistoric animals appear to sink in a black pond. Lucky are the many children who have toured these exhibits, but for those who haven't, this picture essay is the next best thing. Dozens of black-and-white photos and a coherent text lead young readers through a fascinating history lesson and show how paleontologists excavate and study fossils, still an ongoing task. In fact, according to the author, homeowners in Los Angeles' Hancock Park area occasionally find ancient bones while digging in their gardens.

EVERYBODY HAS A BIRTHDAY ("Ceremonies and Celebrations" series, 1987)

Gretchen S. Baldauf

SOURCE: A review of *Everybody Has a Birthday,* in *Children's Book Review Service,* Vol. 15, No. 13, July, 1987, p. 144.

This book is a factual approach to the one holiday nearly everyone celebrates. It recognizes the variety of ways in which people celebrate birthdays, while minimizing the idea of presents. Included are sections on names, the zodiac, customs in other countries, and famous people's birthdays. The full-color illustrations [by Anthony Accardo] are rather busy, but pleasant. A useful addition to holiday collections.

Susan Nemeth McCarthy

SOURCE: A review of *Everybody Has a Birthday,* in *School Library Journal,* Vol. 33, No. 11, August, 1987, p. 63.

Each double-page spread combines merely decorative artwork and several short paragraphs to describe an event or tradition associated with the celebration of birthdays. Text is fragmented into short discussions such as names, birthday parties, birthday customs in other countries, birthdays of famous people, etc. The inclusion of subjects such as prenatal visits and tests to determine sex of the fetus are unnecessary and inappropriate for the intended audience. Other information is sparse and haphazardly chosen. For example, in "Your Name" only 18 names and their meanings are given, these names cited as being popular. They include Clark, Fred, Wayne, and Holly—hardly the most common names today.

GIRAFFE ("Animal Favorites" series, 1987)

Kirkus Reviews

SOURCE: A review of *Giraffe,* in *Kirkus Reviews,* Vol. LV, No. 15, August 1, 1987, p. 1154.

There is plenty to celebrate in these two new titles by the team [Arnold and Richard Hewett] that gave us **Koala** and **Kangaroo,** this time focusing on animals at Six Flags Great Adventure Safari Park in New Jersey.

Giraffe provides intriguing facts and endearing close-up color photographs of adult and infant giraffes—browsing treetops for food using their spectacular 18-inch tongues, playfully necking, galloping, chewing cud, getting down for a drink, and giving birth to a 150-pound baby. The text discusses some of the giraffe's special features, including the 25-pound heart which pumps blood up its long neck, blood pressure which is the highest in the animal kingdom, and the patterns of spots which are as unique as fingerprints.

Publishers Weekly

SOURCE: A review of *Giraffe,* in *Publishers Weekly,* Vol. 232, No. 9, August 28, 1987, p. 82.

Most photos of giraffes are interesting: that powerful neck and the long slim body that go with it make every movement unusual. Here they crane toward their favorite food—leaves from the acadia trees, posing awkward-

ly to drink water without tipping over in one picture, then galloping gracefully with all four legs off the ground in the next, twisting around in a knot for a drink of mother's milk. The concise text offers a general introduction to the giraffe and includes a close-up look at a newborn calf (young giraffe). Arnold also passes on other information, like the animal's zoological name, which translates to "camel leopard."

Osiris W. Boutros

SOURCE: A review of *Giraffe,* in *Science Books & Films,* Vol. 23, No. 4, March-April, 1988, p. 252.

Giraffe is an excellent addition to the juvenile literature. Arnold describes the natural habitat of giraffes as well as their food habits and social and reproductive behavior as observed in a large, open-air wildlife park in New Jersey. The origin of the giraffes and their functional adaptations to the environment are also discussed. Scientific information, such as the giraffe's body measurements and its oversize heart and lungs, are accurate and interesting. No two giraffes have exactly the same patterns of neck markings, the book explains, so this is how the park keepers identify them.

KANGAROO ("Animal Favorites" series, 1987)

Sr. Barbara Anne Kilpatrick

SOURCE: A review of *Kangaroo,* in *Catholic Library World,* Vol. 59, No. 2, September-October, 1987, pp. 86-7.

"From the back porch of their country house in Wellington Point, Queensland, Irma and Les Melton could see the Pacific Ocean where it met the Australian shore. The trees nearby were noisy with the calls of magpies and parrots, and next to the flowers in the garden below, a young kangaroo contentedly nibbled the green grass."

Irma and Les Melton share their experiences of raising an orphaned kangaroo, Sport. His first year with the Meltons tells how he is prepared to be on his own. They bottle fed him, made a pouch out of burlap and sheepskin, and took him for walks in a backpack.

Kangaroo introduces young readers to the day-to-day life, habits and perils of a marsupial. The kangaroo family, their characteristics and behavior are discussed. Forty extraordinary photographs [by Richard Hewett] accompany this fascinating essay that will appeal to all animal lovers.

Arlene Bernstein

SOURCE: A review of *Kangaroo,* in *Appraisal: Science Books for Young People,* Vol. 21, No. 1, Winter, 1988, pp. 11-12.

LIBRARIAN: *Kangaroo* is a beautiful addition to that group of science books that follows a year in the life of a wild animal that is "adopted" by an individual due to a "family tragedy". Sport is an eastern gray kangaroo who was cared for by a family in Queensland, Australia, after his mother was killed by hunters. As Arnold relates Sport's year with the Melton family, she describes in detail the characteristics and habits of these marsupials. Close-up color photographs abound in this slim, fact-filled volume which, because of its detailed index, will be a useful source of information for elementary reports. A minor flaw, unfortunately, is the lack of a pronunciation guide for several of the words used in the text.

Glenn M. Cohen

SOURCE: A review of *Kangaroo,* in *Science Books & Films,* Vol. 23, No. 3, January-February, 1988, pp. 175-76.

In this true story, "Sport," a kangaroo, is orphaned after his mother is killed by hunters. Fortunately for "Sport," the Meltons adopt him and nurse him back to health. Sport is released into a wildlife reserve when he turns one and is able to care for himself. *Kangaroo* focuses on raising Sport but also manages to describe the origins of marsupials and the different species of kangaroos without burdening the story with excessive detail. The author is clearly sensitive to the plight of marsupials but is not melodramatic. The book needs at least a hint of humor to lighten its somber tone, however. Young children will grasp the story through the photographs even though they will not understand some of the vocabulary. Older children will understand the vocabulary but will need explanations of the biological terms.

📖 *KOALA* ("Animal Favorites" series, 1987)

Thomas A. Cole

SOURCE: A review of *Koala,* in *Science Books & Films,* Vol. 23, No. 2, November-December, 1987, p. 106.

This book traces the life cycle of a specific koala female and the natural history of the species with a simple text and 39 excellent photographs [by Richard Hewett]. As a "picture book," it may be read to preschoolers with success by modifying a few words and some sentence structures. For young readers, the volume is a good challenge; most sentences are straightforward. The book covers such topics as Australian settlement by humans, endangered species and koala preserves, scientific names, varieties of koalas, physical characteristics of sexes of koalas including marsupial traits, Australian flowers and eucalyptus-tree varieties, and the aborigine origin of the name "koala." The unstated, underlying principles of ecology and conservation are supported by the story line, which leads to the transport of the young koala to the

San Francisco Zoo in an effort at conservation. An index is included. Parents and grandparents will read the book themselves before giving it to their children and grandchildren. This volume would also be a good addition to the children's section of public libraries and to school libraries.

Martha B. Mahoney

SOURCE: A review of *Koala,* in *Appraisal: Science Books for Young People,* Vol. 21, No. 1, Winter, 1988, pp. 11-12.

LIBRARIAN: The book jacket picturing a mother koala and her child draws both children and adults into this book. They will not be disappointed. It is filled with excellent photographs and interesting facts about the koala.

The text covers the life of Frangipani and her baby Karen. As the author describes stages in this family's life, the illustrator, photographer Richard Hewett, details the life accurately. There are clear explanations in the text. The illustrator has depicted the concept of size well. For example, when the baby first comes out of its pouch, it is eight inches long. The illustration shows Karen cupped in two hands. Not all of the illustrations are captioned, yet the text on the facing page or above/below the illustration is appropriate.

Emphasis is placed on problems the koalas have in their natural environment and how Lone Pine Koala Sanctuary is trying to help these animals survive. A certain number are sent to zoos each year and others returned to the wild. The animals must be quarantined before they go to a zoo in order that no disease will be transmitted.

The terminology used is accurate. Any technical words are explained through the text in a satisfactory manner. The index includes a key word and photograph list, thus making it readily accessible for research.

I feel this book would be a very good addition to an elementary school or public library.

Donna M. Zannelli

SOURCE: A review of *Koala,* in *Appraisal: Science Books for Young People,* Vol. 21, No. 1, Winter, 1988, pp. 11-12.

SPECIALIST: Caroline Arnold and Richard Hewett have combined their extraordinary talents in the writing and illustrating of their new book *Koala.* Arnold factually follows the conception, development, birth and growth of this species of marsupial by telling the story of just one female and her offspring. By following Frangipani's adventures on the reserve in Australia, Arnold gives a homey feeling children will respond to.

However, this book's greatest asset is the collection of fabulous photographs taken by Hewett. He successfully captured the beauty of the koala. Moreover, his ability to catch these elusive creatures in both natural and staged poses enables children to see that koala bears are not really the cuddly stuffed animals they picture all the time. Hewett demonstrates how dangerous these wild animals can be by showing the ferocious nature of their teeth and claws. One the other hand, Arnold seems to overlook this aspect of their nature altogether, and instead supports the image put forth by Quantas Airways.

Overall, I believe that this book would enhance any wildlife book collection. . . . The text is enjoyable to read and has a lot of factual information to offer young readers never before exposed to the life cycle of the marsupial.

AUSTRALIA TODAY (1987)

Jean Gregory Martin

SOURCE: A review of *Australia Today,* in *The Book Report,* Vol. 6, No. 4, January-February, 1988, pp. 55-6.

This up-to-date, comprehensive work details the geography, people, government, daily life, resources, economy and wildlife of Australia. The author includes some history, but the focus is on the life and lifestyles of the people. Frequent comparisons are made between Australia and the United States. In a simple, straightforward style, the author portrays Australia as a modern, forward-moving country. She attributes advances in transportation, communication and technology with much of the transformation of the once uncharted continent into a vital and important country.

A WALK ON THE GREAT BARRIER REEF ("Nature Watch" series, 1987)

Phillis Wilson

SOURCE: A review of *A Walk on the Great Barrier Reef,* in *Booklist,* Vol. 84, No. 21, July, 1988, p. 1831.

Australia's Great Barrier Reef, along with the diversity of creatures that depend on it, is one of the natural wonders of the world, though the reef is in constant danger from humans who disturb the delicate balance of life. This undersea wilderness lies along the northeast coast of Australia, extending in a chain for over 1,200 miles. It is home to multicolored fish, sea creatures both huge and tiny, reptiles, and many kinds of birds. The author provides discussion and clear, cross-section drawings of the three kinds of coral-reef formations: fringing reef, barrier reef, and atoll. Many of the unusual creatures—pincushion sea star, crown-of-thorns sea star, sea cucumber, and sea hare—are stunningly photographed,

[by Arthur Arnold and Marty Snyderman] emphasizing their vibrant colors in a richly textured environment. Above-water shots of the beautiful reef balance the effect. Though practical as curriculum support, this new offering in the fine Nature Watch series, will be a browsing student or photographer's delight.

Ellen Fader

SOURCE: A review of *A Walk on the Great Barrier Reef,* in *School Library Journal,* Vol. 34, No. 11, August, 1988, pp. 99-100.

The fascinating plants and animals of Australia's Great Barrier Reef are described in a straightforward way and illustrated with stunning, clear full-color photographs. Additional information about the growth of coral and the formation of reefs makes this useful to a wide range of readers. Maps and labelled diagrams enhance and extend the presentation of information. Potentially difficult terms appear in boldface and, although ably defined in the text, are also included in a glossary. Arnold does a credible job of explaining relationships within the habitat of the reef community.

Nancy Marie Payne

SOURCE: A review of *A Walk on the Great Barrier Reef,* in *Appraisal: Science Books for Young People,* Vol. 22, Nos. 1 & 2, Winter & Spring, 1989, pp. 9-10.

SPECIALIST: If you know nothing about The Great Barrier Reef, then this book will very simply explain the where, what, why and how, of coral reefs in general, and the Great Barrier Reef in particular.

All the ecological principles are there. The author explains, in a very straightforward manner, the delicate balance needed between sunlight and water to support a coral ecology, the interdependence of plant and animal life, the food chain of a reef society, and human influences on that society. There is a nice evolutionary progression of coral reef inhabitants, starting with the coral itself. Most of the major reef inhabitants are covered, from the algae, through the gastriopods and bivalves, up through fish and ending with the birds. This verbal progression is accompanied by beautiful photographs. At one point the author talks about octopi and sea hares while the photograph on the same page is of cowries, which are univalves. That page is somewhat confusing because it breaks from the norm of picture and text together.

All the phylum names are given for the individuals covered. Although all young readers may not understand what this means, it is good scientific training for them to be aware of such names. . . .

This is your basic ecology book with all the correct information; done in a simple readable format for children. The problem is that the information can be found elsewhere in much more creative styles. There isn't any reason for me not to recommend this book—just no overwhelming reason why I'd want to.

Nancy R. Spence

SOURCE: A review of *A Walk on the Great Barrier Reef*, in *Appraisal: Science Books for Young People*, Vol. 22, Nos. 1 & 2, Winter & Spring, 1989, pp. 9-10.

LIBRARIAN: Not everyone has the opportunity to walk on The Great Barrier Reef, but this latest book by Caroline Arnold in the "Carolrhoda Nature Watch" series is a good substitute. Informative, straightforward text and outstanding full-color photographs take the reader along in investigating this living wall 1250 miles long on the northeast coast of Australia. Our exploration begins with the picture of two people walking on a reef flat; and by the concluding picture of a sunset over the reef, we have learned how a reef is formed and have seen up close the diversity of the plant life, sea creatures and birds which depend on it for food and protection. . . . All in all, a memorable visit.

📖 *COPING WITH NATURAL DISASTERS* (1988)

Meryl Silverstein

SOURCE: A review of *Coping with Natural Disasters*, in *School Library Journal*, Vol. 35, No. 9, June-July, 1988, p. 120.

A general treatment that provides information not always available in one source. The opening chapter lists government and private organizations that entirely or in part are involved in disaster relief. A history of each, its work, and its funding are briefly described. Each following chapter discusses a different natural occurrence, but the treatment is uneven. For instance, "Hurricanes and Floods" features Hurricane Agnes, a vignette of a family and the agency which aided them, and describes the natural causes. But the chapter "Avalanches and Blizzards" devotes less than a page to blizzards. Surprisingly, the involvement of most of the agencies in the opening section are not discussed in the specific cases appearing later. The final chapter gives a list of home emergency supplies and recommendations for actions to take. Thus the first and last chapters are useful for reference. Although many science-oriented books are available for specific disasters, they do not generally cover the social, political, and disruptive consequences that people face.

Shirley Bathgate

SOURCE: A review of *Coping with Natural Disasters*, in *Voice of Youth Advocates*, Vol. 11, No. 4, October, 1988, p. 197.

One of 38 books for young people written by Arnold, *Coping with Natural Disasters* is as well written as Arnold's *Pets without Homes* and *Saving the Peregrine Falcon*, a 1985 ALA Notable Book. The author limits the book to natural disasters which occur suddenly—hurricanes and floods, earthquakes, tsunami, volcanoes, avalanches, tornadoes, and forest fires. She deftly mingles general and specific information. Although Arnold presents specific disasters such as the 330,000 homeless as a result of Hurricane Agnes and the destruction of 230 buildings by the tsunami which struck Hilo, Hawaii in 1960, it is the more general back-ground information that sets *Coping with Natural Disasters* apart from most disaster books. Readers learn, for example, that hurricanes produce as much energy as a half million atomic bombs, and that tornadoes are the most uniquely American weather disaster. The book is also unique in that her emphasis is not on the facts of the disaster or the destruction itself but on how people recovered and rebuilt lives and cities. The work of the Red Cross, CARE, UNICEF and other relief agencies is explained. A final chapter provides an extensive list of emergency supplies and steps to be taken to prepare for possible disasters.

George C. Hartmann

SOURCE: A review of *Coping with Natural Disasters*, in *Science Books & Films*, Vol. 24, No. 2, November-December, 1988, p. 81.

Natural disasters occur frequently and unpredictably, but people generally worry about them only after the fact. This short book conveys information about environmental disruption to stimulate discussions about coping with it. A review of specific agencies that participate in disaster relief is followed by descriptions of seven kinds of natural disasters, their causes, effects on society, and specific efforts to aid the afflicted. Suggestions on how to prepare for emergencies and avert calamity are given in the last chapter. The text is well organized and clearly written. Numerous anecdotes are obviously meant to catch the interest of the young reader. This is not a natural science book, however, since it deals primarily with social concerns and only touches on the physical causes of natural disaster. Some of the illustrations are blurred or lacking in contrast. Nevertheless, students will find this to be a very informative supplement to junior-high level social studies courses and general science courses in which the effects of ecological disruption on human society and culture are discussed.

📖 *LLAMA* ("Animal Favorites" series, 1988)

Eva Elisabeth Von Ancken

SOURCE: A review of *Llama*, in *School Library Journal*, Vol. 35, No. 1, September, 1988, pp. 187-88.

Arnold's photo-essay shows the birth and subsequent life of a baby llama named Gypsy. Although Arnold discusses llamas in their native setting, all but one of the photographs are of ranch raised or zoo specimens. The text and illustrations [by Richard Hewett] discuss the uses of llama wool and llamas as burden carriers on backpacking trips. There is even a section on "showing" llamas and an obstacle course race. The full-color photos are mostly clear but often static. Although there is much information to be found, the lack of chapters or even logical divisions tends to make the whole confusing. The style ranges from chatty to dryly informational. However, a thorough index does help organize the material for research.

Mark S. Rich

SOURCE: A review of *Llama,* in *Science Books & Films,* Vol. 24, No. 3, January-February, 1989, p. 167.

Here Arnold uses the true story of the birth and growth of a llama on a California llama ranch to present information about llamas and other South American cameloids. (There are 4 humpless members of the camel family, including 2 domestic forms (llama and alpaca) and 2 wild species (vicuna and guanaco).) Domestic llama management is presented in a scientific manner suitable for young readers, and the narrative should hold their interest. The 40 closely related color photographs unfortunately include a few that seem slightly out of focus or somewhat poorly reproduced. Despite the lack of drawings, tables, or charts, factually accurate information is imparted in a way that will be of interest to young readers.

Martha B. Mahoney

SOURCE: A review of *Llama,* in *Appraisal: Science Books for Young People,* Vol. 22, No. 4, Autumn, 1989, pp. 6-7.

LIBRARIAN: Caroline Arnold and photographer Richard Hewett have teamed up successfully to present a study of the llama, an animal raised in this country as a pet, for wool, and to carry gear for hikers.

This photo essay follows the life, on a California ranch, of a llama named Gypsy. It also mentions the llamas associated with the Indians of the Andes. The other members of the lamoid family (alpaca, guanaco and vicuna) are pictured and physically described. They are all plant eating, social animals, and they all live in herds.

On the ranch, the reader follows the life of a newborn llama until the time when it is sheared and its wool spun. Llamas are taken to exhibitions in the United States and judged by set criteria. Then they are valued, and some sold or used in breeding.

This is an entertaining, and rather touching book highlighting a remarkable creature.

Jim Maland

SOURCE: A review of *Llama,* in *Appraisal: Science Books for Young People,* Vol. 22, No. 4, Autumn, 1989, pp. 6-7.

SPECIALIST: To most of us North Americans, the llama is a distant and perhaps exotic South American creature. Arnold and Hewett, however, bring this wonderful animal closer to reality. Now found in zoos, ranches, and as pets across the United States, the gentle, good-natured llama is making its mark. In beautiful photography, Hewett captures, and describes, in some detail, the birth of a llama, and the subsequent six months of motherly nurturing. Complemented with excellent photography, the author discusses the intriguing anatomy, behavior and history of the llama. No longer found in the wild, the fate of this animal rests solely with humans. Its beautiful wool, pleasant disposition, and wonderful companionship will, I trust, ensure its survival.

This is an entertaining, and rather touching book highlighting a remarkable creature.

📖 *JUGGLER* (1988)

Denise M. Wilms

SOURCE: A review of *Juggler,* in *Booklist,* Vol. 85, No. 5, November 1, 1988, p. 476.

Arnold introduces Jahnathon Whitfield, a professional juggler who teaches his skills to eager classes. The magical ease an able juggler brings to his performance is demystified by photos and text showing Whitfield explaining a little of the history of juggling and then leading his audience through elementary juggling maneuvers. Later, readers watch the man perform at a renaissance fair and see him at a juggler's convention. The black-and-white photographs [by Richard Hewett] capture the fun of juggling and the earnestness of the novices that Whitfield coaches, but some shots are grainy and others weakly composed. Aspiring jugglers probably won't mind, though, and there is lots of practical advice to get beginners started.

Christine Behrmann

SOURCE: A review of *Juggler,* in *School Library Journal,* Vol. 35, No. 4, December, 1988, pp. 113-14.

Arnold gives a routine presentation of a juggler in action. Jahnathon Whitfield of the California Juggling Institute is depicted as he gives a demonstration at a library; teaches juggling to a class; performs at a Renaissance Fair; and attends a convention sponsored by the International Jugglers' Association. This allows Arnold to give her readers some information on the rudiments of the art of juggling and the many venues in which it is practiced. The present-tense text is simply written. Arnold is especially effective in conveying the instructions given to a novice juggler, a section which will give younger readers some insight into the art itself. . . . One page tells where to obtain more information on juggling classes, equipment, and organizations and lists two other books on the subject. Useful in the main, but not particularly inspiring or distinctive.

📖 *PENGUIN* ("Animal Favorites" series, 1988)

Ellen Fader

SOURCE: A review of *Penguin,* in *The Horn Book Magazine,* Vol. LXV, No. 1, January-February, 1989, p. 89.

Arnold and [Richard] Hewett once again prove themselves outstanding partners in producing photo essays for young readers about animals. As in the similar volumes *Giraffe, Zebra, Kangaroo,* and *Koala,* the new accounts describe the life cycle of one particular species, including information on how the species lives in the wild and in captivity. . . . The Magellanic penguins, which inhabit the Tuxedo Junction exhibit at the San Francisco Zoo, are the subject of *Penguin.* The hatching and care of two chicks form the basis of the intriguing volume.

Mark S. Rich

SOURCE: A review of *Penguin,* in *Science Books & Films,* Vol. 24, No. 3, January-February, 1989, p. 167.

Flightless aquatic birds that walk upright and resemble little dressed-up people appeal to children, and this book will too. Its story line revolves around the birth of a pair of Magellanic penguins at the San Francisco Zoo. Included are excellent explanations of the zoo's husbandry practices for this world's largest captive group of Magellanic penguins. Some mention is also made of the natural history of this species and of all penguin species in the wild. I found no factual errors and enjoyed the 40 excellent color photographs, despite the fact that they are rarely captioned; they are self-explanatory and follow the text, in any case. All measurements include English and metric equivalents. Anthropomorphism is kept to an acceptable level and, when employed, does help to present captive animal management in a readable, scientific manner that young people will relate to. In sum, this is an excellent introduction to penguins and the scientific management of them in captivity.

Lavinia C. Demos

SOURCE: A review of *Penguin,* in *Appraisal: Science Books for Young People,* Vol. 22, No. 3, Summer, 1989, p. 7.

SPECIALIST: This fine book skillfully weaves a great deal of information about penguins in general into the story of Uno and Squeaker, two Magellanic penguin chicks born at the San Francisco Zoo. Outstanding color photographs of penguins accompany the text on each page. I found the information on caring for penguins in a zoo setting especially interesting. In addition, the reader learns a lot about the geographical distribution of various species of penguins, mating and nesting behavior, feeding, bodily structure and function, swimming ability, and dangers to survival. The text is well written and straightforward, but not dry. The text is continuous; I think chapters or paragraph headings, and a map showing penguin distribution would be helpful for a young researcher.

Gwyneth E. Loud

SOURCE: A review of *Penguin,* in *Appraisal: Science Books for Young People,* Vol. 22, No. 3, Summer, 1989, p. 7.

LIBRARIAN: Here are penguins in a man-made environment—the zoo. Magellanic penguins are frequently chosen for life in captivity because they come from the coast of South America, and can easily adapt to our temperate climate. This group has been hand reared in a zoo nursery, given individual names, and studied in much the same way we've become accustomed to reading about in dolphin research. The zoo habitat makes it easier to produce first class detailed photographs, and a great many are included here, all in color. The close observation of a single species makes the book particularly readable, while providing contrasting information about other penguin groups as well.

Two interesting bits of penguin lore are as follows: First, they have to drink salt water when they live in the wild so penguins have special glands to remove the salt from the water after they drink it. It comes out in liquid form and drips down grooves in the side of their beaks. Second, male and female penguins are so nearly identical that nobody can tell which is which for about two years when some of them lay eggs!

📖 *TULE ELK* ("Nature Watch Book" series, 1988)

Kirkus Reviews

SOURCE: A review of *Tule Elk,* in *Kirkus Reviews,* Vol. LVII, No. 12, June 15, 1989, p. 912.

The author of many nature titles describes the history, anatomy, and habits of the smallest of the three elk subspecies in North America. Once nearly extinct, this little-known member of the deer family now flourishes on several preserves in California. While the species' genealogy *is* complex, the writing here at times seems unnecessarily cluttered: " . . . in Europe, the animal North Americans call a moose is called an elk, and the animal North Americans call an elk is called a deer." Meanwhile, as Arnold explains at length the naming of each tine of the antler, she provides little information on the elk's special adaptations of teeth, palate, stomach, and hoof.

Carolyn Angus

SOURCE: A review of *Tule Elk,* in *Appraisal: Science Books for Young People,* Vol. 23, No. 1, Winter, 1990, pp. 72-4.

LIBRARIAN: In **Tule Elk** Caroline Arnold discusses the natural history of Cervus elaphus nannodes, the smallest of the three subspecies of North American elk. Pioneers in California's Central Valley in the 1800s called them tule elk because they frequented the cattail swamps, or tule reeds. In considering anatomy, life cycle, and habits, Arnold compares the tule elk with the Roosevelt elk of the Western coastal rainforests as well as the Rocky Mountain elk. One of the elk's special adaptations, its antlers, is described in detail; the inclusion of a labelled diagram would have been useful. Considerable attention is given to the history of the tule elk: its near extinction in the mid-1880s and its recovery: The tule elk is protected by law and herds now thrive under wildlife management on several California preserves.

John R. Pancella

SOURCE: A review of *Tule Elk,* in *Appraisal: Science Books for Young People,* Vol. 23, No. 1, Winter, 1990, pp. 72-4.

SPECIALIST: On first glance, **Tule Elk** seems to be the least motivating of the three books [in the "Nature Watch Book" series]. Some of the photographs are long distance views and a few are less distinct than the usual high quality ones in the rest of the series. Unless it is reviewed closely, this volume may seem to have only regional appeal, perhaps where deer, elk, or their relatives live. The text includes individual and herd behavior, feeding habits, protection, life cycle, and physical characteristics. The predominant message of the book, however, is worth noting. Here is an excellent study of the majesty of an endangered species that once abounded on free range in the U.S. west. Highlighted are its near extinction due to human migration west in the 1800s, and its gradual recovery beginning in the early 1900s. Less than 500 of this smallest of three North American species now exist under wildlife management on California reserves.

Mary Alice Smith

SOURCE: A review of *Tule Elk,* in *Science Books & Films,* Vol. 25, No. 4, March-April, 1990, p. 212.

This story about tule elk in California presents the characteristics of this animal as well as the history of the species and the impact of a changing environment on the survival of these animals. The text is well written, although sometimes confusing when it switches from descriptions of the past to those of the present. There are two major themes: the characteristics of the tule elk (as well as other members of the deer family) and the concept of conservation. . . . The story of how the tule elk were saved from extinction, largely through the efforts of one man, would make an excellent introduction to a classroom discussion on conservation and the impact that humans have on wildlife.

THE TERRIBLE HODAG (1989)

Publishers Weekly

SOURCE: A review of *The Terrible Hodag,* in *Publishers Weekly,* Vol. 226, No. 15, April 14, 1989, pp. 67-8.

Ole Swenson and the other lumberjacks fear the terrible Hodag, a beast with the head of an ox, the feet of a bear, the back of a dinosaur and the tail of an alligator. They never work in the woods at night, when the creature roams the forest. Then their boss demands that an entire hillside be cleared and the logs hauled to the sawmill before he will pay them. Ole accomplishes that with the help of the Hodag, who is not so terrible, but only worried that the forest—his home—will vanish. Ole assures him it will be preserved. The tale of cooperation and tolerance fits nicely into the northwoods setting; the Hodag looks like a close relation of Babe the Blue Ox. [Lambert] Davis's painterly illustrations depict the lumberjacks as a hale and hearty bunch—an interesting crew to add to the folkloric tradition.

Susan Scheps

SOURCE: A review of *The Terrible Hodag,* in *School Library Journal,* Vol. 35, No. 10, June, 1989, p. 82.

From the lumber camps of northern Wisconsin came stories of the terrible Hodag–a talking beast 40 feet tall with the head of an ox, the feet of a bear, the back of a dinosaur, the tail of an alligator, and red eyes that glow like fire. Arnold has created a tale of how the Hodag helped the men of one lumber camp to cut an entire hillside of trees and take them to the sawmill. It is a simply told story of brave Ole Swenson, a lumberjack who accidently met the legendary beast in the forest at night and convinced it to help his men to do the impossible tasks set by the boss man of the lumber camp. . . . Davis' Hodag—seen from various angles in a series of illustrations—will appeal to young devotees of dinosaurs, monsters, and such. His large feet, dragon-like tail, and massive profile contrast with the tiny loggers to show his immenseness. As tales of this beast do not appear in collections of American lore and legend, this original story, based on northern campfire tales, has its place in children's literature.

Ilene Cooper

SOURCE: A review of *The Terrible Hodag,* in *Booklist,* Vol. 85, No. 20, June 15, 1989, p. 1818.

Calling on north-woods campfire tales about a creature with the head of an ox, the feet of a bear, the back of a dinosaur, and the tail of an alligator, Arnold fashions her own Hodag story. When lumberjack Ole Swenson and his boys are told by their mean old boss to cut down every tree on the far hillside by Friday, the men protest. They won't go into the forest at night because the Hodag might get them. The boss man doesn't care. It's the trees by Friday, or no pay. So Ole braves the Hodag and finds he's not a bad sort—he topples trees with ease. After the boss man stipulates that the logs must be taken to the sawmill before the men are paid, the huge creature helps again. The lumberjacks, learning that the Hodag is their savior, cheer the creature and vow to leave part of the forest uncut so he can live in peace. It's refreshing to see a monster with such a kind disposition, and Davis does the Hodag justice in his bold art. The lumbering creature, despite its visage, has a sweetness and vulnerability that works well against the background of forest scenes in pure, cool colors. An excellent addition for tall-tale collections.

DINOSAUR MOUNTAIN: GRAVEYARD OF THE PAST (1989)

Phillis Wilson

SOURCE: A review of *Dinosaur Mountain: Graveyard of the Past,* in *Booklist,* Vol. 85, No. 18, May 15, 1989, p. 1642.

Devoted dinosaur fans are sure to be enthusiastic about this vicarious visit to the Dinosaur National Monument quarry in Jensen, Utah. It is a gold mine for paleontologists, as fossils of the 10 different kinds of dinosaurs that lived in North America during the late Jurassic period have been found there. Arnold explains the painstaking work and the variety of tools employed in fossil excavation, restoration, and identification. The text is strongly supported by [Richard] Hewett's dramatic photographs, particularly those showing fossils still embedded in quarry walls. This unique contribution to dinosaur collections will spark anew a sense of wonder about a subject that appears to have a never-ending wealth of secrets.

Kirkus Reviews

SOURCE: A review of *Dinosaur Mountain: Graveyard of the Past,* in *Kirkus Reviews,* Vol. LVII, No. 9, May 15, 1989, pp. 759-60.

The Dinosaur National Monument in Utah includes a museum, a visitors' center, and a working laboratory for paleontologists. A rich source of fossils since its discovery in 1907, over 700,000 pounds of fossils from more than 60 different dinosaurs were excavated from the quarry and then shipped to museums around the country. Today the quarry provides new dinosaur finds and a firsthand look at paleontologists in action. Full-color photographs show them at work with jackhammers, microscopes, and epoxy glue, using specialized methods to document fossil finds and learn more about dinosaurs. These photos capture the viewer's imagination with dramatic reconstructions, enormous bones embedded in rock, and teeth smaller than a grain of rice. Meanwhile, the text is full of the everyday details of the paleontologists' work and the kinds of minutiae about specific dinosaur species that enthrall dinosaur enthusiasts.

Ellen Fader

SOURCE: A review of *Dinosaur Mountain: Graveyard of the Past,* in *The Horn Book Magazine,* Vol. LXV, No. 5, September-October, 1989, p. 635.

Utah's Dinosaur Mountain National Monument is a rich source of fossil impressions and bones where scientists continue to make new discoveries during excavations. Arnold seamlessly blends general information about paleontology with facts about specific finds near the Monument and additionally offers intriguing descriptions of ongoing work. Young dinosaur enthusiasts will long for a visit to the Dinosaur Quarry, a visitor center constructed at the site of the first excavations in the area; the rear wall of the building is actually part of the quarry itself, and visitors can watch paleontologists at work. Hewett's arresting photographs command attention, from the fossilized Allosaurus skull on the front cover to pictures capturing modern methods of work on site and in the laboratory. Even the photographs showing dinosaur models, taken at a variety of museums, are compelling. The inclusion of people in many of the photographs helps prevent confusion about relative dimensions; Arnold is conscientious in her inclusion of size and weight, in metric as well as decimal measurement. The first time each dinosaur is encountered in the text, the correct pronunciation of its name is given. The layout, with brief captions neatly set off from the rest of the text, contributes to the book's attractiveness and ease of use. Lively writing, a dramatic subject, and a sure-fire hit with young readers.

Amy L. Cohn

SOURCE: "Dinosaur Days," in *The Five Owls,* Vol. 111, No. 3, February, 1990, pp. 46-7.

[Paleontological] discoveries happen all the time at Dinosaur National Monument, a quarry visitor center, located in Jensen, Utah. Caroline Arnold's *Dinosaur Mountain: Graveyard of the Past,* illustrated with remarkable full-color photographs by Richard Hewett, introduces children to a special facility where visitors can actually observe researchers uncovering ancient fossils. Even better, children can obtain a Dinosaur Hunting License from the county in which the National Monument is located and try their own luck. On second thought, if a trip to Utah isn't in the family vacation plans for the near future, you may not want to bring this book home. The lobbying to go will be intense!

📖 *CHEETAH* ("Animal Favorites" series, 1989)

Kirkus Reviews

SOURCE: A review of *Cheetah,* in *Kirkus Reviews,* Vol. LVII, No. 12, June 15, 1989, p. 911.

An author-photographer team responsible for many appealing animal studies travels to Wildlife Safari—an open-air game park in Oregon—to focus on Damara, a tame cheetah and to the San Francisco Zoo to study Doodles, a baby hippo.

[The book] provides many clear, full-color photos [by Richard Hewett] plus information on anatomy, life cycle, and special adaptations. *Cheetah* includes information on the endangered status of the powerful cat, which has been associated with man for more than 4,000 years. Damara, hand-raised by her keepers, is shown cuddling with schoolchildren, and there are dozens of other endearing photos of young cheetahs.

Margaret Bush

SOURCE: A review of *Cheetah,* in *School Library Journal,* Vol. 35, No. 15, November, 1989, p. 116.

Once found in Africa, India, and other parts of Asia, the highly endangered cheetah now lives only in limited areas of Africa or in captivity, as shown in this attractive photo essay. Arnold's text begins by introducing a tame female cheetah raised by humans at a wildlife park in Oregon and moves smoothly into a discussion of the history and physical characteristics of cheetahs and behavioral differences between animals in the wild and those in protected habitats. The discussion covers hunting activity, rearing of the young, characteristic marking, genetic weakness as the species declines, and other topics. Fine color photographs, handsomely assembled, accentuate the elegance of the species. Although the material tends to be cursory, leaving readers wishing for more information in many instances, this is an appealing introduction to an animal surprisingly underrepresented in children's books.

B. Gary Hoyle

SOURCE: A review of *Cheetah,* in *Appraisal: Science Books for Young People,* Vol. 23, No. 1, Winter, 1990, pp. 7-8.

SPECIALIST: Focusing on events in Wildlife Safari (an open-air park in Southern Oregon), *Cheetah* follows the natural history of the most endangered of the big cats. Famous for its speed and killing power, the cheetah is actually a rather gentle animal, and its "tabby cat nature" is best exemplified in Damara. This hand-reared cheetah is used by park personnel when they lecture to the public. Damara purrs, and people may even pet her.

Though all the beautiful, full-color photographs were taken in Oregon, they give an impression of animals on the wild African plains. The text also ranges beyond Oregon to give children considerable information on cheetahs in their natural home. The last three pages are thought-provoking. The cheetah is so rare that a considerable amount of inbreeding has taken place; thus, zoos have to keep accurate records to reduce this trend. If not, the captive cheetah of the future may be infertile. It is unknown whether the wild cheetah will exist into the next century.

Martha B. Mahoney

SOURCE: A review of *Cheetah,* in *Appraisal: Science Books for Young People,* Vol. 23, No. 1, Winter, 1990, pp. 7-8.

LIBRARIAN: Wildlife Safari in Oregon is the home of Damara, a tame cheetah used to educate people about cheetahs and wildlife conservation. She is the main character in a book, *Cheetah,* written by Caroline Arnold and photographed by Richard Hewett. This book is an excellent look at the life of the animal, both in captivity and in the wild.

The text reviews the history of the cheetah. Interestingly enough, each cheetah has a unique pattern of spots, just as humans have fingerprints. The descriptions of a running cheetah's body (imagine running at 75 mph), the method of killing its prey, and its teeth are clear. In captivity, the Species Survival Plan is used to ensure that the healthiest cheetahs breed. Mention is made of problems cheetahs have in surviving in the wild due to man's encroachment on their habitat.

📖 *HIPPO* ("Animal Favorites" series, 1989)

Amy Adler

SOURCE: A review of *Hippo,* in *School Library Journal,* Vol. 35, No. 14, October, 1989, p. 127.

As with the other titles in this popular series, *Hippo* explores in words and spectacular photographs the life of a hippopotamus in captivity and presents facts about the animal in the wild. The hippos' habitat, group characteristics, and physical qualities are clearly explained as well as their unique adaptation to life in and near the water. A few facts may be up for debate, e.g. Arnold ranks the hippo as the *second* largest land animal while other sources list it *third* behind the rhino and the elephant. Never mind. Small quibbles won't detract from this book's usefulness and attractiveness. [Richard] Hewett's charming full-color photographs succeed in making this admittedly odd-looking animal as engaging as the other more cuddly creatures in the series. A well-rounded look at the hippopotamus for unsophisticated readers, and one that most libraries will want to consider.

B. Gary Hoyle

SOURCE: A review of *Hippo,* in *Appraisal: Science Books for Young People,* Vol. 23, No. 1, Winter, 1990, pp. 8-9.

SPECIALIST: Centering on the San Francisco Zoo, the author describes the development, daily life and ecology of the hippopotamus. This is an animal well adapted to aquatic life, and thus, relishes its all-day soak in the zoo's concrete pool. Many beautiful color photographs are scattered throughout this little book, some showing hippos in their natural African environment. The text is not restricted only to zoo animals. The importance of hippos in their natural environment is stressed: their paths along the shoreline are used by other animals as a safe access to drinking water; their dung provides nutrients for algae and other water plants; and their antics in the water stir up food materials for fish.

As a whole, this book is a worthwhile addition to a library, but I do wish that a glossary had been included with phonetic spelling, and that the photographs had been labeled.

Martha B. Mahoney

SOURCE: A review of *Hippo,* in *Appraisal: Science Books for Young People,* Vol. 23, No. 1, Winter, 1990, pp. 8-9.

LIBRARIAN: *Hippo* is a delightful science book that takes us to the San Francisco Zoo to visit Doodles, a young hippo and his family, as well as hippos in Africa. Caroline Arnold and Richard Hewett have created a book filled with facts and excellent photographs that will fascinate and inform readers.

Doodles lives in an exhibit at the zoo with his parents, Cuddles and Puddles. The author intersperses information about hippos in the wild and in captivity throughout the text. Its habits, its scientific name, the history of the animal, and its physical characteristics, including adaptations to aquatic life, are covered. Interesting facts relating to the training of the babies and the hippos' role in nature are mentioned. . . .

This book will be very popular and an excellent addition to collections.

LeRoy Lee

SOURCE: A review of *Hippo,* in *Science Books & Films,* Vol. 25, No. 5, May-June, 1990, p. 268.

By tracing the growth of a young hippo at the San Francisco Zoo, the author introduces youthful readers to the natural history of the hippopotamus. A great deal of information is presented in the context of a story, yet the information is not overwhelming. The artistic and technical quality of the photographs adds great value to this book, which young readers will enjoy and will find a good source of information. Equally important, the book lends itself to be read by adults to children.

OSTRICHES AND OTHER FLIGHTLESS BIRDS ("Nature Watch" series, 1990)

Deborah Abbott

SOURCE: A review of *Ostriches and Other Flightless Birds,* in *Booklist,* Vol. 86, No. 13, March 1, 1990, p. 1337.

These latest additions to the Nature Watch series [*Ostriches and Other Flightless Birds* and *Albatrosses of Midway Island*] maintain its high standards. The texts flow smoothly from one topic to the next, and the sharp color photographs have broad appeal. Each book includes nuggets of information on habitat, life cycle, and current status and will intrigue science buffs and general readers alike.

In *Ostriches,* the reader learns about the ostrich in superlatives: for instance, this flightless wonder is the largest living bird (6 to 8 feet tall), it has the largest eyes (2 inches in diameter), and the female lays the largest egg (8 inches long). While most of the book focuses on the ostrich, brief discussions of its relatives—the rheas, cassowaries, emus, and kiwis—are also included.

Lynne E. Kepler

SOURCE: A review of *Ostriches and Other Flightless Birds,* in *Appraisal: Science Books for Young People,* Vol. 23, No. 3, Summer, 1990, pp. 79-80.

SPECIALIST: These two books [*Ostriches and Other Flightless Birds* and *Albatrosses of Midway Island*] provide an abundance of good information about two interesting groups of birds—the albatrosses and the ratites (ostriches, emus, cassowaries, rheas, kiwi, and tinamous). Each book gives details regarding the birds' habitats and geographical locations, physical characteristics, history, courtship and rearing of young. Vocabulary is highlighted and a glossary can be found at the end of each book.

Ostriches and Other Flightless Birds does focus mostly on the ostrich. The remaining ratites are highlighted toward the end of the book. Some of the fascinating items found in this book include the fact that ostriches were once an important food source for native Africans and that the eggs in ancient times were used as drinking cups and containers. . . .

These two books would be worthwhile additions to a library, supplying information for the child who is doing a report or for the child who wants to learn more about these birds.

Martha B. Mahoney

SOURCE: A review of *Ostriches and Other Flightless Birds,* in *Appraisal: Science Books for Young People,* Vol. 23, No. 3, Summer, 1990, pp. 79-80.

LIBRARIAN: *Ostriches and Other Flightless Birds* is a Carolrhoda Nature Watch Book written and photographed by Caroline Arnold and Richard Hewett, who have teamed up successfully on many science books. This is no exception! Readers are given glimpses into the lives of rheas, cassowaries, emus, kiwis and the tinamous. The ostrich is covered in detail.

The reader learns basic information about these birds, including physical characteristics, food, enemies, and breeding. Amazingly enough, ostrich eggshells were used as drinking cups in ancient Egypt and their feathers were used in fashion, leading to over hunting for a time. The photographs dramatically enhance the text. Feathers of ostriches and other birds are compared. An egg is held in a hand, effectively demonstrating its size. Bones of these flightless birds are different. Photographs and text combine to make these concepts clear, as well as others related to their speed, eye size, and preening. . . .

A very good introduction to the bird family Ratitae. . . .

Theresa Knapp

SOURCE: A review of *Ostriches and Other Flightless Birds,* in *Science Books & Films,* Vol. 27, No. 1, January-February, 1991, p. 19.

Nature lovers of all ages will find a wealth of interesting information in this book. Although written for the young reader, it has broader appeal. The photographs [by Richard Hewett] are lavish, beautiful in their detail, and well selected to supplement and illustrate information in the text. A simple, clear two-page map shows the distribution of each of six groups of ratites, or flightless birds. The author presents information about the flightless birds in a logical manner, including their evolutionary history, feeding habits, distribution, and breeding behavior. Important new words are printed in boldface type, explained, and included in a short glossary. Although written for a child, *Ostriches and Other Flightless Birds* is not childish. The book presents fascinating information in a short, attractive text and is a delight to

read. I would recommend its purchase for both elementary and secondary school libraries, and as a gift for a child in grade 4 or above.

DINOSAURS DOWN UNDER: AND OTHER FOSSILS FROM AUSTRALIA (1990)

Betsy Hearne

SOURCE: A review of *Dinosaurs Down Under: And Other Fossils from Australia,* in *Bulletin of the Center for Children's Books,* Vol. 43, No. 10, June, 1990, pp. 231-32.

Like the author's *Trapped in Tar: Fossils from the Ice Age* and *Dinosaur Mountain: Graveyard of the Past,* this is a photodocumentary that reveals as much about paleontology exhibits as about the fossils themselves. The subject here is an Australian exhibit on loan to the Natural History Museum of Los Angeles, and the color photos show steps of preparation, unloading, and reassembly that lead to the educational display. The text then systematically describes examples, both vertebrate and invertebrate, with pictures of skeletons, footprints, and casts or models (including the giant egg of an Aepyornis). This is an especially practical complement to the many titles that don't include Australia's unique species of marsupials and flightless birds. Arnold is careful to include the Aborigines' myth for which the exhibit is named (*Kadimakara: Fossils of the Australian Dreamtime*) and to cite approximate dates for extinction of a number of animals, the fierce meat-eater Megalania and the ostrich-like Genyornis among them, that coexisted with early Aborigines. A concluding series of maps compares shifting positions of the continents over 500 million years, and includes a brief explanation of plate tectonics. The style is somewhat catalogic, but the information is inherently interesting and the illustrations awesome. Dinosaur fans will gape over the marsupial lion, with "sharp teeth and claws good for . . . ripping apart its prey." Short of the three-dimensional experience itself, this offers a next-best opportunity for immediate exposure.

Cathryn A. Camper

SOURCE: A review of *Dinosaurs Down Under: And Other Fossils from Australia,* in *School Library Journal,* Vol. 36, No. 6, June, 1990, p. 127.

The fossil wealth of the world seems, wonderfully, almost inexhaustible, particularly when newfound relics of another continent come to light. Arnold's book introduces Australian fossils (and not just dinosaurs) to young readers, an area as yet not well covered in the children's dinosaur canon. The book covers fossils exhibited in the museum show "Kadimakara: Fossils of the Australian Dreamtime," which was displayed at the Los Angeles Museum of Natural History in 1988. Kadimakara is an aborigine word for tree-living dreamtime creatures who left their bones behind when the trees were destroyed and they died. Arnold explains the mechanics of the exhibit, and then covers the basic categories of vertebrate fossils: fish, amphibians, reptiles, dinosaurs, birds, and mammals. As in her *Dinosaur Mountain: Graveyard of the Past,* the photos of the fossils are clear, colorful, and relevant to the text. The problem is, bones sometimes just aren't enough to convey a picture, and Arnold doesn't elaborate on the details of the beasts. It's a good introduction, but children wanting more information or full-color pictures of the animals will have to turn to Rich and Van Tets' *Kadimakara: Extinct Vertebrates of Australia,* an adult book.

Linda Nolan

SOURCE: A review of *Dinosaurs Down Under: And Other Fossils from Australia,* in *Appraisal: Science Books for Young People,* Vol. 24, No. 1, Winter, 1991, pp. 3-4.

SPECIALIST: The book, *Dinosaurs Down Under,* by Caroline Arnold, is one of a series. This volume offers an interesting look at what goes on behind the scenes at a natural history museum, as well as intriguing details about the fossils of the "Kadimakara: Australian Dreamtime" exhibit assembled by the Queen Victoria Museum and Art Gallery, Launceston, Tasmania. The book, accompanied by colorful photographs and lively text, describes the unpacking of valuable fossils, the setting up of exhibits, and the many duties of the professionals involved in getting the exhibit ready for the public. For young readers the scientific terms are defined, pronunciations are given and comparisons of fossils are made to present-day animals. The author illustrates and describes the movement of continents and how this affected living creatures. The book describes how fossils are our windows on the past. Through them we can learn about ancient landscape, its climate, and what kinds of plants and animals inhabited it.

The book contains an index, and is well written and straightforward, while not being too dry.

Nancy R. Spencer

SOURCE: A review of *Dinosaurs Down Under: And Other Fossils from Australia,* in *Appraisal: Science Books for Young People,* Vol. 24, No. 1, Winter, 1991, pp. 3-4.

LIBRARIAN: Caroline Arnold begins her latest book on dinosaurs by defining just what fossils are, where they might be found, and their value. She explains the title of the exhibit at the Natural History Museum in Los Angeles, "Kadimakara: Fossils of the Australian Dreamtime," by briefly retelling an Aborigine legend. According to the legend, Kadimakara were creatures who lived in the treetops during dreamtime, the period when the

world was created. Coming down from their trees to look for food, the Kadimakara were forced to remain on the ground when their homes were destroyed. When they died, their bones were left on earth.

Arnold follows each step of the exhibit: planning the display space, unpacking and assembling the fossils, placing signs and informational boards, and, finally, affixing the fossils on platforms or in glass exhibit cases. She then discusses each of the fossils found, according to the group of vertebrate animals to which it belongs; fish, amphibians, reptiles, birds, or mammals. Generic names, pronunciations, and size in both English and Metric measurement, are given, as well as similarities and differences among the groups and with those of the present time. Readers will be surprised at just how much information concerning habitat, location, and characteristics of dinosaurs and other prehistoric creatures can be learned from a study of fossil skeletons. . . .

📖 *A WALK IN THE WOODS* ("Natural Science" series, 1990)

Margaret C. Howell

SOURCE: A review of *A Walk in the Woods,* in *School Library Journal,* Vol. 36, No. 11, November, 1990, p. 102.

Less successful than her nature books for middle graders, Arnold here writes down to young readers. She relates general tidbits on all aspects of life in the forest in a heavily illustrated book, resulting in a confusing picture. She often leads readers on an exploration, "Feel the moss growing on the log" and then elaborates, "Moss is a tiny plant found in cool, moist places." This approach could interest children, but after saying that the moss "feels like a soft cushion," Arnold changes the subject to mushrooms. Only a few lines are included on each topic, and the book covers trees and their uses, leaves, needles, animals, birds, and seasons.

Frances E. Millhouser

SOURCE: A review of *A Walk in the Woods,* in *Science Books & Films,* Vol. 26, No. 2, November-December, 1990, p. 128.

This introduction to forest life describes what might be observed during a casual walk through the woods. Pastel illustrations show plant and animal life processes without describing the how or why of these activities. The reader is requested to follow robins into the forest, but the robin guides are never seen again. Then, the reader is exhorted to feel the different kinds of bark on different trees. The illustrations [by Freya Tanz] do not contain different textures, nor is this a field guide to be carried into the forest. After describing the peaceful, symbiotic life of the forest, the book depicts the usefulness to humans of trees cut for making lumber and paper. A two-page green-and-brown world map showing the locations of forests is included. This book is a hybrid, and it doesn't work either as a participatory book to prepare preschoolers for a field trip or as a beginning scientific description of a northern deciduous forest for young elementary school-age students.

Lynne E. Kepler

SOURCE: A review of *A Walk in the Woods,* in *Appraisal: Science Books for Young People,* Vol. 24, No. 1, Winter, 1991, p. 5.

SPECIALIST: *A Walk in the Woods* is a pleasant book, introducing the young reader to the many different habitats found within the woods. In addition to the animals and plants that can be seen, the resources provided by forests and the location of forests worldwide are also discussed. While this all-encompassing format provides much information, it is also distracting. The book might best be used by having children focus only on a couple of pages at a time.

Most of the book is scientifically sound. However, the description of several coniferous trees as pine trees (this term to include spruce and firs) is inappropriate. Calling these trees evergreens would have been better. (Later in the book, the term evergreens is used, but, again, readers could be left with the impression that all evergreens are pine trees.) The other error made in regards to evergreens is the statement that, "Pine trees do not have leaves. They have needles instead." True enough, they are called needles, but I think that young children can understand that these, too, are leaves.

In all fairness, there are many sound facts of forest life, including a description of how to age a tree by counting its rings and how camouflage helps creatures stay hidden.

HEART DISEASE (1990)

Randy L. Moses

SOURCE: A review of *Heart Disease,* in *Science Books & Films,* Vol. 27, No. 2, March, 1991, p. 43.

Heart Disease is a book designed to serve as an introduction to cardiology for young readers. Although the book contains no critical errors, it does have several substantive drawbacks. The book is obviously designed for a young audience, but it is not clear what age group it is best suited for. Although it is simplistically written, and the prose will be easily read and understood by children at an elementary level, such an audience will probably not have the biological background necessary to comprehend much of the information presented. Another problem is the inadequacy of the illustrations. The

anatomical illustrations are of particularly poor quality and contain some erroneous, misleading, and confusing labels. Higher quality illustrations and particularly well-planned diagrams could have vastly improved the presentation of the material. Finally, the selection of the material and time spent on each topic must be called into question. Some relatively rare syndromes, which contribute little to an overall understanding of cardiology, are discussed at relatively great length, while basic concepts such as the mechanism of cardiac contractility, the anatomy of the heart, and cardiac physiology were either omitted or discussed too briefly. Inadequate coverage of these and other topics is serious, since they are integral to an understanding of cardiac disease and it is unlikely that the children for whom the book is intended will have had prior exposure to the topics. In sum, although this book is adequate as an elementary introduction to heart disease, it has too many problems to be recommended highly.

Coralie Clark

SOURCE: A review of *Heart Disease,* in *The Book Report,* Vol. 9, No. 5, March-April, 1991, p. 51.

This excellent guide to the functioning and malfunctioning of the human heart begins with a clear explanation of the circulatory system and the complex processes of heart and blood functions in a healthy body. After pointing out that heart and circulatory system problems are a major cause of death in the developed world, the author looks at heart-related diseases and defects. Topical issues like blood pressure, cholesterol, and heart disease prevention merit whole chapters, and there is a fascinating account of techniques and machinery available to health professionals today. Students will learn why high blood pressure and too much cholesterol are bad, what angina is, and how a heart-lung machine works. The text is concise, with content and reading level well matched.

Renee E. Blumenkrantz

SOURCE: A review of *Heart Disease,* in *Appraisal: Science Books for Young People,* Vol. 24, Nos. 2 & 3, Spring-Summer, 1991, pp. 4-6.

LIBRARIAN: This is a well written, comprehensive text that describes the anatomy and physiology of the normal heart and the prevention, diagnosis and treatment of heart disease. Risk factors, such as high blood pressure, smoking, cocaine use, heredity, cholesterol and stress are discussed. Current diagnostic tools/procedures and regimens are explored: electrocardiogram, cardiac catherization, angiocardiography, magnetic resonance imaging, angioplasty, drug therapies, coronary bypass and transplants. Future perspectives, a glossary, index, and bibliography are included. Black and white photographs and diagrams enhance the text, but more are needed. There is no diagram explaining how an electrical impulse is conducted throughout the heart or any diagrams of structural defects of the heart. Despite this fault, I recommend this text for fifth graders to general audiences.

Kenneth D. Massey

SOURCE: A review of *Heart Disease,* in *Appraisal: Science Books for Young People,* Vol. 24, Nos. 2 & 3, Spring-Summer, 1991, pp. 4-6.

SPECIALIST: In the monograph, ***Heart Disease,*** the author addresses an extremely broad and complex area of medical disorders facing modern society. C. Arnold has done a good job in communicating the importance and scope of heart disease to the reader, not just as a malady afflicting older people, but as a myriad of illnesses with potential impact on individuals in all age groups. The work is well organized, easily read, and leaves the reader with the overall impression that, although heart disease is a serious problem, much has and is being done to further reduce both morbidity and mortality.

The book is organized well. Basic anatomical and physiological considerations of the cardiovascular system are initially presented. In subsequent chapters, the author addresses heart defects associated with childhood infections which afflict all ages as well as the more classical, vessel-related pathologies associated with older persons. Common risk factors, i.e. cholesterol, hypertension, smoking, and stress, are presented as "controllable" factors. Rounding out the overall presentation, commonly used diagnostic and therapeutic interventions are discussed, along with a short treatise on some current research directions.

In making the book readable for its audience in size and content, C. Arnold narrowed the use of technical terms. When incorporated, definitions were generally presented in the text, glossary or both. There were, however, several instances where potentially confusing, yet important, terms were used without definition. For example, in the discussion of cholesterol control, the role of the enzyme HMG reductase is described with no definition of what an enzyme is or what it does. In the process of simplification some concepts or terms, as presented, are misleading. Along the same line, it would have been helpful to have included a pronunciation guide for terms appearing in the glossary. Finally, summaries of the important points in each chapter could also have been included. Some significant points are presented almost too informally in the text. These could have been emphasized in summary fashion. These difficulties are minor in nature and do not represent a significant impediment to the understanding of the material.

Overall, this book is technically sound. The presented information is understandable and up-to-date. Examples used will mesh well with recent topics covered by the media, allowing readers to connect ideas presented in the monograph with other sources of information. The author has done an admirable job in narrowing a broad area into a concise work.

A WALK IN THE DESERT ("Natural Science" series, 1990)

Judith K. Brown

SOURCE: A review of *A Walk in the Desert,* in *Appraisal: Science Books for Young People,* Vol. 24, No. 4, Autumn, 1991, p. 4.

SPECIALIST: As a biologist, mother of a four- and five-year-old, and a resident of the Arizona desert, I found *A Walk in the Desert* entertaining, instructive, and accurate. The children have not put the book down, and continue to "read" the book by naming the various wildlife and plants with which they are familiar. For children who do not have the opportunity to live in or visit the desert, this book represents a fine introduction to young, eager minds; thus, I would rate it as very good. Also, the drawings were particularly appealing.

My only negative comment would be the approach used to describe the Grand Canyon and northern parts of the state—it could have focused more on the wildlife and less on the human-intervention side of things. In addition, I teach my children to be environmentally conscious about natural systems like sand dunes, and would never encourage them to slide down one—the upper crusts of sand dunes are extremely fragile and should not be disturbed, let alone be treated as a ride in an amusement park. Destruction of sand dunes and adjacent lands has led to much land being further engulfed by desert; this may or may not be of concern to many readers, but I feel we must educate our young early on with respect to the fragile nature of our environments. The deserts are especially endangered along with the wildlife which call them home, and every opportunity should be utilized to teach respect for the earth. Educating the young (and adults!) is a huge responsibility!

Sallie M. Erhard

SOURCE: A review of *A Walk in the Desert,* in *Appraisal: Science Books for Young People,* Vol. 24, No. 4, Autumn, 1991, p. 4.

LIBRARIAN: This very colorful book about places that are often considered drab and lifeless can best be appreciated with discussion in a small group. The few sentences accompanying each full page drawing force the viewer to look carefully and discover each detail. The author also uses questions in the text to stimulate the reader into thinking about the pictures. The full color illustrations [by Freya Tanz] are beautiful; the individual examples are well done. By isolating a few creatures at a time, the youngsters can concentrate and understand how these plants and animals can survive in such a hostile environment. . . .

The scientific information given is minimal but sufficient for the very young. My only regret is that there is no mention of the fragility of the desert ecology, and that it is being disturbed by civilization.

A GUIDE DOG PUPPY GROWS UP (1991)

Carolyn Phelan

SOURCE: A review of *A Guide Dog Puppy Grows Up,* in *Booklist,* Vol. 87, No. 16, April 15, 1991, pp. 1635-36.

With a good balance of photographs and text, this book provides an appealing introduction to the subject by following one dog, a golden retriever named Honey, through a guide dog training program. Born in a kennel dedicated to breeding guide dogs, Honey is kept with her mother for a time, then given to Amy, a girl in a 4-H Club, to raise for one year. Next, Honey returns to the kennel for six months of training. She is then introduced to Anne, the blind woman who needs her, and the two learn to work together in the kennel's training program. A graduation ceremony reunites Amy, Honey, and Anne for a fitting conclusion to the book. Using a particular case to explain the program could have resulted in a rather sentimental book; however, full-color photos [by Richard Hewett] make every aspect of Honey's story vivid, and Arnold's clear, direct prose leads readers toward a fuller understanding of the process of training guide dogs and how they're used by the blind.

Margaret C. Howell

SOURCE: A review of *A Guide Dog Puppy Grows Up,* in *School Library Journal,* Vol. 37, No. 5, May, 1991, p. 98.

A photo-essay about the training of a guide dog. Honey, a golden retriever, is born at Guide Dogs for the Blind in California. After initial screening at the school, she is sent to the home of a 4-H member, a little girl, where she stays for about 15 months. Once she is returned, Honey is introduced to and trained again with a new owner. Clear full-color photographs show the transition from puppy to working canine. The text is lucid and brief, highlighting points of this process.

Elizabeth S. Watson

SOURCE: A review of *A Guide Dog Puppy Grows Up,* in *The Horn Book Magazine,* Vol. LXVII, No. 3, May-June, 1991, p. 345.

A first-rate photo-essay team has produced an appealing and informative look at the process that Guide Dogs for the Blind employs. The book follows Honey, a golden retriever pup destined to become a partner to Anne Gelles, a blind teacher. The process involves placing potential dog guides with foster families who raise the pups in a loving home atmosphere, giving them very basic training for the first months. The next stage takes the one-and-a-half-year-old Honey to the Guide Dog campus, where she will begin formal training. After another six months, the dogs meet their blind owners, and the pair attend school together for up to four weeks, culminating in a graduation ceremony. The text is smoothly written, and a great deal of information about the program and aboutthe needs of blind people met by their dog guides is nicely integrated into the narrative.

Mary Lou Burket

SOURCE: "Working Dogs," in *The Five Owls,* Vol. VII, No. 4, March-April, 1993, pp. 96-7.

Perhaps because of its matter-of-factness, Caroline Arnold's book, **A Guide Dog Puppy Grows Up** is especially touching. It reports the long process of preparing a tumbling puppy named Honey to be a sleek and effective guide dog for the blind. Only after many months is Honey matched with a human partner, and then the two must continue to train as a team.

Combined with an informative text, Richard Hewett's beautifully composed and printed photographs provide a suggestive view of what it means to two people to know this dog. Amy is a girl who volunteers to raise Honey as a 4-H Project for more than a year. But Ann is the woman who keeps the dog in the end. In a bittersweet moment, Honey poses between her friends, cheek to cheek.

WATCH OUT FOR SHARKS! (1991)

Kirkus Reviews

SOURCE: A review of *Watch Out for Sharks!,* in *Kirkus Reviews,* Vol. 59, No. 17, September 1, 1991, p. 1166.

For shark fanciers, a look at a Los Angeles Natural History Museum exhibit, *Sharks: Fact and Fantasy.* Now touring the country, it includes models of large and small sharks, many of them swimming in simulated undersea settings. The text follows a group of young museum-goers as they examine shark teeth, fossil sharks, sharks in art, and a living shark embryo; shark anatomy, special adaptations, types of sharks, and some shark facts are also included. Photos [by Richard Hewett] are clear, colorful and engaging. Not comprehensive, but an attractive added purchase.

Frances E. Millhouser

SOURCE: A review of *Watch Out for Sharks!,* in *School Library Journal,* Vol. 37, No. 10, October, 1991, p. 132.

Although strictly speaking this is not a museum exhibit catalog, it does nevertheless focus on the "Sharks: Fact & Fantasy" exhibit that appeared at the National History Museum of Los Angeles County and other museums throughout the country. The text contains interesting facts about many species of sharks, but because it is organized around a specific exhibit rather than by subject matter, its appeal and usefulness are limited.

Julie Corsaro

SOURCE: A review of *Watch Out for Sharks!,* in *Booklist,* Vol. 88, No. 3, October 1, 1991, p. 318.

Excellent color photographs of models of gaping shark mouths filled with razor-sharp teeth will keep young ichthyologists involved in this informative book. While Arnold's focus is on the appearance and physiology of a variety of sharks, she also discusses popular myths, evolution, related fish, habitats, possible extinction, and shark scholarship. Based on an exhibition organized by the Natural History Museum of Los Angeles, the continuous text is clear, and the shark trivia is fascinating.

FLAMINGO ("Animal Favorites" series, 1991)

Robert Leo Smith

SOURCE: A review of *Flamingo,* in *Science Books & Films,* Vol. 27, No. 8, November, 1991, pp. 239-40.

Flamingos are colorful birds, and this book is a colorful introduction to them. *Flamingo* is as much a pictorial essay on the birds as a written one. Photographer Richard Hewett captures the life cycle of the flamingos in photographs that complement the text. The Caribbean flamingo, the subject of the book, apparently was never a breeding bird in the United States, although a free-flying flock has been established at Hialeah Racetrack in Florida. This book is based on the large captive flock at Busch Gardens in Florida. To hold the narrative together, both author and photographer follow the development of a young flamingo from hatching to adulthood. Around its development, the author weaves a great amount of information about flamingo taxonomy, physical characteristics, food and foraging behavior, mating, nesting, and adaptations to a salty aquatic environment in a manner that will appeal to young readers. The author tells about the care of the captive flock and points out the importance of such flocks held in seminatural conditions to the future welfare of the species. The book is accurate and well written, with outstanding photography. It belongs on the natural history bookshelf for young readers.

SNAKE ("Animal Favorites" series, 1991)

Joseph Patrick Kennedy

SOURCE: A review of *Snake,* in *Science Books & Films,* Vol. 27, No. 8, November, 1991, p. 240.

"People who study snakes are called herpetologists, from the Greek word for 'creeping' or 'crawling,' referring to the way snakes move around. You don't have to be a herpetologist to enjoy learning about snakes, though." No, indeed. Juvenile readers, whether they be budding herpetologists or among that group of the uninitiated just awakening to the enjoyment of learning about snakes, will be fortunate to find **Snake.** It is, in general, an adequate introduction to snakes, their characteristics, and their life histories, and includes specific references to snakes' babies, food, life span, movement, predators, reproduction, scales, skin, tails, teeth, temperature, tongues, and venom. Young readers are introduced to a rosy boa used in one of the educational programs at the Los Angeles Zoo, whose staff has cooperated in photographing some of the specimens in their care, including "Baby," a 15-foot python. From the initial photographs and descriptions of "Rosy," it becomes evident that snakes may not be the unsightly, obnoxious creatures that they are often conjured to be. The text and accompanying color photographs [by Richard Hewett] are generally substantive and pertinent. However, including the photograph that appears on page three, with the caption reading only "Vine Snake," may not be prudent. In that photograph, the vine snake is casually held in hand. The bite of certain snakes of this genus have been reported to cause swelling and local pain. Without including appropriate information in the caption, this may not be the best snake for young readers to see being held. Boas and pythons are featured in this book, but there is also information about other families and kinds of snakes, both venomous and nonvenomous.

Karey Wehner

SOURCE: A review of *Snake,* in *School Library Journal,* Vol. 38, No. 1, January, 1992, p. 117.

An enticing blend of concise text and outstanding full-color photographs. Arnold briefly describes the physical and behavioral characteristics of snakes in general, featuring subjects on exhibit in the reptile house at the Los Angeles Zoo. She then discusses special traits of a variety of venomous and nonpoisonous species and their ecological importance. An interesting sidelight is the information on how the zoo cares for the reptiles under its protection. Close to four dozen appealing photos depicting about two dozen species serve as extensions of the succinctly written, well-organized narrative.

Miriam F. Bennett

SOURCE: A review of *Snake,* in *Appraisal: Science Books for Young People,* Vol. 25, No. 2, Spring, 1992, pp. 21-2.

SPECIALIST: **Snake** is a fine example of a biological monograph written especially for young readers. It is informative, while not being pedantic. It includes a good index and the grammar, sentence structure, and style are all very good. The prose is marred slightly by some abrupt transitions, and there are a few teleological comments, as well as a few anthropomorphic statements.

Martha B. Mahoney

SOURCE: A review of *Snake,* in *Appraisal: Science Books for Young People,* Vol. 25, No. 2, Spring, 1992, pp. 21-2.

LIBRARIAN: Caroline Arnold and Richard Hewett have again teamed up to create an absorbing photographic essay that describes Rosy, a rosy boa living at the Los Angeles Zoo, as well as many other varieties of snakes. A clear explanation of reptiles' characteristics is given. Fascinating facts are interspersed in the informative text. The captioned photographs are excellent. The photographs and description of Rosy eating a mouse, and the photographs of the process of shedding, are excellent. Information about endangered species is given with the emphasis on caring for these animals as part of the balance of nature. . . .

This book will be read by snake enthusiasts—maybe it will even inspire a future herpetologist!

SOCCER: FROM NEIGHBORHOOD PLAY TO THE WORLD CUP (1991)

Blair Christolon

SOURCE: A review of *Soccer: From Neighborhood Play to the World Cup,* in *School Library Journal,* Vol. 38, No. 1, January, 1992, p. 101.

A clearly written book that covers basic rules, skills, history, and the World Cup. Even veteran players (those fourth graders who have been playing since kindergarten and think they know it all) will find something here. Possible rule changes in the future, such as "kick-in" instead of "throw-in," will also spark interest. Full-color photos of youthful players as well as soccer stars enhance the book, which concludes with a discussion of the 1994 World Cup game to be hosted by the U.S. More thorough than Grosshandler's *Winning Ways in Soccer,* this timely release will be a fine addition to most libraries.

Stephanie Zvirin

SOURCE: A review of *Soccer: From Neighborhood Play to the World Cup,* in *Booklist,* Vol. 88, No. 9, January 1, 1992, p. 821.

Illustrations, colorful though not always sharp, show young people as well as professional players participating in soccer. Initial sections supply game background—

a bit about rules, equipment, etc.—with succeeding chapters reviewing sport skills, game history, and soccer's place in school athletic programs and organized recreational sports for young people. A look at the sport from the competitive standpoint, in the U.S. and internationally, rounds out the nicely written, straightforward text.

THE ANCIENT CLIFF DWELLERS OF MESA VERDE (1992)

Kirkus Reviews

SOURCE: A review of *The Ancient Cliff Dwellers of Mesa Verde,* in *Kirkus Reviews,* Vol. LX, No. 6, March 15, 1992, p. 391.

From roughly A.D. 550 until A.D. 1300, communities flourished in the region where Utah, Arizona, New Mexico, and Colorado now meet. One of the largest was at Mesa Verde, now on the edge of the Ute Mountain Indian Reservation. Called Anasazi–"ancient ones"—by present-day Navajos, these pastoral, pueblo-dwelling people reached a peak of several thousand and then moved away, leaving cliff dwellings, pots, and the detritus of generations; who they were, where and why they went, and what became of them are mysteries, only slowly yielding to research. Drawing on sources here and abroad, Arnold provides an overview of current knowledge and speculation about the lives and culture of these early people. Aided by [Richard] Hewett's detailed, beautiful color photos of sites, researchers, and artifacts, she describes their dwellings, tools, crops, and daily living patterns, carefully separating fact from speculation. Attractive and useful.

Hazel Rochman

SOURCE: A review of *The Ancient Cliff Dwellers of Mesa Verde,* in *Booklist,* Vol. 88, No. 17, May 1, 1992, p. 1594.

It's a fascinating story: the native Americans in southwestern Colorado, known now as the Anasazi, left their communities on the flat mesa top around 1190 and built their homes in the cliffs of the steep canyons, and then, about 100 years later, they abandoned their cliff dwellings and never returned. Hewett's handsome color photos highlight the setting's rich earth colors and capture the Mesa Verde archaeological preserve today, both close up and within the context of the rocks, plants, and animals of the area. Some pictures show contemporary visitors climbing the ladders to the cliff dwellings; some show the Mesa Verde National Park museum dioramas and the artifacts of daily life. Arnold is scrupulous in distinguishing what is known from what is surmised as she re-creates the daily life of the thriving Anasazi community, but her narrative style is flat, and the swing back and forth in time is sometimes confusing. However, with a teacher's guidance, the book will spark kids' interest in the techniques of archaeology, as well as in the site and the people who lived there. And then there's the mystery: why did they come? Why did they leave? And why did they never come back?

David N. Pauli

SOURCE: A review of *The Ancient Cliff Dwellers of Mesa Verde,* in *School Library Journal,* Vol. 38, No. 7, July, 1992, p. 79.

Chapters include a description of the discovery of the area by ranchers in the late 19th century and the development of the area into a national park. Readers will also see how painstaking archeology has re-created the probable scenario of how people lived when the area was at its height of development and various theories concerning the fate of the Anasazi. An engrossing introduction to the culture, the place, and the time, and how we have learned about them.

 PELÉ: THE KING OF SOCCER (1992)

Dem Polacheck

SOURCE: A review of *Pelé: The King of Soccer,* in *Voice of Youth Advocates,* Vol. 15, No. 3, August, 1992, pp. 180-81.

Accurately summarized as an examination of the life and career of the renowned soccer player from Brazil, this *First Book* is aimed at the younger audience, with full-color pictures complementing the simple narration.

Sheilamae O'Hara

SOURCE: A review of *Pelé: The King of Soccer,* in *Booklist,* Vol. 89, No. 3, October 1, 1992, p. 323.

Arnold does a good job of tracing Pelé's soccer career from early promise through young star to international superstar. However, her accounts of exciting games would be more meaningful if the book contained a brief explanation of game rules. Although retired from soccer, Pelé is again in the news as an announced candidate for president of Brazil.

 ON THE BRINK OF EXTINCTION: THE CALIFORNIA CONDOR ("Gulliver Green Book" series, 1993)

Kirkus Reviews

SOURCE: A review of *On the Brink of Extinction: The California Condor,* in *Kirkus Reviews,* Vol. LXI, No. 4, February 15, 1993, p. 221.

Another outstanding science book from a prolific author, this focusing on efforts to save the largest North American bird from extinction, and greatly enhanced by stunning color photos by the designer of the California condor release program, who's also bird curator at the L.A. Zoo. [Michael] Wallace's knowledge and appreciation of these majestic, ugly relics of an earlier time are evident in his vivid, carefully selected photos. By 1986, habitat destruction, hunters, and poisons had reduced the condor population to 26. A joint effort by zoos and naturalists developed a rescue program that involved trapping the remaining birds and putting them in breeding "condorminiums," where their eggs were removed to stimulate extra eggs, which were incubated; young birds were hand reared and prepared for release to the wild. By year-end 1992, the population had reached 64 and specialists were cautiously optimistic. An inspiring story of scientists in action.

Chris Sherman

SOURCE: A review of *On the Brink of Extinction: The California Condor,* in *Booklist,* Vol. 89, No. 16, April 15, 1993, p. 1512.

Since the passage of the Endangered Species Act in 1973, a number of plans have been developed to study condors in the wild and in captivity, create a safer natural environment for the birds, and educate the public. In her latest work about endangered wildlife, Arnold describes the efforts of the California Condor Recovery Team. Her lucid and interesting account of the history of condors emphasizes the factors that led to the birds' near extinction and explains in great detail the measures that have been taken to reestablish a significant condor breeding population. Wallace's photographs are magnificent. They capture the unusual beauty of the creatures and document the processes of procuring and incubating eggs, rearing the hatchlings, and reintroducing mature condors into the wild.

Margaret A. Bush

SOURCE: A review of *On the Brink of Extinction: The California Condor,* in *The Horn Book Magazine,* Vol. LXIX, No. 3, May-June, 1993, pp. 343-44.

In 1986 just one pair of wild condors remained in California. Few animals have lived on earth as long as this huge, unusual looking bird, and few have been snatched so dramatically from the edge of extinction. In their lucid photo essay Caroline Arnold and Michael Wallace sketch the forty-thousand-year history and twentieth-century decline of the California condor and then follow the intensive efforts of the condor propagation program at the Los Angeles and San Diego zoos. Dr. Wallace, whose extraordinary photographs document the condor's growth and care in this handsome presentation, is director of these programs and credited with designing the condor release program. . . . The care given to incubating eggs and the use of realistic puppet "mothers" to avoid human imprinting add to an interesting, satisfying story—in a few short years captive care has successfully increased the condor population. Yet the condor's future is still in question. Caroline Arnold recounts recent efforts at releasing young birds back into the wild, noting that the outcome is still completely uncertain. Beautifully designed and informative, this tantalizing account leaves the reader wanting to know more and sharing the hope that the condor "may once again grace the skies of western North America."

Amy Nunley

SOURCE: A review of *On the Brink of Extinction: The California Condor,* in *School Library Journal,* Vol. 39, No. 6, June, 1993, p. 113.

Arnold turns her pen to the plight of the endangered California Condor. Although she reveals the sad, stunning fact that in 1986 there was but one breeding pair of condors left in the wild, her book is a work of hope as it outlines scientists' attempts to save the bird from extinction. There is background information about the species' 40,000-year-old existence, its size, color, and eating habits. There are descriptions of the growing population, the shooting of the birds for sport, and the terrible scourge of DDT. The excellent full-color photographs and clear, engaging text are sure to capture the attention of readers; together, they record the daring mission to restore the condor to its rightful place. It would be hard to find better photographs; they show the bird in flight, engaged in courtship, birth, even at home in a giant sequoia tree. This is aimed at an older audience than *Saving the Condor* by Nancy Schorsch. It's a treasure-trove for the eye and for the heart.

Robert L. Smith

SOURCE: A review of *On the Brink of Extinction: The California Condor,* in *Science Books & Films,* Vol. 29, No. 7, October, 1993, pp. 209-10.

The California condor, a relict species from the Pleistocene, nearly became extinct because of habitat destruction, shooting, and poisoning. Conservationists arrived at a controversial decision to capture the remaining birds and relocate them to the Los Angeles and San Diego zoos. There, the birds would be used in a captive breeding program in an effort to save the species from extinction. Author and photographer have collaborated to describe, with a clearly written text and outstanding, informative photographs, the efforts to save the condor. After introducing the reader to the California and Andean condors, they describe the development of techniques of captive breeding, using Andean condors as surrogates. These techniques range from the hatching of young from artificially incubated eggs and feeding them with the use of hand-held puppets of condor heads to the release of the birds back to the wild. Although the captive breeding program is successful, it will be some time before many

condors will be soaring again over their vacated habitat. This book is an excellent reference for young and adult readers about the tedious and expensive methods of captive breeding. It also is one of the best arguments available about why we should not allow a species to reach the brink of extinction before taking remedial action.

DINOSAURS ALL AROUND: AN ARTIST'S VIEW OF THE PREHISTORIC WORLD (1993)

Betsy Hearne

SOURCE: A review of *Dinosaurs All Around: An Artist's View of the Prehistoric World,* in *Bulletin of the Center for Children's Books,* Vol. 46, No. 8, April, 1993, p. 239.

Arnold has had considerable practice with this subject (***Dinosaur Mountain, Trapped in Tar***), and the first half of the book features a cohesive discussion and display of work by Stephen and Sylvia Czerkas, who make dinosaur models for museum exhibits. The latter half becomes a descriptive catalogue of various species (Styracosaurus, Albertosaurus, Tyrannosaurus Rex, Allosaurus, Deinonychus, Compsognathus, and Stegosaurus), which young readers will play along with because of the dramatic color photographs of sculptures sporting long teeth, sharp claws, and hatching eggs. Given the Czerkas's meticulous paleontological research of fossil discoveries such as the patterns of scales on dinosaur skin, the photographed models [by Richard Hewett] are superior to most drawings; they add a lifelike dimension to the book, along with a subtle implication that if you follow your dream as these artists have ("Stephen . . . made his first dinosaur sculpture with mud in his back yard when he was four years old"), you may find it.

Stephanie Zvirin

SOURCE: A review of *Dinosaurs All Around: An Artist's View of the Prehistoric World,* in *Booklist,* Vol. 89, No. 16, April 15, 1993, p. 1507.

Dinosaur fever, which often lasts beyond elementary school, has generated a host of nonfiction and fiction works about the fascinating beasts. This well-written book clearly shows that there are still some intriguing aspects of the subject to explore. With the help of photographer Hewett, Arnold takes a look at the craft of making dinosaur models, focusing on paleoartist Stephen Czerkas, whose miniatures and life-size replicas can be found in many museums. Pictures and text highlight aspects of the craft—from Czerkas's combining of known fact and educated guesswork to create a visual representation of a beast, to his modeling, casting, painting, and setting up a facsimile. The photographs, most of which are of models Czerkas created for two traveling museum exhibitions, are generally good (a few of the close-ups are a bit blurry). They not only capture some of the intricacies of the modeling process, but also show finished replicas of several different beasts Arnold describes individually in the latter portion of the book.

Cathryn A. Camper

SOURCE: A review of *Dinosaurs All Around: An Artist's View of the Prehistoric World,* in *School Library Journal,* Vol. 39, No. 5, May, 1993, p. 112.

Arnold gives readers a look at artists Stephen and Sylvia Czerkas as they use their considerable expertise to conceive and construct lifelike, life-sized dinosaur models. The large, eyecatching full-color photographs and clear text show the artists' research into the creatures' skin and anatomy before they begin their models, and details the process of assembling them. The author includes information about the dinosaurs, but this is secondary to the construction of the museum replicas and seems to be almost an afterthought.

📖 *CATS: IN FROM THE WILD* ("Understanding Animals" series, 1993)

Margaret Chatham

SOURCE: A review of *Cats: In from the Wild,* in *School Library Journal,* Vol. 39, No. 9, September, 1993, p. 237.

A lightweight, pleasant introduction to the physical and behavioral characteristics of cats, emphasizing the similarities between domestic and wild varieties. The format is open and inviting, with plenty of full-color photos [by Richard Hewett]. Sidebars appear on almost every page, with lots of white space, smaller photos and captions, and occasional line drawings to explicate such details as how a cat's claws retract or how it rights itself while falling. A few bold-faced terms are explained in a glossary; a list of species of the world follows the text. This book has no political or environmental ax to grind, although it does mention readers' responsibility to find homes for their pets' kittens.

Allen L. Ingling

SOURCE: A review of *Cats: In from the Wild,* in *Science Books & Films,* Vol. 29, No. 7, October, 1993, p. 209.

This is a pretty little book that presents a quick overview of some basic information about cats. It would be difficult to get into much depth in 50 pages, so do not expect a great wealth of detail. There is no attempt to get into subjects such as health, nutrition, breeds, and so on. The book only tries to touch on the origins and physical and behavioral similarities of the various species of wild and domestic cats. The photographs are good and illustrate the physical appearance of many of

the cat species and also many of their common behaviors. The table listing the cat species with size, range, and status is very handy for a quick reference to where each cat fits in the overall picture. This book would probably be a good supplement to more specific children's library texts on subjects such as cat care and feeding.

📖 *ELEPHANT* ("Animal Favorites" series, 1993)

Elizabeth S. Watson

SOURCE: A review of *Elephant,* in *The Horn Book Magazine,* Vol. LXIX, No. 6, November-December, 1993, p. 759.

As in over one dozen previous volumes in their animal series, this expert team begins each of the new titles by rooting text and photographs in the life of one particular animal living in captivity, then expands the book by describing other examples of the species. Both Asian and African elephants are included in *Elephant.* . . . Sociology, physiology, communication, natural habitats, and care in the zoo are all explained.

Frances Bradburn

SOURCE: "Middle Books," in *Wilson Library Bulletin,* Vol. 68, No. 6, February, 1994, pp. 89-91, 106.

A similar [satisfying reading] experience can take place with two photo-essays dealing with the same subject. *Elephant* by Caroline Arnold . . . examine[s] this most captivating of endangered species. . . . [Arnold] compares the African and the Asian elephants and goes on to describe their habits and habitat, all within the context of Marine World Africa USA in Vallejo, California, where both species are quartered. Actually, it's fascinating how Arnold combines elephant facts with these animals' zoo experience, how she offers information about an elephant's toenails while showing a caretaker filing down the rough edges of the toenail of an elephant in captivity, how she compares the diets of a captive elephant and one in the wild. . . .

While this zoo appears humane, no zoo setting is the ideal location for examining a wild animal. It is hoped that middle readers will sense this and want to seek further information about the elephant in its own habitat.

📖 *KILLER WHALE* ("Animal Favorites" series, 1994)

Margaret A. Bush

SOURCE: A review of *Killer Whale,* in *The Horn Book Magazine,* Vol. LXX, No. 6, November-December, 1994, p. 742.

Each of these excellent photo essays offers an informative introduction explaining the featured animal's behavior in the wild and the crucial roles played by marine parks and rescue centers. The volume on killer whales discusses the part the well-developed senses play in their lives as sea predators and provides good explanations of the structure and use of their flukes, fins, and flippers. This animal is still threatened by practices in the whaling industry, and study of their behavior in captivity leads to better understanding of how to protect them and their environment. The handsome photographs and text show extensive human interaction with the killer whales. . . . Once again Caroline Arnold and Richard Hewett achieve a very high standard of nonfiction.

Patricia A. Livingston

SOURCE: A review of *Killer Whale,* in *Appraisal: Science Books for Young People,* Vol. 28, No. 1, Winter, 1995, pp. 6-7.

SPECIALIST: This book begins with an introduction to the killer whales that live at Sea World in San Diego. The first few pages are devoted to an almost propaganda-like description of the benefits of keeping killer whales in captivity. This might be an attempt to balance the negative image of marine parks that has been disseminated in a recent popular movie about killer whales but the effect is somewhat off-center. The main text of the book, however, deals quite well with presenting information about killer whales and their behavior and relationships in natural settings. The language is easy for children to understand and scientific terms are explained directly in the text. This is the main strength of the book. Although there are plenty of close-up photographs of killer whales, virtually all of them are taken at Sea World. Many of the photographs show the killer whales performing tricks with their trainers. Although children may enjoy going to such performances, showcasing these performances in a book about killer whales does not provide young people with the correct image of these beautiful, wild animals.

Nancy Paul

SOURCE: A review of *Killer Whale,* in *Appraisal: Science Books for Young People,* Vol. 28, No. 1, Winter, 1995, pp. 6-7.

LIBRARIAN: This is a good overview of an animal that seems to intrigue children. The author weaves the story of a mother and her calf at Sea World in San Diego with information about killer whales in the wild. Reproduction, feeding habits and behavior are nicely covered. The scientific order to which whales belong is outlined, and killer whales are placed within this order, along with an explanation of the identifying characteristics of the suborder to which killer whales belong. The difference between baleen and toothed whales is pointed out. The way in which these whales are uniquely adapted to

their environment is well explained. Technical words, such as "echolocation" are highlighted in italics and explained in the text. The book also contains an index that also includes an index to the photographs.

The text conveys a lot of information in "easy to digest," non-textbook fashion, but what will really capture attention are the close-up photographs of killer whales in captivity and in their natural habitat. When you are trying to explain dorsal fins or baleen, a picture is indeed worth more than a paragraph of words.

What is not covered in any depth is the way whaling and environmental pollution threaten these creatures. Only two paragraphs are devoted to this subject. Not all the photographs are captioned. I found myself wishing for a few more captions, particularly in the section on whale coloration. And a chart outlining the order and suborders of whales might have been helpful to readers. But all in all, this is a colorful, easy to read book that is likely to attract the attention of children looking for some leisure reading or doing a report.

CITY OF THE GODS: MEXICO'S ANCIENT CITY OF TEOTIHUACÁN (1994)

Elizabeth Bush

SOURCE: A review of *City of the Gods: Mexico's Ancient City of Teotihuacán,* in *Bulletin of the Center for Children's Books,* Vol. 48, No. 4, December, 1994, p. 119.

This pastiche of archeology, history, and travelogue examines the ruins of the ancient Mexican city whose past is so deeply buried that even the Aztecs speculated about its origins when they named the site City of the Gods. Textual organization is somewhat erratic, with a survey of the geographical setting sandwiched between "Exploring the Ruins" and "Religion," and a chapter on building the city following long after detailed discussion of its monumental architecture. Although Arnold implies that excavation and research continue at the site, rendering many "facts" about Teotihuacán open to debate, readers are not offered varied interpretations of building use or social and religious customs; in fact, no reference to specific field workers or scholars is made at all. Still, there is a motherlode of raw data here waiting to be mined by report writers exploring the earliest American cultures. . . .

Cynthia M. Sturgis

SOURCE: A review of *City of the Gods: Mexico's Ancient City of Teotihuacán,* in *School Library Journal,* Vol. 40, No. 12, December, 1994, p. 117.

A highly readable introduction to Teotihuacán. Arnold's succinct, well-written text relates the cultural and social history of this ancient civilization. Coupled with

[Richard] Hewett's fine full-color photographs, the narrative allows readers to walk the streets, climb the pyramids, and view the artistic splendor of a complex culture that profoundly influenced other Mexican and Central American peoples. Leonard Everett Fisher's *Pyramid of the Sun, Pyramid of the Moon* includes a timeline and map to better orient readers, but Arnold provides more extensive cultural background, and Hewett's numerous, full-color photographs give life to the presentation.

Ilene Cooper

SOURCE: A review of *City of the Gods: Mexico's Ancient City of Teotihuacán,* in *Booklist,* Vol. 91, No. 8, December 15, 1994, p. 747.

Arnold and Hewett bring their expertise to Teotihuacán, the largest and most important city in Mexico and Central America for 800 years. Text and full-color photographs explore the ruins and extrapolate what life was like for the people who lived and worshiped in Teotihuacán. The book spends time describing the gods and goddesses; photos of deities in paintings, in stone (carved large and small), and even in mask form appear throughout, along with the ceremonial centers, including the Pyramid of the Sun and the Pyramid of the Moon. There is also discussion about the civilizations that came after, including the Toltecs and the Aztecs. Students doing reports will find this a good resource, but the arresting photographs will draw browsers in as well.

📖 *SEA LION* ("Animal Favorites" series, 1994)

Patricia A. Livingston

SOURCE: A review of *Sea Lion,* in *Appraisal: Science Books for Young People,* Vol. 28, No. 1, Winter, 1995, pp. 7-8.

SPECIALIST: This book provides a good overview of the basic life history of California sea lions, including diet, behavior, predators and relations to other sea mammals. These details are woven into a description of the activities of the Marine Mammal Center, which is a facility that assists sick or injured animals and returns them to the wild. I particularly liked the text describing the effects that the environment and human activity can have on marine mammals. The close-up photographs of the sea lions are also well done, although not many of them are taken in natural settings. Although the author attempts to draw us into the story by beginning with the plight of two undernourished sea lions brought to the shelter, the book quickly moves into the factual information about sea lions. Scientific terms are explained in a very understandable and straightforward fashion. The overall result is a fairly balanced, comprehensible view of California sea lions that should be interesting to children.

Nancy L. Paul

SOURCE: A review of *Sea Lion,* in *Appraisal: Science Books for Young People,* Vol. 28, No. 1, Winter, 1995, pp. 7-8.

LIBRARIAN: Arnold draws the young readers into the fascinating world of this marine mammal with the story of Pumpkin and Piper, two young California sea lions that must have some help from the Marine Mammal Center in Laguna Beach to survive. This photographic essay covers the basic information on sea lion anatomy, behavior, reproduction, feeding habits, communication, habitat and methods of locomotion. The author explains that the number of sea lions needing rescue has grown due to changing weather conditions, pollution, a diminished food supply due to overfishing and a population boom among sea lions. While this would seem to suggest that things are badly out of balance in the natural environment, this deep topic is left, perhaps wisely, for another time. What a child learns about here is not the balance of nature, but about sea lions. The many photographs [by Richard Hewett] provide an intimate look at sea lions exhibiting a variety of behaviors. Technical terms are in italics, and explained within the text. All in all, the text flows very nicely and will be pleasant reading for a young audience.

It is the photographs that will probably draw the reader into the text. The photographs are engaging and informative. They compliment and expand on the text. This book is likely to be one that children will pick from the shelf for browsing as well as for more formal information gathering for reports and such. As the text concludes, Pumpkin and Piper are released back to the seashore. One can only wonder how they will fare.

📖 *WATCHING DESERT WILDLIFE* ("Nature Watch" series, 1994)

George Gleason

SOURCE: A review of *Watching Desert Wildlife,* in *School Library Journal,* Vol. 41, No. 1, January, 1995, pp. 110, 112.

Although opening comments are made about world deserts, the focus here is on the four U. S. deserts: Great Basin, Sonoran, Mohave, and Chihuahuan. Without explanation, [Caroline and Arthur] Arnold jump from plant to animal, from one desert area, altitude, or region to another. The dictionary definition of "wildlife" (birds and animals) has been extended here to include plants. Exposition is generally clear, except for a comment about flash floods, which gets mixed up with "heavy rain." Also, it is questionable whether clear water of a creek is necessarily "brought by winter storms"; storm water is usually muddy.

Robert G. Walther

SOURCE: A review of *Watching Desert Wildlife,* in *Science Books & Films,* Vol. 31, No. 1, January-February, 1995, p. 19.

This new desert biology work is a welcome addition to juvenile literature. Not surprisingly, the author has written more than 90 books for young readers. Her husband and collaborator [Arthur Arnold] has provided most of the 64 photographs illustrating the text. An excellent map portrays the 17 desert regions of the world, and a glossary lists 20 new terms not discussed in the text, e.g., *arroyos, chlorophyll, habitat, mammals, rain shadows,* and *succulents.* Moving smoothly from one topic to another, the author shows us how "plants and animals that live in desert ecosystems share the challenge of trying to survive in some of the driest places on earth." "What Is a Desert?" discusses the characteristics and composition of deserts. We move quickly from world desert regions to the four major deserts in the southwestern United States: the Great Basin, Mojave, Sonoran, and Chihuahuan Deserts. Finding water and coping with the extremes of temperature are other subtopics. "The Living Desert" shows us how plants, birds, reptiles, and mammals interact for survival. Our deserts shrink each year to a growing demand for crops and cities. As the author rightly concludes: "And only if we ensure their [desert plants and animals] survival will we have the opportunity to learn more about the secrets of their success."

Carol R. Bilge

SOURCE: A review of *Watching Desert Wildlife,* in *Appraisal: Science Books for Young People,* Vol. 28, Nos. 2 & 3, Spring-Summer, 1995, pp. 8-9.

LIBRARIAN: This latest edition to the "Nature Watch" series provides a fascinating account of the desert ecosystem, focusing on the desert regions of North America. Beautiful color photographs are fully integrated into the text. The text is clearly written and organized, with pronunciation keys throughout. Many common misconceptions about the desert are addressed, and little known facts uncovered.

Amber C. Conroy

SOURCE: A review of *Watching Desert Wildlife,* in *Appraisal: Science Books for Young People,* Vol. 28, Nos. 2 & 3, Spring-Summer, 1995, pp. 8-9.

SPECIALIST: This comprehensive book smoothly weaves together the important aspects of desert life with emphasis on biology and geography. The book covers geographic locations of deserts and their defining qualities. The obvious topics of water and temperature are interwoven throughout the text, not treated independently. This is important because aspects of science are difficult to isolate and doing so might be an injustice to the topics and

detract from the scope. Biology is the main focus of the book, including discussion of plants, birds and animals, with distinction of reptiles and mammals. Any shortcomings are easily forgiven, and common topics such as pollination and life cycles of plants are creatively integrated so as to hold the reader's attention. Interesting photograph captions and bold face lettering of unfamiliar terms, their explanation and phonetic pronunciation contribute to easier understanding. Many species of plants and animals are discussed and the author provides a wonderful overview of the ecosystem of the living desert. The aesthetically pleasing color photography and sensible organization make this book a pleasure to read. This is a functional and enticing book of desert wildlife that any library should have.

STORIES IN STONE: ROCK ART PICTURES BY EARLY AMERICANS (1996)

Margaret A. Bush

SOURCE: A review of *Stories in Stone: Rock Art Pictures by Early Americans,* in *The Horn Book Guide,* Vol. VIII, No. 1, July-December, 1996, p. 136.

Boulders and canyons in California's Coso Mountain Range exhibit thousands of ancient drawings suggesting everyday activities and rituals of early Americans. Arnold's discussion of the rock art is uncharacteristically lacking in enthusiasm and cohesion. The pictorial images [photographed by Richard Hewett] are intriguing, and this account will be of interest regionally and in teaching units.

Kirkus Reviews

SOURCE: A review of *Stories in Stone: Rock Art Pictures by Early Americans,* in *Kirkus Reviews,* Vol. LXIV, No. 20, October 15, 1996, p. 1528.

Arnold visits the Mojave Desert's Coso Range for a look at some of the U.S.'s oldest, most durable—and most enigmatic—art. It's a good choice of location, with over 100,000 examples discovered: depictions of sheep, deer, coyotes, lizards, hunting tools and scenes, human figures both plain and adorned with feathers or other regalia, and more abstract images. Arnold describes the clever methods researchers use to date the petroglyphs and deduce who made them, and why; Hewett's large, sharp full-color photographs capture the variety of the art and communicate a sense of their arid, remote setting. More cogent—and better illustrated—than Jennifer Owings Dewey's impressionistic *Stories on Stone,* this offers an intriguing glimpse into an ancient mystery.

Pam Gosner

SOURCE: A review of *Stories in Stone: Rock Art Pictures by Early Americans,* in *School Library Journal,* Vol. 42, No. 12, December, 1996, p. 126.

Another fine collaboration from a talented team. Clear, full-color photographs of the many images inscribed on the canyon walls of the Coso Range in California's Mojave Desert illustrate the rock art of the prehistoric residents of the land. The well-written text gives some background information about the area and the discovery of this, the largest assemblage of rock art in the Western Hemisphere. Also discussed are the methods used to inscribe the pictures, the means for dating them, and what is known about the earliest Americans, as well as what the pictures add to this knowledge. A list of other North American sites with rock art is appended. There is very little written on the hunter-gatherers of this area. Arnold's *The Ancient Cliff Dwellers of Mesa Verde* deals with the Anasazi, who may have been descended from the people who made this rock art; Eleanor H. Ayer's *The Anasazi* is for slightly older readers. An appealing book on a little-known subject.

AFRICAN ANIMALS (1997)

Kelly A. Ault

SOURCE: A review of *African Animals,* in *The Horn Book Guide,* Vol. VIII, No. 2, January-June, 1997, p. 344.

This handsome book features close-up color photographs of animals—furry, feathered, and otherwise—that inhabit the grasslands, forests, and deserts of Africa. Each double-page spread contains a large photograph of an animal and information on its behavior and environment. The book concludes with a paragraph about these creatures' disappearing habitats.

Susan Oliver

SOURCE: A review of *African Animals,* in *School Library Journal,* Vol. 43, No. 3, March, 1997, p. 170.

Superb full-color photography, simple but intelligent language, and excellent organization make this a standout in the growing field of nonfiction for the very young. Almost two dozen African species, mostly mammals, are brought to life and placed in the context of their environs. A brief introduction to this lush continent, and a final note about extinction will get children (and the adults reading to them) thinking about their own place in the world. Animals are grouped by habitat (grasslands, forests, and deserts), and basic locator maps show the extent of each area on the continent. A two-page spread is devoted to each animal, and while it is the spectacular photographs that dominate each spread, the brief, boxed text explicates each picture. The straightforward information succeeds in placing the animal in its own environment while exploring the relationship between the creature and a child's own world. "If you were a giraffe, you would be able to see into a second story window!" Occasional questions provide a natural segue

to open discussion. "How would you like to sleep in a tree at night?" This is a book that youngsters will want to return to again and again. Share it with story-time groups or suggest it for one-on-one reading.

Julie Corsaro

SOURCE: A review of *African Animals,* in *Booklist,* Vol. 93, No. 14, March 15, 1997, p. 1236.

Prolific wildlife writer-photographer Arnold takes a lucid look at 20 African animals. Arranged by habitat (grasslands, forests, and deserts), the book features color photographs of such wild beasts as zebras, warthogs, and gorillas. Given the brevity and simplicity of the text, it is surprisingly informative. Basic characteristics are cited along with questions to the readers: "How would you like to sleep in a tree at night?" Well done.

STONE AGE FARMERS BESIDE THE SEA: SCOTLAND'S PREHISTORIC VILLAGE OF SKARA BRAE (1997)

Kirkus Reviews

SOURCE: A review of *Stone Age Farmers beside the Sea: Scotland's Prehistoric Village of Skara Brae,* in *Kirkus Reviews,* Vol. 65, No. 4, February 15, 1997, p. 296.

A fascinating look at "one of Europe's oldest known and best preserved prehistoric villages," inhabited from 3100 to 2500 B.C., in northern Scotland's Orkney Islands.

Arnold relates how the city, predating the Egyptian pyramids, was buried by sand and rediscovered following a storm 150 years ago. This ancient settlement provides a slice of "human history when people made tools with stone or bone and began to live in settled communities." Accompanied by the clear, informative, full-color photos [by Arthur Arnold], Arnold's narrative deftly recounts the design of the stone houses, how they were built, the daily life of the farming inhabitants, how this prehistoric period of Orkney history ends, and why Skara Brae remains of lasting significance. Readers will be impressed by the details of the painstaking work of archeologists to uncover and preserve this ancient site.

Deborah Stevenson

SOURCE: A review of *Stone Age Farmers beside the Sea: Scotland's Prehistoric Village of Skara Brae,* in *Bulletin of the Center for Children's Books,* Vol. 50, No. 8, April, 1997, p. 271.

Skara Brae, situated in the Orkney Islands off the mainland of Scotland, is an astoundingly well-preserved site of stone-age habitation; Arnold describes the history it contains as well as the history of its discovery. She explains the general pattern of settlement in the area, the building techniques involved in creating the community, details of daily life (clothing, diet, and furniture), burial mounds, and the possible reasons for the eventual abandonment of the habitation. There's a great deal of information here, but it never really comes alive; the neolithic Orcadians seem as distant and as voiceless as Leakey's Lucy (some information about language, in fact, would have been helpful) and far less individual. Young readers may also be unsure whether the settlement's current near-underground state was original design or the result of millennia of land changes, and the book never explicitly addresses the question. The photographs vary in quality, but there are some splendid pictures of the sun-drenched stones and the dramatic island scenery. This may not win new converts to the sciences of anthropology or archaeology, but readers with a taste for the topic will appreciate this closeup of one of its more remarkable showpieces; use it with Olivier Dunrea's *Skara Brae* for a mutually complementary pairing that will bring the stones to life.

Pam Gosner

SOURCE: A review of *Stone Age Farmers beside the Sea: Scotland's Prehistoric Village of Skara Brae*, in *School Library Journal*, Vol. 43, No. 7, July, 1997, p. 99.

One of the earliest prehistoric European sites found, Skara Brae is located on the coast of one of Scotland's Orkney Islands. It was inhabited from 3100 to 2500 B.C., then abandoned; the settlement lay buried for centuries until it was uncovered by a storm in 1850. In an accessible and interesting manner, Arnold describes the finding of the village, as well as what its excavation has shown about daily life in the Stone Age. She also discusses nearby tombs and stone circles. The book's format is straightforward with abundant and appealing full-color photographs (the Arnolds seem to have happened upon a rare period of sunny weather).

HAWK HIGHWAY IN THE SKY: WATCHING RAPTOR MIGRATION (1997)

Kirkus Reviews

SOURCE: A review of *Hawk Highway in the Sky: Watching Raptor Migration*, in *Kirkus Reviews*, Vol. 65, No. 7, April 1, 1997, p. 548.

Each fall and spring scientists and volunteers from HawkWatch International gather at Goshute Mountain, Nevada, to count the thousands of raptors that fly overhead on their annual migratory journey. Arnold describes how scientists classify the various raptors, investigate why and how they migrate, and study and measure birds. At Goshute Mountain, over 10,000 hawks, eagles, kites,

harriers, osprey, falcons, and caracaras are counted annually, and nearly 4,000 are trapped, banded, and released. Full-color photographs [by Robert Kruidenier] provide dramatic close-ups of these magnificent birds, although sensitive readers may find it somewhat disconcerting to see so many of these free-flyers in the grasp of well-meaning volunteers. Arnold concludes with a list of the 31 different species of raptors found in North America and a map. Without size and range information for species, silhouettes, or comparison drawings done to scale, it's difficult to gauge the size of these birds; further, readers will have to know if a bird is a hawk or a falcon in order to locate a species in the brief index. An attractive though specialized volume.

Susan Scheps

SOURCE: A review of *Hawk Highway in the Sky: Watching Raptor Migration*, in *School Library Journal*, Vol. 43, No. 6, June, 1997, p. 130.

This short, informative book details the habits and migration patterns of various raptors and shows, in clear, full-color photos, the capture, measurement, and banding processes used at the HawkWatch International observation site in the Goshute Mountains of Nevada—the busiest raptor trapping and banding location in western North American. Although the book's focus is on migration habits and the capture and tracking of birds, Arnold has included enough information about the classification of hawks, physical characteristics, and habitats of raptors to make this title a good source for reports. Children who are fascinated with birds of prey will be drawn to the many outstanding close-up photos. A thorough index makes locating information easy despite the lack of chapters or headings in the report-style text. A list of raptors organized by family and class, and a map showing some of the migration observation sites in North America, add to the usefulness. An attractive and interesting presentation.

Candace Smith

SOURCE: A review of *Hawk Highway in the Sky: Watching Raptor Migration*, in *Booklist*, Vol. 93, Nos. 19 & 20, June 1 & 15, 1997, p. 1687.

As hawks, eagles, and falcons pass over Nevada's Goshute Mountains, scientists and the volunteers of HawkWatch International observe, catch, and measure the birds, charting statistics and plotting migration patterns. The steps in this process, along with information on habits and habits of the raptors, are lucidly detailed by veteran nature writer Arnold. HawkWatch volunteer Robert Kruidenier's sharply shot full-color photographs (many of them close-ups) work well with Arnold's clear, well-organized text, capturing the fierce beauty of the birds as well as the scientists' painstaking work. A useful breakdown of day-flying raptors and migration sites is appended.

CHILDREN OF THE SETTLEMENT HOUSES ("Picture the American Past" series, 1998)

Shelle Rosenfeld

SOURCE: A review of *Children of the Settlement Houses*, in *Booklist*, Vol. 95, No. 2, September 15, 1998, p. 221.

This title in the "Picture the American Past" series offers an excellent introduction to an important aspect of urban American history and instrument of social change: settlement houses, the turn-of-the-century predecessor to today's community centers. Settlement houses provided the urban poor and new immigrants not just with showers and meals but with a place to learn, play, explore the arts, and gain a sense of community and belonging. The well-chosen black-and-white historical photographs are emotionally affecting and provide a wealth of visual information about the times. The simple text effectively covers the history of settlement houses and includes personal remembrances from those who took advantage of their offerings as children, from New York to San-Francisco. However, the photos themselves make this book a strong, worthy addition to American history collections. For educators and adults, there are suggested tie-in activities to encourage reader engagement. A time line, a glossary, a reading list, and the address of the excellent New York Lower East Side Tenement Museum Web site are included.

Anne Chapman Callaghan

SOURCE: A review of *Children of the Settlement Houses*, in *School Library Journal*, Vol. 45, No. 1, January, 1999, p. 109.

Settlement Houses offers a fascinating look at how poor immigrants in urban settings were helped through community centers that offered classes, sports activities, libraries, and, at some locations, medical services. . . . The books [*Children of the Settlement Houses* and *Working Children* by Carol Saller] are clearly written and chapters are short. Black-and-white photographs (many found elsewhere) on every page enhance the texts. Each title has an appended "Note to Teachers and Adults," with ideas for further activities and study.

EL NIÑO: STORMY WEATHER FOR PEOPLE AND WILDLIFE (1998)

Chris Sherman

SOURCE: A review of *El Niño: Stormy Weather for People and Wildlife*, in *Booklist*, Vol. 95, No. 3, October 1, 1998, p. 326.

Science teachers and students will appreciate this very readable introduction to the El Niño current. In just 48 pages, Arnold explains the complex relationship between the warming of the Pacific current and global weather patterns, describes the effects of the most recent El Niño and notable ones of the past, and discusses the tracking and forecasting of the phenomenon and the importance of scientists' predictions. Difficult concepts and terms are defined in the text and, again, in a glossary, and attractive, full-color photographs and diagrams clearly show El Niño's disruptive effects.

Patricia Manning

SOURCE: A review of *El Niño: Stormy Weather for People and Wildlife*, in *School Library Journal*, Vol. 44, No. 12, December, 1998, pp. 132-33.

The phenomenon known as El Niño (and its cooler sibling, La Niña) have apparently been upsetting the meteorological applecart on a relatively regular basis for many centuries, but it is only recently, with the use of modern technologies, that scientists have correlated these oceanic effects with disconcertingly dramatic weather on a global scale as well. Arnold has drawn on this body of scientific knowledge to present a picture of the atmospheric and ecological import of such shifts in oceanic temperatures. Her readable, informative text describes the physical symptoms of El Niño and La Niña and their widespread effects, ranging from a quiet hurricane season in Florida to severe drought in the rainforests of Indonesia, and what this means both to animal/plant habitats and human economies. Full-color photos, a computer-image series, diagrams, and Internet sources bolster the narrative. (Unfortunately, the text is sometimes printed across page-size photos, making deciphering difficult.) While the latest, very powerful El Niño has made headlines for over a year, this is seemingly the first book for young people in this important area of study. And though La Niña now seems to be in the ascendancy, El Niño will return—as will demand for information on the topic.

BABY WHALE RESCUE: THE TRUE STORY OF J. J. (1999)

Patricia Manning

SOURCE: A review of *Baby Whale Rescue: The True Story of J. J.*, in *School Library Journal*, Vol. 45, No. 3, March, 1999, p. 216.

A recounting of the rescue and rehabilitation of a female gray whale calf, separated from her mother and discovered, hungry and exhausted, rolling helplessly in the gentle surf at Marina del Rey beach in California. Whisked to Sea World in San Diego, the young whale was named J. J. and given professional, loving care for the next 12 months. She thrived, growing prodigiously and learning to "hunt" for food placed on the floor of her tank by her caretakers as they prepared her for a return to the sea. The story of J. J. ends with her last transmitted signal showing her to be heading north on the proper migratory route for her species. This well-researched, readable book is full of information on whale care and gray whale behaviors and lifestyle. Bright, full-color photos [by Richard Hewett] show J. J., her treatment and development, and her final release. A heart-warming story with an excellent scientific focus.

Lauren Peterson

SOURCE: A review of *Baby Whale Rescue: The True Story of J. J.,* in *Booklist,* Vol. 95, No. 13, March 1, 1999, p. 1204.

Youngsters interested in marine life will find this real-life adventure of the rescue of a week-old gray whale fascinating. J. J., as she came to be called, was near death when she was found off the coast of California after becoming separated from her mother. Her rescue, 14-month recovery at Sea World, and exciting return to the ocean are depicted in a readable text, accompanied by numerous color photos of all the action. Arnold and Hewett manage to pack a lot of detail into 32 pages, yet the text has a nice flow and doesn't overwhelm readers with unimportant information. Researchers will still need

to find other resources on the topic for a thorough report, but this is sure to spark more interest in the subject than the average nonfiction book.

SOUTH AMERICAN ANIMALS (1999)

Frances E. Millhouser

SOURCE: A review of *South American Animals,* in *School Library Journal,* Vol. 45, No. 9, September, 1999, p. 210.

Organized by geographic setting—forests, mountain, grasslands, the shore—this picture book introduces some of South America's unique animals. The one- to two-paragraph entries per animal are boxed against stunningly beautiful double-page photographs of the creatures. For example, the black feathers on the toucan's head glisten like jet beads and the emerald tree boa sleeping on a branch is a symphony in green. Each narrative employs an economic use of language yet communicates important details, such as the way the New World monkeys use their tales to grip branches—"Monkeys that live in Africa and Asia can't do this." An attractive browsing book.

Additional coverage of Arnold's life and career is contained in the following sources published by The Gale Group: *Contemporary Authors,* Vol. 107; *Contemporary Authors New Revision Series,* Vol. 24; *Something about the Author,* Vols. 36, 85; and *Something about the Author Autobiography Series,* Vol. 23.

Judith Clarke

1943-

Australian author of fiction.

Major works include *The Heroic Life of Al Capsella* (1988, U. S. edition, 1990), *Al Capsella and the Watchdogs* (1990), *Riffraff* (1992), *Panic Stations* (1995), *Night Train* (1998).

INTRODUCTION

Best known for her humorous novels for middle-schoolers and young adults, Clarke has also written serious novels and tales of the supernatural. Clarke's most successful works have blended humor with a keen understanding of teenagers, and the problems and frustrations they face. Critics have praised her sensitivity in depicting young adults. Ronald A. Van De Voorde commented, "Clarke captures the typical feelings of an adolescent boy very well," and Stephen Matthews noted that "good humor and sympathetic understanding" characterize the author's books. Clarke's characters are insightful and reflective, allowing readers to experience the world through them. A *Publishers Weekly* reviewer remarked about *The Heroic Life of Al Capsella*: "Quietly humorous in places, the book, like *Catcher in the Rye*, emphasizes the main character's internal musings. . . . " Clarke's almost deadpan humor also has been widely applauded by reviewers. Deborah Stevenson commented on the author's "wry yet bubbling humor of observation and coincidence," and Catherine M. Mercier commended Clarke's "vivacious, captivating humor."

Many of the author's books focus on the relationships between teens and their parents, and the conflicts that arise. Clarke told *Something about the Author (SATA)*, "In my novels I'm especially concerned with the relationships between children and adults, with the conflicts of interest, misunderstandings, and the pressures they place on one another." Particularly interested in the anxieties of parents, Clarke also explores these issues through the point of view of the teenager, sometimes provoking laughs at the expense of an adult character. Despite this, as Stephanie Zvirin observed, "[h]er adults are not idiotic cardboard shapes; while Clarke pokes fun at laughable behaviors, she never demeans, and beneath the comic veneer she has created lurks a fondness and respect for people—even parents—despite their strange ways."

Biographical Information

Clarke was born in Australia, which is the setting for all of her books. She received her bachelor of arts degree from the University of New South Wales in 1964, and was awarded a master's degree by the Australian National University in 1966. Clarke lives with her family in Melbourne.

Major Works

Clarke's *Al Capsella* series traces the trials of young Al, a teenager in a Melbourne suburb. In *The Heroic Life of Al Capsella*, readers are introduced to the fourteen-year-old boy, whose main tribulation in life is his eccentric parents. Al longs for a quiet, unobtrusive mother and father; instead, his absent-minded dad allows the garden to become scandalously overgrown, and his mom, wearing embarrassing outfits from her hippie days, occasionally shows up at school to check out Al's classes. Desperately hoping for a more normal family, Al visits his grandparents and realizes that even conservative, "normal" families have their outlandish moments and unique ways of operating. In *Al Capsella and the Watchdogs*, fifteen-year-old Al is troubled by his parents' invasive observation. Protective of his privacy, Al commiserates with his friends about their parents' obsessive pursuit—Al's mother even borrows someone else's dog as a pretense for following her son when he goes out at night. But when Al's maternal grandparents come to stay with his family, the boy realizes that each generation goes through what he's experiencing: the anxious grandparents watch every move Mrs. Capsella makes.

Panic Stations, a collection of seven stories, is also about anxieties. The stories focus on different young adults as they confront their fears and doubts, or their "panic stations"; older adults in the stories are also plagued by worries about their children, particularly as they approach adulthood and independence. *Riffraff*, too, is a book about the uncertainties inherent in everyday life. The novel traces the burgeoning friendship between three misfits: Sophia, a rude and strange-looking girl who says whatever is on her mind, regardless of other people's feelings; Sam, a painfully shy boy who is intrigued by Sophia; and Theodore Snackle, the reclusive writer who brings the two children together. *Riffraff* charts the awkward progress of their relationships through misunderstandings, fears, and eventual camaraderie.

Another of Clarke's novels, *Night Train*, illustrates the serious nature of the pressures felt by young adults. The book chronicles the failures of all the adults in Luke's life to reach him and prevent his suicide. Luke, facing failure at a third high school, is overwhelmed with doubt and anxiety. His father rejects him, and his mother is too involved in her own anxieties to be any help. Likewise, guidance counselors and teachers miss pivotal opportunities to help the boy. Luke sinks deeper into his despair, and finally steps in front of a train. *Night Train*, with its portrayal of many points of view—Luke's, his parents', his sisters'—is a thought-provoking message about the very real difficulties faced by teenagers and their families.

Awards

Friend of My Heart was elected to the shortlist for the Australian Children's Book of the Year Award in 1995. *The Heroic Life of Al Capsella* was a *Booklist* editor's choice in 1990, and was named a Best Book for young adults by the American Library Association in 1992. *Al Capsella and the Watchdogs* was named talking book of the year by Variety Club in 1991, and was named a Best Book for young adults by the New York Public Library in 1992. Both *The Heroic Life of Al Capsella* and *Al Capsella and the Watchdogs* were elected to the shortlist for the N.S.W. Premiers Award in 1989 and 1990, respectively.

GENERAL COMMENTARY

Cathi Dunn MacRae

SOURCE: "The Young Adult Perplex," in *Wilson Library Bulletin,* Vol. 66, No. 3, November, 1991, pp. 92-3.

Al Capsella is an engaging new comic character from Australia, invented by J. Clarke. Al has already been embraced by enough American readers to star in his second YA novel and to be compared with our beloved Holden Caulfield. Al's Melbourne suburb has a K-Mart. His home feels so American that readers have no clue that they're in the Southern Hemisphere until page thirty-seven of *The Heroic Life of Al Capsella,* when Al mentions that it's almost November, nearly summertime.

"Being fourteen is scary" to Al, as it is to many adolescent males, but he is more reflective than most and can tell us why: "It's like being in a fairy tale; you never know what you'll find in the mirror when you wake up in the morning."

Al longs to be normal, but he is plagued with parents whom people notice. "The Capsellas," as Al refers to them, are "readaholics." Mrs. Capsella does not wear nice pleated skirts and stay politely at home or work as other mothers do. She bikes to Al's school in outlandish sixties outfits to check out his classes, since she has plenty of time taking breaks from writing romance novels. Mr. Capsella is a university professor so lost in his ivory tower that he must ask Al to explain what Adidas are. In fact, Al must explain a lot to his parents, such as how their overgrown garden is a neighborhood scandal. Though frustrated, Al is gentle and patient with his perplexing parents. After a visit to his eccentric grandparents in Sydney reveals how frustrated Al's mother is with her perplexing parents, Al realizes that normal is "just a word people used to say what *they* liked was right, and what other people liked was wrong."

In the sequel, *Al Capsella and the Watchdogs,* a year later, Al bemoans his "life of a fugitive" as he and his friends search in vain for privacy. All their parents are afflicted with same version of Mrs. Capsella's "Bunny Lake Is Missing Complex," demanding to know where their teenagers are going, what they are doing, and when they are coming home. Imagining their teenagers' dreadful fates, parents take up jogging or dog walking to keep their offspring safely in view. Al also hides from Sophie, a pretty girl in his class whose attraction merely embarrasses him. Al is so like Ron Koertge's charming adolescent males that one anticipates the next sequel in which Al will surely awaken to his sexuality as vigorously as Koertge's characters do.

Al blends common sense with a sense of the ridiculous. Good-heartedness and wry observations make Al Capsella an entertaining commentator on universal teen trials.

TITLE COMMENTARY

📖 **THE HEROIC LIFE OF AL CAPSELLA (first book in the "Capsella" series, 1988; U. S. edition, 1990)**

Stephanie Zvirin

SOURCE: A review of *The Heroic Life of Al Capsella,* in *Booklist,* Vol. 86, No. 14, March 15, 1990, p. 142.

Clarke, a new voice in young adult fiction, joins a growing number of outstanding writers (Mahy, Duder, Savage, Park) who are bringing life "down under" to American readers. Her comical tale, set in Australia, is a perfectly delightful piece—in spite of the fact that it has virtually no plot. At its heart is 14-year-old Almeric ("You'll be grateful when you're forty") Capsella, observant and long suffering, through whose perspective Clarke introduces her singular cast. Like most of his age-mates, Al wants desperately to fit in with his peers. Unfortunately, he is constantly thwarted by "Mr. and Mrs. Capsella," as Al calls his parents—hoping against hope that the pair actually aren't his mom and dad. His wonderfully understated descriptions of their disorganized, bookish, eccentric ways and of the oddball behaviors of other equally outlandish adults who cross his path (among them, a school librarian who shuts up shop when students need books and a good-natured grandfather who stores table scraps in the freezer so the garbage can won't smell) provoke not only chuckles, but also a good deal of empathy for beleaguered Al, obviously never destined to be "normal." But despite the idiosyncrasies of virtually all her older types, Clarke hasn't aimed poison darts at grownups the way authors of American problem novels did for years. Her adults are not idiotic cardboard shapes; while Clarke pokes fun at laughable behaviors, she never demeans, and beneath the comic veneer she has created lurks a fondness and respect for people—even parents—despite their strange ways.

Publishers Weekly

SOURCE: A review of *The Heroic Life of Al Capsella,* in *Publishers Weekly,* Vol. 237, No. 15, April 13, 1990, p. 67.

The title of Clarke's first novel is misleading; Al's "heroics" are a vague reference to his tolerating his somewhat off-center parents—"The Capsellas are a real liability." (Throughout his narrative, Al indicates his detachment by referring to them only by their surnames.) The boy is deeply concerned with appearing "normal" to others, but the fanciful Mrs. Capsella—a writer of romance novels who wears hippy-style clothing—renders this hopeless. It's not until Al accompanies his mother on a visit to her parents, a rigidly structured, conservative, yet quirky pair, that he appreciates Mrs. Capsella as she is. Although the time is the present and the setting a suburban Australian town, Al comes across as a low-key Holden Caulfield. Quietly humorous in places, the book, like *The Catcher in the Rye,* emphasizes the main character's internal musings, and is more episodic than plot-driven. The pace may slacken occasionally, but the engaging, perceptive Al is a fellow worth knowing.

Ronald A. Van De Voorde

SOURCE: A review of *The Heroic Life of Al Capsella,* in *School Library Journal,* Vol. 36, No. 7, July, 1990, p. 88.

Al Capsella, 14, is concerned about how others view him and desperately craves normal parents and a normal life. But his parents are anything but normal, especially his mother, who writes *Woman's Journal* stories, dresses weirdly, and acts decidedly eccentric. Al is constantly embarrassed by these oddballs. Clarke captures the typical feelings of an adolescent boy very well, but she has Al tell his story with deadpan humor. The climax of the book comes with a visit of Mrs. Capsella and Al to his maternal grandparents, Pearly and Neddy Blount. In this household Al discovers what "normal" is with a vengeance. The picture Clarke gives us of the Blounts must be some of the funniest writing to be produced in recent years; readers are sure to be amused by the portrayals of teachers, including the school librarian, who "came out from America and got her iron grip on the place." The Australian setting should pose no problem for American readers, for the family and school incidents are universal.

Kathryn Pierson

SOURCE: A review of *The Heroic Life of Al Capsella,* in *Bulletin of the Center for Children's Books,* Vol. 43, No. 11, July-August, 1990, p. 261.

Al Capsella wants to be more than a normal teenager more than anything. Unfortunately, he has two major liabilities—Mr. and Mrs. Capsella. They are a "bookish couple" who just don't seem to understand that parents should be "perfectly ordinary and unobtrusive, quiet and orderly, well dressed and polite, hardworking and as wealthy as possible." Instead, Mrs. Capsella writes romance novels, wears thrift-shop clothes, and barges into Al's school whenever she's bored. Quiet Mr. Capsella teaches at the University and is overwhelmed by the overgrown state of his suburban lawn. The funny, cynical, but believable Australian story shows Al's growing tolerance for his parent's foibles. Al's misadventures will make a good middle school readaloud, but be forewarned—from Al's perspective, the adults appear ridiculous, and the most ridiculous of all is the school librarian.

THE BOY ON THE LAKE (1989, revised edition published as *The Torment of Mr. Gully: Stories of the Supernatural,* 1990)

Kirkus Reviews

SOURCE: A review of *The Torment of Mr. Gully: Stories of the Supernatural,* in *Kirkus Reviews,* Vol. LVIII, No. 20, October 15, 1990, p. 1454.

From an Australian writer, 11 stories, each with a chilling, macabre touch. Several feature ghosts, disappearing houses, or menacing old men or women. In the eeriest tales, the young narrators go off the deep end: one drowns the neighbors' baby because they've been mistreating their dog; another insists that Auntie has bitten off her hand, though everyone else can still see it; a third suddenly finds himself indifferent to life, himself, or indeed anything except his little sister. Clarke creates and sustains the requisite ominous atmosphere, even in "Scared Stiff," which (until the end) is almost funny; and achieves some subtle effects in "The Last Strawberries" (told from a ghost's point of view) and in the title story, about a class that harasses an elderly teacher only to learn that he's dying. Not bedtime reading.

Holly Sanhuber

SOURCE: A review of *The Torment of Mr. Gully: Stories of the Supernatural,* in *School Library Journal,* Vol. 36, No. 11, November, 1990, p. 134.

All of the characters in these disquieting, disturbing, and somewhat distasteful stories are tormented in varying degrees—some to death—by their encounters with the supernatural. All are driven in some measure to test the power of the unknown; few have any chance against the capricious malevolence of the uncanny, and none escape unscathed. This bleak landscape, where neither goodness nor innocence triumphs over evil, is coupled with hypnotic storytelling that compells readers to turn the pages, regardless of their apprehension. Horror, like humor, is an idiosyncratic taste. The best stays with readers, chilling the mind long after the covers are closed. This book falls into that category.

Denise Wilms

SOURCE: A review of *The Torment of Mr. Gully: Stories of the Supernatural,* in *Booklist,* Vol. 87, No. 10, January 15, 1991, p. 1052.

There's a cerebral bent to this collection of 11 eerie short stories that hails from Australia, where it was originally published in 1989 in a slightly different form as *The Boy on the Lake.* Cool, restrained language is a deceptive cover for the chills, jolts, and occasional horror that mark the conclusions. A young child permanently disappears into a painted scene; a boy is led to death by a malevolent ghost; and in the title story, a teacher leaves his nasty students with an unexpectedly sobering lesson. The title and supernatural billing are attention getters, but seasoned readers are the ones who will settle down best to the stories' measured style.

Lenora Hobbs

SOURCE: A review of *The Torment of Mr. Gully: Stories of the Supernatural,* in *The Book Report,* Vol. 10, No. 2, September-October, 1991, p. 53.

First published in Australia in 1989 as *The Boy on the Lake,* this collection consists of 11 stories with a common theme: the transformation of the mundane into the weird and sinister. In the title story, students torment their teacher, who is dying. Only after he escapes them do they realize what they have done. Other stories depend more on the supernatural. For example, in **"The Cuckoo Bird,"** a small child is drawn into a picture and is replaced in real life by the child who had been in the picture before. Intriguing as these stories are, they may not satisfy hard-core Stephen King fans. Still, they merit a place in the collection.

📖 *TEDDY B. ZOOT* (1990)

Carolyn Jenks

SOURCE: A review of *Teddy B. Zoot,* in *School Library Journal,* Vol. 37, No. 1, January, 1991, p. 70.

Sarah has a classic case of math anxiety: she is the weakest member of the top group in her class, and so afraid of being put back that she forgets to take home the worksheet that is due the next day. Her teddy bear, a devoted friend, risks jeers from a cat, harm by a dog, and sogginess from the rain to get to school in the middle of the night for Sarah's homework. Teddy is a noble character, single-minded in his purpose and sensitive to others he encounters on his adventure. Readers who share Sarah's concerns will be comforted in knowing they are not unique in their troubles, and will recognize the hope in Sarah's situation as her spirits rise the next morning. Charcoal pencil drawings depict paperdoll-like characters against flat, sketchy backgrounds. An average offering for those making the transition from picture books to chapter books.

Kay Weisman

SOURCE: A review of *Teddy B. Zoot,* in *Booklist,* Vol. 87, No. 11, February 1, 1991, p. 1130.

Discovering that she has mistakenly left her math homework at school, Sarah bursts into tears. Mother says it is too late (and too stormy) to return for the paper, but Sarah (who suffers from severe math anxiety) is certain her teacher will be angry if she comes to class unprepared. After Sarah retires for the night, her ever-loyal teddy bear, Teddy B. Zoot, comes to the rescue, setting off through the pouring rain to retrieve the missing assignment. Along the way, he is attacked by a neighbor's dog and gets help from an educated rat living in the school basement. Finally, the bear returns home with the forgotten work sheet. Awakening the next morning, refreshed and no longer anxious; Sarah completes her sums in time for school. While Sarah's problems seem too conveniently solved, the brave and faithful Teddy will appeal to stuffed-animal fans.

📖 *AL CAPSELLA AND THE WATCHDOGS* (1990; revised edition, 1991)

Kirkus Reviews

SOURCE: A review of *Al Capsella and the Watchdogs,* in *Kirkus Reviews,* Vol. LIX, No. 12, June 15, 1991, p. 786.

In an engaging sequel to *The Heroic Life of Al Capsella,* Al continues his affectionate sparring with parents who are almost as outlandish as they seem to his embarrassed 15-year-old eyes. Mrs. Capsella, successful author of romances, has given Al a notably lumpy, badly sewn, homemade beanbag chair that proves to contain all the "Home Duties presents" (apron, egg-timer, etc.) her mother had forced on her. Worse, she and his friends' parents are forever observing their young, resorting to ruses like borrowing each other's dogs in order to spy on unsupervised parties; they are also taking courses on how to deal with adolescents, resulting in transparently uncharacteristic tact and sympathetic concern. Meanwhile,

Mrs. Capsella's truly bizarre parents come to stay and comment on her every move, precipitating the two younger generations into an alliance of sorts.

The flavor here may be Australian, but the anxieties and fencing between parent and child are universal. What's special is Al's mellow tone: he may find his parents inconvenient or incomprehensible, but he views them with an amused tolerance that's both hilarious and endearing (and, one hopes, contagious).

Stephanie Zvirin

SOURCE: A review of *Al Capsella and the Watchdogs*, in *Booklist*, Vol. 87, No. 22, August, 1991, p. 2140.

"No worries" may be Al Capsella's favorite expression, but as readers familiar with **The Heroic Life of Al Capsella** will remember, Al has problems anyway. His lack of privacy is high on his list of concerns these days. So is attractive Sophie Disher, who's got her eye on him. But, as before, most of Al's difficulties are less his own doing than the result of the behavior of the adults who surround him—in particular his mother, whom he frequently wishes would disappear into the woodwork. Readers unfamiliar with the Capsella family eccentricities, laid out beautifully in the previous book, may have a bit of trouble getting into this part of Al's ongoing story. If they manage the first chapter or two, though, they'll be in line for some very funny stuff—especially when Al's mom has to cope with the idiosyncrasies of her own parents. That's "just desserts" for sure. Once again, Australian author Clarke blends humor with warmth, conjuring up an assortment of peculiar adults—muddled, well-meaning folk—who ring true in surprising, subtle ways. With good-natured, long-suffering Al supplying the narrative stickum, they emerge as a delightfully weird bunch, lending a humorous glow to some of the familiar pressures and embarrassments of being a teen. A joy to read. . . .

Susan F. Marcus

SOURCE: A review of *Al Capsella and the Watchdogs*, in *School Library Journal*, Vol. 37, No. 8, August, 1991, p. 195.

Al Capsella, 15, is an Australian high schooler who, like his friends, longs for an independent social life. However, Mr. and Mrs. Capsella, (as he always calls his folks), like his friends' parents, with every good intention, are a bit overprotective. For example, his mother is not above borrowing a dog to walk as an excuse for trailing Al and his friends to a party, thereby ruining his evening. The boys spend much of their leisure time bemoaning the tactics their parents use to remain involved in all phases of their lives. When Mrs. Capsella's parents are forced by floodwaters to stay temporarily with their daughter, Al observes his moth-

er in turn assuming his role, the child whose parents watch her every move. Whereas the book's prequel, **The Heroic Life of Al Capsella,** elicits some empathy for the unique individuals in Al's life, here the laughs are usually at the expense of the adults, portraying them as foolish and laughable. Although this edition has been revised from the Australian original, numerous terms remain unexplained.

Nina VandeWater

SOURCE: A review of *Al Capsella and the Watchdogs,* in *Voice of Youth Advocates,* Vol. 14, No. 5, December, 1991, p. 308.

Al Capsella, in typical 15 year old fashion, suffers from that perennial biological necessity, parents. His particular problem is his mother, who is a constant "watchdog" over his every move. In Clarke's second novel (following **The Heroic Life of Al Capsella**) about this farcical family, it's Mrs. Capsella's turn to suffer when her own parents come to stay while their house dries out from a flood. This turn of events upsets Al's mother far more than it does Al, even though his grandfather, who "had never quite taken in the fact that I'd been given the ridiculous name of Almeric," calls him Bertie (thinking his name is Albert) while his crusty grandmother just "referred to me as him."

Humorously written by an Australian author (the setting is Melbourne), this fast-reading novel will, nevertheless, not appeal to most teenagers, who may identify with Al's problem, but will not want to read a whole novel about it. While the book's thesis seems to be that every generation is annoyed by its parents, Al remains unbelievably polite and calm amid the adult turmoil in this essentially plot-poor novel that suffers from too much adult angst.

RIFFRAFF (1992)

Publishers Weekly

SOURCE: A review of *Riffraff,* in *Publishers Weekly,* Vol. 239, No. 52, November 30, 1992, pp. 55-6.

"Even as a baby, Sophia had been a nuisance," and now she has grown into a loud, obnoxious and absolutely unflappable girl, the terror of her neighborhood. Sam, in contrast, is "so shy that when he saw someone he knew . . . he'd duck behind a tree or fence or a telephone pole so they wouldn't see him." Not surprisingly, neither of these singular characters has a thriving social life. Through their mutual acquaintance with Theodore Snackle, who hates his name, and whose nose, as Sophia points out thoughtlessly, "would look good on a witch," Sam and Sophia both learn something about the nature of friendship and find that they are destined to be pals. Clarke goes easy on his novel's message, focusing instead on the extremes of behaviour that lead Sophia and Sam into their relationship. Calling to mind both *Pippi Longstocking* and the novels of Beverly Cleary, this humorous import from Down Under is a welcome addition to the ranks of comical middle-grade stories.

Hazel Rochman

SOURCE: A review of *Riffraff,* in *Booklist,* Vol. 89, No. 8, December 15, 1992, p. 736.

Three awkward loners become friends in a funny novel about trying to find a place in a dull and difficult world. There's Sophia, cross and wild, bored with the nice mimsy-whimsies everywhere. She talks nonstop in her loud, rackety voice and offends everybody; yet she just knows she's really beautiful and clever. Sam's the opposite, so shy he won't look in the mirror, convinced he's short and strange, wishing he was ordinary. Sophia fascinates him; he longs to walk right up to her in the playground and ask, "Why doesn't it worry you that you're so funny-looking?" Sophia has liked Sam ever since she caught a glimpse of his strange, wonderful drawings, but she doesn't know how to talk to people without being rude. The man who gets them together is Theodore, a reclusive writer who makes up weird, fantastic fables—one about a teacher so boring he puts the class to sleep; one about a raucous, overprotected cat who thinks she's a Sensitive Soul. As in Clarke's YA novels, such as *The Heroic Life of Al Capsella* the fun is in the characters here, especially, larger-than-life Sophia. Kids will recognize themselves and their classmates in the fumbling for friendship and in the yearning to be both ordinary and strange.

Kirkus Reviews

SOURCE: A review of *Riffraff,* in *Kirkus Reviews,* Vol. LX, No. 24, December 15, 1992, p. 1570.

The author of a YA book about some comically bizarre parents—*Al Capsella and the Watchdogs,* 1991—zeros in on an equally bizarre preadolescent. Though orange-haired Sophia is an almost surreal *enfant terrible*—terrorizing her conventional Australian neighborhood with pungently accurate observations and driving her meek, rather dim mother, Mrs. Throstle, nearly to despair—her story's outcome is less astonishing than she is. One of the neighbors the irrepressible Sophia barges in on is Theodore, who writes books. Unlike her other victims, he welcomes her, though even he is taken aback by her outrageously candid remarks. Meanwhile, Sophia has found that not only reading (which she does only late at night) but also writing relieves her chronic boredom; and she's noticed that classmate Sam, who is as painfully shy as Sophia is gauche, draws wonderful pictures. Pausing along the way for Theodore to tell a couple of amusingly wacky and pointed stories, Clarke maneuvers the kids into friendships with first Theodore and then each other, with a romance for

Theodore himself thrown in for good measure. Broad but lively humor, with a not-too-obvious moral or two.

Ellen Fader

SOURCE: A review of *Riffraff,* in *School Library Journal,* Vol. 39, No. 2, February, 1993, p. 92.

Sophia Throstle, a bored, thoroughly disagreeable but self-satisfied nine-year-old girl, possesses a shock of spiky orange hair, freckles, and a scratchy, irritating voice. She terrorizes her parents, schoolmates, and the neighborhood with her rude, unthinking actions and comments. Sophia makes friends with neighbor Theodore Snackle, a reclusive writer, the only remaining person who will open the door to her. He also befriends Sam Froggett, a shy, artistic boy who is fascinated with Sophia. Tentative moves towards friendship on both children's parts result in misunderstandings. Theodore becomes the agent of their eventual getting together by writing stories; two are included here. A subplot concerning his romantic interest in the corner shopkeeper adds interest. This novel of character moves along quite briskly; however, the funny names, the unsympathetic nature of Sophia's behavior, and the lack of involvement by parents in their children's lives gives the story an air of humor and unreality that, in the end, undermines the triumph of Sophia and Sam's growing relationship. . . . A pleasant, if ultimately unmemorable, novel about a common theme of reaching out and discovering the true nature of another person.

Catherine M. Mercier

SOURCE: A review of *Riffraff,* in *The Five Owls,* Vol. VII, No. 4, March-April, 1993, p. 93.

Each of the three idiosyncratic characters Australian author J. Clarke colorfully portrays in ***Riffraff*** lives as an outsider. With spiky orange hair and commanding green eyes, nine-year-old Sophia Throstle alienates nearly everyone she meets when they bristle against her frank, often judgmental remarks. Sophia's classmate Sam Frogget knows with grounded certainty that he's below even normal-looking. He fears that his mother's worries—about Sam's sensitive, shy nature—may carry too much truth. And the unconventional Theodore Snackle, a writer, protects his privacy but also feels embarrassed by his nose and his name.

More than their shared status as outsiders sparks the interest of these unique characters in each other. Banished from her house and told to find something to do, Sophia enters Theodore's life without preliminary, without regard. Somewhat surprised, he doesn't accept her immediately, but he does suggest she entertain herself as he does and they begin to write stories together. Sophia remains attentive to Theodore partly because his stories are better told, are more fantastic, and are much more fun to read than hers are. She also forms a natural friendship with Theodore because he welcomes her without the drive to change her. And, while Sophia admires Sam's drawings from across her classroom, he misunderstands her attempts to befriend him and runs away from her. Sam, however, willingly and spontaneously finds comradeship with Theodore, thus empowering Theodore to act as the catalyst for the two remarkably dissimilar children.

Like Theodore, Sophia and Sam participate in the reflective, sometimes egocentric, often lonely work of an artist. They may not be appreciated, and in Sophia's case may feel bruised by distinct dislike, yet their individuality persists and their artistic pursuits continue. In discovering each other, these three solitary beings discover the sustaining pleasure and energy of a kindred community.

A vivacious, captivating humor flows through his novel and binds it with a sense of perspective. Readers recognize the inappropriateness of Sophia's actions even as they empathize with her. Sam's drawings border on caricatures which reveal truth through cartoon. Theodore's compelling stories entertain with wit and ingenuity even if his well-intentioned but clearly out-dated "love" letters exceed Sam's needs toward Sophia.

While some aspects of plot and extraneous characters distract in this novel, its humor and vision of artists raise it above "riffraff."

 ***AL CAPSELLA ON HOLIDAYS* (third book in the "Capsella" series, 1992; U. S. edition published as *Al Capsella Takes a Vacation,* 1993)**

Deborah Stevenson

SOURCE: A review of *Al Capsella Takes a Vacation,* in *Bulletin of the Center for Children's Books,* Vol. 46, No. 8, April, 1993, p. 242.

Hapless and humorous Al Capsella, hero of *The Heroic Life of Al Capsella,* is back in another adventure, or rather an anti-adventure. At sixteen, he and his best mate Lou are eager to escape on a parent-free beach vacation, but a slight confusion about place names sends the two of them to a tiny inland town where they stay in a converted chicken house in Mrs. Mulroony's backyard. Pride prevents them from calling for help, so they stick it out in sustainedly funny inactivity, making valiant attempts to cook stewing fowl from the local store, joining their landlady in watching her favorite soap, and conferring about Lou's letters to his sweet and hopefully sultry Swedish pen-pal (who turns out to be perhaps seven years old). Clarke sounds like an Australian Jean Shepherd with her wry yet bubbling humor of observation and coincidence, and the Down Under touches like summer at Christmastime make the book intriguingly exotic to American readers. The

mournfully rollicking rhythm of the story might make this a good readaloud for older listeners, and both Al Capsella fans and new friends will relish a tale of independence gone awry.

Kathy Piehl

SOURCE: A review of *Al Capsella Takes a Vacation,* in *School Library Journal,* Vol. 39, No. 5, May, 1993, p. 124.

Clarke brings Al Capsella, now 16, back for a third wry glimpse of adolescent life in Australia. Al and his friend Lou convince their parents that they can handle a summer/Christmas holiday on their own. Acting on a tip from a classmate, Al persuades his mother to book them a cabin. With visions of beaches, discos, and girls dancing in their heads, the boys make the bus journey to their holiday spot, only to discover that they are miles from surf, parties, or even a restaurant. Rather than admit their mistake, the two contend with snide comments from the locals, inedible meals, and ruined laundry. Although there are laugh-provoking moments reminiscent of Clarke's first two books about Al, the humor is not sustained at the same high level. By removing him from the company of parents and teachers, the author reduces her opportunities for him to reflect upon the adult foibles that provide much high-energy amusement in the earlier novels. The maturing Al has grown a bit reflective, and a new poignancy surfaces in his consideration of the world. Yet even a moderately funny Al Capsella packs a larger humorous punch then most YA novels, and libraries will want to add this account of his latest escapades.

Kirkus Reviews

SOURCE: A review of *Al Capsella Takes a Vacation,* in *Kirkus Reviews,* Vol. LXI, No. 11, June 1, 1993, p. 718.

In his third appearance, the 16-year-old Australian and his friend Lou hoodwink their parents into letting just the two of them vacation at Scutchthorpe, which a friend has glowingly described as a beach paradise with discos and an abundance of compliant girls. Lugging their surfboards, the boys embark by bus for what proves to be a tiny community 200 miles from the coast—where their motel reservations are for the only room in a converted "chook" (chicken) house; the one swimming hole has leeches; they must cook their own meals using the sparse provisions from the general store; and, with nothing else to do, they're reduced to reading women's magazines and doing their laundry. Despite Clarke's considerable gift for wryly comical description, the resulting farce isn't as funny *Al Capsella and the Watchdogs,* nor does it have its predecessors' insightful, bittersweet overtones; here, nothing's more exciting than Lou realizing that his Swedish pen pal may be only seven years old, and the story peters out with the boys seizing the chance to go home early. Fans may enjoy this, but it's a weaker effort all around.

Stephanie Zvirin

SOURCE: A review of *Al Capsella Takes a Vacation,* in *Booklist,* Vol. 89, No. 21, July, 1993, p. 1957.

The thought of spending another Christmas holiday under protective custody of their "watchdog" parents is so totally unappealing that Al and his buddy Lou decide to petition for a vacation alone together. They angle for a place called Scutchthorpe, which they've heard has both beautiful beaches and beautiful girls. But, no sooner do they manage to conquer their parents' misgivings than they begin to have a few of own—tiny ones at first, but ones that soon swell to monstrous size when their rickety old bus drops them, surfboards and all, in the middle of nowhere. It isn't long before they discover the paradise they sought is really somewhere else. Yet even when they know the truth, they'd rather struggle with laundry and cooking and read package labels to relieve their boredom than admit defeat and go home. There's sweet nostalgia in the boys' embarrassing situation and in their determination to keep up appearances, but this book doesn't have the verve of Al's earlier adventures, particularly *The Heroic Life of Al Capsella.* There's more than a touch of realism in the boys' stubbornness, however, and a bit of warm comedy shines through, especially during their encounters with a new crop of vividly fashioned adult characters. What's more, Al's wry, almost deadpan narrative is the perfect vehicle for describing a fantasy vacation gone awry.

Susan Levine

SOURCE: A review of *Al Capsella Takes a Vacation,* in *Voice of Youth Advocates,* Vol. 16, No. 4, October, 1993, p. 215.

In this continuing series about Al Capsella (*The Heroic Life of Al Capsella* and *Al Capsella and the Watchdogs*) Christmas is coming and so is summer vacation with the family (it's Australia), a thought sixteen-year-old Al and his friend Lou find too ghastly. Remembering what a former schoolmate had said about Scutchthorpe, a seaside town where there were plenty of discos, twenty-four-hour action, constant sun, good surf, and no one over twenty-four in sight, the two make plans to vacation there alone. They wrangle permission from their parents, find a bus that goes to Scutchthorpe, and finally arrive—only to discover that their vacation resort is in the middle of nowhere. There is no beach, no action; just fields, a couple of houses, a general store, and a dam. Refusing to admit defeat, they settle down to the vacation from hell.

The book is plain fun to read, with terrific dialogue between Al and Lou, who are both insecure but trying to show some independence. The adults are sketched

enough to show their distinct peculiarities (barely human teacher, kindly landlady, protective mother, sneering store owner, et al.) and add to the fun. The only problem is that Al and Lou, while sixteen, are incredibly naive and act more like thirteen or fourteen-year-olds at best. Why didn't anyone think to look up Scutchthorpe on a map? But then there would be no story and readers would miss the fun.

📖 *FRIEND OF MY HEART* (1994)

Stephen Matthews

SOURCE: A review of *Friend of My Heart,* in *Australian Book Review,* No. 167, December-January, 1995, pp. 54-5.

Judith Clarke's *Friend of my Heart* is a far less ambitious book [than Jenny Pausacker's *Mr Enigmatic*] though it too has the power to stir a tearful reaction. Unfortunately, because of its disjointed structure, some readers may not persist far enough to find their tear ducts tested; the books' 148 pages are chopped up into forty-two short chapters and it's not at all clear at first whose story it is.

Almost all the characters are either in love, or wanting to be, or remembering when they were, but the book thankfully turns out to be more than another story about lovelorn adolescents. When we meet sixteen-year-old Daz, her seventeen-year-old brother William and their grandmother Sheila Thredlow, Daz has deluded herself that she's in love with the handsome, but piggish, Valentine O'Leary; William is unrequitedly besotted with a girl whom he cannot find the courage to approach; and their grandmother, smitten with dementia, is confined to a nursing home (which she takes to be a rather poorly-run, uncooperative hotel) and is pining for her long-lost best friend. The book finally takes shape when Daz begins to understand her grandmother's plight.

By the time the book reaches its unashamedly sentimental conclusion, Daz and William have not only resolved their misbegotten loves and their estrangement from each other but also uncovered the fate of their grandmother's friend. Understanding has flourished and love, in one of its varieties at any rate, has triumphed. Tighter editing should have triumphed too, and more observant proofreading should have intercepted the numerous typographical errors.

Stephen Matthews

SOURCE: A review of *Friend of My Heart,* in *Australian Book Review,* No. 173, August, 1995, p. 60.

Of the books the judges did see fit to choose [for the Children's Book Council award shortlist], *Friend of My Heart* is a surprising but interesting candidate.

Though flawed by its choppy structure, uncertain focus and shaky proofreading, it's redeemed by Judith Clarke's good humour and sympathetic understanding, which transform it from the hackneyed story about lovelorn adolescents it might have been into a touching exploration of what makes people of any age devote so much energy to the pursuit of love.

📖 *PANIC STATIONS* (1995)

Stephen Matthews

SOURCE: "Parallel Dangers: Ends and Beginnings," in *Australian Book Review,* No. 171, June, 1995, pp. 64-5.

The best stories come last in *Panic Stations.* . . . The first three are undemanding to the point of limpness but then Judith Clarke hits her stride, articulating with wonderfully precise insight in the remaining four stories the doubts and uncertainties of young people—their panic stations—on the road to adulthood. Though the stories express the gulf in outlook between old and young adults, their good-humoured perceptiveness helps build the understanding by which the gulf can be bridged. Thus in **"Blue Volvo"**, the eighteen-year-old Andy, manfully proud of passing his driving test, sees his now elderly Year Five teacher and, manliness rapidly diminishing, becomes consumed by painful memories of his school days. Eventually, however, he understands that:

> the slow nod, the gravity, the long level gaze into his eyes hadn't been a put-down but a form of acknowledgment. She'd expected the best from him, not the worst, as he'd imagined. She'd thought he didn't need the smiles she'd given to the others.

"Parting Company" is a story for all adults who have ever been frustrated by a teenager with a gift for mislaying everything, and **"What's There to Eat?"** is for parents afflicted with one of those aging, hungry young adults who hasn't yet felt the urge to experience the advantages of independent living. In the wryly titled **"Living Skills"**, on the other hand, a mother and father constantly worry for the safety of their seventeen-year-old son when he doesn't come home on Saturday nights.

Clarke's ironic observation of the quirks and eccentricities of ordinary people brings to mind the English writer, Jane Gardam. The best of her stories can be appreciated as much by adults as by young people on the cusp of adulthood. A shame then that they're blighted with typographical errors like 'allelulia', 'plummetting' and 'wree' (for 'were'), not to mention uncertainty as to whether a certain relation is an 'Aunty' or an 'Auntie'. A shame too that the weakest, most 'accessible', stories are at the beginning. At least short stories have the advantage that they don't have to be read in the published sequence, as the chapters of a novel do.

📖 *BIG NIGHT OUT* (1995)

Alan Horsfield

SOURCE: A review of *Big Night Out,* in *Magpies,* Vol. 10, No. 3, July, 1995, pp. 26-7.

Moz, Guster and Davo have just about enough money between them for a Big Night Out at the off limits pub. The night quickly turns into a disaster when the money is lost and their deceit is discovered. **Big Night Out** is full of fun, humour and danger that, in the cold light of morning and safety, is recognized for the foolishness that it is. The story is full of the rattle of the suburbs at night and the chilling realization that unconsidered actions have unwanted consequences. The innovative use of language will be sure to impress many readers.

📖 *NIGHT TRAIN* (1998)

Ruth Starke

SOURCE: "Switching Viewpoints," in *Australian Book Review,* No. 199, April, 1998, pp. 55-6.

Not another book about death, I groaned, as the opening pages of **Night Train** landed me in the middle of a funeral. And not just death: yet another teenage suicide. 1997 saw an amazing number of novels for young people written on these subjects; one dared hardly open a book without reaching first for a box of Kleenex. But surely not Judith Clarke, she of the hilarious Al Capsella books and the wry humour of **Panic Stations,** succumbing to the trend for the dark and depressing? Well yes, but in a very Judith Clarke sort of way, and that makes all the difference.

The funeral is for Luke Leman, run over by a train in mysterious circumstances in the early hours of the morning. In attendance are his school friends, teachers, and, of course, his grieving and shocked family: parents Dan and Margaret, sister Molly and baby sister Naomi. The story is told in flashback, and over the course of the next twenty-four chapters we learn the circumstances that have led to the tragedy: the relentless pressure of Year 12 on a bright young mind gradually losing focus and perspective, the awareness of everyone, including Luke himself, that something is terribly wrong, and their ultimate failure or inability to help him.

As a writer, Clarke has always been interested in the tensions and problems brought about by the differing value systems of adults and young people. A typical technique is to switch viewpoints, which may not sound very original but is in fact rare in teenage novels, which usually privilege the young protagonist and eliminate as far as possible any adult voice and perspective. Never in a Clarke novel will any woman, for example, be reduced to the anonymous 'mum' who provides the meals and the clean clothes and has the occasional grizzle about untidy bedrooms. A Clarke mother will have a name and a personality and she'll be lying awake in bed at two in the morning listing in her mind all the possible reasons that her offspring is not yet home:

> Why were they so full of secrets? Why didn't they tell her things, like they'd done when they were smaller? Where did Luke go in the evenings, for instance, when he came home so late? Is he studying at someone else's place? Was he working? What if he didn't pass this time? What was he going to do?

So *Night Train* is not just Luke's story: it is Margaret's and Dan's and Molly's and Naomi's and his teachers' and his girlfriend's. If their stories make frustrating reading at times—so many missed opportunities to help—one of Clarke's strengths is her ability to get inside all these different characters, including the unsympathetic ones, and make you care and feel and understand. Whatever the voice—the alienated father resentful of a son throwing away all the chances he himself never had; little Naomi creeping out each evening to shut all the gates in the street as a good-luck charm to keep her missing brother safe; or Luke himself, branded as lazy by the school counsellor but unable to explain how his brain seizes up and shuts like a padlock when he tries to write—they all ring true and grab your heart.

Jane Connolly

SOURCE: A review of *Night Train,* in *Magpies,* Vol. 13, No. 2, May, 1998, pp. 36-7.

It is obvious that Luke Leman is hurtling towards destruction. His father, in recognising his son's hopelessness, has withdrawn all affection and acknowledgment as punishment. His sister sees he's a loser and does all she can to avoid him. His mother is lost in a haze of worry and indecision. It is only the youngest child, Naomi, who longs for Luke and recognises the frailty which will ultimately destroy him. Thankfully Judith Clarke starts her book at the end of Luke's life thereby expelling any doubt a reader may have about the outcome of this very sad story. If it had been otherwise and Luke's outcome was unknown until story's end then this would not only be a sad story but a truly shocking one also. The quality of the writing is such that it is impossible to remain a dispassionate observer of the end of a young boy's life and it would be cruel to encourage hope for a positive conclusion. By providing the end before the beginning, Clarke changes this story from simply one of despair and ultimate death to an examination of the care we provide or deny young people in obvious need. The story becomes a powerful question about responsibility.

For reasons which are not immediately apparent, Luke, intelligent and once academically capable, finds learning extraordinarily difficult and fails again and again. The story centres around his last few weeks at school, his third following his expulsion and failure at two others.

In a mire of despondency he is unable to focus on tasks important to success in his HSC. He seeks the Luke that was, revisiting a place of happiness from his childhood. This simple act is seen as one of trespass by the insensitive rule-bound deputy of his school who abuses his power and threatens expulsion. Luke knows the effect this would have on his family and sinks further into a state of despondent agitation. The school counsellor is a horrible character and offers no practical help. Indeed all the adults in Luke's life fail him, perhaps none more than his father. His disappointment in his son spills over into a cruel abandonment of the boy. The mother, downtrodden and floundering fears for her son but knows of no way of helping him.

Luke hears the Night train of the title in the early hours of every morning and it becomes for him a symbol of stability. When he discovers however that no one else hears it and doubts its existence he fears madness and sets out on a discovery of self. His youngest sister Naomi is an interesting and empathetic character whose mind, uncluttered with expectations, is able to see the world clearly. She becomes Luke's secret and silent guardian.

This is not a comforting read but is a thought provoking one. It differs from others of its ilk by not only focussing on the feelings of despair but clearly sign-posting reasons for the sense of alienation which results and posing some big 'what if' questions.

THE LOST DAY (1999)

Kikus Reviews

SOURCE: A review of *The Lost Day,* in *Kirkus Reviews,* Vol. LXVII, No. 19, October 1, 1999, p. 1577.

Clark strews this dark comedy with caricatured adults and older Melbourne teenagers clinging to adolescence.

After another Saturday night making the club scene, Jasper (who is 19 and a brick salesman by day) stumbles home, losing his mate Vinny somewhere along the way. He assumes Vinny will show up, but he's wrong; Vinny is not at any of his friends' homes, doesn't pick up his car from Jasper, and doesn't show up for his job at the car wash on Sunday. An anxious hunt begins. Using at least ten points of view, plus a variety of ominous dreams, nameless feelings of dread, and the like, Clarke creates a patchy, faintly suspenseful tale in which the cast's love lives, private yearnings, and apprehension at the looming prospect of adulthood share the front seat with the central mystery. Yet neither the satire nor the cautionary message are delivered with any particular zing. Readers may have dismissed the entire episode by the time Vinny reappears late Sunday night, groggy but unharmed, having blithely accepted at ride and a spiked drink from a seemingly inoffensive stranger, and woken up on a train with no memory of the past 12 hours.

Additional coverage of Clarke's life and career is contained in the following sources published by The Gale Group: *Contemporary Authors*, Vol. 142 and *Something about the Author*, Vol. 75.

Daniel Defoe

1660?-1731

Robinson Crusoe

(Also DeFoe and De Foe; born Daniel Foe) English author of fiction, nonfiction, and poetry; essayist, journalist, historian, and satirist.

Major works include *The Life and Strange Surprizing Adventures of Robinson Crusoe, of York, Mariner* (1719); *The Farther Adventures of Robinson Crusoe: Being the Second and Last Part of His Life* (1719); *Serious Reflections during the Life and Surprising Adventures of Robinson Crusoe, with His Vision of the Angelick World* (1720); *The Fortunes and Misfortunes of the Famous Moll Flanders* (1722); *A Journal of the Plague Year: Being Observations or Memorials of the Most Remarkable Occurrences, as Well Publick as Private, Which Happened in London during the Last Great Visitation in 1665, Written by a Citizen Who Continued All the While in London* (1722).

Major works about the author include *Defoe* (by James Sutherland, 1938, revised as *Defoe: A Critical Study,* 1950), *The Incredible Defoe* (by William Freeman, 1950), *Daniel Defoe: Citizen of the Modern World* (by John Robert Moore, 1958), *Daniel Defoe's Many Voices: A Rhetorical Study of Prose Style and Literary Method* (by E. Anthony James, 1972), *Daniel Defoe: Ambition and Innovation* (by Paula R. Backscheider, 1986), *The Life and Strange Surprising Adventures of Daniel Defoe* (by Richard West, 1997).

The following entry presents criticism on *Robinson Crusoe.*

INTRODUCTION

In his own time, Defoe was known primarily as a journalist, pamphleteer, and social commentator from the merchant class. From 1688 to 1731, he wrote hundreds of essays on diverse topics, including religion, politics, history, trade, crime, and marriage. His pioneering work in the field of periodical publication has earned him the title "father of modern journalism." Though he amassed a considerable body of work in the early part of his career, Defoe did not assume his most famous role until he was almost sixty years old. On April 25, 1719, he wrote himself into the history of the English novel when his *The Life and Strange Surprizing Adventures of Robinson Crusoe, of York, Mariner* was published in London by William Taylor. Here for the first time, Defoe fully revealed his skills as a fiction writer, skills he had previously honed on satires and mock biographies. The book, known today simply as *Robinson Crusoe,* is considered by some critics the first true English novel and by others the immediate precursor to the novels of Samuel Richardson and Henry Fielding. Although deliberately written for adults, *Robinson Crusoe* eventually gained

wide readership among children, especially boys, and spawned an entire sub-genre of children's literature: the adventure/survival tale. Margery Fisher commented on this phenomenon, declaring that "it is amusing to think that this level-headed, practical, sardonic tale of 250 years ago has sired a host of romantic, highly fanciful junior adventures." *Robinson Crusoe*'s themes of adventure and survival in nature have fascinated boys of every generation following its publication. Its appeal for children, as James Sutherland commented in *Defoe,* comes from "the human delight in making things," the satisfaction of "making things do," and "the delight of unexpectedly discovering things." Jean-Jacques Rousseau, the eminent French philosopher and writer, wrote in *Émile* that *Robinson Crusoe* should be the first and most important book in the natural education of each child.

Biographical Information

Defoe was born in London, the son of Nonconformist, middle-class parents. The Nonconformists, or Dissenters, were protestant sects that opposed the official state religion of Anglicanism and consequently suffered persecution. But despite the oppression of Nonconformists during his youth, Defoe enjoyed a relatively secure and religious upbringing. He attended the famous academy at Stoke Newington kept by Charles Morton, where most of the students were Dissenters. He was intended for the ministry, but gave up the ambition after three years and turned to business, establishing himself as a hosiery merchant and traveling throughout England and the rest of Europe. True to his social situation and ambition, he married Mary Tuffley, the daughter of another successful Nonconformist merchant. Defoe's experience as a merchant enabled him to acquire an expert knowledge of trade and economics, and he subsequently entered into a number of financial ventures. One such speculation backfired, and in 1692, Defoe filed for bankruptcy. For the rest of his life, he was haunted by debt collectors and manipulated by shrewd, powerful politicians able to turn him over to his creditors if and when he failed to carry out their programs. It was while spending time in the debtor's refuge of Whitefriars that Defoe first came into contact with the thieves and prostitutes who would be the subjects of much of his later fiction. After his release from prison, Defoe took a position at a brick factory near Tilbury, England, and worked his way up to chief owner. During this time, he published his first essays, using his experience as a businessman and traveler in suggesting a number of radical reforms for the British nation. The suggestions—many of which were eventually enacted over the next two centuries—established Defoe as an acute social observer and progressive thinker.

The first decade of the 1700s marked a period of increased political involvement for Defoe. He published several works in response to the hardships of the Dissenters and the attacks on King William, whom Defoe staunchly supported. His anonymously written satire, *The Shortest Way with Dissenters,* or *Proposals for the Establishment of the Church* (1702), enraged the political and religious leaders it targeted and led to Defoe's arrest and charge with seditious libel. He was found guilty and sentenced to a term in prison and three consecutive days in the pillory, a punishment which occasionally ended in death, for the pilloried were usually stoned or assaulted by a crowd of onlookers. Critics generally believe that the pillory had a lasting effect on Defoe, making him a bitter man and an outcast in his own society. After his release, Defoe became an instrument of the government, serving as a secret agent and political propagandist for the Tories. It was during this time that he wrote and edited *The Review,* a Tory journal considered the forerunner of the *Tatler* and *Spectator* and the most advanced newspaper of its time. Defoe developed his essentially Whiggish beliefs in private and eventually put them to use as a secret Whig agent.

Throughout these years of political activity, Defoe continued his imaginative writing. He began to experiment with realistic dialogue, setting, and characterization in *The Family Instructor* (1715-18), one of his many books on religious and moral conduct; but it was not until the publication of *Robinson Crusoe* that Defoe discovered the proper ingredients for success. This masterpiece, originally published in three volumes, was called by critic Edmund Grosse "one of the most beautiful of the world's romances," and gained Defoe literary immortality as a novelist.

Plot and Major Characteristics

With his previous works, Defoe had been developing the tools of his trade: point of view, dialogue, characterization, and a sense of scene. With *Robinson Crusoe* he put these together for the first time in a continuous creative product. Employing the form of a travel biography, the work tells the story of a man marooned on a Caribbean island. Seemingly fanciful, the story was in fact the result of several worldly inspirations. Defoe lived during an age of sea voyages to the distant lands of Asia and the Americas, and many true stories of marooned voyagers circulated during his lifetime. The most famous of these was the account of Alexander Selkirk, a Scottish sailor who was left on an island off the coast of Chile to fend for himself from 1704 to 1709. Accounts of Selkirk's solitary life were still popular in London at the time Defoe wrote his tale. Also important in the development of the novel was the proposal, in early 1719, by England's South Sea Company to establish a colony near the mouth of the Orinoco River in Guiana—very close to the fictional location of Crusoe's island. Added to this topical inspiration was Defoe's perennial interest in utopian colonies, as well as his search for a literary mouthpiece to give voice to his Christian doctrines.

Robinson Crusoe, the son of a successful English merchant, rejects the family business in favor of a more adventurous career at sea. After a number of mishaps, including a violent storm, capture by pirates, sale into slavery, and escape, Crusoe is taken aboard a Portugese cargo ship and ends up in Brazil where he establishes a plantation. Because of the success of his venture, he decides to travel to Africa to secure some slaves. While sailing off the coast of South America, Crusoe's ship encounters a hurricane and experiences damage. Before the expedition can reach the refuge of an English outpost in the Caribbean, it is hit by a second storm which drives it toward the coast of what is now Venezuela. All hands are lost in the wreck, except for Crusoe, who manages to battle the furious waves until he is washed safely ashore on an island off the mouth of the Orinoco River. When the storm abates the following day, Crusoe is able to salvage provisions from the grounded ship using a raft he fashions himself. The remainder of the first volume recounts Crusoe's struggles to survive and cope with his isolation during his twenty-eight years on the island. Building a raft, he manages many trips back to the wrecked ship to salvage food, water, weapons, tools, lumber, sail cloth, clothing, and various other articles he will need to survive. His first home is a tent on the side of a hill that he encircles with stakes to create a crude fort or stockade. His long-absent contact with humans resumes when cannibals from a nearby island come ashore on Crusoe's beach to feast on an unhappy victim. Chasing them off, Crusoe saves the life of their intended meal, and dubs the man Friday, after the day he is saved. Friday becomes Crusoe's faithful friend and servant, and the two come to the aid of the captain of a mutinous English ship that anchors in the bay off Crusoe's island. Crusoe and Friday leave five members of the mutinous crew behind on the island, and set sail for England.

In a sequel to this story that Defoe quickly assembled after finding his novel to be immensely popular, Crusoe has more adventures. Finding that most of his family in England has died during his long absence, Crusoe and Friday travel to Crusoe's holdings in Lisbon, where Crusoe discovers he has become wealthy from his Brazilian estates. Returning to England, he marries and has three children. But with the death of his wife, he and Friday set out for more adventures on a trading ship bound for China. En route, his ship puts in at his former island, where the mutineers who stayed behind have taken native wives and established a community. At sea again, Crusoe's ship is attacked by pirates and Friday is killed. Crusoe is set ashore in China by the pirate crew, which has grown tired of his preaching at them. There he joins an overland caravan to Siberia, and eventually, an old man near death, Crusoe returns home to England.

Critical Reception

Like all great creative works, *Robinson Crusoe* lends itself to myriad interpretations: an allegorical representation of the British Empire, an attack on economic individualism and capitalism, a further installment in the author's spiritual biography, and a lightly veiled allegory of Defoe's own life. Crusoe has also been seen as a representative of mankind at struggle with nature, or religion, or himself. Many critics also consider Defoe the first "realist" in literature, and it was his sensitivity to detail that gave his art a quality of believability unknown before his time. This realism, along with Defoe's use of common language and his simple, direct style, made *Robinson Crusoe* accessible to the middle and lower classes, who could identify with Crusoe's adventures. Defoe is also credited with popularizing the novel form in England and has been called the "father of the English novel." John Robert Moore noted in an essay in *Twentieth-Century Interpretations of Robinson Crusoe* that before Defoe's book "there was no English novel worth the name, and no book (except the Bible) widely accepted among all classes of English and Scottish readers."

Although Defoe has always enjoyed a wide popularity among the reading public, from critics and scholars he has received ambivalent reactions. During his lifetime, Defoe was looked upon as an imaginative writer at best, although he was usually considered a swindler and moral invalid. Even in the years following his death in 1731, Defoe's works fell victim to the rigorous critical standards of the eighteenth century. Criticism of Defoe's work during this time focused strictly on its authenticity and moral implications—two standards poorly suited for

an appreciation of Defoe. Scholars such as Theophilus Cibber and George Chalmers praised Defoe for his vivid imagination and literary talents, but could not escape the eighteenth-century perception that literature needed to serve a moral purpose in order to be worth reading. *Robinson Crusoe* was even considered un-Christian by some critics. Charles Gildon, in his *The Life and Strange Surprising Adventures of Mr. D— De F— [Daniel Defoe]* (1719), criticized what he believed to be Defoe's "impious" depiction of Crusoe, arguing that "it would be very hard to perswade [sic] us to believe, that a Man, who seems in all Things else innocent enough, should be so very abandon'd in Impiety, as never to pray and acknowledge the overruling Providence of God in all the Transactions of this World." Gildon also attacked *Crusoe* for its improbabilities and misconceptions concerning life at sea. He felt that Defoe "employ[ed] all the Force of his little Rhetoric to dissuade and deter all People from going to Sea," and could not "see any reason why . . . *Crusoe* should think it any more a Crime in him to go to Sea, than in a hundred and fifty thousand more, who constantly use the Sea in these Nations, besides ten times that Number in all the Nations of the World who do the same."

It was nearly a hundred years after Defoe's death before Walter Scott presented the first favorable account of Defoe's merits as a novelist. Scott's essay signaled a major shift in Defoe criticism. No longer was it necessary to authenticate Defoe's novels or to hold up a moral stricture to justify their worth. What made Defoe a successful author, according to Scott, was his ability to present an "appearance of reality" in his works, particularly *Robinson Crusoe*. Other critics began to praise Defoe for his simple style, his common language, his lack of affectation, even his unstructured method of writing, for all these contributed to the sense of reality conveyed by his narratives. Throughout the first half of the nineteenth century Defoe enjoyed an inordinate amount of critical attention, especially when compared to the previous century. His stature rose from an obscure literary mountebank to one of England's greatest authors, superior even to Jonathan Swift, according to Samuel Taylor Coleridge. But by the 1850s Defoe's reputation once again began to wain. Late nineteenth-century critics such as W. C. Roscoe and Leslie Stephen argued that Defoe was a skillful writer, but hardly an imaginative or creative genius. Many concluded that *Robinson Crusoe* was the only novel in which he demonstrated any degree of artistry whatsoever.

For the most part, twentieth-century critics of Defoe's works have tended to be more concerned with structure and meaning than with the author's character. Most often discussed is Defoe's use of irony, his dependence on conventional morality, his economic theories, and his debt to the traditional autobiography. Twentieth-century critics generally consider Defoe an artist struggling with a new medium and dealing with an audience unable to comprehend many of his ideas. He is still criticized for his carelessness, his one-dimensional characters, his moralizing, and his obsession with unnecessary details, but he is also praised for an insight into the nature of his craft that both eighteenth- and nineteenth-century critics failed to recognize. *Robinson Crusoe* is still regarded as one of Defoe's greatest works. Virginia Woolf, in her *Collected Essays,* called it "a masterpiece," and went on to note that "it is a masterpiece largely because Defoe has throughout kept consistently to his own sense of perspective."

While the adult reactions to *Robinson Crusoe* have gone through a variety of phases, including ignoring it altogether, children have continued to hold the story in high esteem since soon after it was published. The authors of *A Critical History of Children's Literature* believed that the episodic narrative "is a form directly natural for children's liking, with no confusing complication of structure, with effortless unity of place and character, and, above all, with vividness of dealing with natural things and natural adventure." Moreover, Crusoe is very much a character with which children can identify, these reviewers suggested. "What he did, though he accomplished wonders," they wrote, "was done as slowly, as laboriously and clumsily as any ordinary boy would do it, with the constant danger of utter failure." The book also popularized the children's adventure/survival tale. These types of stories, as J. S. Bratton noted in *The Impact of Victorian Children's Fiction* (1981), were particularly suited to boys: "There was a handful of adult novels which by the 1860s had come to be regarded as good books for boys, and from them the juvenile writers drew their patterns and methods, establishing a convention strong enough to support many thousands of stories written in the next fifty or sixty years." *Robinson Crusoe* was the first of these stories, which include Robert Louis Stevenson's *Swiss Family Robinson,* whose timeless appeal has weathered the years, even centuries, since their publication. Maximillian E. Novak pointed out in *Dictionary of Literary Biography* that "in *Robinson Crusoe* [Defoe] created a work which was to be read throughout the world. It . . . started a rage for the island tale—the 'Robinsonade'—which has yet to show signs of fading away."

COMMENTARY

Daniel Defoe

SOURCE: A preface to *The Life and Strange Surprizing Adventures of Robinson Crusoe of York, Mariner,* in *Robinson Crusoe: An Authoritative Text, Backgrounds and Sources, Criticism,* edited by Michael Shinagel, W. W. Norton & Company, 1975, p. 3.

[*The following is the preface to Volume I of* **Robinson Crusoe,** *1719.*]

If ever the Story of any private Man's Adventures in the World were worth making Publick, and were acceptable when Publish'd, the Editor of this Account thinks this will be so.

The Wonders of this Man's Life exceed all that (he thinks) is to be found extant; the Life of one Man being scarce capable of a greater Variety.

The Story is told with Modesty, with Seriousness, and with a religious Application of Events to the Uses to which wise Men always apply them (*viz.*) to the Instruction of others by this Example, and to justify and honour the Wisdom of Providence in all the Variety of our Circumstances, let them happen how they will.

The Editor believes the thing to be a just History of Fact; neither is there any Appearance of Fiction in it: And however thinks, because all such things are dispatch'd, that the Improvement of it, as well to the Diversion, as to the Instruction of the Reader, will be the same; and as such, he thinks, without farther Compliment to the World, he does them a great Service in the Publication.

Daniel Defoe

SOURCE: A preface to *The Farther Adventures of Robinson Crusoe,* in *Robinson Crusoe: An Authoritative Text Backgrounds and Sources Criticism,* edited by Michael Shinagel, W. W. Norton & Company, 1975, pp. 258-59.

[*The following is the preface to Volume II of* **Robinson Crusoe,** *1719.*]

The Success the former Part of this Work has met with in the World, has yet been no other than is acknowledg'd to be due to the surprising Variety of the Subject, and to the agreeable Manner of the Performance.

All the Endeavours of envious People to reproach it with being a Romance, to search it for Errors in Geography, Inconsistency in the Relation, and Contradictions in the Fact, have proved abortive, and as impotent as malicious.

The just Application of every Incident, the religious and useful Inferences drawn from every Part, are so many Testimonies to the good Design of making it publick, and must legitimate all the Part that may be call'd Invention, or Parable in the Story.

The Second Part, if the Editor's Opinion may pass, is (contrary to the Usage of Second Parts,) every Way as entertaining as the First, contains as strange and surprising Incidents, and as great a Variety of them; nor is the Application less serious, or suitable; and doubtless will, to the sober, as well as ingenious Reader, be every way as profitable and diverting; and this makes the abridging this Work, as scandalous, as it is knavish and ridiculous; seeing, while to shorten the Book, that they may seem to reduce the Value, they strip it of all those Reflections, as well religious as moral, which are not only the greatest Beautys of the Work, but are calculated for the infinite Advantage of the Reader.

By this they leave the Work naked of its brightest Ornaments; and if they would, at the same Time pretend, that the Author has supply'd the Story out of his Invention, they take from it the Improvement, which alone recommends that Invention to wise and good Men.

The Injury these Men do the Proprietor of this Work, is a Practice all honest Men abhor; and he believes he may challenge them to shew the Difference between that and Robbing on the Highway, or Breaking open a House.

If they can't shew any Difference in the Crime, they will find it hard to shew why there should be any Difference in the Punishment: And he will answer for it, that nothing shall be wanting on his Part, to do them Justice.

Charles Gildon

SOURCE: In his *The Life and Strange Surprizing Adventures of Mr. D— De F—[Daniel Defoe]*, J. Roberts, 1719, 48 p.

[*Charles Gildon, a minor playwright and pamphleteer, disliked Defoe, and the success of* **Robinson Crusoe** *made him jealous. He attacked both the book and its author in a scathing essay published as a pamphlet. This excerpt, taken from Gildon's* The Life and Strange Surprizing Adventures of Mr. D— DeF— *(1719) is intended as a parody of the preface to* **Robinson Crusoe**.]

I have perus'd your pleasant Story of **Robinson Crusoe**; and if the Faults of it had extended no farther than the frequent Solecisms, Looseness and Incorrectness of Stile, Improbabilities, I had not given you the Trouble of this Epistle. But when I found that you were not content with the many Absurdities of your Tale, but seem'd to discover a Design, which proves you as bad an *Englishman* as a Christian, I could not but take Notice in this publick Manner of what you had written; especially, when I perceiv'd that you threaten'd us with more of the same Nature, if this met with that Success which you hop'd for, and which the Town has been pleas'd to give it. If by this I can prevent a new Accession of Impieties and Superstition to those which the Work under our Consideration has furnish'd us with, I shall not think my Labour lost.

I am far from being an Enemy to the Writers of Fables, since I know very well that this Manner of Writing is not only very Ancient, but very useful, I might say sacred, since it has been made use of by the inspir'd Writers themselves; but then to render any Fable worthy of being receiv'd into the Number of those which are truly valuable, it must naturally produce in its Event some useful Moral, either express'd or understood; but this of **Robinson Crusoe,** you plainly inculcate, is design'd against a publick Good. I think there can be no Man so ignorant as not to know that our Navigation produces both our Safety and our Riches, and that whoever therefore shall endeavour to discourage this, is so far a profest Enemy of his Country's Prosperity and Safety; but the Author of **Robinson Crusoe,** not only in the Beginning, but in many Places of the Book, employs all the Force of his little Rhetoric to dissuade and deter all People from going to Sea, especially all Mothers of Children who may be capable of that Service, from venturing them to so much Hazard and so much Wickedness, as he represents the Seafaring Life liable to. . . . I dare believe that there are few Men who consider justly, that would think the Profession of a *Yorkshire* Attorney more innocent and beneficial to Mankind than that of a Seaman, or would judge that *Robinson Crusoe* was so very criminal in rejecting the former, and chusing the latter, as to provoke the Divine Providence to raise two Storms, and in the last of them to destroy so many Ships and Men, purely to deter him from that Course of Life, to which at last he was to owe so ample a Reward of all his Labours and Fatigues, as the End of this very Book plainly tells us he met with.

If this be not a bold Impiety, I know not what is, and an Impiety for which I can see very little ground; for why should he imagine that the Storm was sent to hinder him from going to Sea, more than any other that were in it, and suffer'd any more by it? Nor, indeed, can I see any reason why your *Crusoe* should think it any more a Crime in him to go to Sea, than in a hundred and fifty thousand more, who constantly use the Sea in these Nations, besides ten times that Number in all the Nations of the World who do the same. If Storms are sent by Providence to deter Men from Navigation, I may reasonably suppose, that there is not one of all that vast Number I have mention'd, to whom Providence has not sent the same Warning. At this absurd Way of Arguing, most of the Communication and Traffick of Nations would soon be at an end, and Islanders especially would be entirely cut off from the rest of the World; and if your Doctrine prevail'd, none would venture upon Salt Water, but such as cared not for the Safety either of Body or Soul, both which you all along endeavour to perswade us are more in danger there than any where else. . . . It is plain, that the Seafaring Men are generally (for here we speak only of Generals, and not of Particulars) generally, I say, are more free, open, disinterested, and less tricking and designing than those who never go to Sea; and tho' you are pleas'd often to mention the Wickedness of *Crusoe,* whom, being a Creature of your own, you might have made as wicked as you pleas'd: This very *Crusoe,* I say, does not appear to be guilty of any heinous Crimes; and it would be very hard to perswade us to believe, that a Man, who seems in all Things else innocent enough, should be so very abandon'd in Impiety, as never to pray and acknowledge the overruling Providence of God in all the Transactions of this World; and by consequence in all that did or could happen to him. But after all, if you will needs have him this impious person; for he is a Creature of your making, and not of God's; you have given him *Manners,* as the Critics call it, quite out of Nature, and no ways necessary to your *Fable.*

[You] seem very fond of all Occasions of throwing in needless Absurdities to make the Truth of your Story still the more doubted. What occasion else had you to make *Xury* speak broken *English,* when he never convers'd with any *English* but *Robinson Crusoe*? so that it had been more natural to have made *Robinson* speak broken *Arabick,* which Language he must be forc'd in some Measure to learn; whereas *Xury* had no Motive in the World to study so much *English* as he makes him speak; but this is a Peccadillo and not worth dwelling upon.

I shall not take notice of [*Robinson*] stripping himself to swim on Board [the ship], and then filling his Pockets with Bisket, because that is already taken Notice of in Publick; and in the last Edition, at least, of the Book, you have endeavour'd to salve this Difficulty, by making him keep his Breeches on; tho' why he should do so I can see no reason; and tho' he did do so, I don't find how the Pocket of a Seaman's *Breeches* could receive any Biskets, that being generally no bigger than to contain a Tobacco Pouch, or the like.

I would [also] ask Mr. *Crusoe,* how he could see the saucer Eyes of the Goat in the Cave, when he tells us it was so dark that he could see nothing there; this is not helpt by saying, that a Ray of the Light struck thro' the Mouth of the Cave, for then there was Light, which he says there was not; and if there was, then he might have seen the Goat's Body as well as his Eyes.

Well, *Crusoe* at last, and his Man *Friday,* get away from his Island into *England;* and from thence he makes a Voyage to *Portugal,* where having settled all his Affairs and found himself a Rich Man, in obedience to his secret Hints, he resolves not to go by Sea back, but thro' *Spain* and *France* by Land, and so only cross the Seas from *Calais* to *Dover.* All that happens in this Land Journey worth taking Notice of, is the monstrous Story of his Man *Friday* and the *Bear*; they are passing the *Pyrenean* Mountains thro' a very great Snow, the Roads were so infested with Wolves, that two of them fell upon their Guide, and wounded him and his Horse, before *Friday* could come up and shoot them; but notwithstanding this Wound of the Guide, and the howling of the Wolves all about, and that it was within two Hours of Night, and they had near three Leagues to ride in the Snow, he makes a matter of thirty Passengers, and the wounded Guide stand still in the Cold, to see *Friday make laugh,* as he calls it, with a *Bear,* that by chance came that Way. *Friday* pulls off his Boots and claps on his Pumps, runs to the Bear and takes up a great stone, which he throws at him; but how *Friday* could pick up a great Stone in a Place all cover'd deep with Snow, I know not; nor can I tell, how *Friday* came to know the Nature of the Bear, since that is a Creature, which is never found in such a warm Climate, as *Friday's* Country must needs be, since it was so near the *Equinox*: I believe it is equally true, that the whole Company laugh'd at *Friday's* managing the Bear; but, indeed, this Book seems calculated for the Mob, and will not bear the Eye of a rational Reader. Well, *Robinson* at last gets again to *London,* marries, has three

Children; he is near sixty five Years of Age, which one would think was old enough to leave off Rambling, having especially a plentiful Fortune; ye he tells us, that he takes a Trip, as it were for Pleasure, to his old Island in *America,* and thence to *Brasil,* and so rambles about till seventy five Years of Age, and how much longer I know not, an Account of which he promises in his next Volume. I hope, dear *D—e,* that you have taken more care of Probability and Religion than you have in this; tho' I am afraid you are too harden'd a Sinner in these Particulars, to give us any Proof in your Works of your sincere Repentance, which yet is heartily wish'd you. . . .

Daniel Defoe

SOURCE: A preface to *Serious Reflections during the Life and Surprising Adventures of Robinson Crusoe,* in *Robinson Crusoe: An Authoritative Text, Backgrounds and Sources, Criticism,* edited by Michael Shinagel, W. W. Norton & Company, 1975, pp. 259-61.

[*The following is the preface to Volume III of* **Robinson Crusoe**, 1720.]

As the Design of every Thing is said to be first in the Intention, and last in the Execution; so I come now to acknowledge to my Reader, That the present Work is not merely the Product of the two first Volumes, but the two first Volumes may rather be called the Product of this: The Fable is always made for the Moral, not the Moral for the Fable.

I have heard, that the envious and ill-disposed Part of the World have rais'd some Objections against the two first Volumes, on Pretence, *for want of a better Reason;* That (*as they say*) the Story is feign'd, that the Names are borrow'd, and that it is all a Romance; that there never were any such Man or Place, or Circumstances in any Mans Life; that it is all form'd and embellish'd by Invention to impose upon the World.

I *Robinson Crusoe* being at this Time in perfect and sound Mind and Memory, Thanks be to God therefore; do hereby declare, their Objection is an Invention scandalous in Design, and false in Fact; and do affirm, that the Story, though Allegorical, is also Historical; and that it is the beautiful Representation of a Life of unexampled Misfortunes, and of a Variety not to be met with in the World, sincerely adapted to, and intended for the common Good of Mankind, and designed at first, *as it is now farther apply'd,* to the most serious Uses possible.

Farther, that there is a Man alive, and well known too, the Actions of whose Life are the just Subject of these Volumes, and to whom all or most Part of the Story most directly alludes, this may be depended upon for Truth, and to this I set my Name. . . .

Without letting the Reader into a nearer Explication of the Matter, I proceed to let him know, that the happy

Deductions I have employ'd myself to make from all the Circumstances of my Story, will abundantly make him amends for his not having the Emblem explained by the Original; and that when in my Observations and Reflexions of any Kind in this Volume, I mention my Solitudes and Retirements, and allude to the Circumstances of the former Story, all those Parts of the Story are real Facts in my History, whatever borrow'd Lights they may be represented by: Thus the Fright and Fancies which succeeded the Story of the Print of a Man's Foot, and Surprise of the old Goat, and the Thing rolling on my Bed, and my jumping out in a Fright, are all Histories and real Stories; as are likewise the Dream of being taken by Messengers, being arrested by Officers, the Manner of being driven on Shore by the Surge of the Sea, the Ship on Fire, the Description of starving; the Story of my Man *Friday,* and many more most material Passages observ'd here, and on which any religious Reflections are made, are all historical and true in Fact: It is most real, that I had a Parrot, and taught it to call me by my Name, such a Servant a Savage, and afterwards a Christian, and that his Name was called *Friday,* and that he was ravish'd from me by Force, and died in the Hands that took him, which I represent by being killed; this is all litterally true, and should I enter into Discoveries, many alive can testify them: His other Conduct and Assistance to me also have just References in all their Parts to the Helps I had from that faithful Savage, in my real Solitudes and Disasters.

The Story of the Bear in the Tree, and the Fight with the Wolves in the Snow, is likewise Matter of real History; and in a Word, the Adventures of *Robinson Crusoe,* are one whole Scheme of a real Life of eight and twenty Years, spent in the most wandering desolate and afflicting Circumstances that ever Man went through, and in which I have liv'd so long in a Life of Wonders in continu'd Storms, fought with the worse kind of Savages and Maneaters, by unaccountable supprising [sic] Incidents; fed by Miracles greater than that of Ravens, suffered all Manner of Violences and Oppressions, injurious Reproaches, contempt of Men, Attacks of Devils, Corrections from Heaven, and Opposi[ti]ons on Earth; have had innumerable Ups and Downs in Matters of Fortune, been in Slavery worse than *Turkish,* escaped by an exquisite Management, as that in the Story of *Xury,* and the Boat at *Sallee,* been taken up at Sea in Distress, rais'd again and depress'd again, and that oftner perhaps in one Man's Life than ever was known before; Ship wreck'd often, tho' more by Land than by Sea: In a Word, there's not a Circumstance in the imaginary Story, but has its just Allusion to a real Story, and chimes Part for Part, and Step for Step with the inimitable Life of *Robinson Crusoe.*

Daniel Defoe

SOURCE: "Serious Observations," in *Robinson Crusoe: An Authoritative Text, Backgrounds and Sources, Criticism,* edited by Michael Shinagel, W. W. Norton & Company, 1975, pp. 263-65.

[*The following excerpt is from chapter 1, "Of Solitude," in* **Serious Reflections during the Life and Surprising Adventures of Robinson Crusoe, with His Vision of the Angelick World,** *1720*].

I have frequently look'd back, you may be sure, and that with different Thoughts, upon the Notions of a long tedious Life of Solitude, which I have represented to the World, and of which you must have formed some Ideas from the Life of a Man in an Island. Sometimes I have wonder'd how it could be supported, especially for the first Years, when the Change was violent and impos'd, and Nature unacquainted with any thing like it. Sometimes I have as much wonder'd, why it should be any Grievance or Affliction; seeing upon the whole View of the Stage of Life which we act upon in this World, it seems to me, that Life in general is, or ought to be, but one universal Act of Solitude: But I find it is natural to judge of Happiness, by its suiting or not suiting our own Inclinations. Every Thing revolves in our Minds by innumerable circular Motions, all centring in our selves. We judge of Prosperity, and of Affliction, Joy and Sorrow, Poverty, Riches, and all the various Scenes of Life: I say, we judge of them by our selves: Thither we bring them Home, as Meats touch the Palat, by which we try them; the gay Part of the World, or the heavy Part; it is all one, they only call it pleasant or unpleasant, as they suit our Taste.

The World, I say, is nothing to us, but as it is more or less to our Relish: All Reflection is carry'd Home, and our Dear-self is, in one Respect, the End of Living. Hence Man may be properly said to be *alone* in the Midst of the Crowds and Hurry of Men and Business: All the Reflections which he makes, are to himself; all that is pleasant, he embraces for himself; all that is irksome and grievous, is tasted but by his own Palat.

What are the Sorrows of other Men to us? And what their Joy? Something we may be touch'd indeed with, by the Power of Sympathy, and a secret Turn of the Affections; but all the solid Reflection is directed to our selves. Our Meditations are all Solitude in Perfection; our Passions are all exercised in Retirement; we love, we hate, we covet, we enjoy, all in Privacy and Solitude: All that we communicate of those Things to any other, is but for their Assistance in the Pursuit of our Desires; the End is at Home; the Enjoyment, the Contemplation, is all Solitude and Retirement; 'tis for our selves we enjoy, and for our selves we suffer.

What then is the Silence of Life? And, How is it afflicting, while a Man has the Voice of his Soul to speak to God, and to himself? That Man can never want Conversation, who is Company for himself; and he that cannot converse profitably with himself, is not fit for any Conversation at all; and yet there are many good Reasons why a Life of Solitude, as Solitude is now understood by the Age, is not at all suited to the Life of a Christian, or of a wise Man. Without enquiring therefore into the Advantages of Solitude, and how it is to be managed, I desire to be heard concerning what Solitude really is; for I must confess, I have different Notions about it, far from those which are generally understood in the World, and far from all those Notions upon which those People in the primitive Times, and since that also, acted, who separated themselves into Desarts and unfrequented Places, or confin'd themselves to Cells, Monasteries, and the like, retir'd, as they call it, from the World; All which, I think, have nothing of the Thing I call Solitude in them, nor do they answer any of the true Ends of Solitude, much less those Ends which are pretended to be sought after, by those who have talk'd most of those Retreats from the World.

As for Confinement in an Island, if the Scene was plac'd there for this very End, it were not at all amiss. I must acknowledge, there was Confinement from the Enjoyments of the World, and Restraint from human Society: *But all that was no Solitude;* indeed no Part of it was so, except that which, as in my Story, I apply'd to the Contemplation of sublime Things, and that was but a very little, as my Readers well know, compar'd to what a Length of Years my forced Retreat lasted.

It is evident then, that as I see nothing but what is far from being retir'd, in the forced Retreat of an Island, the Thoughts being in no Composure suitable to a retired Condition, no not for a great While; so I can affirm, that I enjoy much more Solitude in the Middle of the greatest Collection of Mankind in the World, I mean, at *London,* while I am writing this, than ever I could say I enjoy'd in eight and twenty Years Confinement to a desolate Island.

Theophilus Cibber

SOURCE: "De Foe," in *The Lives of the Poets of Great Britain and Ireland, Vol. IV,* by Mr. Cibber and Other Hands, R. Griffiths, 1753, pp. 313-25.

Poetry was far from being the talent of De Foe. He wrote with more perspicuity and strength in prose, and he seems to have understood, as well as any man, the civil constitution of the kingdom, which indeed was his chief study. . . .

The natural abilities of [De Foe] (for he was no scholar) seem to have been very high. He had a great knowledge of men and things, particularly what related to the government, and trade of these kingdoms. He wrote many pamphlets on both, which were generally well received, though his name was never prefixed. His imagination was fertile, strong, and lively, as may be collected from his many works of fancy, particularly his *Robinson Crusoe,* which was written in so natural a manner, and with so many probable incidents, that, for some time after its publication, it was judged by most people to be a true story. It was indeed written upon a model entirely new, and the success and esteem it met with, may be ascertained by the many editions it has sold, and the sums of money which have been gained by it.

Jean-Jacques Rousseau

SOURCE: "Rousseau on 'Robinson Crusoe'," in *Defoe: The Critical Heritage,* edited by Pat Rogers, Routledge & Kegan Paul, 1972, pp. 52-4.

[*In the following excerpt, French philosopher and essayist Jean-Jacques Rousseau discusses the instructive value of Defoe's* **Robinson Crusoe.** *The essay was originally published under a different title in* Émile, ou de l'Education, *176É2.*]

Since books are absolutely necessary, there is one which to my taste supplies the happiest introduction to natural education. This will be the first book my Émile will read. For a long time it will constitute his entire library by itself, and it will always retain a distinguished place there. It will be the text on which all our discussions of the natural sciences will be merely a gloss. It will serve as a check on the state of our judgment as we proceed, and in so far as our taste remains unspoilt, we shall always take pleasure in reading it. What is this wonderful book then? Is it Aristotle, or Pliny, or Buffon? No—it is *Robinson Crusoe.*

Robinson Crusoe on his island, alone, deprived of the help of his fellows and of all artificial aids, yet providing for his own support, for his own safety and even achieving a sort of well-being—this is a matter of interest for any age, which can be made enjoyable to children in a thousand ways. . . . This state, I admit, is not that of man in society, and most probably it will not be Émile's: but it is through this state that he will come to value all others. The surest way of rising above prejudice and ordering one's opinions according to the real relations of things is to put oneself in the place of a solitary man, and to judge everything as he would, having regard to its particular utility.

Stripped of all its nonsense, beginning with Robinson's wreck off his island and ending with the arrival of the ship which is to take him away, this novel will be both instruction and delight to Émile during this period. I would like him to be quite infatuated with it; to busy himself constantly with his stockade, his goats and his crops. I want him to learn in detail everything one would have to know in such a case, not through books but through things. I want him to identify himself with Robinson, to see himself dressed in skins, with a big hat and a broadsword—the whole grotesque paraphernalia of his appearance, except the parasol which he will not need.

The child, when urged to equip himself for the island, will be keener to learn than the master to teach him. He will want to know everything useful, and nothing else; you will no longer have to guide him, only to restrain him. Moreover, we must hurry to set him up on the island, whilst it is enough in itself to satisfy him. For the day is coming when, if he wishes to live there still, it will not be alone; and when Friday, who scarcely concerns him now, will no longer suffice for any time.

James Beattie

SOURCE: "On Fable and Romance," in *Dissertations Moral and Critical*, W. Strahan, 1783, pp. 505-74.

[Beattie was a Scottish poet and philosophical writer whose immensely popular poem, "The Minstrel"—which traced the development of the poet in the early stages of civilization—heralded the beginning of the Romantic revival. In the following excerpt, Beattie discusses the social value of **Robinson Crusoe.**]

Some have thought that a love tale is necessary to make a romance interesting. But *Robinson Crusoe,* though there is nothing of love in it, is one of the most interesting narratives that ever was written; at least in all that part which relates to the desert island: being founded on a passion still more prevalent than love, the desire of self-preservation; and therefore likely to engage the curiosity of every class of readers, both old and young, both learned and unlearned.

Robinson Crusoe must be allowed, by the most rigid moralist, to be one of those novels, which one may read, not only with pleasure, but also with profit. It breathes throughout a spirit of piety and benevolence: it sets in a very striking light, as I have elsewhere observed, the importance of the mechanick arts, which they, who know not what it is to be without them, are so apt to undervalue: it fixes in the mind a lively idea of the horrors of solitude, and, consequently, of the sweets of social life, and of the blessings we derive from conversation, and mutual aid: and it shows, how, by labouring with one's own hands, one may secure independence, and open for one's self many sources of health and amusement. I agree, therefore, with Rousseau, that this is one of the best books that can be put in the hands of children. The style is plain, but not elegant, nor perfectly grammatical: and the second part of the story is tiresome.

Hugh Blair

SOURCE: "Fictitious History," in *Robinson Crusoe: An Authoritative Text, Backgrounds and Sources, Criticism,* edited by Michael Shinagel, W. W. Norton & Company, 1975, p. 285.

[Blair's essay was originally printed in Lectures on Rhetoric and Belles Lettres, *1783.]*

No fiction, in any language, was ever better supported than the *Adventures of Robinson Crusoe.* While it is carried on with that appearance of truth and simplicity, which takes a strong hold of the imagination of all Readers, it suggests, at the same time, very useful instruction; by showing how much the native powers of man may be exerted for surmounting the difficulties of any external situation.

George Chalmers

SOURCE: "The Popularity of 'Robinson Crusoe'," in *Robinson Crusoe: An Authoritative Text, Backgrounds and Sources, Criticism,* edited by Michael Shinagel, W. W. Norton & Company, 1975, p. 286.

[Chalmers was a Scottish historian and biographer whose study of Defoe, The Life of Daniel Defoe, *1790, from which the following excerpt is taken, was the first book-length work devoted to Defoe's life and literature. His comments on Defoe's art anticipate the praise of several nineteenth-century critics, including Walter Scott, Charles Lamb, and Samuel Taylor Coleridge.]*

[T]he time at length came, when De Foe was to deliver to the world the most popular of all his performances. In April 1719, he published the well-known *Life and Surprising Adventures of Robinson Crusoe.* The reception was immediate and universal. . . . It if be inquired by what charm it is that these *Surprising Adventures* should have instantly pleased, and always pleased, it will be found, that few books have ever so naturally mingled amusement with instruction. The attention is fixed, either by the simplicity of the narration, or by the variety of the incidents; the heart is amended by a *vindication of the ways of God to man:* and the understanding is informed by various examples, how much utility ought to be preferred to ornament: the young are instructed, while the old are amused. . . .

John Ballantyne

SOURCE: "On Defoe," in *Robinson Crusoe: An Authoritative Text, Backgrounds and Sources, Criticism,* edited by Michael Shinagel, W. W. Norton & Company, 1975, pp. 286-87.

[Ballantyne, publisher and friend of Walter Scott, published a shorter version of the following excerpt as an introduction to **Robinson Crusoe** *in* The Novels of Daniel De Foe, *edited by Walter Scott, 1810. This more polished excerpt is taken from* The Prose Works of Sir Walter Scott, *1834.]*

Perhaps there exists no work, either of instruction or entertainment, in the English language, which has been more generally read, and more universally admired, than the *Life and Adventures of Robinson Crusoe.* It is difficult to say in what the charm consists, by which persons of all classes and denominations are thus fascinated; yet the majority of readers will recollect it is among the first works which awakened and interested their youthful attention; and feel, even in advanced life, and in the maturity of their understanding, that there are still associated with *Robinson Crusoe,* the sentiments peculiar to that period, when all is new, all glittering in prospect, and when those visions are most bright, which the experience of afterlife tends only to darken and destroy.

This work was first published in April, 1719; its reception, as may be supposed, was universal. It is a singular circumstance, that the Author, * * * after a life spent in political turmoil, danger, and imprisonment, should have occupied himself, in its decline, in the production of a work like the present; unless it may be supposed, that his wearied heart turned with disgust from society and its institutions, and found solace in picturing the happiness of a state, such as he has assigned to his hero. Be this as it may, society is for ever indebted to the memory of De Foe for his production of a work, in which the ways of Providence are simply and pleasingly vindicated, and a lasting and useful moral is conveyed through the channel of an interesting and delightful story.

There scarce exists a work so popular as *Robinson Crusoe.* It is read eagerly by young people; and there is hardly an elf so devoid of imagination as not to have supposed for himself a solitary island in which he could act *Robinson Crusoe,* were it but in the corner of the nursery. To many it has given the decided turn of their lives, by sending them to sea. For the young mind is much less struck with the hardships of the anchorite's situation than with the animating exertions which he makes to overcome them; and *Robinson Crusoe* produces the same impression upon an adventurous spirit which the *Book of Martyrs* would do on a young devotee, or the *Newgate Calendar* upon an acolyte of Bridewell; both of which students are less terrified by the horrible manner in which the tale terminates, than animated by sympathy with the saints or depredators who are the heroes of their volume. Neither does a re-perusal of *Robinson Crusoe,* at a more advanced age, diminish our early impressions. The situation is such as every man may make his own, and, being possible in itself, is, by the exquisite art of the narrator, rendered as probable as it is interesting. It has the merit, too, of that species of accurate painting which can be looked at again and again with new pleasure.

Charles Lamb

SOURCE: "On Defoe's Novels," in *Robinson Crusoe: An Authoritative Text, Backgrounds and Sources, Criticism,* edited by Michael Shinagel, W. W. Norton & Company, 1975, p. 290.

[*The following excerpt is taken from a letter that Lamb wrote to Walter Wilson in 1822.*]

In the appearances of truth, in all the incidents and conversations that occur in them, they exceed any works of fiction that I am acquainted with. It is perfect illusion. The author never appears in these self-narratives (for so they ought to be called, or rather auto-biographies) but the narrator chains us down to an implicit belief in every thing he says. There is all the minute detail of a log-book in it. Dates are painfully pressed upon the memory. Facts are repeated over and over in varying phrases, till you cannot chuse but believe them. It is like reading evidence in a court of Justice. So

anxious the storyteller seems that the truth should be clearly comprehended, that when he has told us a matter of fact, or a motive, in a line or two farther down he repeats it, with his favourite figure of speech, I *say,* so and so, though he had made it abundantly plain before. This is in imitation of the common people's way of speaking, or rather of the way in which they are addressed by a master or mistress, who wishes to impress something upon their memories, and has a wonderful effect upon matter-of-fact readers. Indeed, it is to such principally that he writes. His style is every where beautiful, but plain and homely. *Robinson Crusoe* is delightful to all ranks and classes; but it is easy to see, that it is written in a phraseology peculiarly adapted to the lower conditions of readers. Hence, it is an especial favourite with sea-faring men, poor boys, servant-maids, &c. His novels are capital kitchen-reading, while they are worthy, from their interest, to find a shelf in the libraries of the wealthiest and the most learned. His passion for matter-of-fact narrative, sometimes betrayed him into a long relation of common incidents, which might happen to any man, and have no interest beyond the intense appearance of truth in them, to recommend them.

Charles Lamb

SOURCE: "Estimate of De Foe's Secondary Novels," in *The Works of Charles and Mary Lamb: Miscellaneous Prose, 1798-1834, Vol. I,* edited by E. V. Lucas, AMS Press, 1968, pp. 325-27.

[*The following excerpt was originally published in* Memoirs of the Life and Times of Daniel Defoe, *1830.*]

It has happened not seldom that one work of some author has so transcendently surpassed in execution the rest of his compositions, that the world has agreed to pass a sentence of dismissal upon the latter, and to consign them to total neglect and oblivion. It has done wisely in this, not to suffer the contemplation of excellencies of a lower standard to abate, or stand in the way of the pleasure it has agreed to receive from the master-piece.

Again it has happened, that from no inferior merit of execution in the rest, but from superior good fortune in the choice of its subject, some single work shall have been suffered to eclipse, and cast into shade the deserts of its less fortunate brethren. . . . [In] no instance has this excluding partiality been exerted with more unfairness than against what may be termed the secondary novels or romances of De Foe.

While all ages and descriptions of people hang delighted over the *Adventures of Robinson Crusoe,* and shall continue to do so we trust while the world lasts, how few comparatively will bear to be told, that there exist other fictitious narratives by the same writer—four of them at least of no inferior interest, except what results from a less felicitous choice of situation.

The narrative manner of De Foe has a naturalness about it, beyond that of any other novel or romance writer. His fictions have all the air of true stories. It is impossible to believe, while you are reading them, that a real person is not narrating to you every where nothing but what really happened to himself. To this, the extreme *homeliness* of their style mainly contributes. We use the word in its best and heartiest sense—that which comes *home* to the reader. The narrators everywhere are chosen from low life, or have had their origin in it; therefore they tell their own tales . . . as persons in their degree are observed to do, with infinite repetition, and an overacted exactness, lest the hearer should not have minded, or have forgotten, some things that had been told before. Hence the emphatic sentences marked in the good old (but deserted) Italic type, and hence, too, the frequent interposition of the reminding old colloquial parenthesis, "I say"—"mind"—and the like, when the story-teller repeats what, to a practised reader, might appear to have been sufficiently insisted upon before: which made an ingenious critic observe, that his works, in this kind, were excellent reading for the kitchen. And, in truth, the heroes and heroines of De Foe, can never again hope to be popular with a much higher class of readers, than that of the servant-maid or the sailor. Crusoe keeps its rank only by tough prescription. . . .

Samuel Taylor Coleridge

SOURCE: "Robinson Crusoe," in *Coleridge's Miscellaneous Criticism,* edited by Thomas Middleton Raysor, Harvard University Press, 1936, pp. 292-300.

[*Coleridge remains among the most important critics in the history of world literature. In the excerpt below, written sometime between 1812 and Coleridge's death in 1834, but not published until 1836, he considers* **Robinson Crusoe** *a portrait of "the universal man," and finds that it is this quality which gives the novel its enduring appeal.*]

[*Robinson Crusoe*] always interests, never agitates. Crusoe himself is merely a representative of humanity in general; neither his intellectual nor his moral qualities set him above the middle degree of mankind; his only prominent characteristic is the spirit of enterprise and wandering, which is, nevertheless, a very common disposition. You will observe that all that is wonderful in this tale is the result of external circumstances—of things which fortune brings to Crusoe's hand. . . .

Compare the contemptuous Swift with the condemned De Foe, and how superior will the latter be found. But by what test? Even by this. The writer who makes me sympathise with his presentations with the *whole* of my being, is more estimable than the writer who calls forth and appeals to but a part of my being—my sense of the ludicrous for instance; and again, he who makes me forget my *specific* class, character, and circumstances, raises me into the universal man. Now this is De Foe's excellence. You become a man while you read.

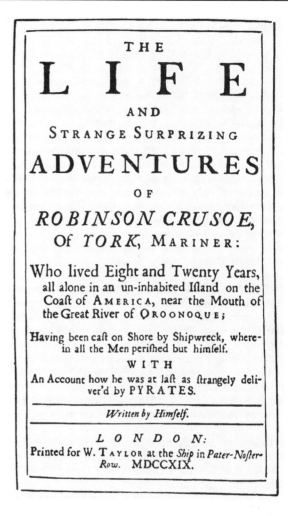

THE
LIFE
AND
STRANGE SURPRIZING
ADVENTURES
OF
ROBINSON CRUSOE,
Of *YORK*, MARINER:

Who lived Eight and Twenty Years,
all alone in an un-inhabited Island on the
Coast of AMERICA, near the Mouth of
the Great River of OROONOQUE;

Having been cast on Shore by Shipwreck, wherein all the Men perished but himself.

WITH
An Account how he was at last as strangely deliver'd by PYRATES.

Written by Himself.

LONDON:
Printed for W. TAYLOR at the *Ship* in *Pater-Noster-Row.* MDCCXIX.

Title page of the 1719 edition of Robinson Crusoe.

De Foe was a first-rate master in periodic style, but with sound judgment and the fine tact of genius, [he] avoided it as adverse to, nay, incompatible with, the everyday matter-of-fact *realness* which forms the charm and character of all his romances. The *Robinson Crusoe* is like the vision of a happy nightmare such as a denizen of Elysium might be supposed to have from a little excess in his nectar and ambrosia supper. Our imagination is kept in full play, excited to the highest, yet all the while we are touching or touched by a common flesh and blood.

One excellence of De Foe among many is his sacrifice of lesser interest to the greater because more universal. Had he (as without any improbability he might have done) given his Robinson Crusoe any of the turn for natural history which forms so striking and delightful a feature in the equally uneducated Dampier—had he made him find out qualities and uses in the before (to him) unknown plants of the island, discover a substitute for hops, for instance, or describe birds, etc.—many delightful pages and incidents might have enriched the book; but then Crusoe would cease to be the universal representative, the person for whom every reader could substitute himself. But now nothing is done, thought, or suffered, or desired, but what every man can imagine himself doing, thinking, feeling, or wishing for. Even so very easy a problem as that of finding a substitute for ink is with exquisite judgment made to baffle Crusoe's inventive faculties. Even in what he does he arrives at no excellence; he does not make basket work like Will Atkins. The carpentering, tailoring, pottery, are all just what will answer his purpose, and those are confined to needs that all men have, and comforts all men desire. Crusoe rises only where all men may be made to feel that they might and that they ought to rise—in religion, in resignation, in dependence on, and thankful acknowledgement of the divine mercy and goodness.

Edgar Allan Poe

SOURCE: "'The Life and Surprising Adventures of Robinson Crusoe'," in *The Complete Works of Edgar Allan Poe: Literary Criticisms, Vol. I*, edited by James A. Harrison, Thomas Y. Crowell & Co., Publishers, 1902, pp 169-73.

[*The following excerpt was originally published in* The Southern Literary Messenger, *1836, as an unsigned review of* **The Life and Surprising Adventures of Robinson Crusoe** (Volume I).]

How fondly do we recur, in memory, to those enchanted days of our boyhood when we first learned to grow serious over **Robinson Crusoe**!—when we first found the spirit of wild adventure enkindling within us; as by the dim fire light, we labored out, line by line, the marvellous import of those pages, and hung breathless and trembling with eagerness over their absorbing—over their enchaining interest!

While Defoe would have been fairly entitled to immortality had he never written **Robinson Crusoe,** yet his many other very excellent writings have nearly faded from our attention, in the superior lustre of the Adventures of the Mariner of York. What better possible species of reputation could the author have desired for that book than the species which it has so long enjoyed? It has become a household thing in nearly every family in Christendom. Yet never was admiration of any work—universal admiration—more indiscriminately or more inappropriately bestowed. Not one person in ten—nay, not one person in five hundred, has, during the perusal of **Robinson Crusoe,** the most remote conception that any particle of genius, or even of common talent, has been employed in its creation! Men do not look upon it in the light of a literary performance. Defoe has none of their thoughts—Robinson all. The powers which have wrought the wonder have been thrown into obscurity by the very stupendousness of the wonder they have wrought! We read, and become perfect abstractions in the intensity of our interest—we close the book, and are quite satisfied that we could have written as well ourselves! All this is effected by the potent magic of verisimilitude. Indeed the author of *Cru-*

soe must have possessed, above all other faculties, what has been termed the faculty of *identification*—that dominion exercised by volition over imagination which enables the mind to lose its own, in a fictitious, individuality. This includes, in a very great degree, the power of abstraction; and with these keys we may partially unlock the mystery of that spell which has so long invested the volume before us. But a complete analysis of our interest in it cannot be thus afforded. Defoe is largely indebted to his subject. The idea of man in a state of perfect isolation, although often entertained, was never before so comprehensively carried out. Indeed the frequency of its occurrence to the thoughts of mankind argued the extent of its influence on their sympathies, while the fact of no attempt having been made to give an embodied form to the conception, went to prove the difficulty of the undertaking. But the true narrative of [Alexander] Selkirk in 1711, with the powerful impression it then made upon the public mind, sufficed to inspire Defoe with both the necessary courage for his work, and entire confidence in its success. How wonderful has been the result!

William Hazlitt

SOURCE: "The Influence of 'Robinson Crusoe'," in *Robinson Crusoe: An Authoritative Text, Backgrounds and Sources, Criticism,* edited by Michael Shinagel, W. W. Norton & Company, 1975, p. 292.

[*Hazlitt's remarks were originally published in a memoir to Defoe titled, "The Life of Daniel Defoe," and prefixed to* The Works of Daniel Defoe, *1840.*]

The first, and by far the most celebrated, of those works of imagination, which have conferred immortality upon the name of De Foe, appeared in 1719, under the title of **The Life and Strange Surprising Adventures of Robinson Crusoe, of York, Mariner;** &c. Next to the Holy Scriptures, it may safely be asserted that this delightful romance has ever since it was written excited the first and most powerful influence upon the juvenile mind of England, nor has its popularity been much less among any of the nations of Christendom. At a period when few of the productions of English genius had been transferred into any of the languages of foreigners, this masterpiece of the homely, unaffected, unpretending, but rich and masculine intellect of Daniel De Foe, had already acquired, in every cultivated tongue of Europe, the full privileges of a native work.

Thomas De Quincey

SOURCE: "The Double Character of Defoe's Works," in *Robinson Crusoe: An Authoritative Text, Backgrounds and Sources, Criticism,* edited by Michael Shinagel, W. W. Norton & Company, 1975, p. 292.

[*De Quincey's commentary was originally published as "Homer and the Homeridae," in* Blackwood's Edinburgh Magazine, *1841.*]

De Foe is the only author known, who has so plausibly circumstantiated his false historical records, as to make them pass for genuine, even with literary men and critics. . . . How did he accomplish so difficult an end? Simply by inventing such little circumstantiations of any character or incident, as seen by their apparent inertness of effect, to verify themselves; for, where the reader is told that such a person was the posthumous son of a tanner; that his mother married afterwards a Presbyterian schoolmaster, who gave him a smattering of Latin; but, the schoolmaster dying of the plague, that he was compelled at sixteen to enlist for bread—in all this, as there is nothing at all amusing, we conclude, that the author could have no reason to detain us with such particulars, but simply because they were true. To invent, when nothing at all is gained by inventing, there seems no imaginable temptation. It never occurs to us, that this very construction of the case, this very inference from such neutral details, was precisely the object which De Foe had in view, and by which he meant to profit. He thus gains the opportunity of impressing upon his tales a double character; he makes them so amusing, that girls read them for novels; and he gives them such an air of verisimilitude, that men read them for histories.

George Borrow

SOURCE: "Inspiration from 'Robinson Crusoe'," in *Robinson Crusoe: An Authoritative Text, Backgrounds and Sources, Criticism,* edited by Michael Shinagel, W. W. Norton & Company, 1975, p. 293.

[*Borrow's remarks were printed in* Lavengro, 1851.]

Reader, is it necessary to name the book which now stood open in my hand, and whose very prints, feeble expounders of its wondrous lines, had produced within me emotions strange and novel? Scarcely, for it was a book which has exerted over the minds of Englishmen an influence certainly greater than any other of modern times; which has been in most people's hands, and with the contents of which even those who cannot read are to a certain extent acquainted; a book from which the most luxuriant and fertile of our modern prose writers have drunk inspiration; a book, moreover, to which, from the hardy deeds which it narrates, and the spirit of strange and romantic enterprise which it tends to awaken, England owes many of her astonishing discoveries both by sea and land, and no inconsiderable part of her naval glory.

Hail to thee, spirit of De Foe! What does not my own poor self owe to thee? England has better bards than either Greece or Rome, yet I could spare them easier than De Foe, "un-abashed De Foe," as the hunchbacked rhymer [Alexander Pope] styled him.

W. C. Roscoe

SOURCE: "De Foe As a Novelist," in *The National Review,* London, Vol. III, No. VI, October, 1856, pp. 380-410.

Totally destitute of the power to fathom any intricacies of human nature, Defoe is familiar with its external manifestations. He may have no conscious picture of *character;* but he has a keen eye for traits of character, and a very vivid idea of *persons.* He takes a man and his life in the gross, as it were, and sets them down in writing; but as it is his characteristic to be mainly occupied with the life, not the man, so this too becomes the main source of the reader's interest. It is not Robinson Crusoe we care about, but the account of his adventures, the solution of the problem of how to live under the circumstances. His name calls up the idea not of a man, but of a story. Say 'Lear,' and you think of a man; you have the image of the white-haired king—the central point, about which the division of his kingdom, the disaffection of his daughters, the terrors of the tempest, the soft pity and sad death of Cordelia, group themselves in subordinate place: say 'Robinson Crusoe,' and you see a desert island, with a man upon it ingeniously adapting his mode of life to his resources; the imagination of a solitary existence, reproduced in a special form with wonderful vividness, consistency, and particularity,—this is the source of our interest. It would be to impugn the verdict of all mankind to say **Robinson Crusoe** was not a great work of genius. It is a work of genius—a most remarkable one—but of a low order of genius. The universal admiration it has obtained may be the admiration of men: but it is founded on the liking of boys. Few educated men or women would care to read it for the first time after the age of five-and-twenty. . . . If a grown man reads the book in after years, it is to recall the sensations of youth, or curiously to examine the secret of the unbounded popularity it has enjoyed. How much this popularity is due to the happy choice of his subject, we may better estimate when we remember that the popular **Robinson Crusoe** is in reality only a part of the work, and the work itself only one of many others, not less well executed, from the same hand. No other man in the world could have drawn so absolutely living a picture of the desert-island life; but the same man has exercised the same power over more complex incidents, and the works are little read.

Wilkie Collins

SOURCE: "'Robinson Crusoe': The Self as Master," in *Defoe's Narratives: Situations and Structures,* by John J. Richetti, Clarendon Press, 1875, pp. 21-62.

[*The following excerpt is taken from Collins's* The Moonstone: A Novel, *1873.*]

You are not to take it, if you please, as the saying of an ignorant man, when I express my opinion that such a book as **Robinson Crusoe** never was written, and never will be written again. I have tried that book for years—generally in combination with a pipe of tobacco—and I have found it my friend in need in all the necessities of this mortal life. When my spirits are bad—**Robinson Crusoe.** When I want advice—**Robinson Crusoe.** In past times, when my wife plagued me; in present times, when

I have had a drop too much—*Robinson Crusoe*. I have worn out six stout *Robinson Crusoes* with hard work in my service. On my lady's last birthday she gave me a seventh. I took a drop too much on the strength of it; and *Robinson Crusoe* put me right again. Price four shillings and sixpence, bound in blue, with a picture into the bargain.

John Stuart Mill

SOURCE: "The Preeminence of 'Robinson Crusoe' in Childhood," in *Robinson Crusoe: An Authoritative Text, Backgrounds and Sources, Criticism,* edited by Michael Shinagel, W. W. Norton & Company, 1975, p. 298.

[*Mill's remarks were printed in his* Autobiography, *1873.*]

Of children's books, any more than of playthings, I had scarcely any, except an occasional gift from a relation or acquaintance: among those I had, *Robinson Crusoe* was preeminent, and continued to delight me through all my boyhood.

Charles Dickens

SOURCE: "The Want of Emotion in Defoe," in *Robinson Crusoe: An Authoritative Text, Backgrounds and Sources, Criticism,* edited by Michael Shinagel, W. W. Norton & Company, 1975, p. 295.

[*Dickens's remarks are taken from John Forster's* The Life of Dickens, *1874.*]

You remember my saying to you some time ago how curious I thought it that *Robinson Crusoe* should be the only instance of an universally popular book that could make no one laugh and could make no one cry. I have been reading it again just now, in the course of my numerous refreshings at those English wells, and I will venture to say that there is not in literature a more surprising instance of an utter want of tenderness and sentiment, than the death of Friday. It is as heartless as *Gil Blas,* in a very different and far more serious way. But the second part altogether will not bear enquiry. In the second part of *Don Quixote* are some of the finest things. But the second part of *Robinson Crusoe* is perfectly contemptible, in the glaring defect that it exhibits the man who was 30 years on that desert island with no visible effect made on his character by that experience. De Foe's women too—Robinson Crusoe's wife for instance—are terrible dull commonplace fellows without breeches; and I have no doubt he was a precious dry disagreeable article himself—I mean De Foe: not Robinson.

Leslie Stephen

SOURCE: "Defoe's Novels," in *Hours in a Library Vol. I,* G.P. Putnam's Sons, 1894, pp. 1-46.

[*Stephen's work was originally published in 1874.*]

It is time, however, to say enough of *Robinson Crusoe* to justify its traditional superiority to De Foe's other writings. The charm, as some critics say, is difficult to analyse; and I do not profess to demonstrate mathematically that it must necessarily be, what it is, the most fascinating boy's book ever written, and one which older critics may study with delight. The most obvious advantage over the secondary novels lies in the unique situation. . . . [The] horrors of abandonment on a desert island can be appreciated by the simplest sailor or schoolboy. The main thing is to bring out the situation plainly and forcibly, to tell us of the difficulties of making pots and pans, of catching goats and sowing corn, and of avoiding audacious cannibals. This task De Foe performs with unequalled spirit and vivacity. In his first discovery of a new art he shows the freshness so often conspicuous in first novels. The scenery was just that which had peculiar charms for his fancy; it was one of those half-true legends of which he had heard strange stories from seafaring men, and possibly from the acquaintances of his hero himself. He brings out the shrewd vigorous character of the Englishman thrown upon his own resources with evident enjoyment of his task. Indeed, De Foe tells us very emphatically that in *Robinson Crusoe* he saw a kind of allegory of his own fate. He had suffered from solitude of soul. Confinement in his prison is represented in the book by confinement in an island; and even a particular incident, here and there, such as the fright he receives one night from something in his bed, 'was word for word a history of what happened.' In other words, this novel too, like many of the best ever written, has in it the autobiographical element which makes a man speak from greater depths of feeling than in a purely imaginary story.

It would indeed be easy to show that the story, though in one sense marvellously like truth, is singularly wanting as a psychological study. . . . De Foe, even in *Robinson Crusoe,* gives a very inadequate picture of the mental torments to which his hero is exposed. He is frightened by a parrot calling him by name, and by the strangely picturesque incident of the footmark on the sand; but, on the whole, he takes his imprisonment with preternatural stolidity. His stay on the island produces the same state of mind as might be due to a dull Sunday in Scotland. For this reason, the want of power in describing emotion as compared with the amazing power of describing facts, *Robinson Crusoe* is a book for boys rather than men, and, as Lamb says, for the kitchen rather than for higher circles. It falls short of any high intellectual interest. When we leave the striking situation and get to the second part, with the Spaniards and Will Atkins talking natural theology to his wife, it sinks to the level of the secondary stories. But for people who are not too proud to take a rather low order of amusement *Robinson Crusoe* will always be one of the most charming of books. We have the romantic and adventurous incidents upon which the most unflinching realism can be set to work without danger of vulgarity. Here is precisely the story suited to De Foe's strength and weakness. He is forced to be artistic in spite of himself. He cannot lose the thread of the narrative and break it into disjointed fragments, for the limits of the island confine him as well as his hero. He cannot tire us with details, for all the details of such a story are interesting; it is made up of petty incidents, as much as the life of a prisoner reduced to taming flies, or making saws out of penknives. The island does as well as the Bastille for making trifles valuable to the sufferer and to us. The facts tell the story of themselves, without any demand for romantic power to press them home to us; and the efforts to give an air of authenticity to the story, which sometimes make us smile, and sometimes rather bore us, in other novels are all to the purpose; for there is a real point in putting such a story in the mouth of the sufferer, and in giving us for the time an illusory belief in his reality. It is one of the exceptional cases in which the poetical aspect of a position is brought out best by the most prosaic accuracy of detail; and we imagine that Robinson Crusoe's island, with all his small household torments, will always be more impressive than the more gorgeously coloured island of [Alfred Lord Tennyson's] Enoch Arden. When we add that the whole book shows the freshness of a writer employed on his first novel—though at the mature age of fifty-eight; seeing in it an allegory of his own experience embodied in the scenes which most interested his imagination, we see some reasons why **Robinson Crusoe** should hold a distinct rank by itself amongst his works. As De Foe was a man of very powerful but very limited imagination—able to see certain aspects of things with extraordinary distinctness, but little able to rise above them—even his greatest book shows his weakness, and scarcely satisfies a grown-up man with a taste for high art. In revenge, it ought, according to Rousseau, to be for a time the whole library of a boy, chiefly, it seems, to teach him that the stock of an ironmonger is better than that of a jeweler. We may agree in the conclusion without caring about the reason; and to have pleased all the boys in Europe for near a hundred and fifty years is, after all, a remarkable feat.

[De Foe] may be said to have stumbled almost unconsciously into novel-writing. He was merely aiming at true stories, which happened not to be true. But accidentally, or rather unconsciously, he could not help presenting us with a type of curious interest; for he necessarily described himself and the readers whose tastes he understood and shared so thoroughly. His statement that **Robinson Crusoe** was a kind of allegory was truer than he knew. In **Robinson Crusoe** is De Foe, and more than De Foe, for he is the typical Englishman of his time. He is the broad-shouldered, beef-eating John Bull, who has been shouldering his way through the world ever since. Drop him in a desert island, and he is just as sturdy and self-composed as if he were in Cheapside. Instead of shrieking or writing poetry, becoming a wild hunter or a religious hermit, he calmly sets about building a house and making pottery and laying out a farm. . . . The portrait is not the less effective because the artist was so far from intending it that he could not even conceive of anybody being differently constituted from himself. It shows us all the more vividly what was the manner of man represented by the stalwart Englishman of the day; what were the men who were building up vast systems of commerce and manufacture; shoving their intrusive persons into every quarter of the globe; evolving a great empire out of a few factories in the East; winning the American continent for the dominant English race; sweeping up Australia by the way as a convenient settlement for convicts; stamping firmly and decisively on all toes that got in their way; blundering enormously and preposterously, and yet always coming out steadily planted on their feet; eating roast beef and plum-pudding; drinking rum in the tropics; singing 'God Save the King' and intoning Watts's hymns under the nose of ancient dynasties and prehistoric priesthoods; managing always to get their own way, to force a reluctant world to take note of them as a great if rather disagreeable fact, and making it probable that, in long ages to come, the English of **Robinson Crusoe** will be the native language of inhabitants of every region under the sun.

Rev. R. P Graves and William Wordsworth

SOURCE: "Crusoe's Extraordinary Energy and Resource," in *Robinson Crusoe: An Authoritative Text, Backgrounds and Sources, Criticism,* edited by Michael Shinagel, W. W. Norton & Company, 1975, pp. 290-91.

[*Graves articulates William Wordsworth's remarks on* **Robinson Crusoe** *in "Reminiscences of the Rev. R. P. Graves, M.A.," in* The Prose Works of William Wordsworth, *1876.*]

[Wordsworth] thought the charm of **Robinson Crusoe** mistakenly ascribed, as it commonly is done, to its *naturalness.* Attaching a full value to the singular yet easily imagined and most picturesque circumstances of the adventurer's position, to the admirable painting of the scenes, and to the knowledge displayed of the working of human feelings, he yet felt sure that the intense interest created by the story arose chiefly from the extraordinary energy and resource of the hero under his difficult circumstances, from their being so far beyond what was natural to expect, or what would have been exhibited by the average of men; and that similarly the high pleasure derived from his successes and good fortunes arose from the peculiar source of these uncommon merits of his character.

William Minto

SOURCE: In *Daniel Defoe,* Harper & Brothers Publishers, 1879, 167p.

In writing for the entertainment of his own time, Defoe took the surest way of writing for the entertainment of all time. Yet if he had never chanced to write **Robinson Crusoe,** he would now have a very obscure place in English literature. His "natural infirmity of homely plain writing," as he humorously described it, might have drawn students to his works, but they ran considerable risk of lying in utter oblivion. He was at war with the whole guild of respectable writers who have become classics; they despised him as an illiterate fellow, a vulgar huckster, and never alluded to him except in terms of contempt. He was not slow to retort their civilities; but the retorts might very easily have sunk beneath the waters, while the assaults were preserved by their mutual support. The vast mass of Defoe's writings received no kindly aid from distinguished contemporaries to float them down the stream; everything was done that bitter dislike and supercilious indifference could do to submerge them. *Robinson Crusoe* was their sole life-buoy.

Edmund Gosse

SOURCE: "Defoe and the Essayists," in *A History of Eighteenth-Century Literature: 1660-1780,* The Macmillan Company, 1889, pp. 176-206.

Defoe lives, and will ever live, by *Robinson Crusoe,* the most thrilling boy's book ever written. . . . He . . . asserts of *Robinson Crusoe* that it is "a just history of fact, neither is there any appearance of fiction in it." . . . These artifices matter little to the reader, who now would rather that Defoe should have written fiction than reported fact, but they throw light on the intellectual character of the author. Defoe had no ambition; he worked as blindly and as restlessly as a mole, and his contemporaries, who saw his writing everywhere, knew nothing of the man himself. He did not wish to win personal distinction; he would have been the first to tell us that he wrote out of zeal for public morality, and to make money. By dint of incessant journalistic work he had attained great skill and fluency in writing, and he had been storing up details in his capacious memory all his life. When his apoplexy withdrew him a little from the hurly-burly, he turned his restless pen to a new sort of trade; and while his hand was still vigorous there was thrown in his way the matchless collection of facts about the solitary man, marooned on the blossoming island, and subduing nature to his wants. The result was that, rather by accident than art, this prosaic and unimpassioned hack produced one of the most beautiful of the world's romances, and tried time after time to repeat his great success, without ever rising again much above mediocrity. Defoe had extraordinary talents, and he retains a not unimportant niche in the history of literature; but it can scarcely be denied that his character exhibits, almost to excess, some of the least pleasing qualities of the eighteenth-century mind and morals.

W. J. Dawson

SOURCE: "The Father of English Fiction," in *The Makers of English Fiction,* Revell, 1905, pp. 7-18.

So like the truth is *Robinson Crusoe* that it was accepted on its publication as a real narrative, and to this day multitudes of the uninstructed probably regard it in the same light. It bears some resemblance to the authentic story of Alexander Selkirk, but it is in theme rather than in incident. What finer justification of Defoe's method can be found than that the invented story of Crusoe appears quite as probable as the real story of Selkirk? Charles Lamb found the story altogether too homely, and said that it was better fitted for the kitchen than the drawing-room. Dickens complained of "an utter want of tenderness and sentiment" in the account of Friday's death, and said that it was the only great novel which excited neither tears nor laughter. Later critics have lamented its lack of psychological interest. But these criticisms, after all, amount to nothing more than this, that Defoe chose to tell his story in his own way. He does not pretend to describe emotions; he is content to relate facts. The state of Crusoe's mind is of less importance than his expedients to get the means of life.

Opportunities of brilliant description such as Stevenson would have seized with eagerness, opportunities such as Tennyson has used to the utmost in his "Enoch Arden," Defoe ignores, as incompatible with his method. Perhaps it would be juster to say that he does not so much as perceive them. He was essentially a bluff, masculine, matter-of-fact man, and he tells his story in a matter-of-fact way. Prosaic accuracy of detail serves him perhaps better than heroics. The man he paints is a sturdy, plain-minded seaman, who sets himself to solve the problem of how to live under conditions which would have overwhelmed a more sensitive mind. It is the indomitable courage of Crusoe which charms us. He is typically Anglo-Saxon in his stolid endurance of fate, his practical grasp of circumstances, his ingenuity, his fertility of resource, his determination to make the best of his unfortunate situation. He behaves after the manner of his race. Having by chance become the monarch of a desert island, he sets himself to govern it to the best of his ability, and to arrange his life with decent orderliness. There is something much more affecting in the indomitable courage of Crusoe than there would be in any amount of sentiment. One supreme imaginative incident illumines the book—the finding of the footstep on the sand; but, apart from this, Defoe is content to kindle the imagination by mere truthfulness of detail in common things. And he does this so successfully that we are affected quite as deeply by Crusoe's painful attempts to keep house and record the passage of time as we are by what may be regarded as the supreme imaginative incident of the book.

James Joyce

SOURCE: In *Daniel Defoe,* translated by Joseph Prescott, State University of New York Press, 1964, pp. 23-5.

[*Joyce delivered the following lecture in Italian in 1912.*]

You will find, if anything, beneath the rude exterior of his character an instinct and a prophecy. His women have the indecency and the continence of beasts; his men are strong and silent as trees. English feminism and English imperialism already lurk in these souls which are just emerging from the animal kingdom.

Defoe's masterpiece, **Robinson Crusoe,** is the full artistic expression of this instinct and this prophecy. . . . The story of the shipwrecked sailor who lived on the desert island for four years reveals, as perhaps no other book throughout the long history of English literature does, the wary and heroic instinct of the rational animal and the prophecy of the empire.

European criticism has striven for many generations, and with a not entirely friendly insistence, to explain the mystery of the unlimited world conquest accomplished by that mongrel breed which lives a hard life on a small island in the northern sea and was not endowed by nature with the intellect of the Latin, nor with the patience of the Semite, nor with Teutonic zeal, nor with the sensitiveness of the Slav. European caricature has amused itself for many years in contemplating, with a gaiety not unmixed with distress, an exaggerated man with the jaws of an ape, checkered clothes that are too short and too tight, and enormous feet; or the traditional John Bull, the corpulent trader with the fatuous, rubicund moonface and the diminutive top-hat. Neither of these lay figures would have conquered a handbreadth of ground in a thousand ages. The true symbol of the British conquest is Robinson Crusoe, who, cast away on a desert island, in his pocket a knife and a pipe, becomes an architect, a carpenter, a knifegrinder, an astronomer, a baker, a shipwright, a potter, a saddler, a farmer, a tailor, an umbrella-maker, and a clergyman. He is the true prototype of the British colonist, as Friday (the trusty savage who arrives on an unlucky day) is the symbol of the subject races. The whole Anglo-Saxon spirit is in Crusoe: the manly independence; the unconscious cruelty; the persistence; the slow yet efficient intelligence; the sexual apathy; the practical, well-balanced religiousness; the calculating taciturnity. Whoever rereads this simple, moving book in the light of subsequent history cannot help but fall under its prophetic spell.

Saint John the Evangelist saw on the island of Patmos the apocalyptic ruin of the universe and the building of the walls of the eternal city sparking with beryl and emerald, with onyx and jasper, with sapphire and ruby. Crusoe saw only one marvel in all the fertile creation around him, the print of a naked foot in the virgin sand. And who knows if the latter is not more significant than the former?

Clennell Wilkinson

SOURCE: "The Author of 'Robinson Crusoe'," in *The New Statesman,* Vol. XIII, No. 320, May 24, 1919, pp. 190-92.

Those—and they are many—who would rather, other things being equal, read a history than a romance know

that there is in the former a certain secret flavour, a kind of "atmosphere," if you like, prized above all things by lovers of history, but never, I think, successfully imitated by a writer of fiction, with the single exception of Daniel Defoe. It is not that these discriminating persons love fact for its own sake. The late Lord Wolseley once confessed in a book of reminiscences that he had never in his life been able to take the slightest interest in any story unless he knew beforehand that it was strictly true. That attitude of mind is happily rare; it is probable that Lord Wolseley was unable to appreciate Defoe. The charm of history is something quite different from this. It is as though all history were written by the same hand. History does not, of course, repeat itself. But all true stories are extraordinarily alike; they are all distinguished by the same restraint; they all eschew the "good curtain," the dramatic *dénouement,* and yet achieve a delightful unexpectedness not to be found in any fictitious drama. True stories may be distinguished from false, not only by their fact, but by their manner. All of them have the same peculiar fascination which makes them "go down" in any kind of company. Thus it is that the most ill-written history (if it be true history and not speculation) is readable. History is historian-proof. But ill-written fiction, as we nowadays know to our cost, is quite often unreadable.

It follows that a true story need not be true in Lord Wolseley's sense; but it must be in Defoe's. The bicentenary of **Robinson Crusoe** affords a good opportunity of studying the methods of its author, that most versatile and prolific of writers, who has been credited with the invention of things so diverse as the leading article and the realistic novel, and who was certainly the father of the historical novel. No one has ever appreciated the value of a true story more than Defoe. Not only did he strive, with unexampled success, to give his romances (or memoirs, as he preferred to call them) an air of verisimilitude, but he constantly asserted that they were true in actual fact. . . . In the case of **Robinson Crusoe,** which was, of course, based upon the actual experiences of one Alexander Selkirk, who spent four solitary years on the island of Juan Fernandez, Defoe was eventually brought to admit that the narrative was not strictly true, but was in the nature of an allegory—an allegory of his own "life of unexampled misfortunes." He accompanied this confession with the following curious homily upon the wickedness of pure invention in story telling:

> This supplying a story by invention is certainly a most scandalous crime, and yet very little regarded in that part. It is a sort of lying that makes a great hole in the heart in which by degrees a habit of lying enters in. Such a man comes quickly up to a total disregarding the truth of what he says, looking upon it as a trifle, a thing of no import, whether any story he tells be true or not.

He must have written this with his tongue in his cheek. For, to be frank, the allegory theory will not wash. **Robinson Crusoe** is no more an allegory than the **Memoirs of a Cavalier** is an original journal, or than **Count**

Patkul was written by a Lutheran minister. They are all creations of Defoe's own brain. It would be doing his memory an evil turn to assume that this pretence of literal truth was a mere device for increasing the sale of his books; they would have sold equally well if no one had believed a word of them. A true story succeeds not because it is true, but because it has a quality that other stories have not. . . .

As for *Robinson Crusoe*, the classic, it does not really matter to anyone whether it be true or untrue. It is sufficient that it has all the charm of a true story. It has been badly treated. It has been cast before schoolboys, who often prefer *Swiss Family Robinson*; publishers classify it among "Tales for the Young." But Crusoe and his man, Friday, have survived, and will survive. As studies in character they are, perhaps, inferior to some of Defoe's own creations, such as William, the Quaker pirate in *Captain Singleton*, Moll Flanders, Roxana and Colonel Jack; but the story is easily the best of its kind that has ever been written.

Robinson Crusoe alone, with its more obvious appeal to the love of adventure, its ingenuity and exuberant imagination, has survived all changes of taste and is, perhaps, as popular now (though with a more limited class of readers) as it was two hundred years ago.

Virginia Woolf

SOURCE: "Defoe" and "'Robinson Crusoe'," in *Collected Essays, Volume I,* Harcourt, Brace & World, Inc., 1925, 359p.

[*Woolf's essays were originally written in 1919.*]

The fear which attacks the recorder of centenaries lest he should find himself measuring a diminishing spectre and forced to foretell its approaching dissolution is not only absent in the case of *Robinson Crusoe* but the mere thought of it is ridiculous. It may be true that *Robinson Crusoe* is two hundred years of age upon the twenty-fifth of April 1919, but far from raising the familiar speculations as to whether people now read it and will continue to read it, the effect of the bi-centenary is to make us marvel that *Robinson Crusoe,* the perennial and immortal, should have been in existence so short a time as that. The book resembles one of the anonymous productions of the race rather than the effort of a single mind; and as for celebrating its centenary we should as soon think of celebrating the centenaries of Stonehenge itself. Something of this we may attribute to the fact that we have all had *Robinson Crusoe* read aloud to us as children, and were thus much in the same state in mind towards Defoe and his story that the Greeks were in towards Homer. It never occurred to us that there was such a person as Defoe, and to have been told that *Robinson Crusoe* was the work of a man with a pen in his hand would either have disturbed us unpleasantly or meant nothing at all. The impressions of childhood are those that last longest and cut deepest. It still seems that the name of Daniel Defoe has no right to appear upon the title-page of *Robinson Crusoe,* and if we celebrate the bi-centenary of the book we are making a slightly unnecessary allusion to the fact that, like Stonehenge, it is still in existence.

The great fame of the book has done its author some injustice; for while it has given him a kind of anonymous glory it has obscured the fact that he was a writer of other works which, it is safe to assert, were not read aloud to us as children. Thus when the Editor of the *Christian World* in the year 1870 appealed to 'the boys and girls of England' to erect a monument upon the grave of Defoe, which a stroke of lightning had mutilated, the marble was inscribed to the memory of the author of *Robinson Crusoe.* . . .

There are many ways of approaching this classical volume; but which shall we choose? Shall we begin by saying that, since Sidney died at Zutphen leaving the *Arcadia* unfinished, great changes had come over English life, and the novel had chosen, or had been forced to choose, its direction? A middle class had come into existence, able to read and anxious to read not only about the loves of princes and princesses, but about themselves and the details of their humdrum lives. Stretched upon a thousand pens, prose had accommodated itself to the demand; it had fitted itself to express the facts of life rather than the poetry. That is certainly one way of approaching *Robinson Crusoe*—through the development of the novel; but another immediately suggests itself—through the life of the author. Here too, in the heavenly pastures of biography, we may spend many more hours than are needed to read the book itself from cover to cover. The date of Defoe's birth, to begin with, is doubtful—was it 1660 or 1661? Then again, did he spell his name in one word or in two? And who were his ancestors? He is said to have been a hosier; but what, after all, was a hosier in the seventeenth century? He became a pamphleteer, and enjoyed the confidence of William the Third; one of his pamphlets caused him to be stood in the pillory and imprisoned at Newgate; he was employed by Harley and later by Godolphin; he was the first of the hireling journalists; he wrote innumerable pamphlets and articles; also *Moll Flanders* and *Robinson Crusoe;* he had a wife and six children; was spare in figure, with a hooked nose, a sharp chin, grey eyes, and a large mole near his mouth. Nobody who has any slight acquaintance with English literature needs to be told how many hours can be spent and how many lives have been spent in tracing the development of the novel and in examining the chins of the novelists. Only now and then, as we turn from theory to biography and from biography to theory, a doubt insinuates itself—if we knew the very moment of Defoe's birth and whom he loved and why, if we had by heart the history of the origin, rise, growth, decline, and fall of the English novel from its conception (say) in Egypt to its decease in the wilds (perhaps) of Paraguay, should we suck an ounce of additional pleasure from *Robinson Crusoe* or read it one whit more intelligently?

For the book itself remains. However we may wind and wriggle, loiter and dally in our approach to books, a lonely battle waits us at the end. . . .

[F]rom anger, fear, and boredom a rare and lasting delight is sometimes born.

Robinson Crusoe, it may be, is a case in point. It is a masterpiece, and it is a masterpiece largely because Defoe has throughout kept consistently to his own sense of perspective. For this reason he thwarts us and flouts us at every turn. Let us look at the theme largely and loosely, comparing it with our preconceptions. It is, we know, the story of a man who is thrown, after many perils and adventures, alone upon a desert island. The mere suggestion—peril and solitude and a desert island—is enough to rouse in us the expectation of some far land on the limits of the world; of the sun rising and the sun setting; of man, isolated from his kind, brooding alone upon the nature of society and the strange ways of men. Before we open the book we have perhaps vaguely sketched out the kind of pleasure we expect it to give us. We read; and we are rudely contradicted on every page. There are no sunsets and no sunrises; there is no solitude and no soul. There is, on the contrary, staring us full in the face nothing but a large earthenware pot. We are told, that is to say, that it was the 1st of September 1651; that the hero's name is Robinson Crusoe; and that his father has the gout. Obviously, then, we must alter our attitude. Reality, fact, substance is going to dominate all that follows. We must hastily alter our proportions throughout; Nature must furl her splendid purples; she is only the giver of drought and water; man must be reduced to a struggling, life-preserving animal; and God shrivel into a magistrate whose seat, substantial and somewhat hard, is only a little way above the horizon. Each sortie of ours in pursuit of information upon these cardinal points of perspective—God, man, Nature—is snubbed back with ruthless common sense. Robinson Crusoe thinks of God: 'sometimes I would expostulate with myself, why providence should thus completely ruin its creatures. . . . But something always return'd swift upon me to check these thoughts.' God does not exist. He thinks of Nature, the fields 'adorn'd with flowers and grass, and full of very fine woods', but the important thing about a wood is that it harbours an abundance of parrots who may be tamed and taught to speak. Nature does not exist. He considers the dead, whom he has killed himself. It is of the utmost importance that they should be buried at once, for 'they lay open to the sun and would presently be offensive'. Death does not exist. Nothing exists except an earthenware pot. Finally, that is to say, we are forced to drop our own preconceptions and to accept what Defoe himself wishes to give us.

Let us then go back to the beginning and repeat again, 'I was born in the year 1632 in the city of York of a good family'. Nothing could be plainer, more matter of fact, than that beginning. We are drawn on soberly to consider all the blessings of orderly, industrious middle-class life. There is no greater good fortune we are assured than to be born of the British middle class. The great are to be pitied and so are the poor; both are exposed to distempers and uneasiness; the middle station between the mean and the great is the best; and its virtues—temperance, moderation, quietness, and health—are the most desirable. It was a sorry thing, then, when by some evil fate a middle-class youth was bitten with the foolish love of adventure. So he proses on, drawing, little by little, his own portrait, so that we never forget it—imprinting upon us indelibly, for he never forgets it either, his shrewdness, his caution, his love of order and comfort and respectability; until by whatever means, we find ourselves at sea, in a storm; and, peering out, everything is seen precisely as it appears to Robinson Crusoe. The waves, the seamen, the sky, the ship—all are seen through those shrewd, middle-class, unimaginative eyes. There is no escaping him. Everything appears as it would appear to that naturally cautious, apprehensive, conventional, and solidly matter-of-fact intelligence. He is incapable of enthusiasm. He has a natural slight distaste for the sublimities of Nature. He suspects even Providence of exaggeration. He is so busy and has such an eye to the main chance that he notices only a tenth part of what is going on round him. Everything is capable of a rational explanation, he is sure, if only he had time to attend to it. We are much more alarmed by the 'vast great creatures' that swim out in the night and surround his boat than he is. He at once takes his gun and fires at them, and off they swim—whether they are lions or not he really cannot say. Thus before we know it we are opening our mouths wider and wider. We are swallowing monsters that we should have jibbed at if they had been offered us by an imaginative and flamboyant traveller. But anything that this sturdy middle-class man notices can be taken for a fact. He is for ever counting his barrels, and making sensible provisions for his water supply; nor do we ever find him tripping even in a matter of detail. Has he forgotten, we wonder, that he has a great lump of beeswax on board? Not at all. But as he had already made candles out of it, it is not nearly as great on page thirty-eight as it was on page twenty-three. When for a wonder he leaves some inconsistency hanging loose—why if the wild cats are so very tame are the goats so very shy?—we are not seriously perturbed, for we are sure that there was a reason, and a very good one, had he time to give it us. But the pressure of life when one is fending entirely for oneself alone on a desert island is really no laughing matter. It is no crying one either. A man must have an eye to everything; it is no time for raptures about Nature when the lightning may explode one's gunpowder—it is imperative to seek a safer lodging for it. And so by means of telling the truth undeviatingly as it appears to him—by being a great artist and forgoing this and daring that in order to give effect to his prime quality, a sense of reality—he comes in the end to make common actions dignified and common objects beautiful. To dig, to bake, to plant, to build—how serious these simple occupations are; hatchets, scissors, logs, axes—how beautiful these simple objects become. Unimpeded by comment, the story marches on with magnificent downright simplicity. Yet how could comment have made it more impressive? It is true that he takes the opposite way from the psychologist's—he describes the effect of emotion on the body, not on the mind. But when he says how, in a moment of anguish, he clinched his hands so that any soft thing would have been crushed; how 'my teeth in my head would strike together, and set against one another so strong that for the time I could not part them again,' the effect is as deep as pages of analysis could have made it. His own instinct in the matter is right. 'Let the naturalists', he says, 'explain these things, and the reason and manner of them; all I can say to them is, to describe the fact. . . . ' If you are Defoe, certainly to describe the fact is enough; for the fact is the right fact. By means of this genius for fact Defoe achieves effects that are beyond any but the great masters of descriptive prose. He has only to say a word or two about 'the grey of the morning' to paint vividly a windy dawn. A sense of desolation and of the deaths of many men is conveyed by remarking in the most prosaic way in the world, 'I never saw them afterwards, or any sign of them except three of their hats, one cap, and two shoes that were not fellows'. When at last he exclaims, 'Then to see how like a king I din'd too all alone, attended by my servants'—his parrot and his dog and his two cats, we cannot help but feel that all humanity is on a desert island alone—though Defoe at once informs us, for he has a way of snubbing off our enthusiasms, that the cats were not the same cats that had come in the ship. Both of those were dead; these cats were new cats, and as a matter of fact cats became very troublesome before long from their fecundity, whereas dogs, oddly enough, did not breed at all.

Thus Defoe, by reiterating that nothing but a plain earthenware pot stands in the foreground, persuades us to see remote islands and the solitudes of the human soul. By believing fixedly in the solidity of the pot and its earthiness, he has subdued every other element to his design; he has roped the whole universe into harmony. And is there any reason, we ask as we shut the book, why the perspective that a plain earthenware pot exacts should not satisfy us as completely, once we grasp it, as man himself in all his sublimity standing against a background of broken mountains and tumbling oceans with stars flaming in the sky?

Karl Marx

SOURCE: "Crusoe and Capitalism," in *Robinson Crusoe: An Authoritative Text, Backgrounds and Sources, Criticism,* edited by Michael Shinagel, W. W. Norton & Company, 1975, pp. 295-98.

[*The following is an excerpt from Marx's* Capital, *1921.*]

Since Robinson Crusoe's experiences are a favorite theme with political economists, let us take a look at him on his island. Moderate though he be, yet some few wants he has to satisfy, and must therefore do a little useful work of various sorts, such as making tools and furniture, taming goats, fishing and hunting. Of his prayers and the like we take no account, since they are a source of pleasure to him, and he looks upon them as so much recreation. In spite of the variety of his work, he knows that his labour, whatever its form, is but the activity of one and the same Robinson, and consequently, that it consists of nothing but different modes of human labour. Necessity itself compels him to apportion his time accurately between his different kinds of work. Whether one kind occupies a greater space in his general activity than another, depends on the difficulties, greater or less as the case may be, to be overcome in attaining the useful effect aimed at. This our friend Robinson soon learns by experience, and having rescued a watch, ledger, and pen and ink from the wreck, commences, like a true-born Briton, to keep a set of books. His stock-book contains a list of the objects of utility that belong to him, of the operations necessary for their production; and lastly, of the labour time that definite quantities of those objects have, on an average, cost him. All the relations between Robinson and the objects that form this wealth of his own creation, are here so simple and clear as to be intelligible without exertion, even to Mr. Sedley Taylor. And yet those relations contain all that is essential to the determination of value.

Let us now transport ourselves from Robinson's island bathed in light to the European middle ages shrouded in darkness. Here, instead of the independent man, we find everyone dependent, serfs and lords, vassals and suzerains, laymen and clergy. Personal dependence here characterises the social relations of production just as much as it does the other spheres of life organized on the basis of that production. But for the very reason that personal dependence forms the groundwork of society, there is no necessity for labour and its products to assume a fantastic form different from their reality. They take the shape, in the transactions of society, of services in kind and payments in kind. Here the particular and natural form of labour, and not, as in a society based on production of commodities, its general abstract form is the immediate social form of labour. Compulsory labour is just as properly measured by time, as commodity-producing labour; but every serf knows that what he expends in the service of his lord, is a definite quantity of his own personal labour-power. The tithe to be rendered to the priest is more matter of fact than his blessing. No matter, then, what we may think of the parts played by the different classes of people themselves in this society, the social relations between individuals in the performance of their labour, appear at all events as their own mutual personal relations, and are not disguised under the shape of social relations between the products of labour.

For an example of labour in common or directly associated labour, we have no occasion to go back to that spontaneously developed form which we find on the threshold of the history of all civilized races. We have one close at hand in the patriarchal industries of a peasant family, that produces corn, cattle, yarn, linen, and clothing for home use. These different articles are, as regards the family, so many products of its labour, but as between themselves, they are not commodities. The

The Juan Fernandez Islands off the coast of Chile is the presumed location of the events that inspired Defoe's novel, Robinson Crusoe.

different kinds of labour, such as tillage, cattle tending, spinning, weaving and making clothes, which result in the various products, are in themselves, and such as they are, direct social functions, because functions of the family, which just as much as a society based on the production of commodities, possesses a spontaneously developed system of division of labour. The distribution of the work within the family, and the regulation of the labour-time of the several members, depend as well upon differences of age and sex as upon natural conditions varying with the seasons. The labour-power of each individual, by its very nature, operates in this case merely as a definite portion of the whole labour-power of the family, and therefore, the measure of the expenditure of individual labour-power by its duration, appears here by its very nature as a social character of their labour.

Let us now picture to ourselves, by way of change, a community of free individuals, carrying on their work with the means of production in common, in which the labour-power of all the different individuals is consciously applied as the combined labour-power of the community. All the characteristics of Robinson's labour are here repeated, but with this difference, that they are social, instead of individual. Everything pro-

duced by him was exclusively the result of his own personal labour, and therefore simply an object of use for himself. The total product of our community is a social product. One portion serves as fresh means of production and remains social. But another portion is consumed by the members as means of subsistence. A distribution of this portion amongst them is consequently necessary. The mode of this distribution will vary with the productive organization of the community, and the degree of historical development attained by the producers. We will assume, but merely for the sake of a parallel with the production of commodities, that the share of each individual producer in the means of subsistence is determined by his labour-time. Labour-time would, in that case, play a double part. Its apportionment in accordance with a definite social plan maintains the proper proportion between the different kinds of work to be done and the various wants of the community. On the other hand, it also serves as a measure of the portion of the common labour borne by each individual and of his share in the part of the total product destined for individual consumption. The social relations of the individual producers, with regard both to their labour and to its products, are in this case perfectly simple and intelligible, and that with regard not only to production but also to distribution.

Raymond F. Howes

SOURCE: "'Robinson Crusoe': A Literary Accident," in *The English Journal,* Vol. XVI, No. 1, January, 1927, pp. 31-5.

Professor Trent, in his *Defoe—How to Know Him,* bewails the fact that to the ordinary mortal the author of **Robinson Crusoe** is known as precisely that and nothing more. That book, says Trent, "while it has made Defoe's name famous, has also, if one may so phrase it, given occasion to weak and lazy mortals to pigeonhole that name." He thereupon lauds this eighteenth-century writer as one of the most prolific and versatile that ever lived.

Perhaps it is natural for a student of Defoe to magnify his accomplishments and minimize his defects. But the question remains: Does the fact that this author wrote much on many subjects entitle him to be called a "titanic genius"? After all, is not the ability to write a few things with consummate artistry more valuable than the power to write a multitude of things hurriedly? May not the world be right in regarding Defoe merely in the light of his masterpiece?

Perhaps we may challenge the statement that Defoe was a great genius still further if we can show that **Robinson Crusoe** itself, that book which has thrilled millions through the ages, that masterpiece on which the fame of its author rests, was partly, at least, the product of circumstances, not a brain-child that sprang full-grown from the head of a literary master. There is little honor, it is true, in trying to undermine an author's reputation, yet there is an undeniable thrill in sticking a pin into what one considers an unduly inflated bubble, even if the bubble in question prove to be solid instead of empty, as at first supposed.

In the first place, the theme of the story was not of Defoe's invention. It is generally recognized that the idea for the narrative was hit upon by chance and developed because it happened to be one in which the public was interested. If Alexander Selkirk had not astonished the world at that particular period by remaining for several months on a desert island without dying or becoming insane, **Robinson Crusoe** would never have been written.

It is true, of course, that the material for the book came largely from Defoe's experience. But Defoe wrote many other stories embellished with accounts of his thrilling adventures, and none have excited even a passing interest except from a comparatively small number of scholars.

Why, then, did this particular story have such a powerful appeal? Why has it lived while other works by Defoe have died? One reason is that it shows, with great simplicity, the struggle of man versus environment. A legion of great novelists have treated some aspect of this them. Dickens wrote of the trials of England's poor; Conrad wrote of civilized men thrown into an uncivilized environment; Hardy personifies environment, and lets his characters fight hopelessly against it; and even such a literary nobody as Horatio Alger sold thousands of trashy volumes because his heroes invariably triumphed over adversity. Hence we find Defoe with a theme of universal appeal thrust upon him. And not only that but the treatment of the theme in the story of an isolated individual was manifestly easier than the complicated technique required when the hero of a story is involved in the tangled affairs of a civilized community. There was little difficulty ahead in working out the plot; all that was necessary was sufficient knowledge of practical expedients to keep the shipwrecked man alive, a knowledge which Defoe fortunately had.

Walter John De La Mare

SOURCE: In *Desert Islands and Robinson Crusoe,* Faber and Faber Limited, 1930, pp. 37-61.

The spell of [Defoe's] enchanting masterpiece is not, of course, mere romance, but the dressing-up of romance to make it look like matter-of-fact. Defoe's passion as a writer of fiction was this craving to mimic life itself, and, in his later books, preferably its wrong and seamy side—a literary craving that is not inactive in our own enlightened day. The comment is hackneyed enough but worth repeating, if only as a reminder, first, that Defoe largely originated the method, though most of the old broadsides and chapbooks were of the same complexion; next, that he was, in much, the first English novelist; and last, that the craft and art of fiction are far from consisting in this alone. Still, in this close lively likeness to actuality Defoe hardly falls short of Pepys and Boswell; and all seems so easy and so natural that one is aware neither of the difficulty nor the skill. . . .

[I]n that 'drab', surprising, go-as-you-please entrancing prose of his, 'everywhere beautiful, but plain and homely'—we too become a kind of second-self. We are cut off completely from the actuality—the chairs, the tables, the walls and the world around us. We see with Crusoe's eyes, hear with his ears, feel in the heat of tropic sunlight the cool air 'whistling under our shirt'. Shut up as it were in one of those matter-of-fact dreams in which we are spectators of our own actions and with no possibility of interruption from within or without, we read on and on and on—hardly conscious either of the book in our hands or of the eyes in our heads. It is as if one had chanced on the story of one's own life, but a life how marvellously renewed, and of how guileless a career. For 'Thou art the man', Crusoe cries on his reader. We can but listen then like a three years' child; the mariner hath his will. . . .

Here to the full is Defoe's compassion for the outcast, the unfortunate, the suddenly abased, the simple and the misled; even though it is seen only in glimpses and is often elsewhere concealed or stifled by the haste and worldliness of the practical man, by that cold and weary indifference which horrified the creator, and destroyer, of Little Nell. And here, also, are seen Defoe's absorption in every aspect of human malady, his delight in the marvellous, his love of detail, his passion for deception, his trade instincts, his social inclinations, and his sense of citizenship.

In his *Crusoe* youth itself swept back into a mind jaded and harassed by years of journalism and politics, and Defoe drank deep of romance at an age when most of us have completely finished with it. When joy and grace appear in his work they are from this well-spring. . . .

According as Crusoe's fortunes set, we are dejected, exalted, horrified, unutterably grateful. We watch his grain in its first green blade, tremble at the footprint, garner his raisins, milk his goats, and all but cry aloud to him in warning when he is in danger. We revel in a reiterated, 'I told you so!'. We sit with heart drawn tight watching fate's insidious perfidies—the ravaged grapes, the prolific cats, the noble hapless venture out to sea, the immovable roll of sheet lead, which we modestly and vaguely surmise Robinson *might* have thought to hack into strips, the sea-caked barrel of powder.

On our own unworthy heads fall the blissful and sometimes even superfluous benefactions of that 'Superior Power' which not even the most impious of Defoe's adventurers ever really questioned—the complete magazine of muskets, the few grains of barley spared by the rats, the sleep of the mutineers; the Cavalier's saddle stuffed with gold, or Jack's hollow tree in the lonely field beyond the *Blind Beggars* at Bethnal Green.

How still and clear that island of Crusoe's is, how near and small. An ample sky must arch it over though we seldom lift our eyes to it. At echo of gun a crying host of birds flies up; then quiet descends again. The sea stretches around us in its concave immensity, and it is with a shocked astonishment that we realize the continent of America is in sight from the hill-top. No, not the continent; only the islands about the mouth of the Oroonoque. But we thought we were alone.

We hearken on and on to winds that toss the leaves in woods of Crusoe's planting and to the crash of breaker; we watch those lights of night and daybreak, tremble at the vast roar of his tropical rains, and start as though transfixed at the voice of the friendly ghost that sups with him, and calls out upon him from the horny bill of his parrot—'Robin, Robin, Robin Crusoe, poor Robin Crusoe! Where are you? Where have you been?'

What wonder such a book as this has been not only translated into every civilized, and into most barbarous languages, but has been brazenly imitated on and on, and bids fair to remain a literary incentive until time is no more. Within a year of its publication it was put into French, and in less than a century into Arabic. In Germany alone 'some fifty' *Robinsonaden* appeared in the nineteenth century. . . .

Nevertheless for those not exclusively intent on life's subtleties Defoe's book never fails to reward even the

most casual of visits. Like honest bread and cheese it will satisfy a natural hunger when richer and rarer kick-shaws may fail to titillate or cheer. His derelict sailor is as original as his name, and he left his theme unexhausted and inexhaustible. 'He is read', says one of his most sympathetic critics, 'by schoolboys and kitchenmaids, by sailors.' Not an exacting circle, at least on the positive side. And yet surely one's mind and taste must have become a little surfeited or belletristic or too, too fastidious, if—when the occasion offers—one cannot be content to shut out even the greatest awhile and all the Muses, and hobnob with Jack in *The Blind Beggars* at Bethnal Green, or with Crusoe and Singleton dare the high seas, bound for Friday, or the sources of the Nile.

And does not a voice out of 'the little nowhere of the mind' astonish every one of us at times with its insistent—'Robin Crusoe! Robin Crusoe! Poor Robin Crusoe! Where are you? Where have you been?' Indeed an hour will come, as it came to Defoe himself in Ropemaker's Alley, on April 26th, 1731, when, braving disaster, we shall be compelled, whether we will or not, to follow it into the unknown, and on the wings of the imagination flee away towards Ultima Thule, skirting latitudes even remoter than that of 9 degrees 22 minutes north of the line.

Anne Thaxter Eaton

SOURCE: "You'll Find that Reading's Very Nice," in *Reading With Children,* The Viking Press, 1940, pp. 11-23.

Robinson Crusoe was written "for fun," in the sense that Daniel Defoe had a story that he wanted to tell. He thought he was writing it for adults, but just as children have shared Lewis Carroll's two Alice books with grown-ups, so *Robinson Crusoe* has become the property of adventure-loving boys and girls.

Paul Hazard

SOURCE: "The Lineage of Children's Literature," in *The Unreluctant Years: A Critical Approach to Children's Literature,* by Lillian H. Smith, American Library Association, 1953, pp. 20-32.

[*Hazard's commentary is taken from* Books, Children, and Men, *1944.*]

What is there so surprising in their seizing upon *Robinson Crusoe,* if they find it to be a story of constructive ingenuity and energy? They also start out in life rather fearful. Like their great shipwrecked friend, they find themselves tossed onto an unknown land whose limits they will never know except by slow exploration. Like him, they are afraid of the darkness that falls. Night arrives and closes them in. Who knows if the sun will appear again tomorrow? They have everything to fear, beginning with hunger, with cold. Little by little they gain poise, are reassured, and begin to live on their own account. Just as Robinson does when he starts out to reconstruct his life.

Elizabeth Rider Montgomery

SOURCE: "The Two Castaways," in *The Story Behind Great Books,* Dodd Mead & Company, 1946, pp. 19-22.

A bearded man, clad in animal skins, kneels on the beach, looking at a footprint. Just an ordinary print of a man's bare foot, yet the sight of it fills the watcher with amazement, delight, and even fear, because for years he has believed himself to be the only human being on the entire island. Whose footprint can it be? It may be friend or foe. He may have a companion in his lonely exile—or he may be forced to fight for his life.

Of course, you know that the solitary man is Robinson Crusoe. The story, *Robinson Crusoe,* has been a classic for so long that the very names of the characters have become a part of our language. Everyone knows what you mean when you speak of someone's "Man Friday" or when a person is called a "modern Crusoe."

Though the story reads like a true account and is completely convincing, we know that *Robinson Crusoe* is fiction, not fact. We, today, are accustomed to fiction which is as believable as fact. But when the book was published, its readers at first accepted it as literally true, because up to that time fiction had been *obviously* fiction. Except for romances of chivalry and fairy tales, fiction was non-existent. There was no such thing as an imaginary story written in a convincing and credible style. Defoe was a pioneer in that line of writing. . . .

As his tale developed, Robinson Crusoe and his island came to be so real to Defoe that it seemed as if he was, indeed, telling a true story. It seemed as if he, himself, were Robinson Crusoe. By the time he had finished writing the book, he almost believed that he had really been shipwrecked just as he told it, and had lived on that island exactly as he described, pitting his wits against the forces of nature.

When the story was finished, Defoe tried to get it published. But it was an entirely new type of book for that day. Prose fiction was something strange and daring. Publishers hesitated to risk it. At last Defoe found one who agreed to take a chance, and *The Life and Strange Surprising Adventures of Robinson Crusoe, of York, Mariner, Written by Himself,* was published in 1719.

The book was an instant success. Everybody ready it, enjoyed it, almost believed it. And everybody has been reading, enjoying, and almost believing it ever since. The fictional story of an imaginary castaway is known the world over, while the true story of [Alexander] Selkirk, who was a real castaway, is practically unknown today.

Ian Watt

SOURCE: "'Robinson Crusoe' as a Myth," in *Essays in Criticism: A Quarterly Journal of Literary Criticism,* Vol. 1, No. 2, April, 1951, pp. 95-117.

We do not usually think of *Robinson Crusoe* as a novel. Defoe's first full-length work of fiction seems to fall more naturally into place with *Faust, Don Juan* and *Don Quixote,* the great myths of our civilization. What these myths are about it is fairly easy to say. Their basic plots, their enduring images, all exhibit a single-minded pursuit by the protagonist of one of the characteristic aspirations of Western man. Each of their heroes embodies an *arete* and a *hubris,* an exceptional prowess and a vitiating excess, in spheres of action that are peculiarly important in our culture. Don Quixote, the impetuous generosity and the limiting blindness of chivalric idealism; Don Juan, pursuing and at the same time tormented by the idea of boundless experience of women; Faustus, the great knower, his curiosity always unsatisfied, and therefore damned.

Crusoe does not at first seem a likely companion for these other culture-heroes. They lose the world for an idea; he for gain. Their aspirations are conscious, and defiant, so that when retribution comes it is half expected and already understood; whereas Robinson Crusoe disclaims either heroism or pride; he stolidly insists that he is no more than he seems, that you would do it too in the circumstances.

Yet of his apotheosis there can be no doubt. By the end of the nineteenth century, there had appeared at least 700 editions, translations and imitations, not to mention a popular eighteenth-century pantomime, and an opera by Offenbach. There are other more picturesque examples of his fame. In 1848, an enterprising French industrialist started a restaurant up a tree, a particularly fine chestnut in a wood near Paris; he called it 'Robinson', and now restaurateurs vie for the title in a village of that name. And 'un robinson' has become a popular term for a large umbrella.

Nor, as Virginia Woolf has pointed out, is he usually thought of as a hero of fiction. Instead, partly because of Defoe's verisimilitude and partly for deeper reasons, his author's name has been forgotten, while he himself has acquired a kind of semi-historical status, like the traditional heroes of myth. When his story appeared it is reported to have been 'universally received and credited as a genuine history'; and we today can surely apply to it Malinowski's description of primitive myths. 'It is not of the nature of fiction, such as we read today in a novel, but it is a living reality, believed to have once happened in primeval times, and continuing ever since to influence the world and human destinies.'

Almost universally known, almost universally thought of as at least half real, he cannot be refused the status of myth. But the myth of what? . . .

Percy Muir

SOURCE: "'Adopted' Books," in *English Children's Books 1600-1990*, B. T. Batsford Ltd., 1954, pp. 40-4.

The desert-island theme was a sure-fire winner. Its popularity is not yet exhausted, although in a world of such shrunken dimensions as ours, in which, nevertheless, everything must be always bigger and better than before, the modern castaway must be wrecked on a planet, his vessel a space-ship. But it is all basically Defoe, hotted up, if not necessarily improved. It is amusing to note, in passing, that a French translator, in 1721, added a section to the story in which Crusoe is given a "vision du Monde Angélique", to which the illustrator, possibly Picart, responded with a frontispiece of the hero, his redingote and tricorne hat not in the least disturbed by his passage through the solar system, well on his way to Saturn.

Adaptations of the Crusoe story in every modern language are virtually countless. J. H. Campe, a German author, was the first to adapt the story, and his *Robinson der Jüngere* was published at Hamburg in two volumes in 1779-80. The author himself translated it into English and French; but the best English edition was Stockdale's in four volumes, 1788, with cuts by John Bewick, Thomas's less famous, but greatly gifted, younger brother.

The *Swiss Family Robinson* in its modern form is a composite work. Originally conceived by the Swiss Lutheran pastor, J. H. Wyss, and published in 1812-13, it was first translated into English in 1814, probably by William Godwin, who also published it. In 1814 and 1824-26 also, Madame de Montolieu, the translator of Jane Austen, produced a French version, in which she added further incidents and characters of her own devising, notably the donkey, with the rather contemptuous consent of Wyss himself. W. H. G. Kingston enlarged it still further.

There have been boy Crusoes, girl Crusoes, arctic Crusoes, and even a dog Crusoe. Indeed the *Robinsonnade* became a world phenomenon, and the writer of a preface to one of them puts it very effectively when he says: "The word Robinson has for some time replaced for us Germans the French word *aventurier*. It describes for us a creature for whom the world holds an infinity of possibilities, fortunate and unfortunate."

Walter Allen

SOURCE: "Daniel Defoe," in *Six Great Novelists: Defoe, Fielding, Scott, Dickens, Stevenson, Conrad*, Hamish Hamilton, 1955, pp. 9-37.

[I]t is enough that it was from [Alexander] Selkirk that Defoe got the germ of the part we always remember of *Robinson Crusoe*, a book which deals, as we sometimes forget, with its hero's 'life and strange surprizing adventures' as a whole and not with his experiences as a castaway alone.

It is the latter, however, that has captured the imagination of the world. It has done so in the first place because, as Coleridge said, Crusoe is the 'universal representative, the person, for whom every reader could substitute himself . . . Nothing is done, thought, suffered, or desired, but what every man could imagine himself doing, thinking, feeling, or wishing for.' We normally think now, partly as a result of *Robinson Crusoe,* of uninhabited tropical islands as romantic places. But Crusoe does not see his island as romantic. For him it represents a situation in which he must either endure or go under, a desperate situation in which he can prevail only with the aid of good luck and his native wit and ingenuity. On his island Crusoe is man against nature. He triumphs, and the triumph is heroic because of the very matter-of-factness with which he sets out to fight nature. Crusoe is the unheroic hero, and this makes him all the more acceptable to us; his ordinariness brings what he does, heroic though it is, down to the level of what any of us might be capable of in similar circumstances. Or so we feel. As Coleridge points out, in what he does, Crusoe arrives at no excellence. He is content in the end to have made a serviceable pot—and how long it took him; how many botchings were necessary before he could achieve even that!

But there is another, and deeper, reason for the enduring fascination of the book, one that we miss when we read it first as children but that strikes home to us with tremendous force when we take it up again later in life. Quite simply, Defoe was right when he claimed that *Robinson Crusoe* was an allegory; but it is an allegory not only of his own life but of every man's. In the last analysis, we are each of us alone, condemned to solitariness. We manage most of the time to forget this is so, but it is the fundamental condition, the realization of which we can never escape entirely, and which we discover anew in our moments of most intense experience. This condition Defoe symbolizes in the sharpest possible way when he sets Crusoe down on his island, alone, with himself, and with God. *Robinson Crusoe,* then, is a dramatization of universal experience: we are all Crusoes, for to be Crusoe is the human fate.

Books do not achieve universality, though, merely because of their themes. The greatest subject will count for nothing if it is poorly expressed or, in the case of a work of fiction, inadequately or unconvincingly embodied in the lives of its characters. Imagination, in other words, must be matched with a technique as powerful. For what he wanted to do, Defoe's technique was unrivalled. In *Robinson Crusoe* he has somehow to persuade us that the impossible is in fact not merely possible but actually happens. Crusoe is on his island twenty-eight years, two months and nineteen days. The very exactness is a clue to Defoe's method. He is the master of the literal. His illusion of complete reality is obtained by his employing, all the time and as a matter of course, a mass of detail, of circumstantial evidence of a kind we feel no one would bother to invent. Whatever happens to Crusoe, whatever Crusoe does, Defoe describes, and describes in minute particulars, so that it seems impossible that he is not describing what he has experienced at first hand.

Lillian H. Smith

SOURCE: "An Approach to Criticism of Children's Literature," in *Children and Literature: Views and Reviews,* by Virginia Haviland, Lothrop, Lee & Shepard Co., 1956, pp. 395-96.

The success of *Robinson Crusoe* . . . revealed that the subject matter of shipwreck on a desert island was one of great interest to the reading public, especially to children. A host of imitators seized on the idea and stories of castaways appeared in great numbers. Most of these have fallen by the wayside and passed into oblivion, while *Robinson Crusoe,* after over two centuries, continues to be "the best desert island story ever written." Defoe created in *Robinson Crusoe* a fundamental and universal conception which his imitators never achieved.

Ian Watt

SOURCE: "'Robinson Crusoe,' Individualism and the Novel," in *The Rise of the Novel: Studies in Defoe, Richardson and Fielding,* University of California Press, 1967, pp. 60-92.

[Watt's essay was originally printed in 1957.]

We have until now been primarily concerned with the light which Defoe's first work of fiction sheds on the nature of the connections between economic and religious individualism and the rise of the novel; but since the primary reason for our interest in *Robinson Crusoe* is its literary greatness, the relation between that greatness and the way it reflects the deepest aspirations and dilemmas of individualism also requires brief consideration.

Robinson Crusoe falls most naturally into place, not with other novels, but with the great myths of Western civilisation. . . . [Crusoe] has an exceptional prowess; he can manage quite on his own. And he has an excess: his inordinate egocentricity condemns him to isolation wherever he is.

The egocentricity, one might say, is forced on him, because he is cast away on an island. But it is also true that his character is throughout courting its fate and it merely happens that the island offers the fullest opportunity for him to realise three associated tendencies of modern civilisation—absolute economic, social and intellectual freedom for the individual.

It was Crusoe's realisation of intellectual freedom which made Rousseau propose the book as 'the one book that teaches all that books can teach' for the education of Émile; he argued that 'the surest way to raise oneself above prejudices, and order one's judgement on the real relationship between things, is to put oneself in the place of an isolated man, and to judge of everything as that man would judge of them according to their actual usefulness.'

On his island Crusoe also enjoys the absolute freedom from social restrictions for which Rousseau yearned—there are no family ties or civil authorities to interfere with his individual autonomy. Even when he is no longer alone his personal autarchy remains—indeed it is increased: the parrot cries out his master's name, unprompted Friday swears to be his slave for ever; Crusoe toys with the fancy that he is an absolute monarch; and one of his visitors even wonders if he is a god.

Lastly, Crusoe's island gives him the complete *laissez-faire* which economic man needs to realise his aims. At home market conditions, taxation and problems of the labour supply make it impossible for the individual to control every aspect of production, distribution and exchange. The conclusion is obvious. Follow the call of the wide open places, discover an island that is desert only because it is barren of owners or competitors, and there build your personal Empire with the help of a Man Friday who needs no wages and makes it much easier to support the white man's burden.

Such is the positive and prophetic side of Defoe's story, the side which makes Crusoe an inspiration to economists and educators, and a symbol both for the displaced persons of urban capitalism, such as Rousseau, and for its more practical heroes, the empire builders. Crusoe realises all these ideal freedoms, and in doing so he is undoubtedly a distinctively modern culture-hero. Aristotle, for example, who thought that the man 'who is unable to live in society, or who has no need because he is sufficient for himself, must be either a beast or a god', would surely have found Crusoe a very strange hero. Perhaps with reason; for it is surely true that the ideal freedoms he achieves are both quite impracticable in the real world and in so far as they can be applied, disastrous for human happiness.

It may be objected that Robinson Crusoe's achievements are credible and wholly convincing. This is so, but only because in his narrative—perhaps as an unconscious victim of what Karl Mannheim has called the 'Utopian mentality' which is dominated by its will to action and consequently 'turns its back on everything which would shake its belief'—Defoe disregarded two important facts: the social nature of all human economies, and the actual psychological effects of solitude.

The basis for Robinson Crusoe's prosperity, of course, is the original stock of tools which he loots from the shipwreck; they comprise, we are told, 'the biggest magazine of all kinds . . . that was ever laid up for one man'. So Defoe's hero is not really a primitive nor a proletarian but a capitalist. In the island he owns the freehold of a rich though unimproved estate. Its possession, combined with the stock from the ship, are the miracles which fortify the faith of the supporters of the new economic creed. But only that of the true believers: to the sceptic the classic idyll of free enterprise does not in fact sustain the view that anyone has ever attained comfort and security only by his own efforts. Crusoe is in fact the lucky heir to the labours of countless other individuals; his solitude is the measure, and the price of his luck, since it involves the fortunate decease of all the other potential stockholders; and the shipwreck, far from being a tragic peripety, is the *deus ex machina* which makes it possible for Defoe to present solitary labour, not as an alternative to a death sentence, but as a solution to the perplexities of economic and social reality.

The psychological objection to *Robinson Crusoe* as a pattern of action is also obvious. Just as society has made every individual what he is, so the prolonged lack of society actually tends to make the individual relapse into a straightened primitivism of thought and feeling. In Defoe's sources for *Robinson Crusoe* what actually happened to the castaways was at best uninspiring. At worst, harassed by fear and dogged by ecological degradation, they sank more and more to the level of animals, lost the use of speech, went mad, or died of inanition. One book which Defoe had almost certainly read, *The Voyages and Travels of J. Albert de Mandelslo,* tells of two such cases; of a Frenchman who, after only two years of solitude on Mauritius, tore his clothing to pieces in a fit of madness brought on by a diet of raw tortoise; and of a Dutch seaman on St. Helena who disinterred the body of a buried comrade and set out to sea in the coffin.

These realities of absolute solitude were in keeping with the traditional view of its effects, as expressed by Dr. Johnson: the 'solitary mortal', he averred, was 'certainly luxurious, probably superstitious, and possibly mad: the mind stagnates for want of employment; grows morbid, and is extinguished like a candle in foul air'.

In the story just the opposite happens: Crusoe turns his forsaken estate into a triumph. Defoe departs from psychological probability in order to redeem his picture of man's inexorable solitariness, and it is for this reason that he appeals very strongly to all who feel isolated—and who at times does not? An inner voice continually suggests to us that the human isolation which individualism has fostered is painful and tends ultimately to a life of apathetic animality and mental derangement; Defoe answers confidently that it can be made the arduous prelude to the fuller realisation of every individual's potentialities; and the solitary readers of two centuries of individualism cannot but applaud so convincing an example of making a virtue out of a necessity, so cheering a colouring to that universal image of individualist experience, solitude. . . .

'We covet, we enjoy, all in privacy and solitude': what really occupies man is something that makes him solitary wherever he is, and too aware of the interested nature of any relationship with other human beings to find any consolation there. 'All that we communicate . . . to any other is but for their assistance in the pursuit of our desires': a rationally conceived self-interest makes a mockery of speech; and the scene of Crusoe's silent life is not least a Utopia because its functional silence, broken only by an occasional 'Poor Robinson Crusoe' from the parrot, does not impose

upon man's ontological egocentricity the need to assume a false façade of social intercourse, or to indulge in the mockery of communication with his fellows.

Robinson Crusoe, then, presents a monitory image of the ultimate consequences of absolute individualism. But this tendency, like all extreme tendencies, soon provoked a reaction. As soon as man's aloneness was forced on the attention of mankind, the close and complex nature of the individual's dependence on society, which had been taken for granted until it was challenged by individualism, began to receive much more detailed analysis. Man's essentially social nature, for instance, became one of the main topics of the eighteenth-century philosophers. . . .

Just as the modern study of society only began once individualism had focused attention on man's apparent disjunctions from his fellows, so the novel could only begin its study of personal relationships once *Robinson Crusoe* had revealed a solitude that cried aloud for them. Defoe's story is perhaps not a novel in the usual sense since it deals so little with personal relations. But it is appropriate that the tradition of the novel should begin with a work that annihilated the relationships of the traditional social order, and thus drew attention to the opportunity and the need of building up a network of personal relationships on a new and conscious pattern; the terms of the problem of the novel and of modern thought alike were established when the old order of moral and social relationships was shipwrecked, with Robinson Crusoe, by the rising tide of individualism.

John Robert Moore

SOURCE: "Robinson Crusoe," in *Robinson Crusoe: An Authoritative Text, Backgrounds and Sources, Criticism,* edited by Michael Shinagel, W. W. Norton & Company, 1975, pp. 335-42.

[*The following excerpt was first published in* Daniel Defoe: Citizen of the Modern World, *1958.*]

The most significant date in Defoe's literary career was April 25, 1719, when the first volume of *Robinson Crusoe* was published. Before that there was no English novel worth the name, and no book (except the Bible) widely accepted among all classes of English and Scottish readers. *The Pilgrim's Progress* had many elements of great fiction; but it was intended as a work of religious instruction, it was meant for humble readers, and for a century it was despised by literary critics.

The impact of *Robinson Crusoe* was greater, and in some ways quite different. There were doubts about whether it was a genuine travel book, a fraudulent travel book, or a legitimate work of fiction, so that Defoe resorted to improvisations and equivocations to evade questions about its truth to fact. But the esteem in which it was held in the literary world is shown by the praise it received from Alexander Pope, by its immense influence on *Gulliver's Travels,* and by Dr. Johnson's including it as one of the three books by mere man which anyone would wish longer. Its popularity among the lowest classes of readers was a source of jealousy which sought relief in a pretense of scorn: "there is not an old woman that can go to the price of it, but buys thy *Life and Adventures,* and leaves it as a legacy, with *The Pilgrim's Progress, The Practice of Piety,* and *God's Revenge against Murther,* to her posterity." For *Robinson Crusoe* not only created a new literary form; it created a new reading public.

Because of its popularity among the semiliterate, there was a chance that it might sink to the level of the little chapbooks sold by itinerant peddlers. The Rev. James Woodforde purchased it with a life of a gypsy, *The Complete Fortune Teller,* and *Laugh and Grow Fat,* from "a traveling man and woman who sold all kinds of trifling books, &c." However, in 1806 the Rev. Mark Noble, hostile to Defoe as a Dissenter, admitted its almost universal acclaim: "I have never known but one person of sense who disliked it. Rousseau, and after him all France, applauded it."

Harvey Swados

SOURCE: "Robinson Crusoe—The Man Alone," in *The Antioch Review,* Vol. XVIII, No. 1, March, 1958, pp. 25-40.

[*The following excerpt is from* Daniel Defoe: Citizen of the Modern World, *1958.*]

Tough-minded journalist that he was, Daniel Defoe would have blanched if he had known that future generations would classify him snugly as the Father of the Novel. Indeed it was precisely in his greatest works of fiction that he was at pains—because the temper of his time demanded it—to claim that he was only setting down the unvarnished facts, and that he had no intention of concocting romances or other questionable works of the imagination. But if this is a historical oddity it is hardly the most remarkable paradox psychologically of this complicated man: one must be particularly struck by the disparity between the materials he sought out so methodically and the literary uses to which he put them. This disparity is most intriguing in the case of *Robinson Crusoe;* an examination of it may perhaps reveal to us a little more, not just about the personality of Defoe, but about the vaster problem of human loneliness, which spreads like a stain as more and more of us are pressed closer and closer together.

In the spring of 1944 I was cycling along the North Sea coast with several companions, equipped with neither map nor guidebooks, only with a turkey and other picnic necessities borrowed from the merchant ship on which we were employed. One of the most pleasant occurrences of that delightful day in peaceful County Fife was our sudden discovery of a statue about the size of a cigar-store Indian standing forthrightly on the front lawn of a

modest row house in the town of Largo. There was barely room for the statue, and when we saw that it had been erected in memory of Alexander Selkirk, we nodded wisely, exchanged some comments about *Robinson Crusoe,* and continued on our way.

But that statue remained in a corner of my mind, obstinately, as such things will. The world is full of statues of all sorts, and I have stared at my share: statues of authors and statues of their creations, statues of Montaigne and Balzac in Paris and of Tom Sawyer and Huck Finn in Hannibal. But I am not aware of many statues erected to the memory of those who have inspired the authors of great works, or who have served as the models for their characters. Is there a statue of Gogarty in Dublin, of Mrs. Wolfe in Asheville, of Thalberg in Hollywood, or of that little piece of Madeleine in Paris?

I knew rather vaguely, I suppose, that Alexander Selkirk had been a seafaring man, that he had been shipwrecked for a time, and that Defoe had somehow made use of his adventure, but it was not until, browsing through Walter Wilson's rambling three volume *Life and Times of Defoe* (1830), I came upon a hair-raising footnote, that I began to sense what kind of fellow Selkirk had been. After he was rescued from his desert island, he returned in 1712 to Largo. There, says Wilson casually, "His parents, who were still living, received him with joy; but his recluse habits induced him to shun the haunts of men, and he constructed a cave in their garden, where he sought repose in solitude. . . . "

The fact is that, far from having been shipwrecked, he had had himself put ashore on a desolate island at his own request—and there he remained alone for four and a half years before being taken off and returned to happy little Largo, his parents' garden, and the cave which he hastened to dig. This voluntary commitment has been amply commented on (although I don't think it has been interpreted quite as I interpret it), but I am unaware that any modern writer has so much as mentioned the cave in the garden, with the exception of Walter De La Mare, in his wonderfully engaging *Desert Islands.* . . .

After eight long months of melancholy and horror, in which he was "scarce able to refrain from doing himself violence," he vanquished his blues, as De La Mare puts it, and set to work. He burned all-spice wood, fed on fish, turnips and goats' meat, and came gradually to cope creatively with life on Mas-a-tierra. He had a couple of narrow escapes, once from a fall of a hundred feet, another time from marauding Spaniards, and when his ammunition ran out he raced barefoot after the island's goats and their kids, capturing and killing no less than five hundred of them.

On the 31st of January, 1709, he was picked up, scarcely articulate but otherwise healthy, by two more marauding ships, the *Duke* and the *Duchess,* on one of which was no other than Dampier. Selkirk was made mate of the *Duke,* and subsequently master of one which the marauders captured, and returned home with about eight hundred pounds of prize money, or plunder. As De La Mare notes, this "prince and prototype of all cast-aways" was "not so happy, he said, as when he hadn't a farthing." Selkirk enjoyed considerable notoriety after his return to England in October of 1711. He was interviewed by Richard Steele, was made the subject of a paper in *The Englishman,* and had several narratives of his life written, as well as four published accounts of his adventures. . . .

Scholars are apparently still arguing as to whether Selkirk and Defoe actually met. Thomas Wright says categorically that Defoe "made a journey from London to Bristol apparently for the express purpose of seeing" Selkirk at the house of a Mrs. Damaris Daniel, and that Selkirk "placed in Defoe's hands all his papers." On the other hand, back in 1916 William P. Trent was arguing in his *Daniel Defoe* (an intelligent and enlightening book, but so steeped in the dying genteel tradition that its author could not bring himself to reproduce the full subtitle of *Moll Flanders,* much less to quote from it or to recommend it to general readers) that "the makers of myths have not hesitated to affirm that Defoe made use of the papers of the returned sailor—who has not been shown to have had any—and cheated him into the bargain. A meeting with Selkirk has also been affirmed by some, and the house where the supposed conference took place has been pointed out in Bristol."

Well, whatever the truth as to the possible encounter, we do know that Defoe was thoroughly up on the adventures of the Scottish sailor, that he was a careful researcher, and that in many, many of its details *Robinson Crusoe* does parallel Selkirk's story. I would prefer to think that they met, if only because I enjoy imagining the confrontation, in the comfortable home of the lady with the elegant name, of the dour adventurer and the dapper, elderly word-slinger; but I must admit that it really doesn't matter. What counts is that this profile-writer, who was in journalism for money as he had been in half a dozen other enterprises to support his wife and six children, from hosiery to jobbing to spying to editing, worked up yet another in his incredible series of true-life romances, with no other purpose than to pick up some quick cash, and that from his re-imagined version of the travail of the neurotic castaway came one of the great pure classical tales of all time. . . .

If we think of Daniel Defoe as a typical Englishman, a typical Londoner, perhaps a typical Cockney (he was even born within hearing of Bow Bells), and of his tale of a man on an island as a typical English novel, with its emphasis on factuality, fortitude, and optimistic common sense, we find that we are cheered on by English critics of all persuasions, from Sam Johnson to Virginia Woolf to V. S. Pritchett (let us except Macaulay, who said coldly of Defoe: "Altogether I don't like him"). Indeed, it is precisely those writers who one might think would harbor reservations about Defoe's genius who are most fervent in their adulation, who support most fervidly Daudet's estimation of Defoe as England's national author and Robinson Crusoe as "the typical Englishman par excellence, with his adventuresomeness, his taste for travel, his love of the sea, his piety, his commercial and practical instincts," and so on and so on. . . .

The real question, it may be argued, is why *Robinson Crusoe* has persisted in its popularity in the several hundred years since its first printing, down through a time when interest would seem more likely to center not on what this ingenious islander does with his goats and his salvaged tools, but rather on his dreams and nightmares, on what he substitutes for female companionship for more than twenty-eight years, and on the symbolic richness of his punishment and redemption. . . .

But now, in our own day, something does seem to be happening. The book which Maxim Gorky characterized apothegmatically as "The Bible of the Unconquerable" is being turned over to the kiddies. It is not being shared with them, like *Alice in Wonderland* or even *Huckleberry Finn;* in an age in which hillbillies gape at the Sadlers Wells Ballet on their barroom screens and intellectuals leaf desperately through their expensive paperbacks in search of entertainment which will not be entertaining, *Robinson Crusoe* does not seem to be often read by those past the age of confirmation. . . .

The reader who has been patient this long may now begin to suspect, with reason, that what I have been attempting to do is to push *Robinson Crusoe* for the adult trade. (Children have as yet no need to be so instructed—although even *that* audience is becoming so violently sophisticated that one may tremble for its future capacity to be enthralled by the doings of a single man, neither bubble-headed nor space-gunned, who teaches a parrot to talk and learns by trial and error how to bake bread and fire pottery.) To be sure, there are many ways of awakening, or re-awakening, reader interest in a classic work. We may rhapsodize over the plot, or story development, but only, it seems to me, if we can be reasonably certain—as in the case of a Portuguese or Tibetan classic—that it has remained generally unknown. We may linger admiringly over the author's periods and cherish the subtleties of his rhythmic ebbs and flows, but not, it seems to me, when the author wields the serviceable but uninspiring "prose of democracy." We may fall in with the current fad of playing locksmith, fumbling among the unwieldy bunch of keys that constitute our critical armory for the one that will magically unlock the work and reveal the symbolism presumably hidden within—but Thomas Wright, who maintained stoutly for years (basing himself on an offhand remark of Defoe's) that *Robinson Crusoe* was a deliberate allegory, a direct reflection of Defoe's own life, and that Defoe for nearly twenty-nine years had led a life of silence, was at length forced to admit that he had been the victim of his own theorizing; and I have no desire to lay the foundations for such a future admission.

We may finally—which is what I have attempted—look to see if, how, in what way, the passions and problems of the author have paralleled ours so many years later. If we then find Defoe to be contemporary—not in manner necessarily, nor even in outlook, but in *preoccupation*—then surely he merits pride of place alongside those in our time who have been preoccupied too with loneliness and isolation but who, much more torn than he with the agony of doubt, have hesitated to address themselves to the Unconquerable and so have become the tribunes of the Unsure.

Here, however, we enter other realms. I would not contest the obvious truth that *Robinson Crusoe* has been read over the years not primarily because of what it says, or omits, about loneliness, but because it appeals to the busy child in us all, because it is a practical and entertaining manual in the domestication of nature, and because it is a painless and un-frightening guide to the exotic. To the extent that it continues to be read, it can be seen as still providing the same kind of refreshment to the same kind of people. But I have been addressing myself in these lines I suppose to the Unsure, to those who increasingly attempt to distinguish themselves from the masses (among other ways) by ignoring escapist literature, even classical escapist literature, in favor of those books which do grapple with the problems of loneliness.

In the emerging mass society, the *angst* of the solitary intellectual is now being experienced, if confusedly, by ever-lengthening lines of bumper-to-bumper megalopolitans trained to dread nothing more fiercely than loneliness. Will *Robinson Crusoe,* with its cheery accent on the positive, still find acceptance among either the hypersophisticated or the great ordinary anonymous mass who have been its cherishers, as they have been the cherishers—at least until the coming of the mass society—of most great writings throughout the ages? One can only guess. It is entirely possible, for example, that it may be on the verge of yet a new wave of popularity for just these reasons, that now it will be read not as an epic of man's indomitability, but as a nostalgic revery of those old days when it was possible to conceive of the vanquishing of loneliness and the disappearance of doubts, when it was possible to conceive that by conquering nature you had conquered all.

Francis Watson

SOURCE: "Robinson Crusoe: An Englishman of the Age," in *History Today,* Vol. IX, No. 11, November, 1959, pp. 760-66.

For admirers in all countries—and Defoe's masterpiece has probably earned more translations than any other book except the Bible—the slightest excuse is good enough for going back to *Robinson Crusoe:* not perhaps to the *Farther Adventures* and the *Serious Reflections,* which are admittedly formidable, but at least to the full version of the *Life and Strange Surprising Adventures,* as the book first came from the printers in 1719. The tercentenary of the casting of Crusoe on his island on September 30th, 1659, offers a peculiarly apt excuse. Not only was Defoe himself much taken with the significance of dates and anniversaries; but the popular and enduring

inclination to accept Crusoe as a real, rather than an imaginary figure provides the final vindication of Defoe's craftsmanship. . . .

In 1898, at the Universal Exposition in Chicago, a Governor of Tobago sponsored the display of a model of Robinson Crusoe's cave, together with the skeleton of the old goat that he found dying there, and a cast of the immortal footprint in the sand. Crusoe's cave, ten miles west from Scarborough in Tobago, is listed today among the island's attractions, in defiance both of the claims put forward for other islands—including Juan Fernandez, nearly three thousand miles away—and of the book's title-page and text. Defoe's island had to be believed, not identified. That was a technical requirement for a book presented as a history of travel and adventure, in competition with the records of voyages that brought profit to booksellers during the early eighteenth century. It was, of course, many other things; and Charles Gildon's contemporary sneer at its immediate success suggests that it also found a place on the shelf of popular religion. But as a record, "written by himself," Robinson Crusoe's story contains an exact statement of the island's latitude—nine degrees and twenty-two minutes north of the Equator, and thus at least a hundred miles *south* of Tobago. . . .

What is the value, then—apart from the absorbing fun of the game—of research into *Robinson Crusoe*? The fact is that, the more that comes to light about Defoe, his motives and methods of writing, where he found his material and how he used it, the more interesting does he appear to the historian. Over the past thirty years, a vast amount of research has been devoted to "the great polygrapher," particularly by American scholars. William Minto's famous appraisal of Defoe, as "a great, a truly great liar," was made in 1879, and distorted echoes of it are heard even now.

Without much difficulty, we forget the moral. This is an adventure story; and there is testimony to its effectiveness in the biographies of many famous Englishmen. But, ostensibly, it attempts to *dissuade* headstrong young persons from leaving an assured security to seek a doubtful fortune. This may be no more than a stock device, just as Defoe's later description of *Robinson Crusoe* as a close allegory of the author's life, was a device intended to rebut the damaging charge of having written imaginative fiction. Yet, in effect, the contrary impulses achieve a kind of polarity. Behind it lie Defoe's own arguments with himself and with Providence. Crusoe's father, in a passage often quoted by social historians, sets out the advantages of "the middle station of life." No doubt Defoe's intention was serious; but he speaks no less clearly both in the prodigal and in the penitent. The values postulated may be class values; but the man groping among them is human. Even as we decide that the successful Brazil plantation represents what Defoe, "the typical Englishman of his day," was searching for, we hear Crusoe describing it as "an employment quite remote to my genius." It was the island that attracted him, and the hazards and hardships that he found there. Understandably so; for Robinson Crusoe is a true-born Englishman.

G. M. D. Henderson-Howat and Francis Watson

SOURCE: In "Letters to the Editors: *Robinson Crusoe,*" in *History Today,* Vol. X, No. 1, January, 1960, p. 51.

[*This exchange of letters from* History Today *was provoked by an article written by Francis Watson for that publication regarding a popular tourist attraction in Tobago known as "Robinson Crusoe's Cave."*]

GENTLEMEN,

The other evening I happened to be showing my son the family photograph album and, in particular, a snap of himself sitting inside Robinson Crusoe's cave in Tobago. It was an odd coincidence that brought *History Today* the next morning with Mr. Watson's most interesting article.

I recall a difficult and lengthy climb down to the cave with an infant on my back and, at the time, I went to some trouble to trace the origins of Tobago's claim. I write now without any notes or references to hand but, as I remember, the claim largely amounted to Defoe's having read and used the geographical descriptions of Tobago (including the cave) in a book recently published. If this was so, Tobago's claim to have provided the "setting" for the book seems justifiable. Perhaps Mr. Watson would be good enough to comment: I hope (as a professional historian) I have not been guilty of passing on error—even as a bedtime story.

> Yours, etc.,
> G. M. D. HENDERSON-HOWAT,
> *Kelly College, Tavistock, Devon.*

Mr. Francis Watson writes:

It seems very probable that Defoe, who read so much, knew the book by Capt. John Poyntz called *The Present Prospects of the Famous and Fertile Island of Tobago.* This was published in 1683—thirty-six years before **Robinson Crusoe**—and gives a fairly full description of the island, and recommends it as a little paradise for quiet retirement. There were other available sources, of course, for knowledge of Tobago, and Defoe's habit of talking to sea captains in waterfront inns must have given him much that research among print can never trace. There are correspondences with the Poyntz account which have encouraged the Tobago claimants, but Defoe must have known what he was doing when he established a different position by latitude and other observations. Whatever he took from Tobago (and from many other islands, including Ceylon) to build up his picture, he avoided the identification.

Bettina Hurlimann

SOURCE: "Robinson: Dreams and Educational Methods," in *Three Centuries of Children's Books in Europe,* translated and edited by Brian W. Alderson, Oxford University Press, 1967, pp. 99-112.

Title page for Defoe's Robinson Crusoe.

'Robinson Crusoe'—is there anyone whose heart is unmoved at the sound of that name? And when we consider that literate humanity has been moved by it for some 250 years we realize just how curious a phenomenon this is.

Defoe's **Robinson Crusoe** first appeared in 1719 as a serial publication and shortly afterwards as a book. It depicts in the form of a novel the life of a young man who is initially wicked, lazy, and disregardful of parental authority, but who is brought back to good fortune and godliness through enormous exertions, all very realistically described, and through twenty-eight years of loneliness. It is all too obviously a moral tale, but at the same time it is in its first part a lively portrayal of colonial trade in Africa and South America in the days when you could barter pocket-knives and coloured glass for gold, pearls, and slaves. The whole book bears the stamp of documentary exactitude, while remaining a novel of breathtaking tension. But is that sufficient to turn the book into one of the most popular of the eighteenth century and one of the greatest favourites among children's books of all time, even though one must bear in mind that Defoe was the first truly significant English novelist and, at the same time, was to become through *Robinson* the founder of an international literary genre—the so-called *Robinsonnades*—which were of importance not only to children?

No; all this is not sufficient to explain the magic of this book, nor the emotion that we feel when we see this creature standing in front of his cave with his furry breeches and his hide umbrella; this wicked fellow who has run away from home in the most unfeeling way and has now escaped as the sole survivor from a whole ship full of men.

And what does this fine gentleman do who has turned his back like this on the middle-class comforts of his parental home and has suddenly come into possession of nothing more than the tattered clothes he stands up in and the few bits and pieces left behind by the shipwreck? What does he do? In three decades he creates from all this nothingness a life which is morally unobjectionable and which emphasizes all the middle-class values such as tables and chairs and beds and cupboards—everything pedantically organized and bearing the stamp of good non-conformist piety.

Just at the right moment God sends him a companion, the magnificent Friday, 'the splendid savage', who will play an important part in literature from now on. And, of course, with Friday the whole process repeats itself, but with even more attention paid to instruction. The 'good' savage who was no stranger to cannibalism and had himself almost become a victim of the practice, learns to put on trousers, to pray, and to go around with a gun.

Finally the reformed good-for-nothing returns to human society, but not without leaving behind on his island a model administration in the form which humane colonial governments usually take. And after a number of difficulties it is augmented by a jumbled population of English and Spanish mariners, adventures of every kind and even a number of women.

Thus, in most exemplary manner, one human being, without goodness, piety or material possessions, portrays in half a lifetime the development of the human race. The simple man first discovers the mutual dependence of neighbours and is ultimately brought before the problems of human society, of justice, and of marriage, propagation and government. All this takes place in the unspoilt, untouched natural surroundings of a lonely island, far surpassing all other pastoral pieces and the 'back to nature' movements right down to our own day. . . .

In 1711 the newspapers of the day had carried the personal accounts of a Scottish mariner, Alexander Selkirk, who had been marooned on an island off the Chilean coast after a disagreement with the captain of his ship. Here he had set up house for himself through four years of utter loneliness. He had then been discovered by an English captain and brought to London, where Defoe heard of his adventures and supposedly even met him. It is therefore possible to say that Selkirk gave the initial impetus to the novel and that the island of Juan Fernandez off the Chilean coast is Robinson's island. Defoe himself disavows such a geographical location, although the island now possesses a monument to the event and a cave, which is described as being Robinson's.

Thus far the facts take us and thus we now see this man for ever on his island: a permanent ideal for his own age and for countless generations, interpreted by men according to their own designs through two hundred years.

Cornelia Meigs

SOURCE: "Three Tales of Travel," in *A Critical History of Children's Literature, Revised Edition,* by Cornelia Meigs and others, Macmillan Publishing Company, 1969, pp. 41-51.

Defoe's was an amazing output—histories, biographies, accounts of apparitions, a record of a *Journey to the Land of the Moon,* and a series of tales for the reading and moral improvement of rogues and criminals. He had among his many gifts an extraordinary faculty for assuming different personalities. His biographies, some of them semifictional, some of them wholly so, were nearly all presented as journals or first-person accounts. In them he identified himself with his subject so completely that in many cases it has never been known how much, if any, was the contribution of the central figure and how much was pure Defoe. He was fifty-eight years old, expert in his craft, and full of worldly experience when he turned himself to his greatest impersonation of all, the writing of *The Life and Strange Surprising Adventures of Robinson Crusoe of York, Mariner* (1719). It made him immortal, a result as unexpected as had been his landing in the pillory from the publication of an ill-judged political pamphlet.

In 1712 had been published the account of the sojourn of a sailor, Alexander Selkirk, on the Island of Juan Fernandez. He had deserted his ship and had lived alone for four years, until a chance vessel came by and took him back to England. The narrative was meager in detail, given at secondhand by the captain of the rescuing ship, but the fact of the adventure and the man's problem of survival struck Defoe's fancy and he set out to become, in imagination, a simple-hearted British mariner cast suddenly into this solitary and dangerous situation.

As a book for adults, *Robinson Crusoe* was immensely popular in its own time and has been highly regarded ever since. The loosely jointed, episodic narrative has become a model to all later literature for that kind of biographical yarn. It is a form directly natural for children's liking, with no confusing complication of structure, with effortless unity of place and character, and, above all, with vividness of dealing with natural things and natural adventure. It was exactly that for which children had looked so long in vain. It is as a tacit declaration of independence of all that their elders would thrust upon them that young readers have so firmly and persistently supported the books which they have chosen for themselves.

A man thrown on his own resources on a desert island is an irresistible subject, but this man was peculiarly appealing in his ways and methods. He was no marvel of knowledge and inventiveness, as is the paterfamilias of *The Swiss Family Robinson.* What he did, though he accomplished wonders, was done as slowly, as laboriously and clumsily as any ordinary boy would do it, with the constant danger of utter failure. His most inefficient and long-drawn out method of building his bower, his constructing of a boat that, in the end, was too large for him to move, his making of pots which were "ugly things" are none of them the work of any superman. But the baking of the clay in the fire is one of the dramatic episodes in the book; in the end he had "three very good, I will not say handsome, pipkins" after which life goes on to more ingenuities.

The pioneer spirit still dwells in the human race in spite of crowded civilized surroundings, and in no portion of mankind does it dwell so lustily as in children. The instinct of survival is ever-living in human beings, and the why and how of achieving it is no matter of course to the young. Any boy reader (or any girl with a little stretch of wishful imagination) can, without a great leap of fancy, see himself as Robinson Crusoe, building his house, capturing his goats, teaching Friday to talk to him. Little by little the reader becomes so identified with Crusoe, just as Defoe was, that he can see himself at the end in command of the final dramatic situations of great hazard, called governor of the island, giving orders to captains of ships and always looked up to as the leading spirit, the rescuer.

It is doubtful which is the more fascinating figure, Crusoe dealing with cannibal savages or Crusoe in his solitary existence, a grotesque picture with his goatskin costume, his umbrella, his attendant goats and parrot. The real charm of the story is in knowing just how he did everything, and so convincing is Defoe in his explicit descriptions, that we quite overlook some of the things which he does not explain. We are not told how Crusoe got fire, even though we see him cooking goat's flesh and baking red pots. Only long after, he speaks of having a tinder box, but it was made with "wild-fire" which he must have got in the forest rather than from the ship. He says it was very necessary to have an umbrella that will open and shut but "However, at last, . . . I made one to answer," is as far as Defoe can go. He is vague, too, in the matter of baskets.

One does not expect this denizen of eighteenth century London to be omniscient in the matter of life on a desert island, even though he sets himself up to be. The real heart of the story is the fact that there is never a dull moment; when the exercise of ingenuity has lost its novelty there are the earthquake, the explorations in the

little boat, finally the footprint in the sand. Almost anyone who looks back upon the book from maturity has the indefinite memory that the footprint was Friday's, but in real fact of narration it was five years later and in quite another part of the island that Friday first made his appearance. The story ends in a fine welter of battles, escapes, meetings, surprises, and final departure. Even the journey back to England has its hazards and adventures, but Crusoe arrives at last, very satisfactorily, for he has picked up, here and there, a fortune of almost thirty-three thousand pieces of eight. Pieces of eight are Spanish silver dollars, such as have been absorbed into our own currency, but which will always be a romantic measure of fortune and success.

So great was the prestige of the first **Robinson Crusoe** that it was followed by a host of others, so that a generic name has been applied to them, Robinsonnades. The earliest, published in 1727, was *The English Hermit or Unparalleled Sufferings . . . of Mr. Philip Quarll* by Longueville. The story begins with a wealth of detail about the hermit's establishment as discovered by a traveler, before one gets any glimpse of the hermit himself as a center and focus of the description. Defoe on the other hand, makes us so interested in Crusoe and so sympathetic with his misfortunes that every small matter of what he does and how he does it becomes the object of our curiosity. *The Swiss Family Robinson* by Johann Wyss, published in English in 1814, is the most famous of these followers of Crusoe; it is typical of its age, full of moralizing and lecturing by Robinson Senior, with complete unreality as to natural facts. Not even a child reader will believe that every fruit and every animal of temperate and tropical climes could have come together on a single island. There is even an *American Family Robinson,* so poorly written that there is no need to mention more than its existence.

Writers in all later times have taken inspiration not only from the form, but from the content of **Robinson Crusoe.** *Treasure Island* unconsciously borrows even some of its phrases and some scenes, but none the less is most gloriously Stevenson's own. And what is even more important, small boys everywhere and in all places have played at being Crusoe themselves, even as Tom Sawyer did. It is a far cry, but Mark Twain could hardly have found a better romantic substitute for Juan Fernandez than an island in the Mississippi River.

James Sutherland

SOURCE: "The Writer of Fiction," in *Daniel Defoe: A Critical Study,* Houghton Mifflin Company, 1971, pp. 117-74.

As every schoolboy used to know, the prototype of Robinson Crusoe was a stubborn and refractory Scottish sailor, Alexander Selkirk (1676-1721), who while cruising on a privateering voyage under the command of William Dampier, quarreled with the captain of his ship, and had himself put ashore in 1704 on the uninhabited island of Juan Fernandez. After some initial difficulties, Selkirk managed to make a life of it, and when he was rescued in January 1709 from his self-inflicted exile by Captain Woodes Rogers, he was in good health and apparently quite satisfied with his island life. He consented, however, to sail with Woodes Rogers, who appointed him mate of his ship. Later he was given command of another ship, and returned at last to London in October 1711. Accounts of his life on Juan Fernandez were published in 1712 by Woodes Rogers and by Captain Edward Cooke, and on 3 December 1713 Steele devoted a whole paper to him in his periodical *The Englishman.* Defoe must have known some or all of these accounts, and it is odd that with his interest in voyages and pirates he made no reference to Selkirk in the *Review* or elsewhere. Steele claimed to have had frequent conversations with Selkirk when he came back to London in 1711, and although nothing is known of Defoe having ever met the Scottish sailor, it seems unlikely that he would not seek him out and learn his story from his own lips.

At all events, *Robinson Crusoe* shares with most of Defoe's later fiction a firm basis in actuality: while his fiction *is* fiction, it often starts from, and in some cases stays very close to, a fact or series of facts. Selkirk's story gave Defoe the situation of a marooned mariner and a few accompanying circumstances—the goats which he tamed, the goatskin clothing, the cats, etc. In Steele's account it is related of Selkirk that he went through a period of deep depression, "grew dejected, languid and melancholy," until gradually "by the force of reason, and frequent reading of the scriptures, . . . he grew thoroughly reconciled to his condition." Selkirk's progress from dejection to equanimity is paralleled by that of Crusoe; but Defoe was quite capable of imagining Crusoe's state of mind without having recourse to Selkirk's. On the other hand, Crusoe's description of his religious exercises may owe something to Steele's account of how Selkirk had formed the habit of using "stated hours and places for exercises of devotion." On any count, however, Defoe's indebtedness to the Selkirk narratives was small; and indeed it was essential for him as a writer of fiction to conceal it as much as possible, since Selkirk's strange experience was comparatively fresh in the public mind. . . .

In Defoe's own day readers of all classes—from Alexander Pope to every "old woman that can go to the price of it"—enjoyed *Robinson Crusoe* as a story of "strange, surprising adventures." Twentieth-century critics have seen it as more than just that; but it is primarily as an adventure story that it still lives, and its continuing vitality is largely due to the skill and narrative confidence with which Defoe told it. . . .

Ultimately, much of the power of *Robinson Crusoe* lies in its appeal to the permanent feelings and essential interests of the human race. In this story Defoe achieved a drastic simplification of society and social relationships, and by stripping life of its inessentials he got down to the roots of human experience. This return to

the essential can hardly have been difficult for him: he was never far from it in his own life. He had none of the artificiality and little of the sophistication of the polite writers of the day; he habitually wrote plain English, called a rogue a rogue, and a whore a whore, and continually reduced moral and religious problems, political issues, and economic policies to the simplest terms . . . Defoe's black-and-white view of things undoubtedly leads at times to oversimplification (however effectively it enabled him to make his points as a controversialist), but in *Robinson Crusoe* it tends rather to clear the way for an uncomplicated vision of life lived on its simplest and most essential terms. . . .

As a story, *Robinson Crusoe* has the firm and satisfying structure of a man triumphing over difficulties, creating his own little cosmos out of what, if he had been merely idle and despondent, must have remained chaos. In most of Defoe's fiction the situation is that of the hero or heroine alone against the world, surviving by dint of perseverance and ingenuity and sheer native energy; but nowhere is that situation brought home to us more forcibly than in *Robinson Crusoe.* The hero has his moments of self-pity and even despair, but these have the effect of intensifying our awareness of his desperate plight. . . .

So much do we tend to think of *Robinson Crusoe* as a desert-island story that most readers probably forget that almost a quarter of the book is taken up with other matters—Crusoe's early voyages, his capture by the Sallee rover, his subsequent escape with his boy Xury, his rescue by the Portuguese merchantman, his life as a tobacco-planter in Brazil, and finally, when he leaves the island, his return to Europe and his journey across the Pyrenees in winter. The Pyrenees episodes, in which Friday demonstrates his unexpected expertise with a bear and in which the whole party is nearly devoured by ravenous wolves, have the sort of narrative interest that Defoe could always impart to adventures by land or sea, and enable him to give his readers another view of Friday, translated from his native tropics to "the severest winter all over Europe that had been known in the memory of man."

Kenneth Rexroth

SOURCE: "'Robinson Crusoe'," in *The Elastic Retort: Essays in Literature and Ideas,* The Continuum Publishing Company, 1973, pp. 59-63.

It is very fashionable nowadays—or was at least in the heyday of the faddist exegesis of Kafka, Kierkegaard and Henry James—all confused together as though they were one author—to write of *Robinson Crusoe* as though it were written by San Juan de la Cruz, an allegorical spiritual autobiography with dark nights of the soul and ladders of illumination. Defoe as a matter of fact states quite plainly that Crusoe's vision of an avenging archangel was due to a surfeit of turtle eggs. His terrors and panics of which so much has been made are no more than would be engendered in the most normal of men by simple loneliness, and they die out as he becomes habituated to his total isolation. The psychology of a man in solitary confinement is accurate. Crusoe is afraid of what men might do to him because year after year men do nothing to him whatsoever. He is terrified by an inexplicable footprint, but master of himself when the real cannibals finally show up.

The sense of sin that haunts the early part of his narrative is no more than what would be expected of a man of his time brooding on the reasons for his predicament. As time goes on, it ceases to be a predicament. It is fruitless to search for an allegorical original sin in Crusoe's opening pages. He says what it was. He didn't want to go into business. He least of all wanted to be a member of the middle class, that "best of all states" in his father's words, and he ran away to sea. "Of man's first disobedience and the fruit"—indeed. If this is original sin no boat would ever have been invented and put out to sea. . . .

Crusoe has been called a kind of Protestant monk and it is true that he turns the chance of his isolation into an anchorite's career. The story is one of spiritual realization—almost half a lifetime spent in contemplation works profound changes, whatever the subject's religion. We can watch Crusoe become, year by year, a better, wiser man. He writes little about his interior development and when he does his vocabulary is mostly inappropriate. We see it happen behavioristically. Defoe has been accused of insensitivity because Crusoe shows little compassion for Friday or sorrow at his death. But Defoe is portraying a true-born Englishman whose vocabulary cannot cope with the deepest personal emotions if they cannot be translated into the symbolical language of Dissenting piety.

At the end of the story as it first stood we watch Crusoe grow foolish again. He is back in the world of men and their commerce. It is only when human relationships escape from commerce that the spiritual wisdom he spent so many years acquiring as a hermit has a chance to show itself. Of course he has considerable worldly wisdom and the sequel is largely the story of a Ulysses of many devices who happened to have spent a few years by accident in a Zen monastery.

Samuel Johnson said that *Don Quixote, The Pilgrim's Progress* and **Robinson Crusoe** were the only three books a mature man wished were longer. In his time he was close to being right. **Robinson Crusoe** may still be the greatest English novel. Surely it is written with a mastery that has never been surpassed. It is not only as convincing as real life. It is as deep and as superficial as direct experience itself. The learned but incorrigibly immature will never see in it anything but a well written boys' story interspersed with out-of-date moralizing, best cut out when it is published as an illustrated juvenile. Others will believe that Defoe placed himself on record just this once as an unneurotic Kierkegaard, others as a critic beforehand of Montesquieu and Rousseau, others

will see Crusoe as the archetype of Economic Man. The book is all these things and more. It is what Defoe intended, a true life narrative.

Margery Fisher

SOURCE: "Robinson Crusoe," in *Who's Who in Children's Books: A Treasury of the Familiar Characters of Childhood,* Holt, Rinehart and Winston, 1975, p. 309.

Robinson Crusoe, the generalized figure of a castaway, fur-clad and practical, quickly became the property of children through chapbook simplifications of Defoe's story. It is the practical, adventure aspect of the story that has always attracted children, the well-documented, journalist's account of how a castaway builds a new, comfortable and well-organized life and even reconciles the alien Friday to it. Most of the many eighteenth- and nineteenth-century imitations and offshoots of **Robinson Crusoe** pursue the idea of the castaway either as a man finding God through suffering and solitude or as an allegory of the slow march of civilization. The Robinsonnades written for children in the present century are very different. Whether they are set properly on a desert island or in some comparable geographical outpost, whether Crusoe is represented by a solitary figure or (most often) by a group, the emphasis is on the do-it-yourself adventure. . . .

Barbara Hardy

SOURCE: "Robinson Crusoe," in *Children's Literature in Education,* Vol. 8, No. 1, Spring, 1977, pp. 3-11.

Robinson Crusoe is a marvellous story and a great novel. Unlike those other great books which appeal to all ages—*Don Quixote, A Pilgrim's Progress, Gulliver's Travels*—its appeal is one and indivisible. When we grow up, we discover profundities and complexities we missed in Cervantes, Bunyan, and Swift, and look back on the childhood charm as simple and easy, a mere selection from a vast and rich experience. But, although there are some things in **Robinson Crusoe** which are omitted in abridgement, or skipped by children, all the most important things can be appreciated and shared by people at all ages. The story of Robinson Crusoe's religious conversion to a faith in Providence is an important subject and structural principle, but it is of little interest to the child, and it is not the centre of the book's power and originality. Henry James once tenderly described the grown man's response to Stevenson's *Treasure Island* as being like reading the story over a boy's shoulder. When we re-read **Robinson Crusoe,** it is to remember and include the experience of the child. We are still moved and gratified by the fantasy of defiance, escape, solitude, making and making believe, companionship, rescue, and survival. **Robinson Crusoe** is a fuller and deeper novel than *Treasure Island,* and no one outgrows it. At a time when books are written either for adults or children, it offers particular pleasure.

It is a great adventure story, with many perils—storm, shipwreck, cannibals, wild animals, war, and exposure. But what makes its adventures more than mere thrills is the presence, at the heart of the action, of the adventurous man. The dangers and exploits of Robinson Crusoe are linked with great narrative skill in a pattern of tension, expectation, surprise, kept up in an astonishingly sustained creation of excitement. More important, they are presented from the inside as well as the outside. There is a chain of events, and a circulation of feeling. The adventures are not baldly or externally related, events that are important only as events. They happen to a man, and the tension is not only our breath-held expectation of the next event, it is Robinson Crusoe's. Clearly, our fear is created through his fear, our relief, curiosity, and courage are provoked and particularised by character. . . . We delight in Crusoe's cleverness, as he settles in, surrounds himself with necessaries and luxuries, salvages things from the wreck, and uses the raw materials to provide shelter, food, clothes, furniture, writing materials, a calendar, and other aids to survival. The game changes from games that are played with imaginary environments to constructional games. The child's brick-building, jigsaws, and imitations of the manufactured adult world, are both fun and learning. Defoe's precise and careful descriptions of making are sometimes blueprints for doing it yourself. I am not suggesting that we learn from the making in the novel, but that we rather associate ourselves with Crusoe's learning. His achievements are not only, as Ian Watt has insisted in *The Rise of the Novel,* steps in technological development, but are games, too, to be played painstakingly, clumsily, sufficiently, like the making of planks (one plank each tree); ingeniously but also stupidly, like the building of the first boat; and by scientific observation and experiment, like the making of cooking pots. Crusoe is the one who learns, by trial and by error. And some things he never learns to make, like a thing so important to writers—ink. The borderlines of skill and clumsiness, achievement and failure, make the environment game credible and exciting. The making of a thing, like the building of the card-castle or meccano bridge, is a feat, another kind of adventure.

Children do not only make replicas and models, they also use things to make makeshift and make-believe worlds, secret places, private habitations. Robinson Crusoe makes several houses, and lucidly reminds us of the psychological need for the making. Like the imaginary houses, refuges, and secret gardens we all make, here and there, and everywhere, are Robinson Crusoe's magazines, castles, town- and country-houses. They are really made and really make-believe, so giving us a double delight. They are nests, without either mates or babies, and they resemble play-houses, real and imaginary. Crusoe loves caves and tree-houses, for their physical shelter and imaginative gratification. His dwellings meet deep psychological needs for privacy, comfort, seclusion. They are cosy wombs.

The secret houses are full of things, and though the things are mostly necessary to Robinson Crusoe, they have a special charm. The identity and accumulation of things is fascinating to the child, for reasons both obvious and arcane. The child gets to know the use of things, but the childhood feeling for objects, happily not vanishing completely in adult life, has a sense of the individuality of objects, radiant, funny, startling, or terrifying. Robinson Crusoe caters to the lively interest in individual things. We see the making, almost from scratch, of the world of things we take for granted, except on desert islands. We see the special qualities of Crusoe's resourcefulness, patience, good temper, intelligence, and piety, as he makes and handles things. But there remains something, too, of that extra delight in the individual faces of things, which is gratified by the flotsam and jetsam of the island. There are odds and ends, like three little things Crusoe has with him when he is first swept on to the island—a knife, a pipe, and a little tobacco in a box. There is all the joy of salvage and treasure-hunting in a whole wreck, with its goods at his disposal. . . .

There is all the pleasure of finding the larder full of food. . . .

There is all the pleasure of rummaging amongst miscellaneous and useless things. . . .

And there is the invention and fun of dressing up. . . .

To the child, things have a peculiar and pure fascination. To the adult, their economic meanings and moral ironies take over. Both child and adult enjoy the things, the same things, the things Defoe specifies so solidly. And just as adult and child enjoy the sense of discovery, accumulation, and manufacture, so, too, both enjoy the strong if less solid satisfactions, of a world of fantasy. Robinson Crusoe makes believe one dwelling is home, one is a fortress, one a castle, one a country-house. He plays king with his domestic animals as living toys. Later on, he enacts more practically and dangerously the fantasies of kingship and colonisation, but in the early days the fantasy is strongly rooted in childhood needs for privacy, isolation, self-discovery, and escape.

Whatever the psychological interpretations, however, Defoe's overt presentation is simply and strikingly nonsexual. Since he could be sexually candid, gross, and prurient when he choses, as in *Moll Flanders* and *Roxana,* it seems possible to insist on an absence of sexuality in *Robinson Crusoe*. . . . Crusoe's island is a world of matter-of-fact making, adventure, and companionship, which offers either its innocence or its blandness to the innocence or blandness of childhood. Its fantasy is strong, but it is not a sexual fantasy.

Violent adventure, a game of making environments and things, a fantasy of escape, solitude, and self-possession. The hero of these adventures, creations, and dreams, is Crusoe, whose simplicity makes him just the right hero for a story that appeals to the child. Crusoe's simplicity is one of nature, not caricature. His simplicity is healthy, and vital, compared with that of crude or gross supermen. It is compatible with intelligence and a rich emotional life. Although Crusoe is contaminated with capitalist energy and imperial pride, he also possesses admirable qualities of good humour and friendliness. Unlike the heroes so brilliantly analysed by David Holbrook in his essay on C. S. Lewis in *Children's literature in education,* Crusoe is loving, self-critical, and moral. When he longs to destroy the cannibals, second thoughts rebuke him, and his aggressiveness is rationally and imaginatively restrained. The novel has violence in it, but it is neither sensational nor amoral in presentation. We are never crudely stimulated by fear or hostility, but shown the workings of fear and hostility in Robinson Crusoe. He is simple enough to be Everyman, and simple enough to have an unmysterious emotional life which is accessible to the child, but sufficiently vivid and various for the adult. . . .

Defoe's artlessness . . . has a strong appeal. The story and the character shine through a transparent medium, radiantly and purely, with no assertion of decoration or artifice. There *is* artifice, but as always in Defoe, it is most thoroughly concealed and assimilated. The simplicity of story and language is enhanced by the relaxation of rhetoric. There is a directness and modesty which can delight the adult by its restraint, and never irritate the child. If we want the borderline between fact and fiction blurred, then we will find that excellent blurring in **Robinson Crusoe.** Its adventures, its solid world and objects, its manifold fantasy, its simple but individual hero, are presented in perfectly candid form and style. But the novel has all the cunning and advantage of art. Of all great novels, **Robinson Crusoe** is the novel we can share most easily and completely with our children.

Bob Dixon

SOURCE: "Empire: Fiction Follows the Flag," in *Catching Them Young 2: Political Ideas in Children's Fiction,* Pluto Press, 1977, pp. 74-119.

Before literature aimed especially at children began to be written in any quantity—towards the middle of the eighteenth century—they had to make do with what they could find to their taste from literature written for adults. (We shouldn't forget that most children couldn't read, anyway, in those days.) One of the first of such books, which they took over for themselves, happens to be a blue-print for colonisation. It's Defoe's **The Adventures of Robinson Crusoe.** Of course, it isn't hard to see the attractions such a work had, and still has, for children—with their desire for privacy, their love of hideouts and their wish to organise and control their lives—especially when all this is told with Defoe's careful attention to the most minute details. In fact, such is the strength of this aspect of the book that we are apt to forget its whole framework, and equally, perhaps, the class of children—the aspiring bourgeoisie—to whom it first made its appeal. The first part was published in 1719.

About half-way through, there's a typical insight into the way Crusoe thinks: 'how like a king I looked. First of all, the whole country was my own mere property, so that I had an undoubted right of dominion. Secondly, my people were perfectly subjected—I was absolute Lord and lawgiver.'

At this point, of his 'three subjects', Friday has already been converted to Protestantism, his social and cultural destruction having been begun by Crusoe with no loss of time. Friday was renamed and Crusoe was to be known as 'Master'. The instruction of Friday in English language and customs is soon started. He's clothed, trained as a gun-dog and cured of cannibalism. Crusoe begins to instruct him in 'the knowledge of the true God' although it's clear that Friday already has a religion, his god being 'Benamuckee' and his priests the 'Oowookakee'. Defoe's cheap disparagement here needs no further comment. However, it's amusing to note how sorely tried Crusoe is by some of Friday's innocent questions about Christianity.

Crusoe sets up the rescued Spaniard as the overseer of Friday and his father in the cutting down of trees to make a boat. Later, Friday, having no option on whether to join his 'nation' or even stay with his father, whom he loves, goes to England with Crusoe.

Then, great details are given of the finances of Crusoe's plantation in Brazil. Finally, he sells it and is rich, now referring to the island as 'my colony'. Certainly, he's come a long way from his first exploration of the island as 'King and lord' with 'a right of possession' and his later development of 'plantations' and a 'country seat'.

Now, we can turn to look at racism, a constant and, I'd think, inevitable feature of empire-building, since it seems impossible to subject people to an alien rule without believing in their inferiority. We have it in **Robinson Crusoe,** at the beginning of the literary tradition. After the cannibals have visited the island, Crusoe resolves 'to get one of those savages into [his] hands' as a 'servant' to help him, Crusoe, to escape. Before, when a large and obviously white man's ship had been wrecked on the island, Crusoe had longed for a 'companion' and 'fellow creature' but the idea of a 'servant' had not struck him.

His chance comes. He rescues Friday, being 'called plainly by Providence to save this poor creature's life' and Friday gradually approaches him. Then, we read 'he kneeled down again, kissed the ground, and laid his head upon the ground, and, taking me by the foot, set my foot upon his head: this, it seems, was in token of swearing to be my slave for ever.'

There are degrees in racism in British literature, other races becoming more acceptable in so far as they approach the north-west European type. In the first book of empire, Friday 'had all the sweetness and softness of an European in his countenance . . . especially when he smiled. His hair was long and black, not curled like wool . . . his nose small, not flat like the Negroes; a very good mouth, thin lips.' Finally, as far as Friday's concerned, this devoted servant, who'd been reduced to a mere extension of the will of his master, is killed carrying out Crusoe's wishes.

I've already mentioned a religious streak in **Robinson Crusoe.** It continues, in strong measure, throughout the book and almost throughout the tradition. Crusoe's first thought after seeing, and being revolted by, the remains of the cannibal feast has a Pharisaical tone about it: 'I looked up with the utmost affection of my soul, and, with a flood of tears in my eyes, gave God thanks, that had cast my first lot in a part of the world where I was distinguished from such dreadful creatures as these.' Crusoe has several religious debates with himself as to whether it's right to kill cannibals. However, when they are about to eat a *white* man, the matter is decided at once—a fine blend of religion and racism.

Killing, in fact, is an important and clearly unavoidable part of the tradition and, towards the end of the edition I'm using, which includes *The Further Adventures of Robinson Crusoe,* the killing increases. In a type of scene which will be repeated again and again, enormous slaughter is carried out between rival groups of 'savages' and, later still, terrible havoc is wreaked upon the Madagascans when the trouble had been originally started by an English sailor. Crusoe professes horror at the massacre but we are treated to a description of it nevertheless, a type of hypocrisy, or of having it both ways, which, again, is common to this type of literature. Violence and sadism of all kinds, as a matter of fact, are rife in imperialist literature for children and usually it's cloaked in religion, racism, or patriotism, or combinations of these.

Slavery plays a big part in the book. Robinson Crusoe, very early in his adventures, is, as he puts it, a 'miserable slave', kept by a Turkish ship's captain. However, he's by no means ill-used and the experience doesn't prevent him, very soon after his escape, from setting up as a plantation-owner (which meant, in effect, the same thing as a slave-owner) in Brazil: 'the first thing I did,' he tells us, 'I bought me a negro slave' and, very soon, 'for trifles', he buys blacks from the Guinea coast 'in great numbers'.

For the most part, women don't appear at all in imperialist literature. It's a man's world—that is, if you consider murder, brutality, enslavement and the collecting of as much wealth as possible as quickly as possible to be manly attributes. Women can't be kept out entirely, however, and apart from that, the views that emerge about them, whether consciously or unconsciously held, are very interesting. Towards the end of Robinson Crusoe's adventures, the five Englishmen who have become part of his ever-growing 'colony' draw lots to choose five native wives. The women don't have a say in the matter. On Crusoe's return to the island, arrangements are made for the Christian marriage of these couples and for the Christianising of the wives (as well as of the 37 subjected 'heathens' on the island). Fortunately, a priest happens to be around. Obviously, racism enters into the

proceedings here but white women fare little better. 'For my Spaniards' Crusoe tells us a little later 'I engaged three Portugal women to go; and recommended it to them to marry them, and use them kindly. I could have procured more women,' he goes on, but 'there were but five of the Spaniards that wanted' and he remembers that a Brazilian planter, fleeing to the island from the Inquisition, has two daughters. No doubt they'll do.

So almost all of the main elements of the tradition are here, in **Robinson Crusoe,** at the beginning. It remains for us, now, to see what different forms they take as the years go by and the empire grows.

J. S. Bratton

SOURCE: "Books for Boys," in *The Impact of Victorian Children's Fiction,* Croom Helm, 1981, pp. 102-47.

There was a handful of adult novels which by the 1860s had come to be regarded as good books for boys, and from them the juvenile writers drew their patterns and methods, establishing a convention strong enough to support many thousands of stories written in the next fifty or sixty years.

Pre-eminent among these books, occupying a special place in the ancestry of the boys' story, was **Robinson Crusoe.** Just as the strictest Evangelical ban upon fiction for the young made an exception of *The Pilgrim's Progress,* so **Crusoe** was the one fiction which all followers of a rationalist, Rousseauian theory of education gave to their pupils, on the authority of *Émile* itself. Its continued popularity after the strictly doctrinaire period had gone by was founded on its fictional appeal. In shape hardly removed from true accounts of adventure at sea, it had the vital fictional addition of a hero in whose character and fortunes the reader was interested, and moreover included an episode, Crusoe's life on the desert island, so powerful and compendious as story and as symbol that it was capable of holding interest through infinite numbers of imitations, repetitions and adaptations.

Margery Fisher

SOURCE: "Daniel Defoe: 'The Life and Strange Surprising Adventure of Robinson Crusoe of York, Mariner' (1719)," in *Classics for Children & Young People,* The Thimble Press, 1986, pp. 49-50.

A long-haired gentleman dressed in goatskins and carrying an umbrella gazes in astonishment at a single footprint on a stretch of empty sand. This ideogram of the castaway is all that many children will ever know of Robinson Crusoe—this and the fact that he has a black servant oddly styled Friday. What do they miss by not reading the story in a respectable version (for instance, in the Dent C.I.C. edition of 1903, which is only slightly shortened)? First, circumstantial detail. From the memorable day (30 September 1659) when Crusoe, a rebel from his father's ideal of the 'middle station of life', was cast away on an uninhabited island, he tells us everything—exactly what he saved from the ship before it broke up, how he contrived shelter, recorded time, domesticated goats, observed weather. Then, most simplified versions omit the emotional aspect of the tale. Defoe offers an ironic picture of a seventeenth-century bourgeois who survives solitude by re-creating the methodical life he has left (and by becoming self-styled ruler of the island, an early imperialist). The satiric implications of Defoe's book and its basic veracity will only be apparent if young readers realize the story in its full spread: it was almost a year before Crusoe visited the other side of the island, nearly four years before he made a canoe to venture from its shores, more than twenty-five years before he found a servant and subject (incidentally, in the present sensitive climate the whole subject of Friday is better understood in historical perspective in the full narrative). Crusoe's survival is ideal rather than probable; his mercantile outlook is historically valid; the physical circumstances of his castaway life remain the inspiration for hundreds of junior adventure yarns in which children triumph happily over danger and deprivation. It is amusing to think that this level-headed, practical, sardonic tale of 250 years ago has sired a host of romantic, highly fanciful junior adventures.

Margery Fisher

SOURCE: "Desert Islands," in *The Bright Face of Danger,* The Horn Book, Inc., 1986, pp. 293-317.

The huge genre of junior adventure stories which has justly been given the name of 'Robinsonnade' is eternally enlarged and refreshed by new motives, new circumstances, new settings, but in whatever latitude the particular desert island is located, whether it is an isolated inland valley or truly surrounded by water, some combination of sand, coconut palms and heat will usually be found. These elements are not wholly derived from the primal source, *Robinson Crusoe.* As the centuries passed and the salient points of Crusoe's adventure settled into the literary consciousness, they became almost like signals evoking in readers a Pavlovian response. In a popular Robinsonnade of seventy years ago, H. de Vere Stacpoole's *Bird Cay,* the boy of fifteen who tells the story asserts the influence of that marooned hero on him:

> I could have read that book upside down, I believe, if it had been given to me to read it in no other way; as it was I had read it through, and backwards and forwards, and here and there. It was a heavy old copy with a blue and gilt cover, and two pictures were missing; but little I wanted with pictures when I could see, as clearly as though I were looking through air, the island, and the goats, and the grapes, drying in the sun and turning into raisins, Friday's footprint, and Robinson's fur cap, his two guns, and the sea washing in on the beach—I who had never seen the sea.

In fact this story of a stowaway's adventures in search of buried gold, his encounters with greedy rivals and

venal sea-captains, offers little atmosphere to the reader, who is left to supply his own imagined setting from a predictable sequence of sand and skeletons, waves and wickedness.

As it has developed over two and a half centuries since *Robinson Crusoe* was published, the Robinsonnade has used settings varying from the strictly geographical to the frankly fantastic; to some extent at least these settings have been predominantly decorative in the case of books for entertainment, less luxurious with more philosophical works. The usual mental picture of a coral island, fertile and hospitable (the picture reflected in its most stereotyped and suggestive form in the television advertisement for the Bounty chocolate bar), is very distant from Crusoe's island. Though Defoe based his sturdily matter-of-fact fiction on the true circumstances of Alexander Selkirk's ordeal on Juan Fernandez, off the west coast of South America, he landed his fictional hero on an island in the Gulf of the Orinoco within sight of Trinidad in a part of the world he called the Brazils. It was at first sight a barren place, where rocks predominated and available food consisted of wild goats and turtles. If Crusoe could be excused for his lack of response to this unpromising place, we may allow ourselves to be surprised that it was not until almost a year had passed that he ventured inland and discovered a green and fertile valley where he picked limes and was later able to harvest melon, sugar cane, wild tobacco, grapes and lemons.

Although he was refreshed by the contrast between the open savannah and close forest and the bleak shore on which he had landed, he never showed any kinship with the land or any desire to adapt himself to its atmosphere. He was a survivor, not an explorer. His first reactions to the pleasant valley are typical:

> . . . the country appeared so fresh, so green, so flourishing, everything being in a constant verdure, or flourish of spring, that it looked like a planted garden. I descended a little of the side of that delicious vale, surveying it with a secret kind of pleasure (though mixed with other afflicting thoughts), to think that this was all my own; that I was king and lord of all this country indefensibly, and had a right of possession; and if I could convey it, I might have it in inheritance as completely as any lord of a manor in England.

The national and mercantile impulse to acquire the island (the legal term 'convey' is precisely chosen) is tempered by a moderation which is at the centre of Crusoe's character. It is also, presumably, at the centre of Defoe's irony, as he points to the stolid, unimaginative, tenacious middle-class readers to whom he is offering 'strange surprising adventures'. He has drawn the portrait of a man thrown entirely upon his own resources in unknown country, completely alone for fifteen years and then with a companion not judged to be his equal, who is not basically changed by his experience—that is, neither the strangeness nor the solitude affect him permanently. When there are storms, he flinches and repents of his misspent life; his desire for companions is intermittent and brief; he suffers no superstitious fears of unknown presences, no mystical experiences, but an entirely natural and practical access of alarm when Caribs from the mainland visit the island. He is concerned to survive and to build a life of routine, helped by the tools and stores he has been able to carry from the wrecked ship and by the comforting measurement of time on a tally-post.

Indeed, the affecting initial entry in his journal:

> September 30th, 1659 . . . I, poor miserable Robinson Crusoe, being shipwrecked, during a dreadful storm in the offing, came on shore on this dismal, unfortunate island, which I called the ISLAND OF DESPAIR; all the rest of the ship's company being drowned and myself almost dead. . . .

has a contrived air about it, for by the time the passage has been indited (on paper and with ink recovered from the ship), Crusoe has already made a shelter, a table and chair and shelves for his possessions; he has, in short, established a bourgeois home in which to settle down in the kind of moderate, middle station of life which his father had recommended to him but which, in the wildness of youth, he had rejected for the anticipated freedom of the sea.

Robinson Crusoe is hardly a romantic book, with its sturdy recitation of domestic matters and its compact, controlled moments of emotion, but equally, it cannot be called realistic, as Walter de la Mare pointed out:

> . . . if Defoe had really faced, as he might have tried to face, the problem set in *Crusoe,* his solution could not have been in that book's precise terms. All praise and thanks that it is what it is, a triumph in its kind; and yet one may pine for what, given a more creative imagination and a different Crusoe, the book might have been if the attempt had been made to reveal what a prolonged unbroken solitude, an absolute exile from his fellow-creatures, and an incessant commerce with silence and the unknown, would mean at last to the spirit of man. A steadily debasing brutish simplicity? Hallucinations, extravagances, insanities, enravishment, strange guests?

> Selkirk after but four years' silence was scarcely articulate. Crusoe after his eight and twenty years addresses the three strangers whom he finds trussed up on the beach with the urbanity of a prince, the courtesy of an Oriental, and in faultless Spanish . . .

'A triumph in its kind'—de la Mare clearly read *Robinson Crusoe* not as a study in religious regeneration (one modern interpretation) nor as a definition of a particular social class, but as the adventure story which children, and many adults, have taken it to be, establishing as fixed points of the plot the fur hat and umbrella, the tame parrot and submissive Friday. De la Mare commented:

Defoe descends with limpid ease to the level of the boy latent in old men and active in his heroes, and so within this narrow range comes near to being the most imaginative author the world has ever seen.

His speculation about the equilibrium which Defoe allowed his hero *was* just speculation about an approach which, as he realised, Defoe never intended. His remark about articulacy needs to be considered in a different light, since this is the kind of outward symptom of an inner condition which Defoe, given the factual cumulation of his fiction, could hardly ignore. Defoe did offer at least a partial explanation for Crusoe's hold on the power of speech. First, he could address the dog which had survived the wreck, in words a degree less unsatisfying than total monologue. Then, the parrot could be taught to repeat phrases and so an illusion of conversation could be maintained. We are to accept that when after fifteen years Crusoe acquired a human companion, his tongue was therefore sufficiently well exercised to be a proper means of communication with Friday who, within the conventions of fiction, is a quick learner.

Defoe makes us believe that Crusoe remained fully articulate on his island by the same trick of offering disarmingly concrete details which he used in his other stories: we need not be aware, unless we wish to be, that he has avoided any question of mental disintegration as a result of prolonged solitude. On the contrary, he makes it clear that when Crusoe does acquire companions—after Friday, Friday's father and a Spaniard, both rescued from Carib enemies—he does not welcome them for the sake of wider conversational opportunities but for quite different reasons:

> My island was now peopled, and I thought myself rich in subjects. And it was a merry reflection, which I frequently made, how like a King I looked. First of all, the whole country was my own mere property, so that I had an undoubted right of dominion. Secondly, my people were perfectly subjected; I was absolutely lord and law giver; they allowed their lives to me, and were ready to lay down their lives, if there had been occasion for it, for me. It was remarkable, too, I had but three subjects, and they were of three different religions: my man Friday was a Protestant, his father was a Pagan and a cannibal, and the Spaniard was a Papist: however, I allowed liberty of conscience throughout my dominions.

Defoe did what he set out to do, no more and no less. . . .

Zena Sutherland

SOURCE: "Robinson Crusoe," in *Children and Books,* Scott, Foresman and Company, 1986, p. 68.

One book emerged from the Puritan world to mark not only the increase of cheerfulness but the beginning of contemporary adventure tales. It was Daniel Defoe's *Robinson Crusoe,* one of the most popular books in all English literature.

Defoe (1659-1731), with a wisdom far in advance of his times, wrote on banks, insurance companies, schools for women, asylums for the insane, and all sorts of social problems. He turned out bitter political and religious satires which landed him in the pillory. He rose to wealth and fame and sank to penury and prison more than once. Writing was his passion, and few men have written more continuously. His most famous book, *The Life and Strange Surprising Adventures of Robinson Crusoe,* appeared in 1719, when Defoe was sixty and nearing the end of his turbulent career. We are told four editions of it were printed in four months, and for once the old fighter enjoyed fame with no unhappy repercussions of any kind.

Why has this book commended itself to children of each succeeding generation? It was addressed to adults and originally contained masses of moral ruminations that the children must have skipped with their usual agility in the avoidance of boredom. Most children's editions today omit these tiresome reflections and get on with the story.

Here is a book that satisfies children's hunger to achieve competence. Identifying with Robinson Crusoe, they win an ordered, controlled place in the world by their own efforts and foresight. With the coming of Friday, they have the love of a friend whom they in turn nurture and protect. The theme itself is irresistible: man pitted against nature, one man with a whole world to create and control. He must obtain food, provide himself with clothes and shelter, fight off wild animals, reckon time, keep himself civilized and sane.

Michael Seidel

SOURCE: "'Crusoe' and Defoe," "The Importance of the Work," and "Critical Reception," in *Robinson Crusoe: Island Myths and the Novel,* Twayne Publishers, 1991, 130p.

Whenever I teach my large lecture course in the history of the English novel I ask my students how many have heard of *The Life and Strange Surprizing Adventures of Robinson Crusoe, of York, Mariner.* All have. When I ask whether any have read the book in its complete, original version many readily admit that they have not. What they know they have absorbed from the cultural residue of Crusoe's fame, or from shortened, edited, and expurgated children's versions of the novel, or from comic books, movies, even *New Yorker* cartoons. I then ask another question. Of those who have heard of *Crusoe* and have not read it in its original form, how many can describe the basic plot of the story? Again, the bare elements of Crusoe's story as island castaway are known by all, but the rest of the book is a blur. What happened to Crusoe before his shipwreck? Where is the book set? When did its events occur? What were the sequence of events on the island? What happened to Crusoe after his rescue? What place does *Robinson Crusoe* hold in the history and literary history of its own time? What was Daniel Defoe like?

Illustration from the 1923 edition of Defoe's Robinson Crusoe.

The quality of the Crusoe myth, its seeming absorption into the culture as one of its founding stories, is both an advantage and a disadvantage in thinking about the complete original version of Defoe's novel. Reading the book as Defoe wrote it challenges students in a number of ways they may not have anticipated or suspected. For one thing, the narrative in its fullness introduces matters of wide and complex appeal that are not always as familiar as the rudiments of the castaway plot: speculations on maritime and international law, on plantation husbandry, on slavery and cannibalism, on economic theory. For another, Defoe is a figure of fearless engagement with his age and boundless energies that are worth studying in conjunction with his famous castaway story. . . .

As a mirror of contemporary issues and pressures, the novel form had no sustaining practitioner before Defoe to boost it to a place in the literary hierarchy. Shoddily written fictional true-to-life accounts existed in the culture much like the flotsam and jetsam of Crusoe's shipwreck before he fashioned his coherent island estate.

And, of course, preexisting narrative forms of epic and romance, those deriving from classical sources in Greece and Rome or from aristocratic feudal cultures of medieval and Renaissance Europe, existed as timeworn narrative models. But these proved unsuitable for Defoe's charting of the contemporary record, his documentation and inscription of life in the late seventeenth and early eighteenth centuries, perhaps because none was able to do what the last great epic work in England, Milton's *Paradise Lost,* did: combine a compelling narrative event with the awakening reality of individual conscience in modern society. . . .

The centrality of the Crusoe story in the collective mind of this culture—indeed, in the collective mind of so many of the world's cultures—is astounding. Perhaps no single book in the history of Western literature has spawned more editions, translations, imitations, continuations, and sequels than *Crusoe.* To follow its paper trail over the centuries is an adventure almost as daunting as the one Crusoe faces on his island. There have been hundreds of adaptations in dozens of languages, from *Swiss Family Robinson,* to an Offenbach operetta, to Luis Buñuel's brilliant film version, to J. M. Coetzee's *Foe.* Crusoe's adventures form the basis of everything from a jokebook to a cookbook; he even appears in animal narratives as a dog. By the end of the nineteenth century, English language editions alone topped two hundred, with editions of translations abroad multiplying that number threefold. Any book translated into languages as remote from one another as Eskimo, Coptic, and Maltese must be making a deep impression on someone.

In terms of what opinion polls call recognition factor, Crusoe's name is magic. The castaway Crusoe appears everywhere, from Karl Marx's *Das Kapital* to television ads for permanent-press slacks. What is the appeal of his archetypal story? Is a man alone, stranded, outcast, exiled on a temperate desert island somehow an emblem of the organizing capacities of mind and body? How does a human being in isolation combine the resources of nature and culture? What does the mastery of spatial domain have to do with well-being? What does the lone individual need? These questions are so basic that *Robinson Crusoe* is a primer for the science of man, a field study for the anthropologist, the psychologist, the economist, the political scientist, the sociologist, the geographer, the engineer, the agronomist, the theologian, and even, as the story develops, the military strategist.

Crusoe's experience, as Samuel Taylor Coleridge put it, is a staple of fantasy projection, "a vision of a happy nightmare." A soul alone on a desert island turns to self-generated resources; free space and free time provide for the disposition of material life and for the release of psychic energies. Defoe, of course, is aware of the psychological appeal of his narrative. Here, for example, are a few sentences as Crusoe explores an inland paradise on his island, much more lovely and beautiful a place than his settlement nearer the shore: "I descended a little of the Side of that delicious Vale, surveying it with a secret Kind of Pleasure, (tho-mixt with my other afflicting Thoughts) to think that this was all my own, that I was King and Lord of all this Country indefeasibly, and had a Right of Possession; and if I could convey it, I might have it in Inheritance, as compleatly as any Lord of a Mannor in *England*."

What does a secret kind of pleasure mean? The place is an island spot within an island setting—Crusoe loves enclosures within enclosures—and Crusoe's pleasure is an expression of subliminal and activated desires. He takes a piece of paradise and makes it a sovereign state. He is king of vale, lord of the country, squire of the manor. Visionary spots such as these are narcissistic and, as befits the dreams of the material man, owned, protected, held. Crusoe's pleasure in paradise has something of the same relation to the rest of his life as Defoe's novel has to the lives of those who read it. The imagination seeks its sovereign territories, its islanded fictions, and Defoe works that notion into his extraordinary story for all it is worth.

Crusoe's story is a fable of controlling physical space, of organizing time, of making, crafting, fabricating, of fearing and mastering. His fate and his opportunity touch a responsive chord in all those who ponder the course of a life and value the appeal of alternative or substitute worlds. As Crusoe remakes himself in a space that he inscribes, that space becomes him. To think of the man is to think in terms of the whole phrase, "Crusoe on his island." Conjuring up an empty space and setting out its contours is therapeutic, satisfying, and liberating. Indeed, those in long captivity often sustain themselves by imagining an empty plot of land and building a house brick by brick or board by board in their mind's eye. As time goes by, they will landscape the space, possibly add an addition or create an entire compound. It is the rare human being who is not compelled by this kind of projection.

Crusoe's story is emblematic for the genre of the novel in England, which Defoe's narrative, in a sense, inaugurated. . . .

The form of the novel in England did not burst into existence solely as the imp of Defoe's genius, though it might appear so. For decades the later seventeenth and earlier eighteenth century struggled to find a form of literary expression in which some of the strong fervor of contemporary historical events, domestic consciousness, social analysis, and the new psychology of John Locke and others might manifest itself. When in his late fifties Defoe began writing volumes of fiction that did a little of all these things, the English could not even find an adequate name for his narratives. Novel was the last thing anyone would call Defoe's works. In point of fact, the term *novel* usually referred to the stylized, ornate, and time-distanced French romance. The circumstantially particularized, recognizable, and roughly contemporary stories Defoe told, beginning with *Robinson Crusoe* and continuing with *Memoirs of a Cavalier, Moll Flanders, Colonel Jack,* and *Roxana*, were a conglomerate of lives, confessions, memoirs, accounts, true histories, and diaries.

"The editor," writes Defoe in the preface to *Crusoe,* "believes the thing to be a just History of Fact; neither is there any Appearance of Fiction in it." He means what he says—the whole may indeed be fiction, but there is no "appearance" of fiction in it. Appearances are what count for Defoe. The distinction between something being a lie and something appearing to be a lie holds a world of difference. The truth is not the record of what happened merely, but the believability of the mode of writing that conveys it, or something like it. The writing can be true and the events fiction. That is why the editor believes there is "no appearance" of fiction in the writing; he is making a stylistic comment as much as a judgment about content. And that is why *Crusoe* comes down through the centuries as special and novel, though only well after Defoe and most of his contemporaries were dead would critics call his works what he himself would have shuddered to call them, novels.

Robinson Crusoe did not address itself at first to an audience well schooled in how to read it as fiction. It passed itself off as a counterfeit memoir and was published by a house that specialized in everything but fiction. . . .

Whatever Defoe's first readers thought they were getting in *Crusoe,* they read it with fervor. The narrative was something of a landmark text within a year of its publication. Its first issue of between 1,000 and 1,500 copies, entered in the Stationers' Register for 23 April 1719 and available two days later, quickly sold out even at the relatively high price of five shillings. Defoe's bilious enemy, Charles Gildon, commented soon after *Crusoe*'s publication, "There is not an old Woman that can go to the Price of it, but buys thy *Life and Adventures*, and leaves it as a Legacy, with the *Pilgrims Progress,* the *Practice of Piety,* and *God's Revenge against Murther,* to her Posterity." Before the end of the year, the first volume of *Crusoe* had run through four editions, 12 May, 6 June, and 8 August, each with multiple issues. . . .

Determining the effect of a book is not merely a matter of counting the copies sold, though Defoe's bookseller surely did that and reacted accordingly. The impact can also be measured by the breadth of awareness, by extracts, piracies, foreign editions, and translations, by the range of response in intellectual circles, in coffeehouse society, in manorial kitchens, and in town house salons. On this basis, and within a matter of decades, *Robinson Crusoe* had reached an audience as wide as any book ever written in English. It had become a part of the literary consciousness of European civilization, a favorite work of such diverse figures as Cotton Mather, Jean-Jacques Rousseau, Benjamin Franklin, and Samuel Johnson. Johnson put it in a very special category: "Was there anything yet written by mere man that was wished longer by its readers, excepting *Don Quixote,* **Robinson Crusoe,** *Pilgrim's Progress?*"

Part of any great work's legacy is the degree to which other works of genius are based upon its premise, even if that premise becomes the grounds for a systematic critique of its values. Such was the case almost immediately for *Robinson Crusoe* in that Jonathan Swift's great narrative, *Gulliver's Travels,* required Robinson Crusoe's fame for the experiences of his own Lemuel Gulliver to carry full satiric force. Swift charts in Defoe's *Crusoe* a kind of formalized egomania, and Gulliver is a Crusoe figure who comes apart at the subjective seams, an adventurer whose ego destroys him, whose self-absorption is a mental travesty, whose compulsion is a human failing, whose neuroses take him right out of body and mind. Gulliver is doomed from the beginning because he traffics in all the goods that make up Defoe's new store for narrative—obsessive realism, mindless psychologizing, inordinate detail, self-valorization. . . .

Of course, early readers like Gildon worry less about the techniques of novelistic impersonation and story telling than about the abuses Defoe has perpetrated on a receptive audience. For Defoe to mask the economic wreck of his life in *Crusoe,* as Gildon charges in *The Life and Strange Surprizing Adventures of Mr. D— De F—, of London, Hosier,* is the worst of fictional illegitimacies. Legitimate travel experiences are one thing; adventures fabricated out of thin air are another. A travel memoir in which bogus adventures are substituted for the exigencies of one's life is trash. Gildon's objection reveals a basic dilemma for readers of Defoe's fiction. What is the status of something that claims to be real and yet is recognized as serving other potential realities? Or of something that exchanges one realistic pattern of circumstantial reality for another implied and hidden one? Gildon made his charges against *Robinson Crusoe* without a fully developed sense of the flexibility and variety of realism in fiction, but his question still haunts a good deal of Defoe criticism today.

Gildon attacked on the basis of an unexamined assumption that writers of fiction should not be pretenders to true historical writing. Those writing in the memoir tradition, those recording lives andadventures, those mapping travels have precious little leeway to invent, especially when the invention of one set of facts serves to sneak in another. But he fails or refuses to see that Defoe is writing a different kind of novel than had ever been written before, that realism is never a simple or simpleminded substitution of pretense for fact but a full imitative circumstantial scene that provides new contexts for interpreting the psychological and material pressures of reality. Precisely because Defoe could write a fully convincing and detailed rendering of the life of a shipwrecked adventurer on a remote island he could also draw into his fable parallel topics and issues ranging from personal biography to natural law, economic theory, religious conversion, colonial policy, and animal and plant husbandry.

The question that critics ought to have asked, if they had the critical wherewithal to ask it or if the form in which Defoe was working had a more pronounced history, was much more daring: What is a novel? In 1719 this was not an easy question; perhaps it is not an easy question now, but, at least, some of Defoe's work has made it a different question. An early reader such as Charles Gildon simply did not recognize the complexity of his reaction to *Crusoe,* though, curiously, Gildon guessed at its interpretable qualities and, more important, guessed that the texture of reality created in it was the beginning of an important experiment in narrative. Defoe was setting new relations between the claims made by history and those made by fiction. The mask of truth may be the strangest fiction of all, and the best fiction may masquerade as something quite different from invention.

Brian Stimpson

SOURCE: In a preface to *Robinson Crusoe: Myths and Metamorphoses,* edited by Lieve Spaas and Brian Stimpson, Macmillan Press Ltd., 1996, pp. viii-xi.

Fascination with the story of Robinson Crusoe—either as the basis for a creative rewriting or as the subject of critical enquiry—remains undiminished with time. As Pat Rogers has written [in *Robinson Crusoe,* 1979], 'Robinson Crusoe has now been in the world for well over 250 years, and continues to show rude health.' If one of the functions of a myth is to spawn a series of variations upon itself while remaining faithful to the underlying paradigm, then *Robinson Crusoe* may indeed be thus considered. Not merely the epitome of 'the whole Anglo-Saxon spirit' as Joyce would have it, nor just the embodiment of 'the characteristic aspirations of Western man' as Ian Watt has argued, the myth of *Robinson Crusoe* has continued to resonate across many ages and many cultures, as the essays in this book amply demonstrate.

The story has been rediscovered and reinterpreted through successive generations in a series of variations and modulations on the crucial themes of solitude, survival, the relation to nature and the relation to others: in short, the mythic value of *Crusoe* has become a pretext over many centuries for an examination of some of the fundamental problems of existence. In *Crusoe,* these issues are reduced to an extreme form of simplicity, yet remain susceptible to forms of reinvention and retelling that question or challenge the assumptions of race, class, gender and culture so commonly attributed to Defoe. Even these, it will be seen, are not as clearly delineated as might previously have been thought, as is evident in the still lively debate between those who view the story as a survival narrative, as religious allegory or as economic parable; to which must be added the dimension of a spiritual, even mystical discovery.

But, if *Robinson Crusoe* has attained the status of a myth, a story rediscovered and reinterpreted through successive generations, it remains a problematic narrative: is it a children's story, a traveller's tale, a religious diary or a myth for adults, or all those things at once? Though Crusoe may seem to reinvent the means for his survival, the primitivism is deceptive; the text is not innocent. As a being endowed with language and

culture, the forms of life he adopts are ideological reflections of the society he has left. The genesis of social behaviour, so admired by Rousseau, was primarily fictional, a manifestation of the anti-social instincts that condemn the 'other' to slavery. It is thus that the story may be seen at once as a comment upon the relationship between the individual and society; an heroic rejection of the old world order; a piece of pre-colonialist propaganda; a tale raising archetypal problems of 'otherness', of 'naturalness', of 'inequality', of 'origin'. For if Crusoe's removal from his social milieu invokes all the more effectively a critical judgement upon that society, it reveals at the same time another dimension at once more intimately personal and more powerfully universal: it is a mediation upon the nature of being and the relationship between self and non-self. Alone on the desert island that lies within the deepest recesses of the self, what happens to consciousness itself?

While critical enquiry has uncovered the implicit spiritual quest within the face of adventure and the view of Crusoe as pre-capitalist exploiter has been much refined, more recent versions have unpicked and reversed the master-slave relationship and gender studies and post-colonial studies have redirected attention upon aspects of the narrative previously little considered. The strength and fascination of the story, encapsulated by Defoe but not restricted to his telling, is that it escapes all ideological strictures and continues to suggest alternative readings and prompt rewritings from alternative vantage points.

A myth, perhaps, cannot be 'created', but exists only insofar as its potential for reinvention remains alive. Hence the link affirmed in the title of this book between myth and metamorphosis which cannot be seen as distinct categories. Defoe's *Robinson Crusoe* was itself already a metamorphosis: the urge to discover an uninhabited island, and to relive a transition from nature to culture, is attested in stories which existed well before he wrote his novel. As Francis Fergusson says [in *Myth and Literature,* 1966] 'One of the most striking properties of myths is that they generate new forms (like the differing children of one parent) in the imaginations of those who try to grasp them. Until some imagination, that of a poet or only a reader or auditor, is thus fecundated by a myth, the myth would seem to exist only potentially.' Myth *is* transference, adaptation, passage through language.

In the pejorative sense, a myth is one that forgets or denies that it is a myth, a symbolic image or a belief system transformed into a mental idol. For is mythification not a collective assent to mystification? Its currency is language and its creditworthiness depends upon collective credulity. But in a positive sense, a myth may be a way of recognising that there are certain spheres of knowledge and depths of experience more readily accessible to the imagination than to the cold logic of reason. A myth may make it possible to say something about the human experience through its capacity to articulate an experience that is at once singular and universal, present and absent, a lived unique experiential reality and a self-reflecting cognisance of the fictional, mystifying process that is an inherent part of all mental activity. Language is germane to the whole process: 'Myth is everything which is inseparable from language', writes Valéry. Thus in modern writing the affirmation of the myth is at the same time the means by which the mythic process is called into question, a recognition of the manner by which language is indissolubly linked to the mythic functioning of the mind. . . .

Clearly the mythic value of *Crusoe* lives in its capacity to be rewritten and to generate new forms, in its potential for metamorphosis.

Richard Phillips

SOURCE: "Introduction: Adventures in the New World" and "Mapping Adventures: Robinson Crusoe and Some Victorian Robinsonnades," in *Mapping Men and Empire: A Geography of Adventure,* Routledge, 1997, pp. 1-44.

Arthur Ransome, author of adventure stories such as *Swallows and Amazons* (1930), sketched out a genealogy of modern British adventure in a reading list intended for children who had enjoyed his own books. The list begins with *Robinson Crusoe,* which Ransome says is 'a very important book for those of you who want to know what to do on a desert island. It is also good about shipwrecks and voyages.' . . .

Among the books of travel and discovery published in the modern period, none has made a greater impression on geographical imaginations than *Robinson Crusoe,* the single most famous, representative and influential adventure story of the time. Popular since its publication in 1719, Daniel Defoe's original novel has since been transformed and redefined, with many different editions, abridgements, imitations and readings. The production of 'Robinsons' was most prolific in the nineteenth century when the story took its place among the foundational myths of British culture. It held that place until after the Second World War, when one critic argued that 'Almost universally known, almost universally thought of as at least half real, [*Robinson Crusoe*] cannot be refused the status of myth' . . .

Despite its immediate success, *Robinson Crusoe* was not to make its greatest impact, and its greatest impression upon geographical imaginations, until the nineteenth century. . . . Not until the nineteenth century was 'popular literature' truly popular across most of the geographical and social spectrum. While forty-one editions of *Robinson Crusoe* were published in Britain within forty years of its publication, the total had risen to at least 200 by the end of the nineteenth century. The production of Robinsons peaked in the Victorian period, with an average of more than two per year. In addition, 110 translations appeared in print before 1900, alongside at least 115 revisions. These assumed every conceivable form, ranging from *Robinson Crusoe in Verse* to *Robinson Crusoe in Words of One Syllable.* Godolphin replaced Bible, for example, with the mono-syllabic 'Book of God's Word,' and after the title she made only two exceptions to the one-syllable rule. Typical of many nineteenth-century Robinsons, *Robinson Crusoe in Words of One Syllable* was written in simple language, illustrated with crude colour illustrations, and aimed at very young children. A survival story and spiritual biography, the *Robinson Crusoe* story was canonised as the archetypal modern adventure story, and as a foundational myth of modern, enlightened, imperial Europe. In the eighteenth century, Jean-Jacques Rousseau (1762) became one of the first to endorse Defoe's story, which he saw as 'a complete treatise on natural education' that would 'serve as our guide during our progress to a state of reason' [according to Rousseau in 1762]. Many famous (and not-so-famous) writers and literary critics—including Karl Marx, John Ballantyne (Robert's uncle), Samuel Taylor Coleridge, James Joyce and Virginia Woolf—followed Rousseau, reading new meanings into *Robinson Crusoe* and helping to canonise it as a 'great' literary work, perhaps as a myth. . . .

Since shortly after *Robinson Crusoe* was first published, relatively few readers have encountered Defoe's complete original work, and fewer still have seen the two sequels he wrote (*The Farther Adventures of Robinson Crusoe,* 1719, and *Serious Reflections During the Life and Surprising Adventures of Robinson Crusoe,* 1720). Most who have read *Robinson Crusoe* have read a one- or two-hundred-page abridgement of some description. Many have read a children's, perhaps a boy's edition, shortened and simplified for the juvenile market, typically undated and anonymous, attributed neither to Defoe nor to the editor (who abridged and/or adapted the story). . . .

Pared down to selected essentials, *Robinson Crusoe* survives in the abbreviated form familiar to most modern readers. It is reduced to the short, simple story of a man who is shipwrecked on an island, where he learns to survive and then to prosper, where he overcomes fear, where he becomes a Christian, and where he saves and converts to Christianity a cannibal he calls Friday. Eventually, after twenty-eight years on the island, Crusoe is rescued by a passing ship. . . .

Through its narrative of colonisation and transformation on and of an island, *Robinson Crusoe* represents, promotes and legitimates a form of colonialism. When, after twenty-eight years, Crusoe finally leaves the island (on a British merchant ship he has helped save from mutineers), he leaves behind him an idealised British colony, which he hands over to the group of mutineers, whose merciful punishment it is to be left there. Before leaving, he 'talked to the men, told them my story, and how I managed all my household business.' Crusoe gives the men his story, the story of how he colonised an island. He intends the story to guide the new colonists, inspiring their practical acts and imaginatively framing their colonial encounters. Crusoe gave his story not only to the mutineers, but also to British readers. Some readers were surely inspired to go off to sea, to seek adventure in distant lands, perhaps to settle in Canada or Australia, and ultimately help to build an empire. 'To many [readers, *Robinson Crusoe*] has given the decided turn of their lives, by sending them to sea', wrote one Scottish observer in 1834. In the middle of the nineteenth century, another prominent British observer called *Robinson Crusoe*

> a book, moreover, to which, from the hardy deeds which it narrates, and the spirit of strange and romantic enterprise which it tends to awaken, England owes many of her astonishing discoveries both by sea and land, and no inconsiderable part of her naval glory.

But while *Robinson Crusoe* inspired many colonial acts, its influence was not limited to the minority of Britons who were directly engaged in such acts. To the majority of Britons who stayed at home, *Robinson Crusoe* was a powerful geographical fantasy but also a colonial myth, a myth that represented British colonialism to the British people, as well as to the colonised peoples. Crusoe's island was a Christian utopia, a middle-class utopia, a colonial utopia. The island and the adventurer represented Britain and British colonialism—including colonial land grabs and colonial violence—in the best possible light, conservatively legitimating, powerfully mapping. To the reader in nineteenth-century Britain, Crusoe's island became an image of Britain and the British Empire, not as they had been when Defoe wrote, but as they had become by the nineteenth century.

Additional coverage of Defoe's life and career is contained in the following sources published by The Gale Group: *Authors and Artists for Young Adults,* Vol. 27; *DISCovering Authors; Dictionary of Literary Biography,* Vols. 39, 95, 101; *Junior DISCovering Authors; Major Authors and Illustrators for Children and Young Adults; Something about the Author,* Vol. 22; and *World Literature Criticism.*

Franklin W. Dixon

Hardy Boys series

Collective pseudonym of more than a dozen American and Canadian authors of fiction.

Major works include the "Hardy Boys Mystery Stories" series (1927-), "Ted Scott Flying Stories" series (1927-43), "Nancy Drew and Hardy Boys" series (with Carolyn Keene, 1984-), "Hardy Boys Case File" series (1986-).

Major works about the authors include *Ghost of the Hardy Boys: An Autobiography* (by Leslie McFarlane, 1976), *Tom Swift and Company: "Boys' Books" by Stratemeyer and Others* (by John T. Dizer, Jr., 1982), *Stratemeyer Pseudonyms and Series Books: An Annotated Checklist of Stratemeyer and Stratemeyer Syndicated Publications* (by Deidre Johnson, 1982), *The Secret of the Stratemeyer Syndicate: Nancy Drew, the Hardy Boys, and the Million-Dollar Fiction Fantasy* (by Carol Billman, 1986), *The Mysterious Case of Nancy Drew and the Hardy Boys* (by Carol Kismaric and Marvin Heiferman, 1998).

The following entry is devoted to criticism on the Hardy Boys series.

INTRODUCTION

For more than seventy years, the pseudonym Franklin W. Dixon has been synonymous with the Hardy Boys series, a multivolume set of mysteries for readers in the middle grades through high school that Jonathan Cott of *Esquire* has called "the most popular boys' books of all time." The authorial collective, a group of ghostwriters that were generally employed as part of the Stratemeyer Syndicate by publishing magnate Edward L. Stratemeyer or his daughter Harriet Stratemeyer Adams, is responsible for composing stories about the exploits of two teenage brothers, Frank and Joe Hardy, who are both all-American boys and brilliant detectives. Edward L. Stratemeyer applied Henry Ford's assembly-line approach to automobile production to the creation of books; the Stratemeyer Syndicate used hundreds of uncredited writers to saturate the marketplace with series titles. In addition to the Hardy Boys, the Stratemeyer Syndicate created such well known series as Nancy Drew (the series closest to the Hardy Boys in popularity), Tom Swift, the Bobbsey Twins, and the Happy Hollisters. The Franklin W. Dixon name was also used for the Ted Scott Flying Stories, a series of adventures about an intrepid airman modeled after Charles Lindbergh. Stratemeyer created the concept of the Hardy Boys in the mid-1920s, hiring a pool of talented writers to flesh out the titles and plots that he devised; Harriet

Stratemeyer Adams continued the tradition after her father's death. Although the Hardy Boys were Stratemeyer's creation, it is generally thought that the initial writer of the series, Leslie McFarlane, gave the series its distinctive character and helped to ensure its success with young readers. A Canadian novelist, short story writer, journalist, and filmmaker, McFarlane, who wrote the first eleven volumes in the series, as well as ten additional Hardy Boys mysteries, decided to invest the books with a more sophisticated structure and style than was usually associated with escapist literature. McFarlane filled his works with suspense and humor and gave the teenage sleuths a decidedly antiauthoritarian attitude. After McFarlane's retirement from the Syndicate, the series became more modernized and faster-paced. Several of the initial volumes were revised to make them relevant to contemporary readers while excising racial and ethnic stereotypes.

A preface in each volume of the Hardy Boys books states the philosophy of the series: "Believing that right will triumph—that lawbreakers can be brought to justice—the Hardys work day and night to accomplish their goals." In Edward L. Stratemeyer's original concept, Frank and Joe Hardy—sons of Fenton Hardy, a respected New York City criminologist who has begun his own agency in Bayport, a small town on the Atlantic coast—are sixteen and fifteen years old respectively. Later volumes of the series depict the Hardy Boys as eighteen and seventeen, while the "Hardy Boys Case File" series, stories directed to young adults, picture the characters as twenty-two and twenty. The boys, who have inherited their father's investigative ability, are distinguished by their personalities and appearance: Frank is dark-haired, rational, and dependable, while Joe is blonde, passionate, and more of a swashbuckler. Working as a team, the brothers solve crimes—murder, drug peddling, kidnapping, auto theft, hijacking, espionage, and terrorist acts, among others—while their father is otherwise engaged. In earlier volumes of the series, the boys concentrate on local cases such as smuggling and counterfeiting, but, in more recent volumes, the brothers investigate criminal activities with a high-tech flavor, such as the retrieval of stolen Pentagon papers and hijacked nuclear cargo, and work internationally with the CIA and Scotland Yard. The Hardy Boys always bring the perpetrators—several of whom hide out in the caves and cliffs surrounding Bayport—to justice through their facility with straightforward detection; in addition, the brothers use their fists (both boys are talented boxers), a variety of gadgets, occasional weapons, and fast cars, boats, and motorcycles. The sleuths are aided in their quest for justice by their "chums," who include Chet Morton, a chubby, wisecracking farmboy with a voracious appetite; his sister Iola, who is Joe's loyal girlfriend; Callie Shaw, a blonde attracted to Frank whom Louis Phillips of *Armchair Detective* called "a paradigm of purity, chastity, and all-American girlhood"; Phil Cohen, a stouthearted Jewish boy who is an electronics whiz; Tony Prito, a fearless young Italian immigrant; and Allen "Biff" Hooper, an athlete who can always be counted on in a fight. In later books in the series, Asian-American and Jamaican boys are featured as "chums." The Hardy family is completed by mother Laura, a home-maker who is constantly worried about her sons, and her sister Gertrude, a sixtyish spinster with an acerbic man-ner but a heart of gold. The Hardy Boys solve their cases with little help from adults, most notably the Bayport police force. Originally, Leslie McFarlane por-trayed this group as particularly obtuse, a quality that made them the butt of much of the humor in the series. However, after Edward Stratemeyer asked him to tone down the Keystone Kops-like characterizations of the officers, McFarlane did so while retaining the healthy regard of the young detectives for bureaucratic ineffi-ciency. At the end of each novel, the Hardy Boys are rewarded, often with a large check or a banquet and always with the approval of their father.

Biographical Information

Edward L. Stratemeyer, the creator of both the Hardy Boys and the pseudonym Franklin W. Dixon, was born in New Jersey in 1862. The son of German immigrants, Stratemeyer began writing at twenty-six, penning a story on wrapping paper while working in his brother's tobac-co shop. When he sold this story to a magazine for seventy-five dollars, Stratemeyer saw the money-making potential in publishing. He began writing dime novels, pulp fiction that preceded cloth-covered books. In the 1890s, he edited a popular boys' weekly magazine pro-duced by Street and Smith, the publishing house respon-sible for the novels of Horatio Alger. In 1899, his employers asked Stratemeyer to complete some of Alg-er's unfinished novels as a ghostwriter and to create a few original works; one of the latter contained the sub-title "Frank Hardy's Road to Success." In the same year, Stratemeyer created the Rover Boys, a juvenile series that set the tone for the Hardy Boys books by featuring two heroes (instead of the usual one) who had thrilling adventures and who operated without adult in-terference. Stratemeyer launched the Rover Boys series by publishing three books simultaneously, a concept that circumvented the problem of waiting until several volumes were on the market before a series made an impression with buyers. Realizing that he could make more money by hiring a stable of writers, he founded the Stratemeyer Syndicate in 1906. Stratemeyer adver-tised for writers who needed fast money and then sent them sketches of settings and characters along with a chapter-by-chapter outline of each plot. Writers had a few weeks to write their copy; the books were then edited by Stratemeyer, who paid his authors an average of fifty to one hundred dollars per title and published their works pseudonymously. In their contracts, writers were asked to waive all residuals from their books.

In 1926, Leslie McFarlane, a twenty-three year old reporter and short-story writer who had moved to the United States from northern Ontario, responded to Strate-meyer's ad for an experienced fiction writer to work from a publisher's outlines. McFarlane was hired to write about Dave Fearless, a deep-sea diving detective. In 1927, Stratemeyer asked McFarlane to write three novels in a new series about two crime-fighting broth-ers, the Hardy Boys. McFarlane wanted to invest the series with attributes lacking in other series titles. In his autobiography, *Ghost of the Hardy Boys,* he recalled, "It seemed to me that the Hardy Boys deserved some-thing better than the slapdash treatment Dave Fearless had been getting . . . [D]id the new series have to be all that hack? There was, after all, the chance to con-tribute a little style, occasional words of more than two syllables, maybe a little sensory stimuli. . . . They were written swiftly, but not carelessly. I gave thought to grammar, sentence structure, choice of words, pace, the techniques of suspense." He added, "I decided against the course of common sense. I opted for Quality." After publishing the first three volumes of the series—*The Tower Treasure, The House on the Cliff,* and *The Secret of the Old Mill*—in 1927, Stratemeyer waited to see if the Hardy Boys would reach their audience before ap-proving a fourth title. The Hardy Boys volumes were immediately successful, and Stratemeyer continued to send outlines for new adventures to McFarlane.

Stratemeyer established rules for the Hardy Boys series: there was to be no sex, profanity, or serious violence, and every episode must end with a cliff-hanger. While remaining faithful to Stratemeyer's dictates, McFarlane added his own touches to the series, including the Dick-ensian cast of police officers, the brothers' cavalier at-titude toward the constabulary, and the character of Aunt Gertrude, a figure beloved by most readers of the nov-els. McFarlane continued to write about the Hardy Boys—getting as much as $150 per adventure—while publishing adult novels and short stories. In 1930, Edward Strate-meyer, who never met Leslie McFarlane, passed away; at the time of his death, Stratemeyer had published over eight hundred books for children, two hundred of which he had written himself. Harriet Stratemeyer Adams, a writer and Wellesley graduate, took over the Syndicate. In the mid-1930s, Adams asked McFarlane to write several volumes of another detective series, the Dana Girls, under the pseudonym Carolyn Keene; this pseud-onym was also used for the Nancy Drew series. McFar-lane stopped working for the Stratemeyer Syndicate in the late 1940s; his last published Hardy Boys book was *The Phantom Freighter* (1947). After his retirement, McFarlane began writing radio plays for the Canadian Broadcasting Corporation (CBC) and writing and direct-ing films for the National Film Board of Canada. Mc-Farlane's script for the documentary short *Herring Hunt* was nominated for an Academy Award and his feature film *Royal Journey* received a British Film Academy Award. In 1953, he became chief editor for television drama at the CBC; in the late 1960s, he worked in Hollywood as a screenwriter for the *Bonanza* television series. McFarlane also continued writing novels; one of his books, *McGonigle Scores!* (1966), is often considered the best hockey book ever written for children. McFarlane did not confess that he was the architect of the Hardy Boys series until 1976; after his death the next year, he was called Canada's best-selling author. McFarlane was surprised that his novels about the Hardy Boys were considered controversial. In *Ghost of the Hardy Boys,* he wrote, "It never occurred to me that these scenes could be construed as subversive, that educators and librarians—mighty sour folk at the time—might scream that my belly-buster was deliberately calculated to shatter any respect the kids might have for the sacred institutions of law and order. I wasn't writing for educators and librarians; I was writing for youngsters."

Harriet Stratemeyer Adams, who herself contributed to the Hardy Boys series, hired a number of successors to Leslie McFarlane, most notably Andrew E. Svenson, a newspaperman who became a partner in the Syndicate, and James Duncan Lawrence, a scriptwriter for radio and a writer of newspaper comic strips. Adams died in 1982; after her death, the Stratemeyer Syndicate was disbanded, and the Hardy Boys series became the joint property of two publishers, Simon and Schuster and Grosset and Dunlap. The novels are still produced today by a new crop of ghostwriters. In the 1950s, the series was adapted for television by Walt Disney Productions in a live-action program that appeared on the *Mickey Mouse Club.* In the late 1960s, the Hardy Boys became an animated cartoon, while in the late 1970s, the series was again adapted for television, this time by the American Broadcasting Corporation. The Hardy Boys was also turned into a syndicated television series in the mid-1990s. In addition, the series has inspired many spin-off products, including games and comic, coloring, and activity books.

Critical Reception

The Hardy Boys series is considered a phenomenon of both children's literature and popular culture. Its popularity—the series has sold over two hundred million copies in both hardcover and paperback—is undisputed, while its place in literature continues to be debated, although with a somewhat less negative emphasis than in the past. The Hardy Boys books are viewed as heirs to the pulp fiction genre and the adult mystery novels of such authors as Ellery Queen and Erle Stanley Gardner, as well as to traditional series for boys such as the rags-to-riches stories of Horatio Alger and Edward L. Stratemeyer's own Rover Boys adventure tales. By blending mystery, suspense, and humor with a minimum of introspection, the Hardy Boys novels are credited with bringing the genre of the adventure story to a new level, one that focuses on detection while creating a successfully repeatable formula. The Hardy Boys series is often noted for its exciting plots, fast-paced action, evocative atmosphere, and cliff-hanging suspense. In addition, the novels authored by Leslie McFarlane are acknowledged for their upgraded literary style, cultural allusions, and insouciant attitude toward authority. Although some critics have

noted that subsequent volumes of the series are just simple narratives with no discernible style, others praise the crisp dialogue and fresh descriptions that accompany the action in the books. Since its inception, the series has had its detractors. Librarians and parents often considered the books to be without literary value, while reviewers berated the conventional gimmickry, stilted phrasing, underdeveloped characterizations, predictability, and lack of depth of the series. The Hardy Boys books have also been criticized for containing racial stereotyping, although they are also defended for their consistent inclusion of ethnic characters. In 1959, Harriet Stratemeyer Adams decided that the earlier volumes of the series needed to be revised for both literary content and political correctness. The new texts removed objectionable material while featuring a faster pace and a more concise writing style. Overall, the new volumes were poorly received; for example, Mark Caldwell of the *Voice Literary Supplement* stated, "Revision eviscerated the books." In the 1960s, the Hardy Boys loosened up a bit, playing in a rock band and having more of an eye for the opposite sex. However, critics slammed the series for its WASP-ish family structure and for the one-dimensional personalities and secondary roles given to Laura Hardy, Iola Morton, and Callie Shaw. The Hardy Boys themselves were often considered anachronistic characters locked into a state of perpetual boyhood not unlike that of Peter Pan. In 1991, facsimile editions of the first three Hardy Boys novels were published by Applewood Books to great critical acclaim.

Despite the objections of some adults to the Hardy Boys series, the books have always been beloved by young readers, particularly for the adventure, action, and humor of the series. In addition, the Hardy Boys are often considered role models for young people: their everyman quality—ordinary boys performing extraordinary feats of detection—is often regarded as an important reason for their longevity as literary characters. These teens solve mysteries and defeat bullies while driving fast cars and acting without adult supervision, characteristics that still attract children. The Hardy Boys series is often credited with encouraging youngsters to read, and it is especially popular with reluctant readers. Moreover, the novels are praised for their positive stance toward moral issues: in the Hardy Boys books, evil is always defeated. While some critics still dismiss the series as low-quality literature, others acknowledge the value of the Hardy Boys. In her book *The Secret of the Stratemeyer Syndicate,* Carol Billman concluded, "Readers need to spend quiet hours in such a retreat—a moratorium, if you will—during which they can amass latent energy for the last stage of growth and adulthood. The readily available, jam-packed, and familiar mystery adventures of Frank and Joe Hardy fill that time to a T." Mark Caldwell further commented that the books "occupied a niche unique to this day in kiddie lit." Writing in the *Beaver,* Shane Peacock stated, "The Hardy Boys, warts and all, and lowbrow, are a part of the history of our popular culture. To change them is to try and re-write history. . . . There is no shame in writing books that give such pleasure. In fact, it is an accomplishment worth a fortune." Louis Phillips noted, "F. W. Dixon knew what he was doing every step of the way. . . . I would rather a child read these books than the works most librarians and teachers would recommend." Maya Ilyse Amster added, "Almost every boy wishes he could be a Hardy."

AUTHOR'S COMMENTARY

Leslie McFarlane

SOURCE: In *Ghost of the Hardy Boys: An Autobiography,* Methuen, 1976, 211 p.

[*A Canadian journalist and freelance writer, McFarlane was contracted by Edward L. Stratemeyer, head of the productive literary syndicate that bore his name, to launch the "Hardy Boys" detective series under the pseudonym Franklin W. Dixon, a name that all writers of Hardy Boys mysteries would adopt. Stratemeyer sent McFarlane an outline of the first volume in the series,* The Tower Treasure, *which was published in 1927. McFarlane wrote the first eleven titles, as well as ten additional Hardy Boys mysteries.*]

I received a communication from Edward Stratemeyer. . . . It consisted of an outline of two chapters of a book and a cryptic note suggesting that I try my hand at the two chapters by way of a trial run. He pointed out again that the assignment did not involve money, but added that if the two chapters met his standard, he would be pleased to offer me a contract to finish the book for a total payment of $100. All rights to the book would become the exclusive property of the Stratemeyer Syndicate. . . .

The outline of this new, as yet unwritten volume, called *Dave Fearless Under the Ocean* (or *The Treasure of the Lost Submarine*) ran for three pages of single-spaced typescript and went something like this:

CHAP. 1–Dave and Bob cruising off Long Island in launch Amos run into fog—mention first and second volumes of series—engine fails—ring reminds Bob of adventures on Volcano Island—mention other volumes—boys discuss Lem and Bart Hankers, believed dead—sound of foghorn is heard—ocean liner looms out of fog—collision seems inevitable.

CHAP. 2—Ship veers off in nick of time—boys hear warning bell and see lighthouse—fix engine—almost pile up on dangerous reef—night and darkness—searchlight suddenly reveals mass of wreckage dead ahead—launch crashes into wreckage and catches fire—boys dive into water—boat blows up—Dave looks for Bob.

It went on for twenty-three more chapters, each loaded with action. When I put down the outline pages my head

was swimming. My impression was that *Dave Fearless Under the Ocean* called for more perils and narrow escapes than a normal diver would encounter in several lifetimes. It all seemed pretty frantic.

I had sense enough to realize, however, that Mr. Stratemeyer was not hiring a critic. The creator of Dave Fearless knew what he wanted and was willing to pay for it. True, the payment would be modest even by the 1926 Consumers' Index, but it added up to more than two weeks' earnings at the *Republican*.

That night, after everyone had gone home for the day, a sheet of paper went into the typewriter and the keys began to clatter.

DAVE FEARLESS UNDER THE OCEAN

or

THE TREASURE OF THE LOST SUBMARINE

by

Roy Rockwood

CHAPTER 1

THE MENACE FROM THE MIST

After a few moments of meditation and perusal of the outline, the keys clattered again.

Dave Fearless looked out over the rolling waves and frowned as he saw a greasy cloud rolling in from the horizon.

"There's a fog coming up, Bob."

"Looks like it. Do you think we had better turn back?"

"Perhaps we should," agreed Dave. "We want to be back at Quanatack in time for supper."

The two chums, Dave Fearless, young deep-sea diver, and Bob Vilett, marine engineer, were cruising off the coast of Long Island in Dave's motor boat, the Amos. Now, as Dave remarked, a fog was rising and they were a long way from home.

So much for the narrative hook, in the standard tradition of pulp fiction. Get your story going on the first page with a passage of action and dialogue. Introduce your chief character in a dramatic situation.

But this wasn't pulp fiction. This was a book series. The outline stipulated mention of the first and second volumes. It was time to leave Dave and Bob in the fog for a while and give a summary of *Dave Fearless After a Sunken Treasure,* thoughtfully provided by Mr. Stratemeyer. Not too much. Just enough to let the young readers know where they stood, and enough to tempt them into blowing their dimes on the whole series. Then, back to the fog. . . .

I mailed the two chapters to Stratemeyer and awaited his verdict with confidence. I felt that the chapters were every bit as good as anything in *Dave Fearless Among the Icebergs*. Better, in fact. I pictured Edward Stratemeyer tossing his hat in the air and shouting, "Hurray! I have found my man!"

Shortly after, the quietly zealous Emerson C. Lowell invited me into his office to reveal some information he had uncovered on our mysterious Mr. Stratemeyer.

"Have you ever heard of *The Rover Boys*?" he asked.

"Of course. I read a couple of them when I was a kid . . . Stratemeyer wrote *The Rover Boys*?"

"Among other things. I haven't read any of them, of course. I understand that some twenty titles in the series have sold upward of five million copies."

"But they're awful!"

"Naturally. You see, Stratemeyer took over from Alger."

"Horatio Alger?"

"There is only one Alger."

"What do you mean by saying Stratemeyer took over?"

"There seems to be a little controversy about this matter, that is, if one can say the issue is worth being controversial about. Before Alger died in 1900 it seems he had published more than 100 books, which sold in the millions. Biggest selling writer in America, no question about it. But after he died, more Alger books came out. There seemed to be no stopping them. About eleven new Alger books appeared before it was revealed that Stratemeyer had a hand in them. Stratemeyer used to be one of Alger's editors, besides being a writer of the same kind of stuff himself, and a friend of Alger. He said Alger had appointed him his literary executor and that the new books were written from outlines found in Alger's papers."

Mr. Stratemeyer, however, had another claim to eminence.

"It seems," said Lowell, "that Stratemeyer runs a fiction factory."

"A factory?"

Lowell explained that Edward Stratemeyer was responsible—"or to blame, if you like"—for most of the inexpensive juvenile books published in America.

"He sets up ideas for series, sells the ideas to publishers and then hires people to write the books. Nearly all the popular juvenile series such as Tom Swift and the like come straight from Stratemeyer's assembly line. Mass-produced. Mass-merchandized. Typical American idea."

"That's very interesting," I said, but didn't bother to explain my interest.

Mr. Lowell rummaged through a desk drawer and handed me a pamphlet entitled "The Winnetka Survey."

"The head of the Winnetka public school system—that's in Illinois—made a survey in 1914 for the American Library Association. Nearly 40,000 pupils in thirty-four cities were asked about their reading preferences. The results were alarming. The kids voted almost unanimously for junk." He checked the pamphlet. "Ninety-eight percent."

"*The Rover Boys* were right up there?"

"Not quite. *Tom Swift* nosed them out."

"Tom Swift, the boy inventor. Victor Appleton, author."

Mr. Lowell nodded his head in agreement "I have it on good authority that Victor Appleton is Edward Stratemeyer. These books are published in series. They sell for fifty cents. All the series books swept the Winnetka Survey. Apparently that's what young America is reading nowadays," he sighed.

"Better than nothing."

"I doubt it. The argument is that they encourage the reading habit and that when youngsters outgrow *The Rover Boys* and *Tom Swift* they'll go on to bigger and better things."

"It sounds reasonable."

"I'm afraid they merely go on to Harold Bell Wright, who wrote *The Winning of Barbara Worth,* which qualifies him to be regarded as our very worst writer. Frankly," he confided, "the more I learn about the publishing business the more I wonder what I'm doing in this office."

"Maybe the Winnetka Survey will do some good."

"Some libraries have banned the fifty-cent juveniles. You realize what that means."

"The kids will read better books."

"The kids will stop going to libraries, where they might be exposed to better books. Instead of taking out a *Tom Swift* on loan they'll buy it. The sales will boom. I wish you hadn't brought up the subject." Mr. Lowell reached for his hat. "I find the whole situation so revolting that it will take a couple of stiff drinks to restore my faith in the future of the Republic. Will you join me in a little trip around the corner?"

In the speakeasy Mr. Lowell insisted on proposing a toast to the damnation of Edward Stratemeyer. To refuse would have involved explanations I didn't care to give at the moment. In my turn I proposed a toast to F. Scott Fitzgerald, who had recently published *The Great Gatsby,* and Mr. Lowell cheered up immediately and decided that American literature was flourishing in spite of everything. . . .

It turned out that I *could* count on Edward Stratemeyer. Before the week was out a long envelope brought another outline, accompanied by a letter explaining his "other plans." He had observed, Stratemeyer wrote, that detective stories had become very popular in the world of adult fiction. He instanced the works of S. S. Van Dine, which were selling in prodigious numbers as I was well aware. S. S. Van Dine was neither an ocean liner nor a living man but the pseudonym of Willard Hungtington Wright, a literary craftsman who wrote sophisticated stories for Mencken's *Smart Set.*

It had recently occurred to him, Stratemeyer continued, that the growing boys of America might welcome similar fare. Of course, he had already given them Nat Ridley, but Nat really didn't solve mysteries; he merely blundered into them and, after a given quota of hairbreadth escapes, blundered out again. What Stratemeyer had in mind was a series of detective stories on the juvenile level, involving two brothers of high-school age who would solve such mysteries as came their way. To lend credibility to their talents, they would be the sons of a professional private investigator, so big in his field that he had become a sleuth of international fame. His name—Fenton Hardy. His sons, Frank and Joe, would therefore be known as . . .

The Hardy Boys!

This would be the title of the series. My pseudonym would be Franklin W. Dixon. (I never did learn what the "W" represented. Certainly not Wealthy.)

Stratemeyer noted that the books would be clothbound and therefore priced a little higher than paperbacks. This in turn would justify a little higher payment for the manuscript—$125 to be exact. He had attached an information sheet for guidance and the plot outline of the initial volume, which would be called *The Tower Treasure.* In closing, he promised that if the manuscript came up to expectations—which were high—I would be asked to do the next two volumes of the series.

The background information was terse. The setting would be a small city called Bayport on Barmet Bay "somewhere on the Atlantic Coast." The boys would attend Bayport High. Their mother's name would be Laura. They would have three chums: Chet, a chubby farm boy, humorist of the group; Biff Hooper, an athletic two-fisted type who could be relied on to balance the scales in the event of a fight; and Tony Prito, who would presumably tag along to represent all ethnic minorities.

Two girls would also make occasional appearances. One of them, Iola Morton, sister of Chet, would be favorably regarded by Joe. The Other, Callie Shaw, would be tolerated by Frank. It was intimated that relations between the Hardy boys and their girl friends would not go beyond the borders of wholesome friendship and discreet mutual esteem.

I got the message. There was to be no petting, as it was known at the time. None of the knee-pawing, tit-squeezing stuff that was sneaking in to so much popular fiction, to the disgust of all right-thinking people. Wholesome American boys never got a hard-on. (Why was that?)

I skimmed through the outline. It was about a robbery in a towered mansion belonging to Hurd Applegate, an eccentric stamp collector. The Hardy Boys solved it.

What a change from Dave Fearless! No man-eating sharks. No octopi. No cannibals, polar bears or man-eating trees. Just the everyday doings of everyday lads in everyday surroundings. They didn't go wandering all over the seven seas, pursued by imbecile relatives. They stayed at home, checked in for dinner every night like other kids. They even went to school. Granted, they didn't appear to spend very much time at school; most of the outline seemed to be devoted to extracurricular activities after four and on weekends. But they went.

I was so relieved to be free of Dave Fearless and his dreary helpers that I greeted Frank and Joe Hardy with positive rapture, and I wrote to Stratemeyer to accept the assignment. Then I rolled a sheet of paper into the typewriter and prepared to go to work.

Then I paused and gave the project a little thought. The sensible course would have been to hammer out the thing at breakneck speed, regardless of style, spelling or grammar, and let the Stratemeyer editors tidy it up. Bang it out, stuff the typed sheets in an envelope and put it in the mail, the quicker the better, and get going on the next book. In this sort of business, at the payment involved, time was money, output was everything.

Writers, however, aren't always sensible. Many of them enjoy writing so much that they would go on doing it even if deprived of bylines and checks, which is why agents are born. The enjoyment implies doing the best one can with the task in hand, even if it is merely an explanatory letter to the landlord. (There is no special virtue in this. Writers just can't help it.)

It seemed to me that the Hardy boys deserved something better than the slapdash treatment Dave Fearless had been getting. It was still hack work, no doubt, but did the new series have to be all that hack? There was, after all, the chance to contribute a little style, occasional words of more than two syllables, maybe a little sensory stimuli.

Take food, for example. From my boyhood reading I recalled enjoying any scenes that involved eating. Boys are always hungry. Whether the outline called for it or not, I decided that the Hardy boys and their chums would eat frequently. When Laura Hardy packed a picnic lunch the provender would be described in detail, not only when she stowed it away but when the boys did. And when the boys solved the mystery of the theft, Hurd Applegate wouldn't stop at a mere cash reward. He would come up with a lavish dinner, good for at least two pages of lip smacking. Maybe even belches.

And then there was humor. There hadn't been so much as a snicker in the whole Dave Fearless series. This stood to reason: a man-eating shark is no laughing matter. Next to food, however, boys like jokes. Why not inject a few rib ticklers into *The Tower Treasure*? Chet Morton was described as a "fun loving lad," and, as he was supposed to be "chubby," it followed that food interest might be maintained by making him a glutton. The cast of characters also gave passing mention to Chief Collig, head of the Bayport Police Department, and his associate, Detective Smuff. While the outline did not suggest that these lawmen were comical fellows, it did seem that anyone named Collig had to be a pretty stodgy cop and that Smuff would simply have to be a dunderhead.

I could hardly wait to get at them.

But why go to all this trouble? If *The Tower Treasure* was a little better written than the usual fifty-cent juvenile, who would get the credit? The nonexistent Franklin W. Dixon. If better writing and a little humor helped make the series a success, who would benefit financially? The Stratemeyer Syndicate and the publishers. The writer who brought the skeleton outline to life wouldn't get a penny even if the books sold a million—which, of course, seemed impossible at the time.

So what? I decided against the course of common sense. I opted for Quality.

The typewriter clattered: "Chapter One: The Speed Demon."

As the boys jounced noisily on their way to the village of Willowville they discussed their mutual ambition to follow in the footsteps of their father, Fenton Hardy, internationally famous private sleuth. The whole passage of dialogue, improbably conducted over the racket of two motorcycles, depressed me. I put an end to it as quickly as possible and moved into the heavy action: the lads were being overtaken by an automobile apparently driven by a maniac. Normally the situation would merely call for evasive action (taking to the shoulder), but a normal situation wouldn't do, as any old hand from the pulp diggings knows. It is necessary to arrange the topography so that an abnormal situation will prevail.

I decided to conjure up a very steep cliff towering above the road on the left and balance it with a very steep declivity dropping off precipitously on the right, straight down into the waters of Barmet Bay. Without a shoulder for refuge, the situation now contained the essential elements of peril, as the pursuing car and lunatic-in-charge gained rapidly on the Hardy boys.

They looked back again. The car was being driven so recklessly that it bounced all over the road, weaving from side to side. It lurched toward the cliff in a cloud of dust. It veered to the other side of the road and almost took off into the sea. The Hardy boys decided to pull over to the shoulder only to find—thanks to my topographical arrangements—that it had been replaced by a 200-foot drop to Barmet Bay, straight down, as the skidding car hurtled right at them.

End of Chapter One.

There may have been some readers who broke into a cold sweat at this stage and couldn't wait to read Chapter Two to find out if the lads met instant death. If so, they were very young, deplorably naive or perhaps a little backward. Before they finished *The Tower Treasure* they would have learned the main fact of life in the world of juvenile fiction: no peril, no danger, no catastrophe, however grim and apparently inescapable, is ever as bad as it seems. These innocents were no doubt vastly relieved when the car missed the boys by inches in the second paragraph of Chapter Two and went bounding and skidding on its errant way.

But not before a clue was planted. The boys saw that the driver of the car had "a shock of red hair." On the way to Willowville they discovered a wrecked car, minus license plates, in the ditch. After checking, like good citizens, to make sure no one was pinned in the wreckage, they went on to Chet Morton's place, "a big, homelike, rambling old farmhouse with an apple orchard at the rear."

This apple orchard was important as a source of provender for the amiable Chet. Whenever he appeared in a Hardy Boys book, from that day onward it was invariably noted that he was eating an apple, which established him as a bit of a glutton. He gobbled up the produce of the whole orchard every year.

The boys found their chum, Chet, in a wrathful mood. Some scamp had just stolen his brand-new, yellow roadster. Tally-ho! All three boys piled onto the Hardy motorcycles and roared away in search of the thief. First, however, they paid another visit to the wrecked car in the ditch where the Hardy boys discovered something they had unaccountably failed to notice the first time: this was the very car that had nearly bounced them into Barmet Bay. They figured it all out in a jiffy: the red-haired speed demon, after coming to grief in the ditch, had pinched Chet's car.

Tally-ho again, pausing only once to make inquiries along the way. This gave me a great opportunity to work in a little comedy by way of some over-the-fence dialogue with four rustics toiling in a field. These yokels were so obtuse that they debated solemnly the issue of whether the car that had recently gone by was a roadster or a delivery truck. Then they engaged in a wild argument over the respective merits of touring cars and coupes, reaching the brink of combat, when the boys departed unenlightened.

A real knee-slapper, that passage, with its not-so-subtle reflections on the mentality of the agricultural community. In the 1920s, stereotypes in humor were predictable: Negroes were always cowardly, shiftless, lazy and unlettered; Irishmen were incredibly dumb; Jews were avaricious; Scots were stingy; farmers—otherwise known as hayseeds—were credulous idiots. A smart-ass comedian never wanted for targets.

About two pages later, when the boys reached Bayport and headed for the police station to report the theft of Chet's car, I had another gold-plated opportunity to exercise my comic itch. Cops were always good for laughs. And here were two of them—Chief Collig and Detective Smuff.

Chorting happily, I typed my way through a rib-tickling encounter between the boys and two of the dumbest cops I could dream up. That scene, I told myself with pardonable pride, could be guaranteed to send every kid lucky enough to read it into hysterics. A belly-buster.

It never occurred to me that these scenes could be construed as subversive, that educators and librarians—mighty sour folk at any time—might scream that my belly-buster was deliberately calculated to shatter any respect the kids might have for the sacred institutions of law and order. I wasn't writing for educators and librarians; I was writing for youngsters.

In any case, the big comedy scene was interrupted by the arrival of Ike Harrity, ticket seller at the steamboat office, reporting a hold-up, and a witness who said the hold-up man had driven away in a yellow roadster and that the fellow was redheaded. The only trouble was that Harrity had described the man as dark haired.

When great confusion and argument ensued, the Hardy boys went home to consult their father. The internationally famous detective wasn't very helpful, although he gave them a lecture to the effect that a good detective must be very observant and pay attention to details. As an object lesson he embarrassed them by asking them the color of the school superintendent's hair. Joe said it was brown; Frank said it was black.

Fenton Hardy, who had seen the superintendent only once in his life while crossing a street, humbled his sons by informing them that the superintendent was bald and wore a chestnut wig. He added that the pedagogue wore buttoned shoes, was a member of the Elks and a great fan of the late Charles Dickens. He had learned these facts in five seconds flat, by one observant look. All this was straight out of Sherlock Holmes. In fact, Sherlock would probably have muffed the elk's tooth clue and wondered, instead, why superintendent Norton was wearing a lousy tooth as a watch-charm on his waistcoat.

It was not until Chapter Seven, however, that the book got into high gear when Hurd Applegate, an eccentric philatelist who lived with his sister, Adelia, in the Tower Mansion on the outskirts of Bayport, was robbed of $40,000 worth of jewels and securities. Understandably, he had so little confidence in the Bayport police force with its assorted stumblebums that he took his troubles to Fenton Hardy.

First, however, he fired his caretaker, Henry Robinson. It appeared that honest Henry had just paid off a $900 bank loan. This automatically made him a suspect character. As a result young Perry Robinson, school chum of the Hardy boys and therefore an upright lad of high moral character, had to leave school and go to work in a grocery store to support the family. As a further consequence, the Robinsons were kicked out of their living quarters in the Tower Mansion and forced to set up housekeeping in "a poor quarter of the city." (Bayport wasn't rich enough to afford slums.)

The sad situation now provided material for an affecting scene in which Frank and his girl friend, Callie Shaw, went to visit the afflicted family. Clearly, Henry Robinson was unjustly accused. Out of work, he was also ineligible for unemployment benefits, welfare or food stamps because the Coolidge administration hadn't created these benefits. Frank and Callie were touched by Mrs. Robinson's gallant efforts to keep the humble cottage clean and neat, as well as by her faith in husband Henry's innocence. The fact that this lachrymose chapter was based on practically every book Horatio Alger ever wrote didn't bother me a bit.

Fenton Hardy latched onto a clue and disappeared on the trail of a rascal named Red Jackley, an ex-con with a weakness for burglary and red wigs. Red Jackley was now lying unconscious and on the point of death in an out-of-town hospital, and might recover just long enough to make a death-bed confession.

Then the Bayport Keystone Kops showed up. They too had heard about Jackley and now declared themselves in on any death-bed confessions that might be floating around. Clearly, if Fenton Hardy was to claim credit and reward, somebody had to prevent Chief Collig and Detective Smuff from boarding the seven o'clock train. This problem paved the way for one of my great comic set pieces—the Great Fruit Stand Bomb Hoax—established on the shaky premises that all cops are dumb and that any immigrant who hasn't mastered the English language is just naturally an object of mirth.

It was Chet Morton's idea to plant a bomb in the fruit stand of Rocco, a character of infinite humorous possibilities because he tacked an "a" to the end of every verb, was highly excitable and had a very silly fear of the Black Hand organization, the 1926 forerunner of the Mafia. The bomb, of course, was merely an alarm clock in a shoebox, but when the Hardy boys and their merry chums called Rocco's attention to the ticking noise and suggested that Rocco had incurred the enmity of the

Black Hand, instant comedy erupted. The frantic Rocco danced in the street, shrieking his apprehensions in splintered English and yelling for the police. Chief Collig and Detective Smuff lumbered to the scene, all bluster and bravery until they heard the oranges ticking away, whereupon they dissolved into abject cowardice. Now, to their relief, an even more comic member of the Bayport constabulary came plodding around the corner in the person of Constable Con Riley, who was promptly ordered to locate and dispose of the bomb.

Over the years, dozens of small boys have told me that the Bomb Hoax has always been high on their private list of Select Comic Readings of All Time. Snickering, they recalled their glee when Con Riley poured about forty buckets of water on the fruit stand, quaking while Collig and Smuff urged him from a safe distance and promised him a staff funeral if the oranges blew up. Grown men have assured me that they still remember the scene with affection.

In any event, the Hoax served a double purpose. It made the kids laugh and it made Collig and Smuff miss their train.

Fenton Hardy was the only person at Jackley's bedside when the criminal rallied long enough to confess that the loot was hidden "in the old tower."

At this point it appeared that the case was all wrapped up. All the Hardy boys had to do now was search the towers of Hurd Applegate's mansion and recover the gems and securities. Then they could pocket the reward and go around town taking well-earned bows. But this was merely the end of Chapter Sixteen. With eight more chapters to go, any reasonably bright reader would understand that it wasn't going to be all that easy. And it wasn't.

When the Hardy boys ransacked the towers, they drew a blank. Hurd Applegate and Sister Adelia threw them out. Fenton Hardy was "dumbfounded." Even Con Riley subjected the lads to public ridicule when he caught up with them on a downtown corner. Mr. Robinson, instead of being cleared by Red Jackley's confession, was arrested all over again as an accomplice. Son Perry, instead of showing up at Bayport High on Monday morning, checked back in at the grocery store. Mrs. Robinson canceled the order for the moving van, reviewed her recipes for hamburg and scrubbed the floor of the humble abode all over again. As for Collig and Smuff, they laughed and laughed.

However, it all turned out fine by Chapter Twenty-four.

For the benefit of any who have unaccountably forgotten the denouement that delighted them so many years ago, they need only be reminded that Frank and Joe came up with a brilliant feat of deduction. They directed their search toward an abandoned water tower by the railway tracks. ("In the old tower." Get it?) There they found the loot, right where Jackley had hidden it. Every gem and every bond.

Chapter Twenty-four wrote itself: Henry Robinson got out of jail again, this time for keeps; Chief Collig bawled out Detective Smuff for stupidity; Perry Robinson resigned from the grocery store and went back to school; the Robinson family returned to their old quarters in the Tower Mansion; and Hurd Applegate forked over a reward of $1,000, which was mighty good money for those days (readers even heard his pen scratching as he wrote two $500 checks for the Hardy boys).

Then he invited the lads and their chums to dinner.

At least that's what the outline indicated. Just dinner. But why skimp? What Franklin W. Dixon provided was a banquet, a feast. He saw to it that young readers savored the sight, smell and taste of roast chicken "crisp and brown" with huge helpings of mashed potatoes and gravy. He served them pickles, vegetables and salads. He encouraged seconds. And when it came to dessert, he didn't take the easy way out and settle for a couple of cartons of ice cream. He whomped up half a dozen kinds of pie *with* ice cream.

Young readers learned then and there that when it came to food, Franklin W. was not a man to count the cost. No cheapskate, he. At one stage he lost his head completely and even allowed the lads to put their elbows on the table. Millions of dismayed mothers probably wondered about the national decline in juvenile table manners which swept the nation in 1927 and subsequent years. Now they know. . . .

Weeks later, a fat envelope came from Stratemeyer. It contained outlines for two more Hardy boys books: *The House on the Cliff* and *The Secret of the Old Mill.* There was also a letter, a check and a document that looked vaguely legal. The document, a contract, was very simple—it covered everything. It was a release form absolving me of any rights to any volumes already written or any that might be written in the future for the Stratemeyer Syndicate. It covered the plots, the titles, the Roy Rockwood name, the name of Franklin W. Dixon and the manuscripts, forever and ever. Furthermore, it included a promise that I would never under any circumstances divulge to anyone the fact that I had ever written a Dave Fearless book or a Hardy Boys book under any title or pen name for anyone.

The penalty for such a revelation wasn't spelled out. I assumed that it had something to do with boiling in oil.

I had no hesitation in signing this document. As a matter of fact, I had been doing a little thinking about the matter. The release saved me the trouble of asking Stratemeyer to do me a similar favor. No sworn affidavits—merely his signature to a promise that he would never tell anyone I ever wrote books for him.

I was glad we understood each other.

Then I turned to the letter, which acknowledged and paid for *The Tower Treasure.* As usual, Edward Stratemeyer managed to keep his emotions well under control. If he thought *The Tower Treasure* was great stuff, jam packed with humor and suspense, he was able to curb any expression of his enthusiasm. Maybe he thought an order for two more books spoke for itself. Perhaps I should have regarded it as the equivalent of an unrestrained burst of applause, but I didn't.

I thought that I had written a hell of a good book—of its kind—and that it rated at least a line of favorable comment. Surely Stratemeyer, being an author himself, realized that writers do not live by bread alone, that without praise they perish. Then it occurred to me that Stratemeyer, of course, regarded *The Tower Treasure* as *his* book and that it would be indecorous of him to come right out and say it was a lallapaloosa. Even so, he didn't have to be all that modest.

Accustomed to the commercial plugs that adorned opening and closing chapters of the Dave Fearless saga, I was prepared for his instructions about the advertising matter I would have to weave cunningly into the texture of my prose.

As for the obligatory plug for Volume Four, Stratemeyer was uncommunicative. This disappointed me. I was curious about the title of Number Four, which suggested that I was getting hooked myself.

Then I recalled my letter from Mr. Lowell, and everything became clear. The three books were breeders. Stratemeyer was launching the Hardy Boys in the same way he had launched his immortal Rovers, with a triple-barrel blast. The three books would be published simultaneously. A kid who read one book would be tempted to read the others. Edward Stratemeyer and the publisher—whoever *he* turned out to be—would bide their time and wait for the sales report. Then, and only then, would there be a decision about Volume Four. After that, with any luck at all, Volume Five would be added in a sort of snowball effect, rolling on and on, the series accumulating more and more readers. Perhaps there might be a Volume Ten. My imagination stopped there.

This merely proves that I wasn't Thinking Big. That there would be a Volume Sixty nearly half a century later was quite beyond my power of fancy. Imagination is fine but you've got to keep it within limits. There is such a thing as being ridiculous. . . .

I furnished my new office in Haileybury with a desk and chair bought from a politician who had just closed his campaign quarters after a disastrous election. He was glad to retrieve ten dollars from the wreckage. The desk is still in use, which works out at about twenty-one cents a year and more millions of words than anyone would believe. It was time to get going on the final book of the Hardy Boys trilogy, Volume Three, *The Secret of the Old Mill.*

Again, an old building was to be the site of strange goings-on. This one was an abandoned flour mill on the out-skirts of Bayport.

I had a feeling that if the series went on for many more volumes Bayport would soon be a disaster area and our lads would qualify as authorities on crumbling architecture.

The abandoned flour mill was about as abandoned as the Old Polucca Place: the ramshackle edifice sheltered a gang of counterfeiters. It didn't have to be spelled out to the young reader that counterfeiters were very Bad Guys indeed. Young readers knew that if you couldn't depend on a five-dollar bill you couldn't depend on anything, and all commerce would crumble. As for smuggling, if the kids didn't know exactly *why* smuggling was wrong, it was enough that the United States government said it was. When the Hardy boys rounded up that gang of smugglers in Volume Two, obviously they performed a great public service. You had the Excise Department's word for it.

I was learning about villains. By and large, the villains who showed up in the abandoned buildings of Bayport were a fairly decorous bunch, a little choosy about their line of work. They didn't go in for the crude and impolite sort of thing, such as murder. Their skullduggery was on a much higher plane, involving crimes against property. Any normal lad knew that smuggling and counterfeiting were really serious offences because they struck at the very foundations of society.

The book began when the Hardy boys, on their way to the store to buy pie plates for their mother, were stopped by a stranger who needed change for a five-dollar bill. Always willing to lend a helping hand, they obliged, only to find out at the store that the bill was not legal tender. Then Fenton Hardy told them that, by an odd coincidence, he had been asked by the government to do something about a wave of counterfeit money sweeping the country.

Next, Callie Shaw's aunt, who ran a beauty shop, got hit for fifty dollars. To top it all, even Laura Hardy was taken when she sold a valuable rug for $800, every dollar of it bogus. This is probably the only time Laura was ever allowed to get in on any of the action.

Naturally the lads went after the counterfeiters with considerable zeal. With a little help from Fenton Hardy and their chums, they found a counterfeiting plant in the old mill, and went on to round up the ring of evil men who threatened the financial stability of the United States. A grateful government gave them their usual one thousand dollars by way of reward. Fenton Hardy's contribution was not recognized, but there was no need. One could assume that he clobbered the Treasury with a staggering fee.

None of this was achieved easily. The malefactors of the Old Mill were not clapped in handcuffs until Frank and Joe survived their quota of misadventures. These setbacks were invariably bloodless. A pattern had been established. No matter how ruthless and antisocial the criminals in a Hardy Boys book, nobody was ever shot, stabbed, blown up or bludgeoned to death. The Hardy boys could face extinction by fire or water, they could tumble through trapdoors and they could be pushed off cliffs, they could be captured, tied up, imprisoned and knocked on the head. But blood never flowed. We had our own code of nonviolence long before television.

Profanity, it went without saying, was a no-no. A Hardy boy or a Hardy chum might cut loose with a "gosh" or even "golly" under extreme provocation, but that was as far as he went. Even the villains, when duly captured—and they were *always* duly captured—never cursed their lot. Not even a d . . n or a h . . l, such as one might find in the racier adult novels of the day. Usually, they just grumbled that they would have escaped scot-free if it hadn't been for "those confounded Hardy boys," which was mighty strong talk one had to admit.

As for booze and tobacco, if a Hardy Boys' villain ever took a snort or broke open a pack of fags he did it on the sly between chapters. This probably created no end of puzzlement for young readers who attended movies, where the bad guys always did their plotting in smoke-filled dives and drank rotgut straight, using the empty bottle to smash someone over the head, and where even the good guys rolled their own and bellied up to the bar like everyone else. Literature these books were not but, by God, they were Moral! You could fault them on any grounds you liked, but never on turpitude!

For the interest of students, it should be recorded that *The Secret of the Old Mill* introduced the stout, seaworthy craft that was to go roaring through so many subsequent volumes—the lads' own motorboat, the *Sleuth*. No longer would they be restricted to adventures on land areas accessible only to motorcycles. The whole Atlantic Ocean was at their disposal.

They bought the *Sleuth* with their own money. After all, those thousand-dollar rewards were piling up. Fenton Hardy, stern parent that he was, handed down an edict that they could not dip into their bank account to buy gas, but they seemed to manage. They never appeared to be inhibited by lack of funds when the situation called for chasing some scalawag all over Barmet Bay. If I had thought of it, they could have invented the credit card.

The book had another novelty. The Hardy boys, hitherto existing only on weekends, were actually seen at school. The outline didn't call for this departure, but just for the hell of it I tossed in an episode about the lads hitting the books and undergoing the torments of cramming for exams. It seemed about time.

When the script was packed off to East Orange it was duly acknowledged and a check was sent out, but Stratemeyer made no comment on my startling burst of originality. That was when I realized that these outlines weren't any more sacrosanct than the Dave Fearless specifications. . . .

Next came a package . . . —three books, published simultaneously by Grosset and Dunlap of New York, in hard covers, bound in red, each with its frontispiece illustration by one Walter S. Rogers, who couldn't draw worth a damn. The art work in *The Tower Treasure* depicted Frank and Joe being introduced to Adelia Applegate by her brother Hurd, the stamp collector. Mr. Applegate was a weedy gent with a string tie and a vacant look. Miss Applegate, standing in a curtained archway with a flight of stairs in the background, was wearing elaborately flowing robes that seemed to have come right out of Godey's *Ladies Book* and the Hardy boys were clutching their caps in a nervous sort of way. On the whole the scene appeared to represent an elderly pimp making a pitch on behalf of a couple of youthful clients to the madam of a fashionable whorehouse. Although it was, no doubt, an interesting illustration, I thought Mr. Rogers hadn't read the book.

On the next page, in a box under the heading by Franklin W. Dixon, the three breeder titles were listed in order. A bracketed line underneath noted in small type that other volumes were in preparation. All three volumes were identical in format, with illustrations equally lacking in talent. At the back were several pages of advertisements for other publications of Grosset and Dunlap. Each page was devoted to an entire series and each series had its long list of titles. . . .

In spite of first-hand knowledge that Edward Stratemeyer managed a whole stable of writers, I was still so innocent that the Grosset and Dunlap imprint fooled me. I thought the volumes advertised at the back of the book were Grosset and Dunlap books not necessarily from the Stratemeyer production line.

Innocent? I was just plain *dumb!* I really believed in Victor Appleton, Allen Chapman and James Cody Ferris, although I had just unwrapped three books by Franklin W. Dixon, whom I knew didn't exist because he was me. Believe it or not, I didn't realize that *all* the advertised books came from the Stratemeyer fiction factory and that, indeed, they represented merely a small part of a prodigious output.

However, there lay the three books, my first hardcovers, in highly visible crimson binding, good readable type, more than 200 pages each, copyrighted in the Library of Congress, looking a good deal more imposing and far more durable than any of the Dave Fearless characters.

I think they sold for seventy-five cents. I am uncertain about this because I never bought one. It was a long time before a Hardy Boys book reached Haileybury, perhaps because they were banned by the local library as deleterious to young minds. On my occasional visits to Toronto it never occurred to me to look for them in real bookstores.

Now they were launched on the sea of juvenile opinion. Would they be greeted with apathy, politely tolerated or rejected with scorn? On the other hand, would they be received with enthusiasm, read with joy, applauded by boyish huzzahs? This may have been of concern to Edward Stratemeyer, Alex Grosset and George Dunlap. It was of absolutely no concern to me. I was merely a ghost. Does a wraith have anxieties? Does a spook fret about sales? No one could have cared less.

I gathered that the breeders must have done reasonably well in the marketplace when Stratemeyer sent along another outline called *The Missing Chums*. Who was missing? Chet Morton and Biff Hooper, held for ransom by a bunch of bank robbers.

It hinged on a big mistake. The robbers thought all along that they were kidnapping the Hardy boys. When they discovered their error, it was too late to say: "Sorry, kids. We thought you was two other guys." The mistake cost them, of course, because the Hardy boys were free to spend the whole book working on the case and there could be only one outcome. The bank robbers were captured, the chums were set free and Frank and Joe snaffled another handsome reward.

With the outline, however, came a disturbing letter. It concerned my beloved Keystone Kops. Stratemeyer felt that the volumes already written suggested a grievous lack of respect for officers of the law! He regretted that I seemed to regard Messrs. Collig, Smuff and Riley as figures of fun. He did not think this was wise. The effect on growing boys must be considered. In future volumes it would be well to treat the Bayport constabulary with the respect to which they were entitled.

I couldn't believe it. There was something wrong with this drastic change of attitude. Why, for example, had Stratemeyer bestowed the name of Smuff on that defective detective in the first place if he wanted the fellow to be held in respect? How could any lad with a scrap of intelligence stand in awe of a cop called Smuff? If the Hardy boys went around tugging their forelocks whenever they encountered Detective Smuff, all young readers would just naturally regard them as stupid. Even stupider than Smuff himself!

And why, if Stratemeyer felt so strongly about the matter, hadn't he done a little editing on the scripts? The cops were already on the printed record as bumbling imbeciles. Five minutes with a blue pencil could have sanctified them, made them grave enforcers of the law, devoted to their trade. Definitely, something had happened when the books went on sale. Maybe Franklin K. Mathiews had pounced again.

I groaned. There went my best source of comedy material. I had been counting on the Bayport Bluecoats for at least four chapters of surefire laughs per book, and if I had any strong conviction about the Hardy Boys Series at all, it was that where kid readers were concerned you couldn't go wrong by larding the action with a little funny stuff. However, when a sheet of paper went into the machine for the opening page of *The House on the Cliff,* I realized glumly that Collig & Co. would have to shape up and the Hardy boys would have to be polite to the cops if it killed them.

But I had my own thoughts about teaching youngsters that obedience to authority is somehow sacred. Where did it say that kids shouldn't size up people for themselves? Was it written in the Bible, the Talmud, the Koran, the British North America Act and the Constitution of the United States that everyone in authority was inflexibly honest, pious and automatically admirable? Would civilization crumble if kids got the notion that the people who ran the world were sometimes stupid, occasionally wrong and even corrupt at times? Was it a favor to let them grow up dumbly assuming that all is for the best in the best of all possible worlds? Wouldn't every kid be the better for a little shot of healthy skepticism at an early age?

Of course. And a lot of good that philosophy did me. Chief Collig suddenly became the sagacious head of an efficient police department. Detective Smuff miraculously acquired wisdom in spite of his name. Constable Riley was strangely transformed into a lovable cop on the beat and a friend to all.

Unexpectedly, however, just as I was choking on these mandatory developments, a ray of sunshine appeared. It had become clear to Stratemeyer, just as it had long been obvious to me, that Laura Hardy was a very pallid character. The outlines practically ignored the good woman and, for the life of me, I couldn't find very much for her to do. She seemed to spend most of her time making sandwiches to go. She served as an admiring listener whenever the men of the family came home long enough to discuss their exploits of crime-busting in the great world, but this function as sounding board was pretty limited.

And now, of all things, Stratemeyer decided that she needed help. Because Fenton Hardy and sons were scheduled to be away from home for long stretches of Volume Four, he suggested that a maiden aunt should come a-visiting to keep Mrs. Hardy company.

Gold! Pure, gleaming, high-grade gold!

I doubt if Stratemeyer intended her to be amusing. If he did, he may have considered that if I insisted on being funny the ribaldry had better be kept in the family rather than directed at the Bayport Police Force. If I couldn't contain myself in the presence of Detective Smuff maybe a domestic lightning rod might help. If that was his thinking, it worked. I looked on the visiting relative as a godsend, spat on my hands and joyfully went to work making Aunt Gertrude a Character.

She arrived in Bayport on the afternoon train one day toward the end of Chapter Six, complete with handbags, parcels, a mountain of luggage and a yellow cat named Lavinia. She climbed out of a cab in front of the Hardy home, bawled out the driver in a dispute over the fare, bellowed for the Hardy boys to come carry her luggage and then gave them hell because they didn't hustle. She went right on giving them hell during every scene in which she appeared for the rest of the book, and I saw to it that she had more scenes than kindly, sandwich-spreading Laura Hardy had achieved in all the previous books or the series put together. She certainly livened up an otherwise routine narrative and more than compensated for the transmutations of Collig and Company.

If there was a turning point in the series this was it. Maybe a turning point wasn't needed. Maybe the series would have plodded along without her but it wouldn't have been the same. Whether the Hardy Boys sales zoomed upward after the arrival of Aunt Gertrude in Volume Four, I can't say for sure but it is highly probable, because after that volume Stratemeyer gave instructions that Aunt Gertrude was to be a permanent member of the cast.

He never actually came right out and complimented me on Aunt Gertrude. You could always count on him to keep his head and steel himself against giving writers fancy notions about their importance. It was enough that the lady appeared in every outline thereafter.

For a while she merely showed up from time to time on visits. After a time she settled in as a member of the household where she asserted herself so formidably that Laura Hardy receded farther into the background.

Kid readers who had merely tolerated Laura Hardy just loved Aunt Gertrude. They knew there was a heart of gold under that crusty exterior. When she bawled out the Hardy boys, which she did continually, she was actually telling them she loved them. Had she come right out and said so, the while smothering them with big, fat, slobbery kisses, young readers would have been disgusted. As it was, she made them feel that here was one who really cared.

In fact, in the late Thirties, when there was a project to launch a Hardy Boys radio program based on the books, it was to have been called "Aunt Gertrude and the Boys." The old termagant had pushed the kids right out of stage center. The death of Edna Mae Oliver, who was to have been the star, terminated the project. It was inconceivable that anyone else could have played Aunt Gertrude. Even in recent years, when the Hardy boys made it in television as cartoon characters in primary colors with their own rock theme blaring away and two completely altered plots jammed into one program (a ridiculous show that polluted the morning air for nearly a year), Laura Hardy was not among the characters but Aunt Gertrude survived.

A school teacher told me a while back that when she asked her class to name their favorite characters in fiction she found Aunt Gertrude right up there with Huckleberry Finn. This caused her no little embarrassment. She had never heard of Aunt Gertrude and didn't care to lose face by asking. Obviously she had been living far outside the mainstream of juvenile culture. She had to sidle off and make inquiries of the principal. He enlightened her but gave her a very strange look. "As if he thought maybe I was too dumb to be teaching English," she said.

By the time I had finished *The Missing Chums,* another outline had arrived: *Hunting for Hidden Gold.* The lads were packed off to the Far West, where they ended up in the usual ruined structure, of course—this time an abandoned mine.

Without realizing it I had acquired systematic work habits and a professional attitude. The morning chapter rolled out of the typewriter every day until the book was done, the order filled, the merchandise delivered. Of the material written during the other working hours, fewer stories came back. The gloomy tale about the settler and his family didn't win the big prize in the all-Canadian short story contest, but it shared third. That was no great honor but it earned a good deal of publicity and an anthologist asked leave to put it in his book. Canadian magazines actually requested material. Bob Hardy, my New York agent, found editors who sent checks.

The professional attitude was difficult to define. If one is willing to accept money for writing a certain kind of material, he should do his best. The young, the uncultured or unsophisticated reader is not to blame for his condition and should not be despised—certainly not by the writer who lives by that reader's nickels and dimes.

The Dave Fearless outlines had been outrageous fantasies, bordering on burlesque. Viewed in one light, they were comic works. "The Hardy Boys" were likewise contrived for wish fulfillment but I had learned not to despise them. They had their lowly place in the world of commercial publishing, with its variety of reading matter as infinite as the mind of man. They were written swiftly, but not carelessly. I gave thought to grammar, sentence structure, choice of words, pace, the techniques of suspense, all within the limits of the medium which was in this case mass-produced, assembly-line fiction for boys. Every kind of writing, from the ancient morality plays to a modern television series, has its own boundaries, and the writer who seeks to earn a living learns the boundaries and works within them. As for the writer of talent, or even genius, perhaps it is better for him and for the world that he earn bread and shelter in any other way than by the sale of words.

I knew I was not a genius and moreover that genius cannot be achieved by effort. I also knew that I was not a writer of great talent, although even a small talent can be improved and developed by diligence. I probably had a knack for story telling, the entertainer's gift which can always be polished to the glow of art. One should be thankful for any gift, however small. I enjoyed using it and there was double enjoyment in the thought that it might give some pleasure to others. One had to guard against self-deception, in mistaking the gift for talent which was somehow deserving of esteem. Honesty was everything. There could be some excuse for poor work but never for dishonest work. Lack of talent might be regrettable but it is not, after all, a mortal sin. The obligation was to do one's best with the gifts one had. . . .

So, I wrote to Stratemeyer and asked him how the Hardy Boys books were doing and how strongly I could depend on them as a source of secondary income. I suggested that the payment was small. An increase seemed in order. Actually I was interested in the sales of the books merely to the extent that they might indicate that I was worth more money.

Mr. Stratemeyer replied that he hoped to publish two Hardy Boys books a year and that he hoped he could count on me to supply them. That was all. He didn't mention money. He didn't mention sales figures. I learned later that Edward Stratemeyer was not a man who ever confided sales figures to his score of ghosts. It wasn't because he was afraid this kind of information would encourage the spooks to ask for more money if a series found favor. He had ways of dealing with that. He simply felt it was none of their business.

A request for a raise wouldn't have done a spook any good anyway. When Stratemeyer struck a price that price was final. A spook could be replaced with alarming ease. Stratemeyer didn't come rightout and say so, but one had a mental picture of a block-long lineup of eager candidates waiting outside his office to pinch-hit for any rebellious Oliver Twist rash enough to ask for more.

Nor would it have helped to seek out a companion spook and compare notes. They were anonymous, invisible, unidentifiable, impossible to find. I met one of them quite by accident years later and he said Stratemeyer conferred with writers only by appointment and that he took good care to see that appointments were judiciously spaced. No two spooks ever found themselves waiting side by side on the bench and in a position to compare notes or even to discover that each was Roy Rockwood or even (God forbid) Laura Lee Hope, renowned since 1906 as authoress of the Bobbsey Twins.

Gloomily, I considered Stratemeyer's reply. Optimistically, then, I told myself that it was only a matter of time before I would be making a hefty income from the magazines and even from book publishers. Until then, Stratemeyer could count on his two books a year. . . .

Although some series were cut from the list during the Depression, and even more were dropped during World War II, the Hardy Boys held firm along with the immortal Bobbsey Twins and Nancy Drew. Somehow the kids—or their relatives—dug up the necessary nickels and dimes so that the little addicts could have their fix. . . .

One day in 1930 a letter from the Syndicate advised that Edward Stratemeyer had died of pneumonia at the age of sixty-eight. His age matched the number of pen names he had used during his life, including forty-seven which had been Stratemeyer Syndicate house names. There were such names among them as E. Ward Strayer, Jim Bowie, Ned St. Myer, Dr. Willard Mackenzie, May Hollis Barton, Laura Lee Hope, Amy Bell Marlow, Carolyn Keene and even Lester Chadwick. One redoubtable pseudonym actually fathered itself when Victor Appleton be-

came Victor Appleton II. Stratemeyer's biography in *Contemporary Authors* ran to two pages of small, closely packed type, more than 3,000 words, of which 2,500 words consisted of the titles of the books with which he had been connected one way or the other. The list ran to more than three of the four columns.

I had never met him, had never even spoken to him on the telephone. At the time of my marriage, he sent a wedding check for $25 and a similar check on the birth of our first daughter. Now the letter said that in his will he bequeathed each of his writers a sum equal to one-fifth of their earnings from the Syndicate. Although he was all business when it came to dealings that involved the Syndicate, he had his kind side. I had a feeling of loss. . . .

As for the Hardy Boys, after *The Short Wave Mystery* (in which the boys went scientific) and *The Secret Panel,* I bowed out with *The Phantom Freighter* which was written in 1946 in motel rooms at night on a location in Nova Scotia when I was directing a film. For me, that was the end of the Hardy Boys. I didn't need them any more, and certainly they didn't need me, because they have continued to this day.

There was no quarrel, no dramatic break with the Syndicate for which I had toiled over a period of twenty years and ground out more than two million words. I merely sent in the manuscript with a note to the effect that I was too busy to take on any further assignments. The Syndicate didn't plead with me to continue. In fact, the Syndicate didn't seem to care much one way or the other. Other spooks were always available. If the parting involved any emotion at all, it was one of relief, as if a couple of relatives who came for the weekend had finally moved on after sticking around for years.

I was pretty bored with the Hardy boys by that time anyway. Not with the books, because I never read them. Whenever a new one arrived I might skim through a few pages and then the volume would join its predecessors on a bookcase shelf. Under glass, like a row of embalmed owls, so the dust wouldn't get at them.

Perhaps a psychologist would have been interested in this extraordinary indifference to the physical evidence of work that had occupied so many hours over so many years (about twenty volumes in all, ending with *The Phantom Freighter*), not counting the Dave Fearless paperbacks, the Dana Girls and assorted extras that have utterly vanished from my memory. But to me it was if some force within my mind insisted on thrusting the books into limbo the moment the final page of a final chapter came out of the typewriter. Not revulsion. Complete indifference. Perhaps this also accounted for the fact that, although I had been in New York many times, I was never tempted to cross the river and drop into the Stratemeyer Syndicate office in East Orange. I had nothing whatever against Edward Stratemeyer or his daughters or the Syndicate people, and I am sure I would have been welcome, but somehow it just never seemed to matter. The dozens of stories I had written for magazines good and bad on both sides of the Atlantic were all carefully collected and bound, some of them occasionally reread, but I never curled up with a Hardy Boys book to spend a happy hour reading it all the way through.

It was not until sometime in the 1940s, as a matter of fact, that I had discovered that Franklin W. Dixon and the Hardy Boys were conjurable names. One day my son had come into the workroom, which had never been exalted into a "study," and pointed to the bookcase with its shelf of Hardy Boys originals. "Why do you keep these books, Dad? Did you read them when you were a kid?"

"Read them? I wrote them." And then, because it doesn't do to deceive any youngster, "At least, I wrote the words."

He stared. I saw incredulity. Then open-mouthed respect.

"Why didn't you tell me?"

"I suppose it never occurred to me."

This was true. The Hardy Boys were never mentioned in the household. They were never mentioned to friends. Maybe it was a holdover from Edward Stratemeyer's long past injunction to secrecy. Habit. I wasn't ashamed of them. I had done them as well as I could, at the time. They had merely provided a way of making a living.

"But they're wonderful books," he said. "I used to borrow them from the other kids all the time until I found them here."

"Other kids read them?"

"Dad, where have you been? Everybody reads them. You can buy them in Simpson's. Shelves of them."

Next day I went to the department store and damned if the lad wasn't right! They *did* have shelves of them. There were **The Tower Treasure, The House on the Cliff, The Secret of the Old Mill, The Great Airport Mystery,** all the remembered titles, the whole score of them, and more I had never heard of. And over on another shelf, a dozen titles in the Dana Girls series, considerably outnumbered by a massive collection of Nancy Drew.

I began to see the Hardy Boys books wherever I went, in small bookstores and large, even in railway depots and corner stores. There seemed to be an epidemic. Whenever I saw a small boy on a train or plane, he was almost invariably absorbed in a bright blue volume, lost in Bayport and environs. "They must have sold a lot of those things," I reflected. "Maybe a hundred thousand or so."

I asked a clerk if the Hardy Boys books were popular.

"Most popular boys' books we carry," he said. "Matter of fact, they're supposed to be the best-selling boys' books in the world."

"Imagine that!" I said in downright wonderment.

Tex W. Dixon

SOURCE: "Ghost Story," in *Texas Monthly,* Vol. 23, No. 9, September, 1995, p. 60.

[*Tex W. Dixon is a pseudonym of a writer from Austin who also has written for the Hardy Boys series.*]

On a summer morning in the mid-fifties, my mother was chatting across the fence with our next-door neighbor, a retired teacher named Mrs. Wood. "You know, I've got a box of books that belonged to son when he was little," Mrs. Wood mentioned. "Your boys can have them if they'll come get them." I scampered next door and came staggering back with a large carton of well-cared-for hardcover books. "You take good care of them, young man," Mrs. Wood told me, "and they'll give you a world of pleasure."

I liked all the books in the box, but my favorites focused on teenage boys who led action-packed lives. One series chronicled the worldwide derring-do of Don Sturdy, an intrepid teen whose explorer father is trapped in the Great Pyramid. Another series recounted the adventures of young sleuths who zipped their roadster around their hometown of Bayport, New York, matched wits with criminal minds, and solved mysteries that invariably befuddled the adult authorities. They were, of course, the Hardy Boys, Joe and Frank, and they helped make me, at age nine, the serious and addicted reader I am today.

I loved the Hardy Boys, although I'm now embarrassed to remember slouching in a living room chair one morning, lost in their latest adventure, and having to lift my bare feet while my mother vacuumed under me. It was always something of a letdown to close the book on Joe and Frank's Bayport and walk outside into my hometown of Bellmead, a blue-collar suburb of Waco. In Bellmead the glaring sun seemed to wash out the color and verve that Joe and Frank experienced. More than anything else, I was intrigued by the author, Franklin W. Dixon. Who was he? How could he dream up such fresh tales? And did he write anything else? I checked the public library and the children's book department at Goldstein-Migel department store, but I never found anything else he had written.

Forty years later, I still have the hand-me-down books, now musty-smelling and yellowed. A price tag on one reads 50 cents. I also have an answer to my childhood question about the identity of Franklin W Dixon: I am Franklin W. Dixon. A couple of times a year, the spirit of the Hardys' creator unlocks the boy's imagination still residing in the mind of this middle-aged man. Together we journey back to Bayport, where Frank and Joe, perpetually arrested in carefree adolescence, eagerly await another adventure—an adventure I get paid to take them on. And I'm not the only ersatz Dixon. Ten to fifteen ghostwriters around the country keep the brothers alive and sleuthing, which is how it has been since they debuted nearly seventy years ago.

You see, Franklin W. Dixon never existed. Neither did Victor Appleton, the author of the Don Sturdy series and of Tom Swift. There was no Laura Lee Hope of the Bobbsey Twins, no Carolyn Keene of Nancy Drew. All the authors and all the books were the brainchildren of an amazing mass-market genius named Edward Stratemeyer. Between 1900 and 1930 Stratemeyer created Sturdy, Drew, and Swift, the Hardys and the Bobbseys, Dave Fearless, Dave Dashaway, the Rover Boys, the Darewell Chums, the Outdoor Girls, the Moving Picture Girls, and numerous other adventure heroes and heroines—as well as their pseudonymous authors. Bruce Watson, who wrote about the relatively unknown Stratemeyer in the October 1991 issue of The Smithsonian magazine, says this mild-mannered "literary machine" produced 125 series and more than 1,300 teen novels. Stratemeyer's lifetime sales, Watson reports, totaled more than 200 million copies.

Realizing that he alone could never accommodate all the youthful characters and exciting plots that sprung from his fertile imagination, Stratemeyer began crafting story ideas into detailed three-page outlines and farming them out to writers. According to Watson, a ghostwriter working for the Stratemeyer Syndicate would produce a novel within a month. Then Stratemeyer would edit it, check it for consistency with previous books, and send it to the publisher. The ghostwriters earned between $50 and $250 per book, signed away all rights to the syndicate, and agreed never to divulge their true identities. We latter-day Dixons make a bit more per book, but we still sign away all rights—to Mega-Books of New York—and we still agree to remain ghosts.

I got into writing Hardy Boys mysteries for the same reason Stratemeyer's ghosts of yesteryear did: I needed the money. I also had a connection. A friend from Austin had moved to New York to write a novel, but she needed to supplement her income, so she took a job at Mega-Books rewriting horrendously written Hardy Boys editions. Overwhelmed with work, she asked me to take an idea fumbled by a Dixon ghost and see what I could do with it. The arrangement suited us both, and now I produce a couple of books a year.

Creating a Hardy Boys mystery is something of an assembly-line process. Once I discuss potential story lines with my editor, she gets Mega-Books' approval, and then I come up with a detailed chapter outline, which usually takes about a week to write. When the outline is approved, I start on the book, which is about a month's worth of work. I rarely have an uninterrupted month to focus on the project, but when I'm "in the zone," so to speak, I'm as oblivious to the rest of the world as I'd be if I were writing *War and Peace.* Coming to the climactic moment of my most recent Hardy tale, I even found myself getting teary when Joe's life was in danger

and Frank was desperately trying to save him. Something about brotherly love must have gotten to me.

My Hardy Boys editor is probably the best editor I've worked with in twenty years as a professional writer. (When she's not pummeling Joe and Frank into shape, she's a travel writer for the *New York Times.*) Her requirements for a rewrite are thorough, exacting, and thoughtful. She pays special attention to the logic and plausibility of the mystery and to making sure the prose is accessible to teens without being condescending.

Although Edward Stratemeyer would still recognize his daring duo, Mega-Books has worked to update them. As the Mega-Books writer's guide ("the bible") urges, we ghostwriters are supposed to jettison the image of the goody-goody Hardy Boys that most of us remember. Frank and Joe now have distinctive personalities, and the crimes they solve are realistic and dangerous, everything from terrorist attacks to industrial espionage.

The Hardys—except for the title, you don't call them Hardy Boys anymore—are still in their late teens, and they still live in Bayport with their mother, Laura, their eccentric Aunt Gertrude, and their father, the internationally famous private detective Fenton Hardy. Their chubby, wisecracking pal Chet Morton still makes an occasional appearance, as does Callie Shaw, Frank's true love.

Among the nineties-style crimes that attract the Hardys are armed robbery, arson, and kidnapping—but no drug crimes. Dialogue no-no's include cursing, double entendres, vulgarity, and taking the Lord's name in vain. No matter how slimy the villain, you'll never hear Joe say, "Jeez, Frank, he's an old rugby player; I was damn sure he had leather balls."

As the Mega-Books bible explains, we writers can focus on murder as long as we keep from delving into the gory details. In other words, someone can be shot and killed, but no puddles of blood. In one of the case files, as the books are called today, the fanatical Assassins blow up the Hardys' car with Joe's longtime girlfriend, Iola Morton, inside.

Whatever the crime, nearly each of the chapters must end in a cliffhanger. In fact, coming up with "cliffs," which usually involve physical danger, is one of the real challenges of being a modern-day Franklin W. Dixon. Not only do they have to be relatively believable and sufficiently hair-raising to keep young, TV-jaded readers turning the page, but they have to be resolved within the first few paragraphs of the next chapter. Like this: An Assassin's bullet penetrates the boat's fuel tank while Joe is at the helm, and as the chapter ends, the craft erupts into a ball of fire; we discover in the next chapter that Joe dived into the shark-infested Gulf of Mexico a second before the explosion. Or this: Helplessly attached to a hang glider, Frank sees a cliff looming before him. As the chapter ends, he closes his eyes and awaits his smashing end; we learn in the next chapter that at the last possible moment a propitious breeze off the Pacific lifted our hero onto a mesa.

My other challenge is the one every mystery writer faces: peeling away deli-thin layers of information so that the reader exclaims "Ah-ha!" at about the same moment the Hardys do. And, as with any novel, it's always a challenge to keep the story moving, the dialogue crisp, and the descriptions fresh—even if the approach is formulaic and my readers are adolescent.

Although Frank, as the bible describes him, is "a Sherlock Holmes in jeans" and Joe "a devil-may-care swashbuckler with a short fuse," the bros today are hip to fast cars, rock music, and the latest computer and video gadgets. They hang out at shopping malls and love fast food. They also have an eye for the girls, although when it comes to sex, the bible is unequivocal: There isn't any. It's not that the guys aren't interested, you understand, but since "thug-busting is a 24-hour-a-day job," the Hardys have little time for socializing. Except for the rare kiss or hug shared with a pretty associate, it's mostly look-don't-touch, with Joe doing the more uninhibited looking. Those female accomplices, by the way, are true nineties women; they're usually just as plucky and resourceful as Frank and Joe.

The Hardys travel more frequently than they did in the early days, usually in the summer or during spring break or Christmas vacation from Bayport High. In *Evil Inc.*, they are in Paris, decked out in black leather combat boots, spiked hair, and gold earrings; they're posing as gunrunning punks so they can infiltrate a band of arms dealers. In *Too Many Traitors,* they fly to Spain and get mixed up with international spies and a beautiful but dangerous operative named Elena. In *Trouble in the Pipeline,* they're in Alaska, where, with the assistance of a hunting and fishing guide named Virgil, they thwart a plot to blow up an oil pipeline.

Joe and Frank also travel to Texas on occasion. In *Web of Horror,* they're in a city just outside of Dallas, where a horror flick being shot on location becomes the scene of a real murder. In *Hot Wheels,* they fly to El Paso, where they compete in a solar-powered-car race and crack a mystery involving sabotage and research theft. In *Shock Waves* a "Nancy Drew and Hardy Boys Super Mystery," the brothers and their famous female friend journey to South Padre Island, where a squad of "resort sharks" has ripped off a fortune in loot. In adventures to come, Joe and Frank will be back on South Padre and in Matamoros, where they'll get caught up with gunrunners, bullfighters, and a beautiful Mexican girl named Rosa. (Only one of the Texas books is mine; I don't know who wrote the others. In fact, we Hardy Boys ghostwriters are as much a mystery to each other as we are to our readers.)

Sometimes I worry a bit that dreaming up boys' adventure tales comes rather easily to me. I'm supposed to be a serious writer; what does this propensity say about my emotional and aesthetic maturity? But then again, who cares? I'm pleased I can do my part in keeping alive two youngsters who are clever, courageous, adventurous, and good. In other words, just the way I wanted to be when I was a boy.

GENERAL COMMENTARY

Gerard O'Connor

SOURCE: "The Hardy Boys Revisited: A Study in Prejudice," in *Challenges in American Culture,* edited by Ray B. Browne, Larry N. Landrum and William K. Bottorff, Bowling Green University Popular Press, 1970, pp. 234-41.

> "Luke Jones don't stand for no nonsense from white folks. Ah pays mah fare, an' Ah puts mah shoes where Ah please."

Luke Jones sounds like a Nat Turner of the Pullman. But he isn't. "He hastily restored his feet to their proper place whenever the conductor came through the car." Luke Jones is no revolutionist, no leader of the people. Luke Jones is simply the "big black fellow" who "done stole de money" in The Hardy Boys story *The Hidden Harbor Mystery.*

Written in 1935 and read by millions of American kids since, *The Hidden Harbor Mystery* is a microcosm of the whole Hardy Boys series. The world of *Hidden Harbor* is that of the Hardys: a world of gross prejudice, of insulting stereotypes, of crude caricature. In this world, where you come from determines what you become; and how you spell your name determines how you speak. If you are fresh off the gondola, then you try to "sella da good fruit at da good price." If a potato famine has driven you here, then you walk a beat, dreaming of corned beef and cabbage dinners. If you are black and know your place, then you become a "shining-faced servant" who dutifully says "Good mawnin', gen'mun" to the teenage Hardys. If you are black and do not know your place, then you become a Luke Jones and bluster that you won't "stand for no nonsense from white folks." But like the guilty Luke, who "cringed and hung his head when he saw his master," you will end up captured by the Hardys, howling for mercy, and headed for jail.

Polarizing this world of prejudice is the Hardy circle. The family itself and most of the close friends are unobtrusively but unmistakenly WASP. (Aunt Gertrude's suggestion that Frank and Joe spend Sunday afternoon discussing *Pilgrim's Progress* is the exception rather than the rule.) Of the Hardy chums only Tony Prito and Phil Cohen are not WASP.

There is little doubt about Tony Prito's ethnic background. His "dark hair, olive skin, and sparkling eyes indicated his Italian parentage, even more emphatically than his name." Characteristically, Tony still stumbles over shibboleths. He says "What's the mattah?" and "I wish is was mine" because "he had not yet been in America long enough to talk the language without an accent." But compared to Rocco the fruitman, Tony is very much assimilated: his father is "one of the most respected citizens in the Italian colony of Bayport," and Tony has his own speedboat, the Napoli. In contrast, Rocco talks like Vanzetti and still lives in fear of "da Blacka Hand." Faithful to his stereotype, Rocco serves as the butt of the vaudevillian jokes. In one episode in **The Tower Treasure** he is duped by the Hardy boys and chums into thinking that a package containing an alarm clock is a time bomb. The high point of the comedy is Rocco "dancing about in the middle of the street, yelling, 'Bombs! Police! Da Blacka Hand!'" Rocco's performance is only natural, however, for "like most of his countrymen, he was of an excitable nature."

Phil Cohen is the most obscure of the Hardy chums. "A diminutive black-haired Jewish boy," Philis accepted by Frank and Joe for the apparent Some-Of-My-Best-Friends reason. Occasionally Phil will play the comic role, and with unmistakable idiom: "Oy! what a fine day you pick for your trip!" But for the most part Phil functions simply as the Resident Jew.

However, the acceptance by the Hardys of a Phil Cohen does not preclude a Charlie Hinchman or a Moe Gordon. Charlie, "a small beady-eyed man with a pointed goatee," owns a candy store in **The Clue of the Broken Blade.** When a car crashes through his store window and Joe Hardy asks him if he's hurt, Charlie answers:

> "No matter about me. Look at my shop! The big sedan—she run right through the window! Oh, oh, she is owing me ten thousand dollars' damages!"

Faithful to the mold, Charlie immediately threatens to get a lawyer and sue the driver who has "ruinated" his shop. But Charlie is not really the avaricious Jew candy store owner of tradition. He is actually an avaricious Jew crook of the 1930s. Charlie specializes in hijacking, but he is not above murder, if there's a profit in it.

Even more rapacious than Charlie Hinchman is his cheese-eating cousin Moe Gordon. For in addition to his hijacking, Moe deals in extortion, knives, and poisonous snakes. Like Luke Jones in **The Hidden Harbor,** Moe preys on a wealthy WASP family. Where Luke steals a diamond ring from his "master," Moe extorts cash from a "friend." Where Luke smashes old people over the head, Moe plants a viper in their room. Each in his own stereotyped way is after WASP money, and both try to destroy WASP families to get it. But criminology not crime pays in The Hardy Boys; the WASP money circulated is always reward money for Frank and Joe.

The blatant Jewishness of Hinchman and Gordon is an exception to the general rule in The Hardy Boys that criminals are ethnically amorphous. Spike Hudson, Taffy Marr, Gus Montrose, Duke Beeson *et al* are names

apparently derived from American criminal mythology and given a slight Dickensian twist. Baldy Turk, Trett Rangle, and Ganny Snackley are more strongly Dickensian, but still cannot be identified ethnically.

Similarly, Bayport's constabulary, Chief of Police Ezra Collig and Detective Oscar Smuff, are Dickensian caricatures. Infallibly fatuous, they read the comics, play checkers, and use "ain't" habitually. To the Hardys and, particularly, Chet Morton they are objects of ridicule—detectives who, according to Chet, can't catch the proverbial cold. If the internationally famous detective Fenton Hardy were not always getting captured by ignorant mobsters, then the disrespect for the law which The Hardy Boys inculcate would be the most amusing irony in the series.

However, Detective Oscar Smuff looks like Alec Leamas compared to Constable Con Riley, Bayport's only visible patrolman. For Con Riley is "thick-headed," very thick-headed. He walks his beat dreaming of the corned beef and cabbage dinner that Mrs. Riley is cooking. As a result he does not notice a pickpocket lifting his handcuffs and nightstick. In the series he suffers every indignity from having his helmet knocked off by a Chet Morton snowball to having his "who done it' corrected to "who did it" by the same Chet. Con naturally speaks with a brogue, and this sometimes creates problems in communication:

> "From what I can learn," said Riley with a severe glance at Chet, "the whole business was a food."
>
> "A what?" said Frank puzzled.
>
> "A food. One of them foods among Chinamen. You know."
>
> "Like chop suey?" inquired Chet, interested.
>
> "A food, I said," declared Riley. "A battle. A war. A food."
>
> "A feud!" exclaimed Joe.

Con Riley is the Stage Irishman, the butt of all the jokes. Con Riley is the man for whom the NINA signs of the nineteenth century were invented. He is Mike of Pat and Mike.

And as painfully as Con Riley is the Stage Irishman, MacBane is "Sandy MacPherson" of Can You Top This immortality; Louis Fong is the No-Tickee No-Shirtee Laundryman gone bad; and all the blacks are Rastus, Remus, or Uncle Tom. A janitor at Bayport High, MacBane is, predictably, "cantankerous" and "dour." When Jerry Gilroy badgers him in **The Secret of the Old Mill,** MacBane lapses into "broad Scotch . . . spluttering unintelligible phrases that could only have been understood in the remotest reaches of Caledonia."

Louie Fong is the most villanous-looking Oriental this side of Fu Manchu:

His head was pointed and almost bald, while a cruel mouth was partly concealed by a dropping wisp of mustache. His eyes were as cold and glittering as those of a snake.

In *Footprints under the Window,* Louie proves that "his evil yellow face" is no lie: he throws around, liberally and accurately, his "long, sharp evil-looking knife"; and he dispatches, frequently and indiscriminately, his "enormous dog, lean and ferocious, with slavering jaws." When Louie Fong is after you, as Tom Wat tells Frank, "Alee samee dead man now."

Louie Fong is not, however, "the worst scoundrel Frank and Joe have ever come across." That distinction goes to Luke Jones. To be a worse scoundrel than Louie Fong, to say nothing of Baldy Turk and Ganny Snackley, is no small achievement. But Luke Jones is actually less interesting psychologically than he is historically and sociologically. For Luke is a nearly perfect example of the Brute Negro stereotype. As Sterling A. Brown described him [in "A Century of Negro Portraiture in American Literature"], the Brute Negro is vicious, ignorant, swaggering, revengeful, gaudily dressed, and—most important—dissatisfied with his place in life and somewhat eager to improve it. First appearing in Reconstruction literature, especially that of Thomas Nelson Page, the Brute Negro is most familiarly, and perhaps most sensationally, illustrated by Silas in *The Birth of a Nation.* The only difference between Silas Lynch and Luke Jones is that the proprieties of the Hardy Boys preclude the raping and the gin-drinking.

For the "black rascal" Luke manifests all the other characteristics of the stereotype: he wears a "suit of extreme collegiate cut, a pink shirt with violet necktie," shiny patent leather shoes, and he flashes a big roll and a sparkling diamond (both stolen). He is always "swaggering," "insolent," and "arrogant." In addition to knocking old Mrs. Rand and old Mr. Blackstone over the head, Luke attempts to murder both Ruel Rand and Chet Morton. This viciousness is not the "motiveless malignity" that Coleridge ascribed to Iago. Luke has his motives, and they are made incontrovertibly clear by his father, an Uncle Tom figure:

> "Evah since he's been up No'th with Massa Blackstone he thinks he's smart. Fine new clothes, big diamon' ring an' he swaggers 'roun' heah lak he own de place."

In fact, so much has Luke been corrupted by the taste of the good life up North that he organizes a Secret Society that out-KKK's the whites. Only the courage, cleverness, and daring of the Hardys prevent these black, "rather stupid looking" rebels from effecting a social coup d'etat.

The message of *The Hidden Harbor Mystery,* 1935, is as self-evident as it is self-condemning; blacks should be kept in servitude because they are an ignorant, violent, immoral people who are as incapable of understanding freedom as they are of fulfilling the responsibilities con-

From The Tower Treasure, *a Hardy Boys mystery written by Leslie McFarlane under the pseudonym Franklin W. Dixon and illustrated by Walter S. Rogers.*

comitant with it. Blatant in the *Harbor,* this message is reinforced over and over in the other Hardy Boys stories. All blacks speak in Uncle Remus dialect, all hold menial jobs, all are anonymous. No black is accorded any respect, no black is entrusted with any responsibility, no black is accepted as a human being.

And the case of the black in the Hardy Boys, as we have seen is an intensification of that of every minority group. Irishmen pound beats, Scotchmen sweep floors, Italians sell bananas. The Applegates and Websters have the money, the Blackstones and Rands have the tradition, the Hardys have the brains. This is the world of the Hardy Boys. This is the American Dream of Franklin W. Dixon.

The influence of the Hardy Boys stories on American thought is as inestimable as their readers are incalculable. Both are enormous. Millions of minds, my own included, have been irrevocably warped by the taken-for-granted caste system. Re-reading the series now, twenty-five years after I grew up with it, is an experience as traumatic as it is embarrassing. For I probably read *The Hidden Harbor Mystery* a half-dozen times in the early 1940's, but I never really saw Luke Jones until two months ago. I know now that I would have accepted it as perfectly natural then if Chet Morton had ever suggested, one day at a carnival, a little eenie-meenie-meinie-moe to see who would throw first in the Hit-the-Coon, Get-a-Cigar game.

Today the Hardy Boys are as popular as ever. Now the stories are being read the world over, from England and France to Iceland and the Argentine. But there is a little hope. For many of the original stories, including *The Hidden Harbor Mystery* and *Footprints under the Window* now bear the following note on the title page verso:

> In this new story, based on the original of the same title, Mr. Dixon has incorporated the most up-to-date methods used by police and private detectives.

The note is slightly misleading. "Mr. Dixon" died about thirty years ago in the person of Edward Stratemeyer; the revision is largely the work of the Stratemeyer Syndicate. Secondly, and far more significant, in the *Harbor* and *Footprints* new "methods" means new book. That is, Louie Fong and Luke Jones have disappeared. There is little, if any, connection between the revised plot of these two stories and the original.

Now it is certainly good and proper that someone in the Syndicate has finally realized that these two stories were extremely bigoted in the original. One only wishes he could be more enthusiastic about the revisions. For although Luke Jones and Louie Fong are gone, and Rocco has become Mr. Rocco, and Con Riley is now Patrolman Riley, the essential nature of the Hardy Boys world has not really changed at all. Mr. Rocco is still selling fruit and he still has an accent. Patrolman Riley is still an Irish cop pounding a beat. And in the revised *Hidden Harbor Mystery,* Mr. Blackstone's door is now answered not by old Uncle Tom Jones but by Minnie, a "young Negro maid."

It is clear that The Hardy Boys are rooted in what Gordon Allport calls "culture-bound traditions." That is, the hierarchic structure of the society and the set of values implicit in it constitute *de facto* prejudice of the worst—because it is so taken-for-granted—kind. Thus, calling the fruit peddler "Mr. Rocco" is about as effective as putting a band-aid over a cancer. Substituting Minnie the Maid for the Brute Negro is removing the cancer and replacing it with a tumor. The Hardy Boys are sick, very sick. In fact, the Hardy Boys are so sick that I doubt that even a heart transplant could make them well.

Arthur Prager

SOURCE: "Rascals at Large," in *Rascals at Large, or, The Clue in the Old Nostalgia,* Doubleday & Company, Inc., 1971, pp. 99-123.

It was during a period of winter inactivity when I was suffering one of my literary bereavements—the death of Sherlock Holmes, the last book in the Tarzan series, or something of the sort—that I came across the Hardy Boys. At that time I had never heard of Nancy Drew (and would not have admitted it if I had) but the boys were more or less counterparts of Nancy's in the teen-ager *qua* detective school of children's literature. They solved mysteries, discomfited bullies, beat up grown criminals, carried firearms, rode motorcycles, camped out, and did as a matter of course almost everything that was forbidden to me and my friends. I asked my mother for money for *The Tower Treasure,* and as soon as I had finished it, for *The House on the Cliff.* Covertly glancing at the inside cover to determine that even then there were more than twenty titles in the series, she sighed her well-known sigh and went to get her pocketbook. I was off on another one. What next?

The early Hardy Boys were written, as I was not to find out until many years later, by the redoubtable Edward Stratemeyer, the uncontested champion of children's series writers, using the pseudonym Franklin W. Dixon. Stratemeyer was a Newark stationer with literary longings who wrote his first story on wrapping paper during a business lull. He was twenty-six at the time. It was 1886, and he sold his story to a shrewd publisher for $75. After that it was good-bye to the stationery store for him. He had started on a career that made his name a household word to kids all over the world—or would have if he had not used more than sixty pseudonyms through the years until his death in 1930. . . .

The Hardy Boys were in their teens at the start of the series. Frank was sixteen, with dark, straight hair, and his brother Joe was a year younger, pink-cheeked with blond curly locks. Joe's eyes were blue and Frank's dark, and both had "firm, good-humored expressions of the mouth." Frank, moreover, had a "clever, good-natured face" although no such claim is made for Joe in any of the books.

The brothers were always on excellent terms with each other, and their teamwork in solving mysteries was well coordinated. No sibling rivalry there. They lived in suburban Bayport, a thriving metropolis of 50,000 souls that rivaled Virginia City or East St. Louis as a lodestone for criminal activities of all kinds. Never were so many assorted felonies committed in a simple American small town. Murder, drug peddling, race horse kidnaping, diamond smuggling, medical malpractice, big-time auto theft, and even (in the 1940s) the hijacking of strategic materials and espionage, all were conducted with Bayport as a nucleus.

The town (which had the worst weather in modern literary history—every mystery reached its climax in a thunderstorm) was on the Atlantic coast, close enough to New York for easy access. It was located on a sheltered bay about three miles inland, and surrounded by cliffs which were liberally riddled with caves that figured importantly in every book. The caves served as criminal hideaways, headquarters and storerooms, often overlapping from book to book, so that the diamond smugglers were able to use the same cave that the car theft ring had used after the latter had been unmasked and jailed by the Hardys.

In 1927 Dr. Sigmund Freud, six years older than Stratemeyer, was practicing in Vienna. It is unlikely that the two men ever met, but the author of the Hardy series understood the fascination that caves have for boys, and used it with his usual lavish hand. The Bayport caves were reached by long, narrow tunnels through which Frank and Joe could crawl unnoticed and eavesdrop on the nefarious plans of their criminal enemies. In a number of the books the caves had entrances (or exits) in innocent-looking buildings, where they were disguised as bookshelves or storage cupboards. Joe (or Frank), about to give up, would lean wearily against a shelf, and a section of wall would swing slowly forward revealing the yawning mouth of yet another tunnel to adventure.

On several occasions, the boys traveled far from good old Bayport—to Mexico and once to the Deep South—but the inevitable caves were there too, for the boys to crawl, eavesdrop, and get captured, bound and gagged in, with the usual hairsbreadth escape.

The Hardy family lived in a large, well-appointed but not luxurious frame house. They kept no servants, but there was plenty of yard and a roomy two-story garage in which Frank and Joe were able to maintain a home-made modern crime laboratory. (This facility was later moved to the cellar for security reasons.) The boys were the sons of the nationally celebrated Fenton Hardy, who had served many years on the New York City police force, and had retired to Bayport to begin a highly successful career as a private detective at the age of forty. Mr. Hardy was tall, with graying hair, keen blue eyes, and a shrewd, clean-cut face. He wore neatly pressed tweeds, and was inordinately proud of his boys. By the third book of the series (*The Shore Road Mystery*) he was regarded as "one of the greatest American criminologists," and numbered among his clients millionaires, generals, high government officials, and notables of all kinds, none of whom seemed at all dismayed when the busy detective handed their cases over to his fifteen- and sixteen-year-old aides.

At first Mr. and Mrs. Hardy wanted Joe and Frank to study law and medicine, but after the boys had displayed their detecting skills and earned several handsome rewards the family relented and the boys were permitted to follow in their father's footsteps. . . .

[T]he reader was never allowed to get close enough to the elusive Mrs. Hardy to find out anything about her at all, except that she had the ability to turn out hearty, delicious meals at the drop of a hat. She was probably in her thirties, but she is never described, and she must have been as much a master of disguise as her distinguished husband, since we find him addressing her as "Laura" in the early books, and as "Mildred" in the later ones. Whether this was the same Mrs. Hardy or whether a divorce and remarriage had taken place is never revealed. In any event, if it was a different Mrs. Hardy, she loved the boys as much and her skills in the kitchen never faltered.

The remaining member of the family was Aunt Gertrude, an eccentric old lady who

> was one of the pepperiest and most dictatorial old women who ever visited a quiet household. She was a rawboned female of sixty-five, tall and commanding, with a determined jaw, an acid tongue and an eye that could quell a traffic cop. She was as authoritarian as a prison guard, bossed everything and everybody within reach, and had a lofty contempt for men in general and boys in particular . . . Underneath this rough exterior was a kindly heart. Her bark was worse than her bite. Joe always said she looked as though her clothes had been chosen by a color-blind saleslady and put on her by a cross-eyed maid with only one arm.
>
> (*What Happened at Midnight*)

This strange relative spent her time dropping in on her kinfolk for visits of indeterminate length, and her brother Fenton and his family had their share. And didn't the boys brush their hair and mind their manners when the old lady was around! In several of their cases she was able to help them by applying feminine intuition to a knotty problem, and she made the best cookies on the Eastern Seaboard.

The Hardys were rarely alone in solving their mysteries, even when Fenton and Aunt Gertrude Hardy were not available. A gregarious pair, they had numerous chums their own age who always seemed to be free to make one of the zigzag, high-speed Odysseys that were essential to mystery-solving in the environs of Bayport. Their set included an ethnic mixed bag worthy of the World War II cinema. There were WASP American farm boy Chet Morton, stout-hearted Phil Cohen, dark, curly-haired Tony Prito, and Biff Hooper in major roles, and a few others in less prominent ones.

There seemed to be a notable lack of Negroes; and Irish Catholics were used only for comedy in those days. The books have all been rewritten now, and reissued in smart, colorful, washable plastic covers, and it can only be hoped that the Hardys have annexed a black chum or two in recent years. The villainous Felix Polucca of *The House on the Cliff* in his 1927 edition has had his name changed to Pollitt in the revised edition, and Frank's remark "I have a sort of hunch that there's a nigger in the wood pile" has become "The boys felt uneasy."

According to Andrew E. Svenson, Stratemeyer partner in charge of revising the series, today's readers will miss the old gunplay of yore, the horseplay and the snide remarks about dumb cops. Now the Hardys respect the police, eschew sidearms in favor of judo, and never make minority groups the butt of jokes. All of the early books have been rewritten. In many cases an entirely new mystery appears under an old title. *The Flickering Torch Mystery* is now about an isotope theft ring at Kennedy Airport and a rock group. *The Clue of the Broken Blade* is now about fencing and voiceprint techniques. *The Mystery of the Flying Express* now deals with hydrofoils and astrology. Aunt Gertrude now appears as a modern woman in her forties but she has, alas, lost much of her pepper.

Principal among the Hardy chums was Chet Morton, who served as the comedy relief for the series. Chet is described as a "fat-cheeked roly-poly youth," and he was possessed of a huge appetite and a vast capacity for trouble of all kinds. Everything happened to Chet. If he took a picture with his new camera, he was certain to step backward right over a cliff. When he sat in a rocking chair, it tipped over. An attempt to put a dead fish in Joe's desk at school resulted in his being caught by the teacher and made to stay after school. When he bought firecrackers for the Fourth of July, they exploded prematurely, scaring the daylights out of a Bayport policeman. On several occasions Chet's proverbial bad luck got him into more serious trouble. He was arrested (falsely) for a movie box office robbery because a wounded and delirious accomplice of the real robber kept mumbling that his colleague's name was Chet. On another occasion, when the boys were off to solve a mystery in Mexico, Chet was denied a passport temporarily because a fugitive felon with numerous offenses just happened to be named Chet Morton.

These trials did nothing to dampen Chet's good spirits and justly celebrated reputation as a boy humorist. No matter what his situation, Chet could always be depended on to come up with a humdinger. . . .

Biff Hooper was the biggest of the chums, strong, athletic, and slow. He was, of course, the natural foil for Chet's humor, but slow or not, Biff was not stupid, and when the chums were graduated from Bayport High in 1930 (*The Great Airport Mystery*) it was Biff who was chosen to deliver a recitation. Tony Prito rendered an accordion solo. A girl (wouldn't you know) was class valedictorian, and the Hardys and Chet were lumped together in a skit. Academic honors were not for the boy detectives, but they didn't care. They were satisfied (as their father put it) to "use their heads for something more than to hang their hats on."

Tony Prito and Phil Cohen, who were "noted at school for their fearless, at times even reckless, dispositions" were practically interchangeable, with Tony slightly more in evidence than Phil. Tony had a starring role in one book (*The Clue in the Embers,* 1955) in which he inherited a curio collection which was promptly stolen by sneak thieves, but Phil remains in the background in the series, content to be mentioned from time to time. He is never described, although Tony is revealed as having "dark hair, olive skin, and sparkling eyes" which "indicated his Italian parentage even more emphatically than his name."

No mention of chums would be complete without a mention of Callie Shaw and Iola Morton, Frank and Joe's special girl friends. Callie, brown-eyed and brown-haired, was "an object of special enthusiasm for Frank," while Iola (Chet's sister) was "all right as a girl in Joe's opinion." In 1927 (*The House on the Cliff*) Iola is described as a plump, dark girl, but by 1950 (*The Secret of the Lost Tunnel*) she has become "slender and good-looking," presumably after twenty-three years of low-calorie meals.

The boys had a hearty, comradely relationship with Callie and Iola (it was Callie, incidentally, who was class valedictorian, and "won the hearts of all by her valedictory address") which included ice-cream soda dates, dancing to phonograph records, parties, and picnics for which the girls prepared the food. There was never any physical contact between them, and certainly no kissing, spooning, lollygagging or similar foolishness. During one group picnic, when Callie and Frank had gone for a walk in the woods and their classmates heard Callie scream, no one suspected for a moment that Frank had been guilty of attempting to steal second base. Everyone knew instinctively that the boy sleuth had been abducted by a pair of red-hots, bundled into the boot of their speedy roadster, and carried off in the direction of the Shore Road caves. . . .

One of the boys' most outstanding characteristics was high-speed mobility. In the first books the Hardys and their chums all had motorcycles, on which they tore in and out of Bayport and the nearby villages, seemingly without arousing the local populace. In those days a teen-ager on a motorcycle was the norm rather than an object of community terror. They were, if truth be told, a juvenile motorcycle gang, although not the first one to appear in boys' books. Stratemeyer had preceded himself (in his guise of Roy Rockwood) with the Speedwell Boys, and (as Andrew Carey Lincoln) the Motorcycle Chums, both pre-World War I, and both very similar to the Hardys. The Motorcycle Chums even had a fat, food-oriented, comical chum to accompany them on their speedy excursions.

Soon after the beginning of the series, the boys put their motorcycles aside in favor of a sleek (but not too dependable) convertible, which they had used in 1928 to trap the members of an automobile burglary ring. The car served them well until 1943, when World War II gasoline rationing had them reduced to bicycles for the duration.

With the reward from one of their first mysteries, Joe and Frank had invested in the *Sleuth,* the fastest motorboat in the Bayport area. They spent a great deal of time afloat, roaring up and down the cave-ridden coast, rescuing drowning women and children (they never embarked without a rescue in the offing somewhere) and nearly losing their lives in Bayport's numerous thunderstorms. As soon as the *Sleuth* appeared, it seemed to stimulate local bullies (who had their own motorboats) to try to run the Hardys down and ruin their boat. They always failed, ending up in the bay amid the splinters of their own ill-fated craft. The Hardys, gentlemen always, would fish the miscreants out and set them ashore with stern admonition to avoid dangerous violence in the future. The same fate seemed to attach itself to their homemade ice boat, the *Sleuth*'s winter replacement, which attracted homicidal maniacs as frequently as its summer counterpart.

When they weren't manning their own vehicles, the boys still traveled fast, and by the early 1930s they had discovered airplanes, making one of the first parachute jumps in boys' literature (*What Happened at Midnight*). Whatever the vehicle, no book ever ended without a smash-up. Motorcycles went off the road, over cliffs, into trees. Cars skidded and spun. Boats rammed other boats. Airplanes sputtered, stalled, and headed for forced landings in wild country. Thrills and more thrills, but the boys (shaken up, knocked about and bruised) always came out in shape for the next chapter.

Lack of official status was the only handicap that prevented the young detectives from functioning with total efficiency, and they frequently tangled with obtuse small-town cops who imagined that their breathless requests for emergency action were boyish practical jokes. After the series was well under way, and newspaper publicity had made the boys famous in and around the Bayport area, it was easier for them to commandeer official help. The Bayport Police Department consisted at first of fat, stupid, nervous Chief Collig, Traffic Officer Riley, another dolt, and Detective Smuff, slow, but friendly. The whole department smarted at being outwitted by the teen-age detectives time and again. The local cops felt that the Hardys' success in mystery solving was due almost entirely to luck. . . .

As the years progressed the police force expanded, and by 1955 Chief Collig was able to field large-scale dragnets and surveillance operations whenever the boys asked for them. Described in 1930 as a "fussy little man with a vast sense of dignity", he had become "fat, genial Chief Collig" by 1955, after having unaccountably been replaced by "fat, genial Chief Finch" in 1941. Today this description has been replaced by a more timely image. Collig is now a keen-eyed vigorous man with iron gray hair, and a veteran of many battles with Bayport's criminal elements.

A typical Hardy case began in one of two ways. Either Fenton Hardy, too busy with other work to pursue a new and urgent assignment, passed it to the boys, or Joe and Frank spotted a suspicious character in Bayport's streets and followed him right smack into the middle of a new mystery. In either event, the action usually began with a warning, phoned, mailed, or tossed through a window of the Hardy domicile by a person or persons unknown. In *The Secret Warning* (1938) it was simply a scribbled "Leave town at once or there'll be trouble." In *The Secret of the Lost Tunnel* (1950) the crook was a little more formal:

Hardy Boys:

Clear out and go back to Bayport if you want to stay healthy. Kids who don't mind their own business end up in the graveyard. If Smith finds the gold, he can't claim it regardless.

The Hardys, of course, were not to be frightened by this kind of fiddle-faddle. They launched into phase two without batting an eye. This usually consisted of some kind of fortuitous coincidence. They met someone on the street who looked like a crook, they overheard two men talking about a crime in a restaurant booth, or some similar evasion. Once a suspect was spotted, they followed him right to the gang's headquarters, and then moved into phase three, trouble. . . .

Now the boys are sure they have found the true criminals, but who will believe them. *Prima facie* evidence is needed, and throwing caution to the winds, they follow the miscreants a little too closely. A favorite surveillance method of theirs is for Joe (or Frank) to lock himself in the trunk of the felons' car.

During their pursuit, a number of extraneous dangers threaten them, and no one, even Nancy Drew, was ever so accident prone as Joe Hardy. In *The Clue of the Broken Blade* Joe is knocked down and hospitalized by a speeding fire truck. In *The Secret Warning* he faces death, and is once again hospitalized by a firebomb explosion in a dry-cleaning establishment. Cattle almost stampede him to death in Texas in *The Mark on the Door.* A drunken pilot buzzes his car off the road in *The Great Airport Mystery.* He falls out of a second-story hotel window in *A Figure in Hiding,* and goes right through a glass canopy, staggering off with superficial cuts. There are car, boat, and motorcycle crashes. In other books Joe is attacked by a giant octopus while deep-sea diving, and drinks water from a poisoned cactus. None of these perils ever seems to affect Frank, who stands by, powerless to do anything except check on hospital visiting hours, and report the latest bloodshed to their father.

There is deliberate mayhem too. The boys are shot at, blinded with a water pistol full of ammonia, and left bound and gagged to starve in caves. An attempt is made to electrocute them by thugs who leave a rifle in the grass after connecting it to a power line. The lifeline on Joe's diving suit is cut. Somehow they always bounce back in good shape for the next rough-and-tumble.

Unlike the Nancy Drew books and other juvenile detective series, the Hardy books had plenty of violence. The boys often carried pistols, and people (always criminals) were shot and killed or wounded. On one occasion the boys dug up a mouldering corpse and then reburied it. There are plenty of heads bashed, jaws punched, and teeth rattled. Frank and Joe, for all their tender years, were always able to overcome full-grown men, because both were adept at the manly art of boxing, and both recognized the superiority of science over brute strength.

Time and again, dodging ponderous, heavy blows from some bull-necked hoodlum, Frank (or Joe) darts in with fancy footwork and plants a scientific left hook that leaves his opponent *hors de combat* for at least fifteen minutes.

Phase four in the books is capture. After peril and mayhem, the boys overstep the bounds of good sense and tumble right into the hands of their enemies. . . . [T]he boys were trussed up to wait for the end, and, of course, rescued in the nick of time by their chums. . . .

And so the final phase of each book began with escape and retribution, punctuated by whines and muttered invective from sniveling felons, and ended with a reward—five hundred dollars, two hundred dollars, a gold watch and chain, a movie camera, the usufruct of a vacation island in the bay, a new vehicle of some kind. No adventure ever ended for Frank and Joe without cash profit and a pat on the back. . . .

We readers knew (and if we hadn't known Mr. Stratemeyer would have told us—he always advertised the next book in each series at the end of the last one) that the young sleuths were already planning their next battle against crime. In all probability a warning note had been tucked into the mailbox, even as Mrs. Hardy sat simpering. Rascals were at large, and the Hardys would fight on until the very last criminal was behind bars. The old readers are grown up and scattered now, and Stratemeyer has gone to whatever special Heaven exists for people who make children happy, but the boy detectives go on thrilling new generations, rewritten, brought "up to date," but still fearlessly making their dad proud of them.

Ed Zuckerman

SOURCE: "The Great Hardy Boys' Whodunit," in *Rolling Stone*, No. 221, September 9, 1976, pp. 36-40.

> "So you boys want to help me on another case?" Fenton Hardy, internationally known detective, smiled at his teenage sons.
>
> "Dad, you said you're working on a very mysterious case right now," Frank spoke up. "Isn't there some angle of it that Joe and I could tackle?"
>
> Mr. Hardy looked out the window of his second-floor study as if searching for the answer somewhere in the town of Bayport, where the Hardys lived. Finally, he turned back and gazed steadfastly at his sons.
>
> "All right. How would you like to look for some smugglers?"
>
> —*The House on the Cliff*

Old Fenton's thoughtful pause didn't fool anybody. Fans of the Hardy Boys knew from experience that, within paragraphs, Frank and Joe would be hot on the trail of smugglers or jewel thieves or forgers or other desperadoes. Bayport was "a pleasant city of 50,000 people on Barmet Bay" (*Footprints under the Window*) yet, as critic Arthur Prager has pointed out, it "rivaled Virginia City or East St. Louis as a lodestone for criminal activities of all kinds. Never were so many assorted felonies committed in a single American small town." And wherever there was a crime, the Hardy Boys were there.

Despite its crime rate, Bayport and its citizens generally had an air of being slightly quaint and dated to one who read of them during the Fifties. That was only natural, as most of the books available then had been written in the Thirties and Forties. The Hardy Boys drove a roadster, whatever that was; they wore caps and neckties; their friends were their "chums"; they listened to radio programs and they carried two-dollar bills. So, when Hardy Boys fans of this generation abandoned them at last and moved on to Raymond Chandler or Henry Miller or Dostoyevsky, the Hardy Boys were left behind in a double past—that of our own childhood and an out-of-focus, adventurous time that preceded even that. The logical conclusion is that the Hardy Boys are dead, or at least moribund, locked in their antique Bayport, doomed to chase the same diamond smugglers in the same roadster until diamonds are as obsolete as roadsters and nobody cares.

It is a shock, therefore, to open *The Flickering Torch Mystery* and find the Hardys and their chums in a rock & roll band.

> The band played for about an hour, doing renditions of songs that had the listeners tapping their toes and snapping their fingers to the varied rhythms. A dance melody led up to the first intermission.
>
> Seymour came over and had a big smile on his face. "Say, gang, you're great!" he said. "Come along. A lot of patrons are dying to meet you. . . . "
>
> Unable to come up with a plausible refusal, Frank led the way down to the dance floor where a crowd was milling around. Each member of the band was promptly buttonholed by a music fan.
>
> An effusive blond teenager engaged Frank in conversation. "I think your combo is too sweet for words," she cooed. . . .
>
> Frank tried to edge away but the girl linked her arm in his. "Do tell me what you're playing next," she begged.
>
> Desperately Frank went through the program. "Now if you'll excuse me, I have to get ready," he said.
>
> "That's the only reason I'd accept," she said archly. "Keep the rhythm coming my way!"

Frank was anxious to break away from this music fan because he had spotted a villain secreting a stolen uranium isotope in his amplifier and, as far as we know, he never saw the young lady again. But a further mystery, beyond the mystery of the stolen isotope, remains: how did she get into *The Flickering Torch Mystery* in the first place? *The Flickering Torch Mystery* was first published in 1943, and anyone who read a copy purchased before 1971 (and that includes most Hardy fans reading this article) did not find a rock band anywhere in it. It was an exciting enough book, having to do with the theft of construction materials near the lab of an eccentric scientist who was developing artificial rubber—big news in 1943—but there were no effusive blond teenagers or uranium isotopes in the neighborhood.

What has happened to *The Flickering Torch Mystery* is a mystery worthy of the Hardy Boys themselves. The trail to its solution leads first to an inconspicuous brick office building in Maplewood, New Jersey, and then on into the past, where the secret of the Hardy Boys is inextricably bound up with the secret of their creator, Franklin W. Dixon. The complexity of the tale would not deter the Hardys. "We'll just have to keep plugging away," Frank counsels Joe in *Footprints under the Window.* "In all the other mysteries we tackled we had plenty of setbacks. Then something usually happened to straighten everything out, and all the points that puzzled us became as clear as day."

In that spirit, we proceed.

The most important thing about Franklin W. Dixon is that he never existed. The first Hardy Boys books were created by a man named Edward Stratemeyer in the late Twenties, and he and his descendants have supervised the actual writing of the books by a succession of anonymous ghost writers ever since. . . .

By the time of his death, in 1930, at the age of 68, Stratemeyer had written more than 200 books himself and presided over the writing of about 800 others. Among his own works were the early adventures of the Hardy Boys, who first breathed the clean air of Bayport in 1927. Their premier appearance came in *The Tower Treasure,* which was written from Stratemeyer's outline. Grosset and Dunlap, Stratemeyer's publisher, fretted that the Hardy Boys, along with Nancy Drew and the others, were too young to die, especially as they had already sold 20 million copies and showed no signs of slacking off. "The publishers were aghast that the empire might crumble," Harriet Stratemeyer Adams, Stratemeyer's daughter, told an interviewer several years ago. "They begged my sister and me to continue." . . .

"The trick in writing children's books," [Andrew] Svenson said in 1974, "is to set up danger, mystery and excitement on page one. Force the kid to turn the page. I've written page one as many as 20 times. Then in the middle of each chapter there's a dramatic point of excitement and, at chapter's end, a cliffhanger."

True to Svenson's formula, the most common phrase in the Hardy Boys books is "Look out!" On page seven of *The Flickering Torch Mystery,* Frank, while flying

the family plane, is nearly struck in midair by another plane piloted by a scar-faced villain. ("'Frank, watch it,' Joe cried suddenly.") Within the next 54 pages an airplane wing drops from a crane over the boys' heads (they leap out of the way), a junkyard truck drives straight at them (they leap again), they strike a log while riding in a friend's boat and are thrown overboard, a big fishing boat careens at full speed toward their boat in a fog (it narrowly misses them), they are buzzed by a low-flying plane (they duck), a stranger with a steel bar tries to sabotage their boat (Joe tackles him), a rope suspending an airplane engine over their heads suddenly breaks (the engine hits a rock and bounces away), Joe's hands begin to slip as he literally hangs over the edge of a cliff (he finds a toehold), and the steering mechanism of the boys' convertible snaps as they drive down a steep mountain road (they stop safely). And that's all in the first seven chapters. To recuperate, the boys go home and eat lunch.

The home the boys go to, a "spacious, three-story clapboard house" at the corner of Elm and High streets in Bayport, could just as easily be located in the section of Maplewood, New Jersey, where the Stratemeyer Syndicate rents a suite of offices. It shares a two-story brick office building with a firm of accountants at the edge of a pleasant tree-shaded neighborhood near the Maplewood Country Club. Mrs. Adams, who is 83, continues her work in an office that's furnished in French provincial style and decorated with original Nancy Drew cover art and signed photographs of her father and Bonita Granville, who played Nancy Drew in four movies in the late Thirties.

Mrs. Adams's M.O., as Fenton Hardy would say, is to pencil a 60-page outline for each book she writes and then dictate from the outline. "The quickest I ever did a book was two weeks," she told the *Wall Street Journal.* "I like two months better, and that's two months of solid work." . . .

The Hardy Boys sold 1,670,000 copies in 1975, second only to Nancy Drew's 2,300,000.

Both series have recently been successfully published in special library editions, marking a breakthrough for the syndicate. Many librarians have contended for years that the Stratemeyer books are badly written and repetitious, and they have been barred from most libraries. Now, says a spokesman for Grosset and Dunlap, librarians are "realizing that these are the only books many kids will read."

The all-time Stratemeyer best seller is Nancy Drew, who has sold more than 60 million books and has been the subject of a spate of articles, including one in *Ms.* magazine that called Ms. Drew "a role model for young feminists." The Hardy Boys, over the 50 million mark, rank second in total sales but have for some reason been out of the limelight since their serialization on the *Mickey Mouse Club* in the Fifties. Unless you're nine years old, of course, in which case the Hardys are as much in view as ever.

But there is a crucial difference between today's Hardy Boys books and the ones we remember, and it has to do with the presence of that blond bombshell in *The Flickering Torch Mystery.* Since 1959, in addition to cranking out a new Hardy adventure once a year, Mrs. Adams and her colleagues, like Soviet historians, have been systematically rewriting the past. The extent of this literary sacrilege is overwhelming: every Hardy Boys book up to and including *The Mystery at Devil's Paw* (number 38) is not the same as it used to be.

Some of the new editions carry the note, "In this story, based on the original of the same title, Mr. Dixon has incorporated the most up-to-date methods used by police and private detectives." But that explanation will not wash. In all the books—both new and old—the boys' main investigative methods are eavesdropping and ducking. Something more fundamental than technique has changed. The Hardy Boys have entered the new age.

The good old Hardy adventures have fallen victim to the march of progress. Grosset and Dunlap say the books have been revised to make them "more relevant," and Mrs. Adams has spoken of "modernizing" them to suit a more "sophisticated" generation of readers.

Some of the resulting changes have clearly been for the common good. The Hardy Boys were never as racist as some other Stratemeyer creations. Nor were the Hardys anti-Semitic; they've had a friend named Phil Cohen from the beginning. But the black train porter in *The Twisted Claw* (1939) who refers to the boys as "Massa" had evidently retired by 1969, when the revised edition came out. And Frank's remark, "I have a sort of a hunch that there's a nigger in the woodpile" in *The House on the Cliff* (1927) has been refined to a narrative comment, "The boys felt uneasy," in *The House on the Cliff* (1959).

In their biographical data, the boys are still basically the same. Frank, "a tall, dark youth of 16, with a clever, good-natured face," is now 18. His blond brother Joe has aged from 15 to 17. But the boys still attend Bayport High School, where they have been good students since 1927.

Their father, the world-famous detective, remains "tall and middle-aged but still youthful in appearance" and still departs frequently on mysterious business trips, leaving the boys behind to mind the store. Their mother, Laura, remains a shadowy figure whose main functions are to cook and worry. And the boys still interrupt their breakneck adventures every dozen pages or so to sit down to a nourishing meal, although the muffins their mother is making to accompany a roast beef dinner in *The Secret Panel* (1946) inexplicably turn into popovers in the revised edition 23 years later.

One persistent theme of the revisions in the new editions has been an overall toning down of excess, perhaps out of a fear of offending, perhaps out of a sense that the times now call for moderation. Whatever the reason, characters who were moronic in the Thirties have become merely a little dumb in the Sixties. The boys' Aunt Gertrude is still peppery but she is no longer dictatorial. Their pal Chet Morton is no longer fat; he is "plump." Accents have been dropped all around, the boys no longer carry guns, and the Tom Swiftian technology has disappeared. In *The Secret Panel* (1938), a gang of thieves opens locked doors with a "shortwave key." In the revised edition, they pick the locks. In the original, a crew of busy good guys "fortified themselves against hunger by eating some concentrated food tablets Mr. Hardy always carried with him." In the revised edition, Mr. Hardy brought some sandwiches from home.

Even the fabled Hardy humor has been toned down. Frank no longer "facetiously" inquires of Joe, "Have you ever seen a barn dance?" But, fortunately for the Hardys' pal Biff Hooper, one joke remains. In *The Secret of the Caves* (1929) Chet turns to Biff upon arriving at an isolated spot and says, "I know what they call this place."

"I don't think it has a name," said Biff.

"Oh, yes, they call this place Fishhook."

"Fishhook? Why?" asked Biff, neatly falling into the trap.

"Because it's the end of the line."

It isn't until the revised edition that Biff comes up with a witty reply: "You really hooked me on that one, pal." Anyone who has ever thought of a snappy comeback five minutes too late can sympathize with Biff, who carried this zinger unspoken in his head for 35 years.

On the morals front, the "modernization" of the books has, predictably, had its limits. "They don't have hippies in them," said Mrs. Adams. "And none of the characters have love affairs or take dope. If they did, I'm sure that would be the end of the series." On the sexual front, however, things have loosened up a little. Frank and Joe have been dating the same girls for 49 years now:

Callie Shaw, a brown-eyed, brown-haired girl, was an object of special enthusiasm with Frank, who was apt to cast an appreciative eye upon the other sex, while Iola, a plump, dark girl, a sister of Chet Morton's, was "all right, as a girl," in Joe's reluctant opinion.

—*The House on the Cliff*

By 1968, Iola has become slim, Callie has become a blond, and Joe has developed enough of an interest in girls to temporarily drop a search for credit card counterfeiters to have a hot dog with a pretty stranger (*Danger on Vampire Trail*). Most extraordinary of all, at a party in 1969 (*The Arctic Patrol Mystery*),

Frank touched Callie's arm. "I'd like to get out for a little fresh air. . . . "

"Me, too," Callie replied. "It's stuffy in here."

The couple stepped out into the star-studded evening.

Only God and Andrew Svenson know what might have happened next, for the couple's walk is interrupted by the arrival of three villains who pounce on Frank in a kidnap attempt. Frank fights them off, but the spell is broken.

It is in the area of politics, broadly construed, that the times have made their greatest mark on the Hardys. Their only contact with Vietnam came when they met a Vietnamese doctor named Cellier in Marrakech (*The Mysterious Carvan,* 1975); but the Cold War came to Bayport soon after it came to Washington and detente has not yet arrived. The old volumes have routinely been replotted, with little concern for literary desecration, to add a national security angle.

A venerable classic like *The Secret of the Caves* (1929), in which the boys track down a college professor who had lost his memory in a train wreck, has been made more "relevant" by having the professor, instead of wandering off in an amnesiac daze, kidnapped by a colleague who, while visiting an "unfriendly" foreign nation, was "brainwashed" into joining a sabotage ring operation on the outskirts of Bayport.

Footprints under the Window (1933) had to do with the smuggling in of "Chinamen" to work in laundries and restaurants. *Footprints under the Window* (1965) has to do with the smuggling in of spies working for a Caribbean dictator named Juan Posada. A mean-looking Latin is pictured on the cover wearing combat fatigues and a beard à la you-know-who.

A corollary to vigilance against spies and saboteurs is respect for your local police. The Hardys didn't always feel this way. In the old days they used to have a great deal of fun at the expense of Bayport's finest, who were invariably stupid or overblown or both. The boys' frequent foil was Constable Con Riley, who "had been a patrolman on a downtown beat but a pickpocket had stolen his handcuffs and nightstick." Riley's superiors were not much better:

> Chief of Police Collig was a fat, pompous official who had never been blessed by a superabundance of brains. His chief satellite and aide-de-camp was Oscar Smuff, a detective of the Bayport police force. As Chet was fond of remarking, "If you put both their brains together you'd have enough for a half-wit."

But all of that is gone now. These are not times for all-American boys to be contemptuous of police. Collig has become "a vigorous, middle-aged man with iron-gray hair who worked closely with the Hardys on various cases." Even Riley has become competent. If the police

are hampered by anything nowadays, it is not their stupidity but the Supreme Court. "We're not saying a thing!" protests a captured thief in a recent book. "We want to see a lawyer. We got our rights, and we'll have your badge for false arrest."

The movement to respect the police was, of course, a reaction to the social revolution of the Sixties. The Hardy Boys kept awfully busy during those years chasing our nation's enemies (and the occasional old-fashioned jewel thief or forger who slipped through), but even they finally took note that something new was in the air. Dope and real sex are still unknown in Bayport, but some elements of the new popular culture have arrived, and they are at first viewed with alarm.

In *The Bombay Boomerang* (1970), there is established a treacherous link between the new rock culture and subversion. A major character, one Teddy Blaze, is a Bayport disc jockey who "plays platters with a real beat" and "uses the slang of the new generation to hold the attention of his audience." Clearly the Hardy Boys are from a different crowd. When they meet Blaze, he gibes, "You fellows look like refugees from the Bach brigade."

The Hardys dislike Blaze instantly, and their intuition is proven correct. It turns out that Blaze's on-the-air "slang" is a cover for coded messages to a subversive gang with plans to explode a stolen missile on a nerve-gas storage site in Colorado. One gang member reveals the plot's horrible final goal: "The nerve gas will knock out enough people to start riots from coast to coast. The government will be overthrown."

(There is, needless to say, no question raised about the government's storing the nerve gas in the first place. "There's been some talk about this," an admiral tells the Hardys, "residents complaining about the danger if an earthquake tremor should split the ground and the stuff got out into the air. One farmer charges that his cattle have already been affected by leakage."

(Mr. Hardy frowns and asks, "Is that true?"

("No," assures the admiral. "All of these accusations are unfounded." So much for kooky environmentalists.)

At book's end, the Hardys smash the gang and save America from the unpatriotic disc jockey. After such a turn of events, one would hardly expect the Hardys to become rock musicians themselves, but by 1971 the Stratemeyer Syndicate had apparently decided that rock & roll was here to stay and that it did not necessarily mean the end of the Republic. In that year's revision of *The Flickering Torch Mystery,* we find the boys in a band and practicing for a Bayport rock festival. They sidetrack to investigate a string of mysterious airplane crashes and end up performing at the crooks' rendezvous.

So the Hardy Boys have even become hip: they still chase traitors but they play folk rock. Bayport adapts— and Bayport survives.

Louis Phillips

SOURCE: "Me and the Hardy Boys," in *Armchair Detective,* Vol. 15, No. 2, 1982, pp. 174-77.

> There, rocking gently in the waves, was a long, graceful craft, white with gilt trimmings, a motorboat . . . There was a flag at the bow and at stern: the fittings glistened; the seats were upholstered in leather, and across the bow was the name of the boat in raised letters: SLEUTH.

The *Sleuth* is a magic craft, for, if you haven't guessed by now, it belongs to the Hardy Boys, to Joe and Frank Hardy, teenaged detectives whose multi-volumed adventures spiced the lives of millions of readers. Created by Franklin W. Dixon, Joe and Frank Hardy, fifteen and sixteen years old respectively, (in later volumes Frank is eighteen and Joe seventeen, perhaps on the assumption that it was not a good idea to permit a sixteen-year-old to have his own hotrod) were, and still are I suppose, the sons of Fenton Hardy, the internationally famous detective, and of Laura Hardy, the not-so-internationally famous housewife. In spite of their father's reputation, the Hardy Boys are the two leading citizens of Bayport, a city of 50,000 inhabitants, a city that is a miracle of civic planning, for, in an age of severe population explosions, Bayport's population has remained unchanged for generations. It has been said that Bayport is located on Barmet Bay, three miles from the Atlantic Ocean, but do not bother to locate it on the map. It does not matter if Bayport is on any chart or upon any globe; as Emily Dickinson so quietly said, true places never are. Let it suffice that, for thousands upon thousands of readers, Bayport was once the literary and adventure capital of the world.

If you have ever read any of the seemingly endless volumes of the Hardy Boys, then there is no need to remind you of how Joe and Frank, with their chums Chet Morton, Tony Prito, Allen Hooper (or "Biff"), and Phil Cohen (notice how the author made certain that different ethnic groups were represented) roared out of Bayport in search of adventure. They were rarely disappointed, for Joe and Frank Hardy encountered and solved some of the most baffling crimes known to man—crimes that, more often than not, had baffled their illustrious father and the not-so-illustrious Bayport Police.

For most young men, mystery and death-defying thrills seem to be a long way off. For the Hardy Boys, however, intrigue was right around the corner. Sometimes they didn't even have to turn the corner:

> "Frank, come here!" Joe Hardy called excitedly to his brother from the front porch of their home.

> It was early afternoon of a hot August day, but tall, dark-haired Frank, eighteen years old, ran down the stairs at top speed. He knew from the tone of Joe's voice that something unusual was happening.

> When he reached the porch, Frank stopped short and stared in amazement. An expressman, who stood there, grinning, had just delivered a burlap crate and a package. Joe, blond and a year younger than Frank, had already removed the burlap. In the crate was a fine, proud-looking hawk.

Not many people receive a hawk in the mail. I've waited a long time, and I never have. To the Hardy Boys, however, such occurrences were mere commonplace. When they didn't seek out mysteries, mysteries sought them.

Now blurbs on the back of the Hardy Boys books insist that Frank and Joe Hardy are to be admired because they are so much like the ordinary twelve-year-old reader. That must be the copywriter's mistake of the century. Actually, my friends and I read the Hardy Boys because, as the above passage suggests, they were not like ordinary twelve year olds at all. The Hardy Boys were what we all wanted to become. Joe and Frank Hardy were not only detectives of great ability, but, more importantly, they were high school students. High School is awesome territory to any sixth-grader. In addition, Joe and Frank had access to hotrods, motorcycles, and to their speed-boat, *Sleuth*. I didn't even own a bicycle. And, as for the Hardy Boys being awarded a thousand dollars for solving a crime—well, a thousand dollars was beyond my ken entirely. The blurbs, therefore, were wrong. Children are always more interested in what they will become, not in what they are. By the time I reached Joe Hardy's age, Dixon's books had long been relegated to a closet shelf.

Whatever the reasons are for reading the Hardy Boys, however, the fact remains that it is virtually impossible to read only one book in the series. Like the potato chips in the famed Bert Lahr commercial, one volume whets the appetite; it does not satisfy it. Hints of other adventures, previous or forthcoming ones, are so skillfully planted in every volume that the ordinary reader is led from one book to another. Browsing through my tattered copy of *The Hardy Boys: Hunting for Hidden Gold,* for example, I come across an especially insiduous dialogue between Joe and Frank:

> " . . . [W]e haven't done too badly so far, anyway."

> "Yes, we had the fun of discovering the tower treasure."

> "And running down the counterfeiters."

> "Yes, and solving the mystery of the house on the cliff and finding out about Blacksnake Island."

If the reader hasn't already encountered the counterfeiters or the house on the cliff, then that poor boy or girl is compelled to purchase the necessary volumes. Since my friends and I were far from rich, we would buy different books in the series and lend them to each other. How sharper than a serpent's tooth it would have been to have had a non-lending friend.

Or, let us consider another side of the same coin. Suppose our hypothetical reader has previously encountered *The Tower Treasure* or *The House on the Cliff.* Imagine that reader's feelings of superiority over his non-reading friends. An immediate bond of intimacy is established between the reader and the Hardy Boys, between reader and writer. After all, literary allusions are a way of patting a reader on his back, a way of complimenting the reader for his magnificent accumulation of wisdom, his breadth of scholarship, his keen eye, and his discerning judgment. Once a young man has his first triumph over a literary allusion, there can be no turning back.

Nor was it only random conversations between Joe and Frank Hardy that influenced my friends to buy more books. The author himself, the phenomenal F. W. Dixon, often casually intruded to provide the faithful reader with encouragement and advice. Often at the conclusion of a typical adventure, a final paragraph would read:

> The Hardy boys were not destined to solve a mystery every week, but it was not long before they were plunged into a maze of events which were fully exciting as those that followed their first visit to the house on the cliff. The story of their next adventures will be told in the next volume of this series, called *The Hardy Boys: The Secret of the Old Mill.*

It has been rumored that the creator of the Hardy Boys was not one man, but many persons writing under one pseudonym. But, whoever he was or is, F. W. Dixon knew what he was doing every step of the way. He knew how to construct a book that can, if it must, stand by itself, but a book that also forms an indissoluble link in a chain. I easily swallowed the bait Dixon cast forth, and thus I soon became an honorary citizen of Bayport, where I sided with Joe and Frank, not only against evil, but also against the most inept and caustic police department in the world.

If I had been slightly older and slightly wiser, I would have recognized that the Bayport Police were distant relatives of the Keystone Kops, police designed not to solve crimes but to show off blundering, mediocre bureaucracies. Ezra Colig, the chief of police, was "a fat pompous official who had never been blessed by a super-abundance of brains. His chief aide-de-camp was Oscar Smuff, a detective." As Chet Morton so characteristically remarked about Colig and Smuff, "If you put both their brains together you'd have enough for a half-wit." Colig was usually discovered reading comic books (a sure sign of mental degradation, since an underlying purpose of the Hardy Boys series was to wean a young man away from the land of Dell), and both Colig and Smuff were naturally hostile to the idea of being outwitted by a group of high school boys. Not even Con Riley, an ordinary cop pounding his beat and often falling victim to a Chet Morton prank, held much warmth for the Hardy Boys' shenanigans. Like Mickey Spillane's Mike Hammer (although, of course, my friends and I could not have known it at the time), the Hardy Boys and the

chums displayed a healthy disrespect for bureaucratic inefficiency. If there were a mystery to be solved, Frank and Joe went ahead and solved it, not always bothering to consult Bayport's comic-book police force. That well may be one of the reasons why Hardy Boys were not displayed on the shelves of our local library.

Of course, if Colig, Smuff, and Riley, that famed vaudeville team, are not shining pillars of intellect, at least they are a far cry from the dastardly villains who provided momentum for the mysteries. Even today, names such as Li Chang, Redhead Blount, John Jackley, Markel, and Weeping Sam do not inspire a multitude of trust. The physical appearances of such characters are no less ominous:

> In the reflected light the boys could see that the speaker was a lean, wolfish-looking man with small calculating eyes, a hatchetlike nose and a thin, cruel mouth.

A crook looked like a crook in those days, and not just like your local congressman. When Mrs. Hardy describes a rug-buyer as

> a queer little fellow, very short and dark. He was a foreigner, you could tell by his appearance. He didn't speak very good English. He was dark and swarthy, with little keen black eyes.

you know it means trouble. In the world of the Hardy Boys, the villain is most likely to be a foreigner. If he is not a foreigner, the villain has red hair. Or if he isn't a foreigner and doesn't have red hair, six times out of nine the villain's name will have a *K* in it. Ganny Snackley, for example. I can no longer remember the more sordid details surrounding Snackley's less-than-legal career, but the very sound of his name fills me with delight. F. W. Dixon was no slacker when it came to creating criminals with notorious names.

With all my emphasis upon criminals and inept police, a casual observer might receive the impression that the Hardy Boys have no normal home life. Such an impression, however, is far from accurate. The Hardy Boys attend high school, worry over exams, and, to the best of their abilities, attempt to remain out of earshot of Aunt Gertrude, "an elderly, crotchety maiden lady of certain temper and uncertain years." Frank even has a girlfriend of sorts—not a real girlfriend, understand, but a let-me-walk-you-home-every-once-in-a-while girl named Callie Shaw. Always carrying cakes and jellies to sick widows, brown-haired and brown-eyed Callie is "Frank's favorite of all the girls in the city," and to this day Callie Shaw remains a paradigm of purity, chastity, and all-American girlhood.

Joe Hardy, like his brother, is not much interested in the gentler sex. The only girl to ever catch Joe's eye is Iola Morton, Chet's sister, and no one in his right mind would dare label Joe's relationship a romance. The closest the poor girl gets to a compliment is the fact that she "had achieved the honor of being about the only girl Joe Hardy had ever conceded to be anything but an unmitigated nuisance." With opium dens and counterfeit coins lying about, no red-blooded American boy is to be distracted by mere women.

Tracking down counterfeiters may be exciting to high-school students, but mothers are not fond of having their sons risk their necks on foolish escapades. Laura Hardy, mother of two great detectives and wife of one, is certainly no exception. One detective in the family is more than enough, so Mrs. Hardy wants her sons to prepare for a career in medicine or for one son to become a doctor and the other to become a lawyer—worthy ambitions, but definitely not as exciting as following in the steps of their father.

In the Hardy household, Laura and Aunt Gertrude, Fenton's sister, sound the note of normalcy, but it is Fenton Hardy who provides a tone of romance. A busy man and a handsome one, Fenton moves across the adventures as an almost shadowy figure, an international figure who always has time for his sons. According to the redoubtable Dixon, Fenton "was not the type of father who maintains an air of aloofness from his family, the result being that he was on good terms with his boys as though he were an elder brother"—and who am I to argue the description with the books' own author?

The best trait of Fenton, however, is his uncanny ability to pop up in the most unexpected places at the most unexpected times. In *The Disappearing Floor,* for example, Joe, Frank, and Chet fall into a deserted cave. No one, seemingly, is around for miles, but who should appear to save the boys from tragedy? You guessed it.

> "Well upon my word! How in the world did you three find your way in here?"
>
> "Dad!" exclaimed Frank and Joe in one surprised breath, while Chet was beside himself with joy.
>
> "Golly, Mr. Hardy," he bubbled, "you found us just in time."

Just in time. True adventurers always get rescued just in time, or they would be wiped out a hundred times over. So Frank and Joe are often rescued by their father, *just in time.* In perilous and chaotic times, how reassuring it is to know that there are at least two boys in the world who are to be looked out for, whose father is only a stone's throw away.

Thus, between the influences of high school, Callie Shaw, Iola Morton, the crochety Aunt Gertrude who never complimented her nephews to their faces, Laura and Fenton Hardy, Joe and Frank were typical adolescents. Well, not quite typical. After all, how many families do you know that have secret identification marks, and how many high school boys get the opportunity to solve murders and robberies? Try as I would,

pray as I might, I turned up no murders in my neighborhood. Joe and Frank had all the luck.

Looking back on my fifth- and sixth-grade reading material, I realize now that the Hardy Boys books are educational in more ways than one. I would rather a child read those books than the works most librarians and teachers would recommend. Nothing is more sad than a person who reads the classics too soon in life; nothing is more sad than a person who reads only what is "best," for classics are what one grows to and into, and the best paths to the classics are not reading lists, not short cuts, not paths clearly marked out, but paths that zig-zag in all directions at once. The Hardy Boys provided me with one such path.

Ah, but I am pontificating, and that will not do, will not do at all. Let me close with fond memories of Frank Hardy rushing to save his brother and another boy from drowning. As Frank rushes forward, F. W. Dixon's prose leaps with excitement:

> Could he reach the two in time? Would the current carry Joe and Lester close enough to the bank to enable him to rescue them? Would he be able to hold them until help arrived?

Anyone who doesn't know the answers to those questions has definitely wasted a misspent youth.

Carol Billman

SOURCE: "The Hardy Boys: Soft-Boiled Detection," in *The Secret of the Stratemeyer Syndicate: Nancy Drew, The Hardy Boys, and the Million Dollar Fiction Factory,* The Ungar Publishing Company, 1986, pp. 79-96.

In 1984 Franklin W. Dixon's eightieth volume in the Hardy Boys series, *The Roaring River Mystery,* was published. Frank and Joe Hardy are about to begin their seventh decade of crime solving today, over seventy million Hardy Boys novels have been purchased, and in the last three years over two and a half million paperback copies of their mysteries were sold—not bad for a series one critic called "nothing more than updated Rover." It is true that the first Hardy Boys title, *The Tower Treasure,* appeared in 1927, one year after the last Rover Boys book. Of more significance, I would say, is the fact that the Hardy Boys were conceived exactly as detective novels by American writers burst onto the market. . . .

The historical development of the Hardy Boys series looks like the genealogy of a very fertile clan. TV shows, coloring books, comic books, and cartoons have been spawned by the novels. The individual titles themselves have been reprinted; and all those written before 1959, substantially revised. . . . As for authorship, Edward Stratemeyer planned and wrote the series until his death in 1930, but a number of others have necessarily contributed to this long-running success story—among them, Leslie McFarlane, Harriet Stratemeyer Adams, and Arthur Svenson. The series is now carried on by a determinedly inconspicuous Syndicate staff.

The covers of the first series volumes are khaki in color and carry, emblazoned in brown, the silhouette of two boys on the prowl on a stormy night. One wears a hat and tie, both have on baggy trousers. Illustrations for the early books likewise depict wavy-haired youth in wide-collared shirts, sweater vests, or full-cut suits. By the late 1950s, Frank and Joe had taken on a new look, younger, clean-cut, more casual; and V-neck sweaters and short hair had replaced pre-World War II fashions. In the 1970s, the boys' hair became tousled. Covers of the current volumes picture preppies in oxford cloth or knit shirts, corduroy pants, even boating shoes. These superficial changes are paralleled by stylistic streamlining of the texts of the Hardy Boys books.

In recent titles there is far less use of dialect and slang in characters' speech, and the occasional stilted phrasing found initially has been ironed out. No such narration as this inelegant passage from the 1932 *While the Clock Ticked* would be printed today: "The boys warmly agreed that jail was much too good for the driver who had so nearly run them down; but as there was nothing they could do about it, the car having vanished before they could take down the number, they dusted their garments and went on their way again." The author's voice, moreover, is sub rosa compared with the chatty persona that used to be. *Footprints under the Window,* written in 1933, concludes in this way: "And have you guessed by this time, my readers, that the footprints under the window were those of the famous detective, Fenton Hardy?" That sort of direct address was rare even at the series' outset, but long-winded summaries of previous series volumes were common narrative intrusions. Now such recapitulation has been tapered down to a quick—usually one sentence in length—reference to the penultimate title. In general, the style shift in the Hardy Boys books might be characterized as a normalization. A style that never really asserted itself, in the manner of Arthur M. Winfield in the Rover Boys series, has given way to virtually invisible writing. Raymond Chandler said of Hammett's work that it "had style, but his audience didn't know it." The Hardy Boys books have no identifiable style, especially the post-1960 volumes, even when searched by a literary critic's keen private eye.

The substance of the Hardy Boys series has undergone alteration as well, regarding both the details of the boys' lives and the kind of crimes they investigate. In the tenth Hardy Boys book, *What Happened at Midnight,* published in 1931, the opening chapter contains an extended description of Bayport's newest building, an automat; in 1941, in *The Mystery of the Flying Express,* the boys are found guarding a hydrofoil; now they play and appreciate rock music. The activities of criminal characters have changed from a never-ending parade of searching for missing treasure, counterfeiting, and auto thefts

to bigger stuff. While still operating from their Bayport base, the two detectives now take on, in addition to more generic cases of kidnapping or stolen objets d'art, work involving international gambling rings, purloined Pentagon documents, schemes of political overthrow, and hijacked nuclear cargo.

Nonetheless, the underlying mystery plot formulas have remained intact throughout the characters' face lifts and the renovations in the form and matter of the stories themselves. The essential ingredients of a Hardys title are fast-paced investigative action and a large dollop of the conventional gimmickry of pulp magazine detection that began with Nick Carter: disguises, ciphers to be puzzled out, rude thugs to be put in their places, crime kits, secret messages, and passwords. . . .

Tony Prito, Biff Hooper, and Chet Morton have supported Frank and Joe Hardy from the series' inception. Since the period of *The Mystery of the Chinese Junk,* minority friends like Jim Foy have made guest appearances in particular titles—in *The Mysterious Caravan,* to cite another example, a Jamaican boy named William gets involved in the Hardys' detecting. Of the regulars, Chet Morton is undoubtedly the most central. As seen in *Chinese Junk,* his role exceeds that typically assigned to fat friends in Stratemeyer books. Beyond providing comic relief through his ever-shifting hobbies, his gullibility, and his indefatigable appetite, Chet is a catalyst for drawing the Hardys into dangerous and suspenseful adventure.

More often than not, Chet replaces the fair sex as the object of a daring rescue. In fact, girls play a decidedly minor role in the Hardy Boys mysteries compared with the status of friends of the opposite sex in either the Rover Boys or Ruth Fielding books. Callie Shaw has been the "object of Frank's affection" for over fifty years without undergoing any character development or appreciable change. (Her hair color has gone from brown to blonde.) Chet's sister Iola has been deemed "all right, as a girl" by Joe for an equal period. (Unlike her brother, Iola has lost weight over the years; once plump, she is now described as slender.) As a Grosset and Dunlap publicity blurb put it in the 1930s, Frank and Joe "think girls are all right—*in their place*!" That place has always been, and still is, window dressing. The only identifiable function served by females in the series is that of rewarder: they are among the first to heap praise on the Hardys' sleuthing at the end of most volumes. . . .

The Hardys and their circle of assistants and well-wishers are high school students, *but* they tackle grown-up crimes, which are usually supplied by their eminent criminologist father. Accordingly, the boys must be ready to fight serious criminal opposition—with their fists, with weapons, with investigative knowhow. . . .

In Franklin W. Dixon's series the adversaries are new in each book—no Josiah Crabtrees to be kicked around decade in and decade out, as was the case in the Rover

Boys fiction. The names of the Hardys' villains sound like those belonging to the felons in the *Dick Tracy* comic strip, which, in fact, began four years after the inception of the Hardy Boys: Mortimer Prince, Baldy Turk, Meeb and Scrabby, Vordo Bleeker, Baby Face, and—in *Chinese Junk*—the Chameleon. These names not only identify the bearers irrefutably as the evildoers, but I think they are also meant to suggest the tough, big-league nature of the cases the Hardys get involved in. No local foes here; Bayport's nasty citizens, like Clams Daggett, invariably turn out to be red herrings. This is not to say that world-class thugs do not carry on their activities in Bayport. As the Chameleon shows, they do—and with phenomenal regularity. A small New England coastal town, Bayport nonetheless holds a magnetic attraction for smugglers, robbers, and extortionists, due no doubt in large part to Fenton Hardy's practice there. Thus, as often as the heroes visit locales like Africa, Mexico, or the Bahamas in the course of their work, big-time crime comes to them in Bayport.

The interaction and conflict between detectives and their opposition is as codified as the characters involved. Arthur Prager suggests that Hardy Boys mystery plots follow a four-part formula. First, Fenton Hardy "hands down" a case. (Alternatively, his sons spot a suspicious character in Bayport.) Second, there is the fortuitous coincidence: the Hardys overhear suspects plotting or spy a potential criminal in a compromising position. Third, trouble develops when the boys follow the trail left by the evildoers. Typically, dirty tricks are enacted against the young detectives, and sometimes these pranks are intentionally deadly: the Chameleon plans to drown the boys in that cavern pool. Fourth, there is the final chapter. Having tumbled into their foes' clutches, the Hardys are miraculously rescued at the eleventh hour. In the meantime, the villains have confessed everything. . . . What keeps readers guessing, moreover, is not so much the outcome of each as the interconnection that will inevitably tie together the disparate threads. The final exposition of the plot(s) is generally lengthy in a Hardy Boys story, as it must be given the number of lines of action and inquiry, and it is ritualistically celebrated by a family reunion, a dance, or, most frequently, a banquet.

Occasionally, the detection in the Hardy Boys books is heightened by an atmosphere of horror . . . As a rule, however, the Hardy Boys series books are without Gothic or espionage embellishments. Their method is straightforward detection, detection accomplished not through deduction but by the search, or chase. At the end of the first series volumes, Grosset and Dunlap ran advertisements, one of which asked this question: "Have You Ever Thought Why You Get So Much Fun Out of Reading the Hardy Boys Stories?" The supplied answer does indeed pinpoint the books' basic attraction:

> It's probably because the Hardy Boys, Joe and Frank, are fellows like yourself. They like action, plenty of it. They are as full of curiosity as a couple of bloodhounds. And just leave a mystery around and they'll be in it before you can say "Sherlock Holmes!" . . .

> It's because they can drive a car and pilot a speedboat and are at home in the great outdoors and keep their heads in an emergency (and an emergency always is just around the corner).

In short, the Stratemeyer Syndicate in the Hardy Boys series had settled on a whirlwind mixture of mystery and adventure that spelled popularity with young readers.

When Tony Prito hypothesized that the junk may have belonged to a Chinese pirate and may contain hidden jade treasure, he is participating in everybody's fantasy adventure, the fantasy that explains in large part the thrill the fast-paced adventure genre has held for boys since the days of *Robinson Crusoe, The Coral Island,* and *Treasure Island.* The secret the Stratemeyer Syndicate hit upon in the Hardy Boys books was the *packing* of timeless adventure-story action into a distinctive, and repeatable, detective fiction pattern. Thus, the novel lure of the detective mystery had at last been thoroughly fused with the earlier adventure tale tradition. In this respect, the Hardys do pick up where the Rovers left off. That older set of brothers, from time to time, hunted treasure and sailed the seas as part of some larger investigation, as in *The Rover Boys Down East;* Frank and Joe make a habit of it.

The Hardys' bayside location leads to numerous expeditions in the *Sleuth,* and other seaside mysteries come along, too—such as **The Phantom Freighter** and **Trapped at Sea.** On or off the water, the Hardys' detection is likely to incorporate some "digging" for hidden treasure, as series titles make clear (**The Tower Treasure, Hunting for Hidden Gold, The Melted Coins, The Secret of Pirate's Hill, The Mystery of Smuggler's Cave,** and others). In fact, the unearthing of treasure is one of the most common climactic moments in Hardy Boys books, the staple ingredient that comes just before the boys fall into the hands of the evil characters, according to the basic plot formula. Frank and Joe's searches for secret goods are, to be sure, more elaborate than the expedition made in a simple tale of treasure hunting. Like Jim Hawkins in *Treasure Island,* the boys must first penetrate the criminal rings who are also after, or have stolen, precious objects, gold, or valuable papers. Hence, they are involved in two activities central to the active (versus the cerebral or contemplative) strain of detective fiction: they spy and they eavesdrop on their opponents. Both these practices are exciting to readers for the very reason that they are secretive endeavors, visual or aural as the case may be.

Where do the Hardy Boys carry out their searches? In archetypal secret places, namely deserted islands, caves, and underground tunnels. *Chinese Junk* makes use of all three hideaways; other titles are self-descriptive—**The Secret of the Caves, The Mystery of Cabin Island, The Secret of the Lost Tunnel.** Islands have long been part of boys' adventure fiction, in part because they are by their very nature set off from the rest of civilization and are often terra incognita, the equivalent of the untamed frontier in western adventure stories. Islands, what is more, according to C. G. Jung [in *Memories, Dreams, and Reflections*], are figures for the self, and explorations of the self, or searches for identity, constitute the major theme in adolescent literature. Caves and concomitant underground tunnels and passageways are secret places by definition. Psychoanalyst Lili Peller has commented [in *"Reading and Daydreams in Latency: Boy-Girl Differences"*] that stories about uncovering secrets are naturals for children, for whom life is full of secrets adults are guarding. More specifically, Prager has suggested [in *Rascals at Large*] a Freudian fascination in the Hardy Boys series with yawning-mouthed caves. It is true that Bayport has an extremely developed system of labyrinthine caverns and passageways, in which stolen goods have inevitably been secreted. But in their use of islands and caves the creators of the Hardy Boys fiction are consciously following not Freud but the example set by nineteenth-century writers of boys' adventure books. And the Stratemeyer Syndicate was not alone in keeping the tradition alive within a new mystery format. . . .

The Hardy Boys series resembles contemporary detective fiction for adults in its blend of adventure and mystery. . . . [T]he American hard-boiled mystery has its roots in the romantic western adventure story. Speaking of this mix, George Grella notes, "the American detective novel, paradoxically, combines its romance themes [good triumphing over evil] and structures with a tough, realistic surface and a highly sensational content." Now the Hardy Boys books also mix romantic adventure plots with a superficial realism, be it the advent of the automat or the boys' love for fast transportation. And the series displays a criminal content sufficiently sensational—viz., armed culprits intent on doing the boys in—to have triggered alarm among librarians and educators. But there is a great difference between the "mean streets" of the adult genre, where murder comes cheap and the entire world is stained by corruption, and the crime-ridden though ultimately comfortable and serene world of Bayport. The social context in which Frank and Joe Hardy operate and the underlying world view in the novels keep them firmly in the realm of the adventure *fantasy*. . . .

At bottom, Bayport is not a place that fires readers' imaginations, as settings so often do in literature for the young, be they realistic or fantastic places. Since Franklin W. Dixon is a cardboard writer, it is, of course, understandable that Bayport remains only a formulaic backdrop, as forgettable as the settings in soap operas or 1950s television situation comedies. Bayport is in fact reminiscent of a place like Springfield in *Father Knows Best*. It's there for characters to live in, it is secure, it throws up no real dilemmas—and Bayport is an especially handy place for the Hardys to be since so many criminals flock there. But it is not a spot that takes on its own life. . . . It is a frozen and fixed world where mysteries come and go, but there is no change or human complexity. . . .

Frank and Joe Hardy have grown a little older; their readers are getting younger. I have found no record of the age group originally projected by the founders of the series, but early to mid-teens is my educated guess. One reader from an earlier generation, John Gardner, has commented on how he outgrew the Hardys, "Dickens I ran into when I was in my early teens, when I began to find the Hardy boys tiresome and unconvincing. . . . The irrealism of two boys having long conversations while riding on motorcycles . . . was more than I could put up with." And in 1932 a writer for *Publishers Weekly* asserted that "publishers today recognize as a fact that boys, of their own accord, stop reading the modern juvenile series two years earlier than their fathers stopped the series of a generation ago." By the era of *The Mystery of the Chinese Junk,* the Syndicate clearly conceived of the Hardys as appealing to ten- to fourteen-year-olds. The back covers of 1960s books say so: "Anyone from 10 to 14 who likes lively adventure stories, packed with mystery and action, will want to read every one of the Hardy Boys stories listed here." In recent years the age level has dropped again: the Simon and Schuster publicity advertises the series as appealing to ages eight to twelve, and membership in the Fan Club run by that publisher bears out these figures. . . .

The boys, too, are, paradoxically, average guys, "fellows like yourself" as the publicity went, even as they perform wondrous feats of detection. They can be likened to Wally and The Beaver or David and Ricky Nelson of the TV sitcoms, rather than the superlative Rovers, who were always at the head of their class. Average fellows from a town that is depicted as a quaint Everytown, U.S.A., right down to the smiling policemen and helpful shopkeepers. But *these* ordinary boys get mixed up in high-level detection and dangerous adventure.

This fantasy scenario offers readers more than escapist thrills. Like the fairy tales, it provides a story in which the young and relatively inexperienced triumph; consequently, it gives an encouraging, confidence-inspiring model for life. Further, the security of the Hardys' existence (though always in danger, they are never seriously harmed) offers comfort as well from the anxieties brought on by the biological and psychological pressures of growing up in a world that most likely resembles Bayport and its extended universe but little. Readers need to spend quiet hours in such a retreat—in a moratorium, if you will—during which they can amass latent energy for the last stage of growth into adulthood. The readily available, jam-packed, and familiar mystery adventures of Frank and Joe Hardy fill that time slot to a T.

Jonathan Cott

SOURCE: "Hale and Hardy," in *Esquire,* Vol. 105, No. 6, June, 1986, pp. 225-26.

Tom Swift, Ragged Dick, the Rover Boys, the Hardy Boys. I remember them all, but it is the last of these whom I, and apparently most men, remember best: for since the first volume (*The Tower Treasure*) describing the adventures of these two teenage brother-sleuths appeared in 1927, the series bearing their name, under the corporate authorship of "Franklin W. Dixon," has sold more than sixty million copies. Reprinted, revised, and rewritten for more than half a century, works like *The Mystery at Devil's Paw, The Haunted Fort,* and *Hunting for Hidden Gold* still sell remarkably well; they are, in fact, the most popular boys' books of all time.

All these years later, however, I ask myself: Why all the fuss? Why did I, at the age of ten or eleven, like so many other boys, get addicted to the Hardy Boys books, devouring the entire series—each volume indistinguishable from any other—like Steinbeck's Tom Joad, who "got into a book, tunneled like a mole among its thoughts, and came up with the book all over his face and hands"? Perhaps that's what being a boy (or even a girl—for girls had Nancy Drew books) meant in those old-fashioned times. And yet, surely, there must also have been the pleasures of the text itself? One way to find out, I realized, was to pay a visit to my local children's-book library, where I picked out some Hardy Boys volumes and perused them. Frank was still "dark-haired," Joe still "blond"; but they were now driving sports cars and mopeds instead of "roadsters" and "jalopies." Later editions, up-to-date vehicles—why not? But something else seemed *very* wrong. Could the style of the books really have been so stultifyingly vapid ("Iola sniffed. 'I don't know about this compliment stuff. There's something on your mind, Joe Hardy!'") or so hyped-up ("'Gator Base to Gator One and Gator Two, do you read me?' Frank Hardy asked tensely. 'Come in, please!'")?

I turned to the various copyright pages and noticed that the editions I had in hand *had* been revised ever since 1959 . . . and some of the early books had been totally rewritten. Luckily, my library had on its reserve shelves a copy of the original version of *The Secret of the Old Mill,* the edition I had read as a kid. And as I turned its musty pages, redolent of old attics and forgotten prepubescent longings, I read:

> The boys started off at last, trudging along the broad highway in the early morning sunlight, whistling away in the best of spirits. They were decorous enough while they were in the city limits, but once they struck the dusty country roads their natural activity asserted itself and they wrestled and tripped one another, ran impromptu races, picked berries by the roadside and laughed and shouted without a care in the world.

The texture of the word "decorous," the leisurely pace, the sense of having world enough and time—all of this had been excised or eviscerated in the flatter or more high-tech versions of recent times.

I felt some morose middle-aged nostalgia but then stopped myself: after all, the early Hardy Boys books were hardly masterpieces of English prose. Compared with works by Arthur Ransome and Laura Ingalls Wilder, they're pretty lame and ignominious stuff.

Still, what I *remembered* having liked about the Hardy Boys books was that paradoxical sense that the series had given me of living in a familiar, secure, protected world, in which one could imagine oneself being as curious, fearless, ingenious, risk-taking, courageous, and righteous as the Hardy Boys themselves—those two action-driven, brotherly ciphers, whose lack of interiority was in fact their most rewarding and positive attribute.

The Hardy Boys were only as real as our imaginations allowed them to be. I suspect that's why nostalgic types like me secretly resent seeing our childhood heroes "made real" on TV—where the Hardy Boys were once serialized and embodied by Shaun Cassidy and Parker Stevenson, or where they still appear, in barely disguised fashion, as *Simon & Simon.* But perhaps that is also why movies like *Indiana Jones* and *Beverly Hills Cop* (think of Eddie Murphy "cracking" the art dealer's drug ring with the help of his police pal, Billy) appeal so strongly to those of us who cannot help but sense in these films' intrepid adventurers the archetypal pattern of the "two bright-eyed boys on motorcycles . . . speeding along a shore road," whose exploits demonstrate—in the words of the Canadian journalist Leslie McFarlane, who pseudonymously wrote the first several Hardy Boys books in a cabin in northern Ontario—what boys' books have always taught us and what boys, then and now, have always wanted to hear: that "no peril, no danger, no catastrophe, however grim and apparently inescapable, is ever as bad as it seems."

Cullen Murphy

SOURCE: "Starting Over: The Same Old Stories," in *The Atlantic,* Vol. 267, No. 6, June, 1991, pp. 18, 20, 22.

In 1959 Harriet Stratemeyer Adams, a Wellesley graduate, a writer, and the owner and president of the Stratemeyer Syndicate, then the nation's largest producer of adventure books for older children and young teens, took a fateful step. She directed that all the books in the company's thirty-two-year-old Hardy Boys series (whose author of record is Franklin W. Dixon—initially a man named Leslie McFarlane) and all the ones in the twenty-nine-year-old Nancy Drew series (whose author of record is Carolyn Keene—initially Adams herself, it once was thought, but in reality a woman named Mildred A. Wirt, who is now eighty-six and lives in the Midwest) be thoroughly and robustly revised. The reason for the overhaul, according to the present editor of the Hardy Boys series, at Simon & Schuster, was to bring the books abreast of various technological developments, and to make them reflect changing "attitudes and approaches" in the larger society. I suspect that another motive was to condense the novels for impatient readers by stripping them down to pure plot; and that yet another was to leach from them their earnest squareness, which calls attention to their age. Whatever the motivations, the upshot is that little remained in the books after their revision which could possibly discomfit anyone (such as dialogue rendered in dialect, humor at the expense of policemen, and big words that might have to be looked up). The bright regiments of Hardy Boys and Nancy Drew books that you see now at bookstores are all reflections of the Great Purge. Needless to say, the scores of new adventures in both series which have been created in the years since 1959—the Hardy Boys corpus now comprises 108 mysteries, the Nancy Drew corpus comprises 101, and both series come in a line of young-adult "Casefiles" as well—also adhere to the revisionist code.

Now, I am not about to dig in my heels about all this. The books are fine, and I have a lot of them in my house. Some of the changes are improvements ("swarthy," for example, is no longer a synonym for "evil"). And many of them (at least many of the ones in the Hardy Boys books, the series I know better) seem to be relatively innocuous. Tony Prito, the immigrant friend of Frank and Joe Hardy, is now able to say "What's the matter?" instead of "What's the mattah?," but after all, he's been in America for sixty years. Another friend, Chet Morton, still plump, now drives a jalopy instead of a roadster, but the word "jalopy" today seems as appealingly old-fashioned as "roadster" always did. Frank and Joe are older now—eighteen and seventeen, not sixteen and fifteen. Growing up, people often remark, takes longer these days. And while the deliberate multiculturalism of the newer books may wink annoyingly at adult readers—"'Hi, Joe!' said the young man, extending his hand for a shake. 'My name is Jason Tanaka'"—younger readers probably don't even notice, and perhaps subtly benefit.

That said, however, I must confess how pleasing it is that the original versions of the first three books in both the Hardy Boys and the Nancy Drew series are about to be republished. The first book in each series—***The Tower Treasure*** and *The Secret of the Old Clock*—will appear this month, thanks to the efforts of the reprint house Applewood Books, which might produce volumes beyond the initial six if the public shows interest. I hope it does. Antiques though these novels be, they deserve a second look, because they're richer than the versions of the same books now in print.

This isn't just some wistful recollection colored by age. Friends have volunteered similar observations, fresh from a session with one of the newer books and a child. One day recently I sat down with my boyhood copy of ***The Tower Treasure*** and a copy of the text you'd buy nowadays at a store, and compared the two line by line. The difference is considerable. Here's the introductory description of Frank and Joe Hardy from the original text:

> While there was a certain resemblance between the two lads, chiefly in the firm yet good-humored expression of their mouths, in some respects they differed greatly in appearance. While Frank was dark, with straight, black hair and brown eyes, his brother was pink-cheeked, with fair, curly hair and blue eyes.

Here's the same passage in the revised text:

> Even though one boy was dark and the other fair, there was a marked resemblance between the two brothers. Eighteen-year-old Frank was tall and dark. Joe, a year younger, was blond with blue eyes.

This doesn't even quite make sense. Here's part of the description of the chief of police, Ezra Collig, from the original version:

> Chief Ezra Collig, of the Bayport police force, was a burly, red-faced individual, much given to telling long-winded stories.

> Usually, Collig was to be found reclining in a swivel chair in his office, with his feet on the desk, reading the comic papers or polishing up his numerous badges, but this day something had happened to shake him out of his customary calm.

Here's what the current version has to say about the chief, in the same place:

> He was a tall, husky man, well known to Fenton Hardy and his two sons.

The entire book has undergone the kind of metamorphosis that these examples suggest. The text of the story, which involves the theft of jewels and securities from the wealthy stamp collector Hurd Applegate, has been substantially shortened. The vocabulary has been diminished. Even the smallest of details has been covered over with smooth vinyl siding. Officers of the law were once "cops"; now they are "the police." The original text was enlivened by comic repartee, which has all but disappeared. So has the occasional evocation of adolescent shyness and awkwardness ("I've been intending to go, but—I sort of—well—you know—," says Frank Hardy to his almost-girlfriend Callie Shaw at one point in the original version). Moments once suggesting emotional complexity ("Frank and Joe, their hearts too full for utterance, withdrew softly from the room") have been replaced by scenes of bland avowal ("Instantly Frank and Joe assured Mrs. Robinson they would do everything they could to find the real thief"). Inexplicably the Hardy boys' taste in sports has been changed. In the old version of ***The Tower Treasure,*** Joe and Frank and their friends play the all-American game, baseball. Today, for some reason, it's tennis. "Of all the impudence!" one is tempted to say with the bilious Hurd Applegate, although he no longer says it.

Besides the loss of narrative texture, the new books suffer from a loss of whole episodes. Gone from ***The Tower Treasure*** are the practical joke played by Chet Morton on Lem Billers, the "bomb scare" that makes Chief Collig and Detective Smuff miss their train and lose a chance to question the dying Red Jackley, and the celebratory feast laid on by Adelia Applegate in the last chapter, when even Chet Morton admits that he's had enough. Gone, too, is the memorable scene, toward the beginning, in which Fenton Hardy, the internationally famous detective, lectures his sons on the importance of training themselves to be observant, and by way of example reveals his insights into Superintendent Norton of the Bayport public schools, a man he has seen but never met. The omission of this long passage is comparable to leaving out the "Science of Deduction" chapter from *A Study in Scarlet,* in which John H. Watson, M.D., has his first long chat with Sherlock Holmes, and Holmes demonstrates and explains the nature of his powers.

I don't want to make excessive claims for the talents of the author of the original Hardy Boys novels. The first "Franklin W. Dixon" was no Trollope or Balzac or Henry James. Leslie McFarlane was a Canadian writer who in the late 1920s lived on the shores of Lake Ramsey, in Ontario, 300 miles north of Toronto, and wrote pulp fiction to support himself even as he tried to compose finer things. His employer was Edward Stratemeyer, Harriet's father, the publishing genius who took Henry Ford's ideas about industrial production and applied them to book production, with stables of writers working from outlines that he himself prepared, turning out an endless line of Tom Swift books, Rover Boys books, Dave Fearless books, and eventually Hardy Boys and Nancy Drew books. McFarlane, who had been writing the Dave Fearless books, was given the assignment to write *The Tower Treasure* (for $125); taken with the concept, he put his heart into the project. "It seemed to me," he recalls in a self-effacing autobiography that does for the craft of ghostwriting what Cellini's autobiography did for goldsmithing and Grant's did for war,

> that the Hardy boys deserved something better than the slapdash treatment Dave Fearless had been getting. It was still hack work, no doubt, but did the new series have to be all that hack? There was, after all, the chance to contribute a little style, occasional words of more than two syllables, maybe a little sensory stimuli.

The year was 1927. George Orwell had yet to write his famous essay on "good bad books," but Leslie McFarlane, it seems, was already determined to write one.

He went on to write some twenty books of the Hardy Boys series. When he quit, in the mid-1940s, it was to become a maker of documentaries for the Canadian Film Board; among the most notable of his films was the short feature "Herring Hunt," which was nominated for an Oscar. McFarlane lived into the 1970s, aware that the work of his early years, done for hire, had been largely bowdlerized by the publishers. For the most part he was publicly unruffled by that fact. "The books are their property, Bob," he stoically reminded one interviewer. "Titles, characters, the author's name, plots—the works." At the same time, though, McFarlane confessed to feeling strangely dispossessed, disinherited: a ghost displaced by a ghost.

Now some of his good bad work, and that of Mildred Wirt, will be once again in print, and in the stores. It is a small occasion, but one worth noting. In his autobiography McFarlane quotes the novelist Frank Norris:

> There is more significance as to the ultimate excellence of American letters in the sight of the messenger boy devouring his *Old Sleuths* and *Deadwood Dicks* and *Boy Detectives* with an earnest, serious absorption, than in the spectacle of a reading circle of dilettanti coquetting with Verlaine and pretending that they understand.

McFarlane believed that, and it shows.

Robert L. Crawford

SOURCE: "Rewriting the Past in Children's Literature: The Hardy Boys and Other Series," in *Children's Literature Association Quarterly,* Vol. 18, No. 1, Spring, 1993, pp. 10-12.

The heart of any discipline is a reliable reference source where primary works are preserved. If this essential bedrock is lost, changed, or falsified, then subsequent work must rely on spurious data, and there is no longer a discipline, a science, but rather chaos and charlatanism. Why then did professional librarians and practitioners in the fields of children's literature and popular culture not arise in outrage at the Stratemeyer Syndicate's publication of altered, revised, and even rewritten versions of their Hardy Boys and other series books as if they were exactly the same as the originals? The originals of these books have been extremely important in developing an interest in reading for hundreds of thousands of children for generations. As such, the study of these books, their characters, idioms, racial and ethnic references, technology, and plots reveals much about the times in which they were written and how society and its values have changed. For a scholar to examine these aspects of the evolution of children's literature, the published past must be available and identifiable in its original form.

Yet the Hardy Boys series, one of the most prolific and important since its beginning in 1927, has been published since 1959 under the original titles and author but with the stories, characters, and dialogue of the first 38 volumes substantially changed. There was little or no notice of this in the earlier printings of the revisions, and now the revised stories are even offered as the "originals"! This complete disregard for the integrity of the written past will create at least two problems for scholars. First, some may examine the new stories thinking they are the originals (as has happened already); second, the original stories could become unavailable except from collectors as the old books are replaced in libraries by the new ones.

The story has been told before, but in a scattered literature; the professional journals seem to have paid scant attention. Ken Donalson briefly discusses the revisions but raises no scholarly arguments against the practice. Strong reaction to the literary mutilation is apparently limited to the popular press and specialty magazines. Ed Zuckerman states that the Syndicate "like

Soviet historians [has] been systematically rewriting the past. The extent of this literary sacrilege is overwhelming . . . ". Cullen Murphy calls it "The Great Purge"; I. R. Ybarra speaks of his "horrified outrage" at the "vandalism"; Fred Woodworth calls it "an almost unbelievably mercenary act". . . .

[U]ntil 1959, *The Tower Treasure,* like all the subsequent volumes, would contain the exact original text. That year, though, the Syndicate began the extraordinary, and to my knowledge unprecedented, scheme to reissue the books in reduced and "modernized" formats but under the original titles. The revision was purportedly to make them more relevant to a modern audience, to deal with anachronous racial and ethnic stereotypes, or to incorporate "up-to-date methods used by police"; another reason may have been as Woodworth suggests: to increase profits by cutting printing costs. The original books averaged 213 pages; the move to shorter books began in 1957 with *The Ghost at Skeleton Rock* which, at 184 pages, was the first in the series to have fewer than 200 pages. The newest titles and the rewrites average about 177 pages. Another mercenary motive was suggested by John Seeback: to ride "on the reputation and success of the original ones by using the same titles" even though "if the Syndicate was bent on writing entirely new stories they should have given them new titles as well." For indeed the books are more than just condensed: the plots and characters are changed; many are completely different, and all are altered to some degree. Subjective appraisals of the literary quality note another important difference: "Sadly, the decrease in length has been accompanied by a decrease in the general descriptive level, the quality of characterizations, and an exchange of depth in background realization for more action. In short, the writing is not what it was" [Robert V. Riordan noted in "A Half Century of the Hardy Boys, or Clues to an Obscure Chronology," 1978]. Jack Bales emphatically agrees with the loss of quality, commenting on "how insipid the series has grown"; "eviscerated," says Jonathan Cott.

Clearly scholars must be certain which version of a work they have in order to make any sort of analysis of the series. The confusion the Syndicate has sown by ignoring the sanctity of the written past is a pitfall waiting to trap future researchers. Even as careful a writer as Billman, who is aware of the story changes, has confused the old and the new versions of *The Mystery of the Flying Express.* . . .

After the death of Harriet Adams in 1982, a complex legal dispute ended with the series in the joint custody of Simon and Schuster and Grosset and Dunlap. The original titles have recently (1989-1991) been reprinted by Grosset and Dunlap with slick plastic-covered bindings. Inside, above a list of titles beginning with the venerable *Tower Treasure,* is this appeal: "Match wits with the Hardy Boys. Collect the *original* Hardy Boys mystery stories by Franklin W. Dixon," (my emphasis added); these stories, advertised as the "originals," are the revisions. On the other hand, Applewood Books

published the genuine original versions of the first three volumes in "The Hardy Boys" and "Nancy Drew" series in 1991; four more of each are planned for 1992. These will be facsimiles of the originals, and the name of the publishing house should make these editions obvious.

The Stratemeyer Syndicate no longer exists to control the rights to the Hardy Boys series or to the other works it has rewritten. Grosset and Dunlap is the publishing house that is now making false claims about the "original" stories. Pressure from academics in library science, children's literature, and popular culture might induce Grosset and Dunlap at least to cease advertising the rewritten books as the originals and to place in the new versions a straightforward statement that the books have been more than just modernized. The present course of Grosset and Dunlap is intellectually and morally dishonest.

Mara Ilyse Amster

SOURCE: "Hardy Boys Series," in *Children's Books and Their Creators,* edited by Anita Silvey, Houghton Mifflin Company, 1995, p. 295.

The crime-fighting team of brothers, Frank and Joe Hardy, was first introduced to the public in three books: *The Tower Treasure, The House on the Hill,* and *The Secret of the Old Mill* (all published in 1927). Edward Stratemeyer, founder of the Stratemeyer Literary Syndicate, developed the Hardy Boys series after noting the popular success during the 1920s of adult detective fiction stories; he correctly assumed that boys' detective fiction would prove just as successful. Using Stratemeyer's outlines, Leslie McFarlane wrote the first eleven books under the pseudonym Franklin W. Dixon. After McFarlane left the syndicate in 1946, the books were ghostwritten by numerous other authors, including Stratemeyer's daughter, Harriet Stratemeyer Adams.

In their original incarnation, it was almost impossible to tell Frank and Joe apart—they were depicted as two sides of the same coin, an inseparable pair who never experienced sibling rivalry. When the syndicate revised the first thirty-eight books (between 1959 and 1972), the characters of Frank and Joe changed dramatically. Eighteen-year-old Frank is rational and careful; he weighs all the options before taking action. He is the high-tech Hardy, an electronics specialist. Seventeen-year-old Joe is impulsive and passionate, never pausing to consider consequences. He is the athletic Hardy, adept at everything from gymnastics to boxing, and he is constantly falling in love.

Plots were also revised to reflect changing times—jewel thieves and buried treasure were replaced by egomaniacal dictators, nerve gas, and evil disk jockeys. Violence is prevalent in the series—bombs are detonated, knives are wielded, punches are thrown. Except for rare occasions, however, neither Frank nor Joe carries or uses a weapon; strength for each is found in brotherhood, not bullets. An adventure with Frank and Joe is seen by some readers as a fantasy come true—days filled with intriguing mysteries and pulse-pounding excitement take precedence over the more mundane aspects of teenage life, such as attending school. Frank and Joe Hardy—stars of the most popular boys' series in juvenile publishing history—are all-American boys next door. Almost every boy wishes he could be a Hardy.

Additional coverage of the writers of "The Hardy Boys" is contained in the following sources published by The Gale Group: *Contemporary Authors,* **Vols. 17-20R,** *Contemporary Authors New Revision Series,* **Vol. 27;** *Major Authors and Illustrators for Children and Young Adults;* **and** *Something about the Author,* **Vols. 1, 67, 100.**

Laszlo Gal

1933-

Hungarian-born Canadian illustrator and author of picture books and retellings.

Major works include *The Twelve Dancing Princesses: A Fairy Story* (retold by Janet Lunn, 1979), *Canadian Fairy Tales* (retold by Eva Martin, 1984; U. S. edition as *Tales of the Far North*), *Prince Ivan and the Firebird* (retold by Gal, 1991), *East of the Sun and West of the Moon* (retold by Gal, 1993), *The Parrot: An Italian Folktale* (retold by Gal, with Raffaella Gal, 1997).

INTRODUCTION

Gal is best known for his intricate drawings and paintings for primary graders that illustrate classic and traditional fairy and folk tales, as well as works written by modern children's authors, primarily Canadians. He has also retold legendary folk tales such as the Russian classic, *Prince Ivan and the Firebird,* and the Norwegian story, *East of the Sun and West of the Moon.* His most popular and highly praised work is a retelling of the Grimms' fairy tale, *The Twelve Dancing Princesses: A Fairy Story.* Although some critics find Gal's narratives to be inconsistent, his illustrations are generally judged to be rich, beautiful, elegant, and delicately drawn. "I like to think that I am a perfectionist," Gal told *Emergency Librarian.* "I work an awful lot at my illustration. I know it's not going to be perfect, but I try to make it as good as possible."

Gal sees the illustrator as the set designer who builds the background for the story. Inspired by each tale, he uses different techniques and media to create unique settings and perspectives. For example, illustrations for *The Twelve Dancing Princesses: A Fairy Story* were inspired by the Renaissance, those for *A Flask of Sea Water* (1989) by Persian miniatures, and *El Cid: Soldier and Hero* (1965) by crumbling and faded Romanesque frescoes. Writing about Gal's work, Virginia Van Vliet noted, "If the chief criterion for judging the work of an illustrator is that his pictures must capture the spirit of the text, expanding it and giving it life, then Laszlo Gal has proven over and over again that his work is worthy to be judged among the best Canada has to offer."

Biographical Information

Born in Budapest, Hungary, Gal was raised by parents who encouraged their children to develop their artistic talents. By the age of nine, he knew that he wanted to be an illustrator, and at the age of thirteen he displayed his work in an international exhibition of youth art in

Paris. For a brief time, Gal set his sights on acting and attended the Budapest Academy of Dramatic Arts, but after being cut from the program he decided his talent lay elsewhere and returned to illustration.

When the government of Hungary changed to a restrictive Communist regime, young people found that they could no longer choose their own careers. Gal was sent by the government to earn an Art Education Diploma at the Superior School of Pedagogy so that he could teach art to children; however, when a political revolution occurred in 1956, Gal leapt at the chance to leave Hungary. At the age of 23 he emigrated to Canada where he took odd jobs until he was able to earn a living as an artist.

Gal worked as a political cartoonist for the *Toronto Globe and Mail*, then in 1958 started what was to become long term employment as a graphic artist for the Canadian Broadcasting Company (CBC). He became a naturalized Canadian citizen in 1961, and in 1962 married a Canadian woman of Italian descent. On a visit to Italy, he showed his portfolio to a publisher there who promptly hired him as an illustrator. He worked in Italy from 1965 to 1969 under a contract to illustrate two full-color books a year.

Unfortunately, Gal's income was not sufficient to support his growing family, and he returned to Canada where he worked as a freelance artist and eventually resumed his job at the CBC. In 1979, after years of frustration with the commercial world of publishing, he finished *The Twelve Dancing Princesses: A Fairy Story* which was a critical success and earned him an international reputation.

Major Works

Gal first achieved international recognition with *The Twelve Dancing Princesses: A Fairy Story*. This classic fairy tale tells the story of twelve princesses whose shoes appear mysteriously worn out each morning, and of the farm boy who discovers their secret, winning half the kingdom and the hand of the youngest princess as a reward. Using two of his daughters as models, Gal labored for two years over the illustrations. He told reviewer Virginia Van Vliet, "I said when I finished that if I don't get any result with this book I will never touch another one." Fortunately, the book was a resounding success, winning the two most prestigious prizes for illustrators in Canada. Irene E. Aubrey commented in *Notable Canadian Children's Books*, "Laszlo Gal's visual interpretation of this enchanted world infuses the retelling with its richness, wonder and strength."

Canadian Fairy Tales, published in the United States as *Tales of the Far North*, presents 12 retellings of traditional folk tales brought to Canada by English and French immigrants. Sarah Ellis called the illustrations, "beautifully conceived . . . executed in Gal's characteristic glowing, grainy, posed style." A *Publishers Weekly* reviewer noted, "Gal's paintings structure space magically, blending past and present, with incandescent colors, and he lifts the reader instantly into a fairy tale dimension."

The story of *Prince Ivan and the Firebird,* retold and illustrated by Gal, is a classic Russian folk tale about Prince Ivan, youngest son of the tzar, who sets out to find the firebird who has stolen the golden apples from the tzar's garden. Helped by a magic wolf, the prince returns home with the firebird, a princess, and a beautiful horse, but is murdered by his jealous brothers. The wolf returns him to life, and he marries the princess and forgives his brothers. In a review for the *Quill and Quire* Ruth Bennett called Gal's illustrations a triumph, "[d]isplaying impressive composition and balance and glowing yet delicate colours, they are a glorious reflection on and enlargement of the exciting tale."

Gal also retold and illustrated the Norwegian folk tale *East of the Sun and West of the Moon*. It is the story of a girl, Ingrid, who passes trials and tests, with the assistance of magic helpers, to free the prince she loves from the power of a troll's spell. Although some critics found both the retelling and illustrations to be flat and unexpressive, most critics found the book to be a fine example of Gal's work. Kit Pearson noted, "[n]ever have his illustrations glowed with such inner light and rich colour, as if they were reflecting the Northern lights of the story's Scandinavian setting."

The Parrot: An Italian Folktale is a story Gal retold and illustrated with his daughter, Rafaella. In this tale within a tale, a merchant's daughter is loved by a magic prince and an evil king. The prince disguises himself as a parrot and tells the girl a story that keeps her so enraptured that she fails to hear a knock at the door, and so does not open it to the king's soldiers when they come to kidnap her. The illustrations show both the parrot telling his tale to the girl, as well as the tale the parrot is telling as envisioned by the girl. All ends well when the merchant returns home and the parrot reveals himself as his beloved's prince. Patricia Morley commented, "The sumptuous, richly colored paintings in pencil, oil, and egg tempera are bold and beautiful, and reinforce the gothic mood of a damsel in danger."

Awards

Gal's artistry is well recognized in Canada, where his books have won numerous awards. He is best known for *The Twelve Dancing Princesses: A Fairy Story,* which won the prestigious Canada Council Children's Literature Prize for Illustration in 1980 and the Governor General's Award for Illustration in 1979, as well as the Amelia Frances Howard-Gibbon Illustrator's Medal from the Canadian Library Association and Best Children's Book of the Year from the Imperial Order of the Daughters of the Empire, both in 1980. He also received many awards for *Hans Christian Anderson's "The Little Mermaid"* (1983), including the Canada Council Children's Literature Prize for Illustration, the Governor General's Award for Illustration, and runner-up for the Amelia Frances Howard-Gibbon Illustrator's Award, all in 1984. Other awards include Best Children's Book of the Year Award from the Canadian Library Association in 1971 for *Cartier Discovers the St. Lawrence* (1970) and Best Children's Book of the Year Award from the Child Study Association of America in 1971 for *The Moon Painters, and Other Estonian Folk Tales* (retold by Selve Maas, 1971). *The Parrot: An Italian Folktale* received an OLA Best Bets citation from The Ontario Library Association Canadian Materials Committee in 1997.

GENERAL COMMENTARY

Virginia Van Vliet

SOURCE: "The Prominent Canadian Illustrator Laszlo Gal," in *Book Bird*, No. 3, 1981, pp. 29-32.

When the ballots were cast for the 1979 Amelia Frances Howard-Gibbon illustrator's award **The Twelve Dancing Princesses** illustrated by Laszlo Gal swept the field. The jury for The Canada Council Award for Children's Literature selected the same book for their illustrator's award. Gal has now won the two most prestigious Canadian awards!

Born in Budapest, Hungary on February 18, 1933, Laszlo was the youngest of six children. There were always books in his home; since times were bad and his family had little money to buy such luxuries they were usually borrowed from the public library. Drawing came naturally to him, and, impressed by the illustrations he saw in these books, he decided at the age of nine or ten that he would become an illustrator. At the age of 13 as the best art student in his school he entered some of his drawings in an international exhibition of children's art in Paris. . . .

[A] friend suggested Laszlo talk to William Toye who was adapting *The Saint Lawrence* as a picture book. Toye liked his work and this partnership launched Laszlo's career as a Canadian illustrator with **Cartier Discovers the St. Lawrence.** This was artwork unlike any seen before in a Canadian history book, carrying with it a sense of huge open spaces against which were rooted sculptured figures of stylized simplicity. Here too Gal's ability to convey texture was immediately apparent, from the shaggy robes of the Indians to the swirling waves of the river.

As a freelance illustrator, Laszlo produced a dozen Canadian children's books, many of which were folktales or legends. A particular favourite was **The Moon Painters and Other Estonian Folk Tales** which reminded him of his Hungarian childhood.

In illustrating legends such as **Why the Man in the Moon Is Happy and Other Eskimo Tales of Creation,** Laszlo naturally turned to Eskimo art for his touchstone, the smooth flowing lines and rough textures of his drawings echoing the Native carvings. To achieve the strong sense of texture apparent in his illustrations for many of these legends and folktales, Gal used a thick brush to paint the surface with gesso which dried into uneven ridges. He then drew on this ridged surface with a soft grease pencil, the colour sinking into the depressions, the raised portions remaining white.

To Gal the illustrator is a kind of set designer who creates the background against which the story comes to life. A brilliant stylist, he seeks his inspiration from within the story itself trying to reflect its individual setting and mood. For example, for the medieval stories of **El Cid: Soldier and Hero** and **Siegfried: The Mighty Warrior,** he captured the texture of the faded, crumbling paint of ancient Romanesque frescoes by painting layers of tempera and then scraping away at the layers with a knife. As pieces of paint flaked off, the various colours showed through one another, resulting in a deep and immensely rich texture. The stylised faces and still gestures of the figures also reflect the medieval influence.

Laszlo's choice of styles is also influenced by the work of those artists whom he admires. Michelangelo is his favourite among the classical artists, reflecting his life-long interest in Italian art. Modern favourites include Chagall and Andrew Wyeth. "I would love to paint as well as he does, but I wouldn't be able to do that. He is just incredible." The children's illustrators whose work has most influenced him are Alice and Martin Provensen who are stern self-critics working and reworking with meticulous care to create a desired effect. Although he still reads magazines such as *Graphics* he is no longer concerned with "trend" artists who reign for a few years and then are forgotten.

The beauty of Laszlo's style is most apparent when he works in full colour; unfortunately, the limited budgets of most Canadian publishers have forced him to design in one or two colours. Although he enjoys working in black-and-white, he finds the process of two colours separation too mechanical. This is especially true when the second colour is worked on the acetate layer in red, a colour which photographs easily, rather than in the shade of ink that will be used in the actual printing. His black-and-white drawings however have winning qualities since he received the 1978 Toronto IODE Award for his illustrations in **My Name Is Not Odessa Yarker, The Shirt of the Happy Man** and **Why the Man in the Moon Is Happy.**

When his work at Mondadori finished his wife was expecting their second child so the family decided to remain in Italy for a while. During this time Laszlo worked on a book of Italian Renaissance fables on "spec." The book was never printed, but when Janet Lunn saw the illustrations nearly a decade later she liked them so much she suggested that Laszlo illustrate her favourite fairy tale, **The Twelve Dancing Princesses.**

For two years Laszlo worked on this book. First he researched Renaissance architecture and costume design: next came page after page of sketches, each building up detail, trying out ideas, experimenting. Finally he was ready to begin to paint, but even then the illustrations were far from resembling their finished form. "When I have the final drawing then I think I know what I am doing: but when I start to paint, I always find it isn't the way I thought it would be. It turns out completely differently." Gal is a meticulous worker, a perfectionist who sets standards for himself, and as he paints his illustrations constantly change, develop and grow. "As I work on each painting my eyes become so critical that as each day passes I want to make it better and better and better. Although I might have liked it the day before yesterday and thought 'That's pretty good,' when I see it the next day in a different surrounding I decide it is not good." It is always a case of "I rework and rework and rework."

The final result of all this meticulous care in **The Twelve Dancing Princesses** is an enchanting book in which soft romanticism swirls from every picture. Using a combination of watercolour with a tempera wash for highlights, Laszlo achieves incredibly rich, muted tones, his drawings seeming almost to glow with an inner light. **The Twelve Dancing Princesses** is a technically brilliant piece of work, but it is also a very personal one. Laszlo's older daughter Anna Maria appears as the princess in the cover illustration, while his younger daughter Raffaella is portrayed in the cameo. Laszlo's love of music finds expression in the beautiful, swirling dance scene in which a filmy veil flows and floats from one dancer to another tying the composition together. This illustration was the most difficult he did for the book, although his own favourite drawing is that of the jester seated before the castle.

The Twelve Dancing Princesses was such a critical success it not only won the Canadian Library Association's Amelia Frances Howard-Gibbon Award for 1979 but also the highly prestigious Canada Council Award for Children's Literature. This acclaim was particularly heartwarming to Laszlo since this book was "like my baby." "I said when I finished that if I don't get any result with this book I will never touch another one." He hopes the success of this work will mark a breakthrough for him into the international market and wider sales. "One has to be very dedicated or just simply crazy to work for two years for practically nothing as I did for this book. That's why you don't find illustrators in this country because nobody makes sacrifices for what sometimes seems a hopeless cause."

Despite the difficulties of being an illustrator in Canada, Laszlo hopes to be able to continue to create high quality books. Currently he is working on another "spec" book, *Farmer Giles of Ham* by J. R. R. Tolkien. Although Methuen is interested in this title, publication is dependent upon whether or not the Tolkien estate will grant copyright privileges. He is again working in watercolour with tempera wash, but this time the tones are earthy browns, golds and greens, and the drawings impart a hearty Breughal-like humour. He wants to integrate the text and illustrations, rather than drawing set pieces as in *The Twelve Dancing Princesses*.

If the chief criterion for judging the work of an illustrator is that his pictures must capture the spirit of the text, expanding it and giving it life, then Laszlo Gal has proven over and over again that his work is worthy to be judged among the best Canada has to offer.

Dave Jenkinson

SOURCE: "Laszlo Gal: Award Winning Illustrator," in *Emergency Librarian,* Vol. 19, No. 4, March-April, 1992, pp. 65-9.

Twice winner of the prestigious Canada Council Children's Literature Prize for Illustration, a youthful Laszlo Gal wanted to be an actor. The youngest of six children, Laszlo was born in Budapest, Hungary, on February 18, 1933. Art was actually Laszlo's first love, and his original career goal was to become an illustrator or poster designer.

"Back in Hungary, posters were a very accepted art form. It's almost like a different cultural form. Poster

designers were very respected people. For some reason, I always had a very strong attraction towards books, not that I really read a lot, but the form of the books, the shape of the books, interested me." . . .

"Bill Toye suggested that I should illustrate *Cartier Discovers the St. Lawrence.* A few weeks later, when I went back to Italy, I found the manuscript there. I remember it was May, 1969, and by August, 1969, we were back in Canada. Immediately I started to work on this book. It took me about three or four months to finish it. I got a flat fee, but I bumped into Bill Toye, and he asked me if I wanted a royalty. Since we were pretty miserable financially when we came back, I couldn't wait for the money to come via royalties in the next ten years." . . .

During Laszlo's second stint with CBC, he was also freelancing as a children's book illustrator. To get his name before that period's many small publishers, Laszlo engaged in what he describes as "calling constantly. It's really a very terrible thing to be a freelance illustrator and there is no publishing. I just had to call all the publishing companies all the time. There were so many artists who were hungry and looking for work that, if you don't keep reminding them you are alive, they might forget about you. I remember some of the art directors or editors were really annoyed when I called again only three weeks later." Laszlo's persistence paid off, however, and he got to illustrate a number of one and two color books "so many small little tiny books which myself I forget because they were not very interesting. Again no royalties. I got a flat fee. I had to hustle for every job."

Looking back to his Mondadori days, Laszlo recalls the influence this period had on his illustrating style. "I tried to accommodate the style of the illustration to fit the text. The text influences my style extremely. Somehow, when I have a bad text, I do bad illustrations. *Aeneide,* because of its Greek background, I tried to do very much like the Greek vase painting. Although the vase paintings were in one or two colors, I tried to make it in full colors. *Chanson de Roland* tries to imitate the fresco paintings of the ancient Romanesque churches."

As Laszlo points out, "I've hardly illustrated any modern stories." Most of the books for which Laszlo has provided the illustrations are retellings of ancient tales and legends. To capture the period of the piece, Laszlo must do research, and he devotes much time to books on costume. "Probably because I wanted to be an actor, I like to read these theatrical things and I like to dress up the books' people." Laszlo's illustrations seem to freeze action, and again he refers to his interest in drama, by saying that his illustration style is "not really that realistic. It's more like a theatrical stage where the people are manipulated."

"I worked on *The Twelve Dancing Princesses* for three years. The originals are huge paintings. I didn't have that much experience at the time, and I used probably the wrong medium, the most difficult medium you can imagine, gouache which is designer's color. It's terrific for posters, but not for these highly detailed illustrations. Every color had to be mixed separately. It's not that it gets mixed on the surface of the painting where one color overlapping the other one creates the third color. Because they are opaque color, whatever I put down will cover up the one which is underneath. I had to use it almost as if it was color pencil and cross hatching."

"I never really considered watercolor that much because it's a very difficult medium. The way I used to know watercolor when I studied in school is that you have to immerse the whole illustration paper in water and soak it overnight and then work on the wet surface. Somehow it doesn't suit the time of the illustrator. I cannot work on wet paper, and, on dry paper, it doesn't come out the same. With *The Twelve Dancing Princesses,* I worked with watercolor in the beginning, and then I went over it with the gouache."

"Only recently I discovered that there is a new type of paint which is called alkyd which can be used the same way as oil paint but dries very fast. I am using that now on paper. Gouache is water-based color, but, because it's opaque, wherever you paint on top of the previous one, it will be eliminated. You have to mix it on a palette. If you screw it up, you have to start that part all over again. I'm sure I must have worked on the gouache cover of *The Twelve Dancing Princesses* for three months." The face of Laszlo's daughter Marika is featured on the *Princess* cover while Raffaella's can be found in the cameo.

The Twelve Dancing Princesses received both the Amelia Francis Howard-Gibbon Award from the Canadian Library Association and the Canada Council Children's Literature Prize for Illustration. Laszlo remains very proud of that work. "I somehow feel that it was really the first full color significant book in Canada. I hadn't seen any full color books before of that caliber. I even feel that book might have started the children's book revolution in this country."

The second Canada Council award for illustration was also presented to a book featuring one of Laszlo's daughters on its cover. However, when Raffaella got her own cover with a retelling of Andersen's *The Little Mermaid,* Laszlo also got some instructions from his publisher. The original cover had featured a mermaid au naturel. "It was much more daring before, and I had to cover the breasts with hair." While American publishers were interested in this book, they did not publish it. "A year later I found out that they couldn't take it because of the 'nudity,' because they cannot sell these books in the Bible Belt. I felt stupid to put a little shell there like a Walt Disney movie."

"I am the one who decides how the book looks. Whether the publisher will accept it or not is a different story. I wanted to have *Pome & Peel,* for instance, horizontal,

and they didn't like the idea. Then I came up with the vertical illustrations. I came up with the arched look again to give the flavor of the Italian architecture. The arch was much more round, but the art director talked me out of it and asked me to make the arches much less rounded. The basic design is mine, but, since I'm not a designer, they are the ones who really make the final refinements. When I have the layouts, the art director tells me, 'This image is too small. Make it larger.' For example, originally *Pome & Peel*'s balconies were smaller. The publisher makes that decision at the point of the pencil sketches. Several times I have to remake the pencil sketches from scratch all over again because they don't like the proportions or the whole thing might not be suitable. Always I use tracing paper. It's really annoying because it's very difficult to draw on tracing paper. It has too much tooth, and you cannot have a gradation of tones. It's a very rough sketch that you have to put up with, but the tracing paper is very useful because you can flip it and you can tear it out and move the figure around."

The illustrations in *The Enchanted Tapestry* project a tapestry feeling. Laszlo explains how that effect came about. "I took out a whole bunch of reproductions of Chinese silk painting and studied them. I don't know if the Chinese were using more colors at the time or not and they just faded out, but they looked very brown but very rich and beautiful. I tried to use those subdued colors that they were using, but I didn't dare to go as far as they did because I thought that maybe it would be interpreted over here as colorless. In fact, some of the American critics said that the book was somehow not colorful enough. But I did that intentionally to make it very subdued."

A Flask of Sea Water's illustrations feature a metallic gold background. "That's a fifth color," explains Laszlo. "The story is oriental, and the Persian miniatures have these gold backgrounds. I asked Oxford if they would be interested in using a fifth color for the background. The gold paint was a gold powder which is mixed into a bronzing liquid. You have to apply it with a brush very fast because it's a very fast drying paint. There was some red underpainting so every now and then, where the paint is chipping off, it gives this richer look."

Asked about his favorite book, Laszlo says, "I think I still like *The Canadian Fairy Tales* the most. The book itself is very beautiful and those borders give an extra special flavor to the wholebook. To put little significant designs into the very narrow ribbon of those borders took me more time maybe than the illustrations themselves." Among his more recent favorites is the Venetian tale, *Pome & Peel,* "because it was very close for me. I lived in Italy, and the surroundings and costumes all came up easier. I lived there for five years, and it was almost like I could illustrate an Hungarian fairy tale. I went to Italy and did photographs on the spot. Some of the drawings are from Northern Italy where my wife comes from."

"I like end papers," says Laszlo. "In Italy, all of the books were done with end papers. I still had this European tradition when I came here. When I started to do end papers for the Canadians, since they didn't have very much experience with them, they thought that a book must have end papers. Now, the Americans don't, but I think it is worth the extra cost." . . .

Despite Laszlo's success as an illustrator, he has again started to make the rounds of publishers' offices, but this time his motivation is different. "I started to call again because of my kids. I have two children and both are in this field. Marika finished Ontario College of Art last year and Raffaella is in third year. They are both very talented. I thought if I go around with their portfolios and my portfolio at the same time, I might be able to pick up some work for them, too." Laszlo's assumption was correct, and, for example, he and his daughters have collaborated on some high school Shakespeare textbooks. "I do the layout, the drawing, and the research. Then, when the pencil sketches are done, I just give it to them and they fill in the 'blanks,' and so we have done it together, the three of us. It's like a little cottage industry." . . .

Coupled with his time difficulties, Laszlo also sets high standards for himself and his work and acknowledges, "I like to think that I am a perfectionist. I work an awful lot at my illustration. I know it's not going to be perfect, but I try to make it as good as possible."

"Unfortunately, I can never satisfy myself because I still think I could do it better, but I don't know how, and that's the problem."

"I am working so hard not for the money. It's for the love of it. If I could give up the CBC and do only this, probably I could do a much better job."

TITLE COMMENTARY

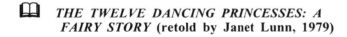

THE TWELVE DANCING PRINCESSES: A FAIRY STORY (retold by Janet Lunn, 1979)

Claire England

SOURCE: A review of *The Twelve Dancing Princesses: A Fairy Story,* in *Canadian Children's Literature,* Nos. 15 & 16, 1980, pp. 140-43.

A handful of books produced in Canada are world class. This is one, a tribute to the collaboration of author, artist, editor, and publisher. Such picture-story books may be reviewed by considering text and illustration as a unit and by comparing them with other editions of the same story. . . .

Laszlo Gal's illustrations help by conveying a sense of real people in a plausible world. His characters have solid bodies; they move and stand naturally. Gal's two daughters served as models for the two most important princesses—the oldest and the youngest. Scenery, castles and costume have either a medieval look or a look of the early 1600's. The princesses favour hats and collars appearing suspiciously like the Italian *punto in aria* lace that became a European vogue in the late sixteenth century.

The colourful pictures have delightful touches. As the princesses descend their secret staircase, both look out at the reader as if making personal contact. One of them is waving. As the princesses dance, with scarves billowing, a balcony orchestra plays on antique instruments.

Denise M. Wilms

SOURCE: A review of *The Twelve Dancing Princesses: A Fairy Story,* in *Booklist,* Vol. 76, No. 12, February 15, 1980, pp. 834-35.

The hushed, misty aura of Gal's double-spread illustrations serves the story well. Muted scenes evoke the enchanted otherworld in which the 12 haughty princesses dance the nights away as richly as they portray the serene discretion of the simple farm boy who discovers the princesses' secret and wins half a kingdom and the hand of the youngest, most perceptive one. Opalescent colors create the effect. Except for a curiously flat opening scene, the pictures are full, dramatic, and commanding in their large-scale presence. From a practical standpoint, the book's use presents the same stop-and-go readaloud problem as Burkert's *Snow White:* two long pages of text alternate with the lush spreads. That is no reason to avoid this, however; it remains a pleasure to read and pore over.

Zena Sutherland

SOURCE: A review of *The Twelve Dancing Princesses: A Fairy Story,* in *Bulletin of the Center for Children's Books,* Vol. 34, No. 5, January, 1981, p. 94.

The pages of an oversize book are used to advantage by Gal for his softly textured and colored paintings of intricately detailed, romantic medieval scenes. Lunn's version of the story focuses on the farm boy who travels along a rainbow path to find the golden palace of which he had dreamed, rather than beginning with the more usual description of the twelve princesses and the mystery of their dancing shoes, but it works nicely although the alternation of print and illustration in double-page spreads gives a staccato effect. Oddly, the jacket copy states that the text is "based on an old French fairy story" while the C.I.P. information correctly attributes the source to the Grimm Brothers; the book won the Canadian Library Association's award as the best-illustrated book of the year.

📖 *CANADIAN FAIRY TALES* (retold by Eva Martin, 1984; U.S. edition as *Tales of the Far North*, 1986)

Sarah Ellis

SOURCE: "News from the North," in *The Horn Book Magazine*, Vol. LXI, No. 1, January-February, 1985, pp. 88-91.

The recent collection *Canadian Fairy Tales* is a fine example of the tradition that is "just a little bit different." Reteller Eva Martin and illustrator Laszlo Gal present a selection of a dozen stories from the English and French traditions, stories collected mainly by folklorists in the early years of this century. All contain elements familiar to the fairy-tale reader. . . .

The relationship between European origin and Canadian retelling is captured by illustrator Laszlo Gal in a beautifully-conceived decorative device. The color illustration that accompanies each tale is executed in Gal's characteristic glowing, grainy, posed style. The settings are universal, populated by peasants with a Brueghel-like sense of solidity. But surrounding each painting is a sketched border featuring Canadian plants, wildlife, landscapes, forts, towns, and farm and household implements. Real life encloses, contains, and focuses the magic of the story. . . .

The afterward to *Canadian Fairy Tales* quotes Italo Calvino: "'The tale is not beautiful if nothing is added. Folktales remain merely dumb until you realize that you are required to complete them yourself, to fill in your own particulars.'" This collection gives the tales beauty by particularity in illustration and by one voice in the retelling. More important, it provides room for storytellers to give the stories life in their own way.

Kay McPherson

SOURCE: A review of *Tales of the Far North*, in *School Library Journal*, Vol. 33, No. 6, February, 1987, p. 81.

A well-written and enjoyable collection of Canadian folk tales in an attractive format. The white French and English settlers of Canada brought with them the folk tales of their native lands, and, like all settlers everywhere, they adapted the tales to the life they developed in their new homeland. Martin retells here 12 of these Canadian folk tales of European origin. Several of them are entertaining variants of "Jack and the Beanstalk," "Bluebeard," the Perrault "Sleeping Beauty," and "The Brave Little Tailor." A version of "Beauty and the Beast" has a nice switch, with "Beauty" being male and "Beast" being female. These variants would make this book a strong choice for children who are studying folktales. One framed, full-page, full-color illustration appears with each story. The people and setting are portrayed in realistic detail, but every once in a while an enchanted detail such as a unicorn or an elfin ear shows up. The pictures serve as a splendid springboard for this outstanding collection.

From East of the Sun and West of the Moon, *retold and illustrated by Laszlo Gal.*

Publishers Weekly

SOURCE: A review of *Tales of the Far North*, in *Publishers Weekly*, Vol. 231, No. 14, April 10, 1987, p. 93.

Martin has compiled and retold tales with familiar motifs that have a Canadian setting, stories that were brought to that country by European settlers. This is a richly compelling collection, replete with cheats, rascals, princesses, fleet-footed horses, tricksters and clever young brothers. Gal's paintings structure space magically, blending past and present, with incandescent colors, and he lifts the reader instantly into a fairy tale dimension. There are but two flaws: the acknowledgments convey much information but are buried in the back; and "The Healing Spring," the first story, is pointless and implausible, throwing off the smooth tone of the book with jarring morbidity.

📖 *THE WILLOW MAIDEN* (written by Meghan Collins, 1985)

Bernie Goedhart

SOURCE: "Picture-books: Some Succeed, Others Better Read Than Seen," in *Quill and Quire*, Vol. 51, No. 12, December, 1985, p. 24.

If you prefer something with more substance and length to read to your children at bedtime, try **The Willow Maiden** by Meghan Collins. A powerful story in the classic fairy-tale tradition, it tells of a young farmer who stumbles onto the Midsummer Night's celebration of the willow people, a magical race that gives life to willow trees. He falls in love with one of them, withstands the test to which her people put mortals such as he, and the two marry—but only after he makes a promise he finds difficult to keep.

The tale is spellbinding, but the illustrations by Laszlo Gal pale by comparison. The award-winning artist's work, as usual, is very precise and beautiful, but the illustrations do little more than just decorate the book. They are predictable, their colours are homogeneously understated from page to page, and—except for a double-page spread showing two nude men struggling under water—they seem flat and stilted.

Hazel Rochman

SOURCE: A review of *The Willow Maiden,* in *Booklist,* Vol. 82, No. 8, December 15, 1985, p. 625.

On Midsummer Night's Eve in the Whispering Woods, Denis stumbles on the feast of the Willow people; he and Lisane, the Willow maiden, fall in love and dance as if they are all alone. Instead of luring him to the doom that other young men have suffered, Lisane helps him win his trial of strength. They marry at the time of the harvest moon and live together through fall and winter. Her father, the Willow King, has warned that she must return to her willow tree every spring and summer so that the tree can live. When the time comes, Denis cannot let her go. In anger, he is about to chop down her tree when he realizes that his act might kill his wife—he must let her go free and she will return. Collins's original fairy tale incorporates many elements from traditional tales, myth, and romance. Except for the occasional jarring use of colloquial modern idiom ("Well, calm down"), the language is direct and resonant: "their parting was for each of them like a tearing of roots." In Gal's highly romantic illustrations, rich with soft colors predominantly of blue and green, the dreamy lovers blend with the foliage in moonlit landscapes. Both humans and nature are defined sharply, from the texture of individual grass stems to the grave-faced father-king. Placement of text within the many full- and half-page double spreads, showing branches that reach outward, reinforces the story's underlying sense of connection between the natural and human worlds.

Jean Hammond Zimmerman

SOURCE: A review of *The Willow Maiden,* in *School Library Journal,* Vol. 32, No. 5, January, 1986, p. 55.

A romantic and beautifully illustrated fairy tale picture book. On a showery Midsummer Night's Eve, a young woman named Lisane welcomes Denis to the Whispering

Woods and tells him that the people feasting there are the Willow people, who live as trees except for two nights a year. He agrees to return to wed Lisane on the night of the harvest moon, even though she can live with him only during the fall and winter months. The two live happily through the winter but, as spring comes, Denis finds he cannot bear to let Lisane leave. He resolves to cut down her tree but changes his mind when he realizes that he could kill Lisane as well and that he must let her return to her people. The story is a well-crafted combination of dialogue and description which can be read aloud. Using watercolor washes, gouache and colored pencils in soft greens and blues, Gal has created an enchanted forest filled with gravely handsome people in medieval costumes and delicately drawn animals and birds. The illustrations possess the elegance and grace of his artwork for Janet Lunn's version of **The Twelve Dancing Princesses** and are a perfect accompaniment to the text.

M. Maran

SOURCE: A review of *The Willow Maiden,* in *Books for Your Children,* Vol. 21, No. 2, Summer, 1986, p. 11.

A beautiful picture book for children of all ages from nine to ninety. The paintings on every page are rich, sometimes incorporating the text, sometimes a full page, sometimes a double-page spread. The words and pictures tell a story of magic, romance, life and freedom. The handsome young hero comes to realise that, although he can be in love with her, the world is diminished if he tries to possess the beautiful willow maiden. One ten year old told me that she thought it was a *"soppy fairy story."* I thought it was magnificent. There's no accounting for taste!

THE ENCHANTED TAPESTRY: A CHINESE FOLKTALE (retold by Robert D. San Souci, 1987)

Publishers Weekly

SOURCE: A review of *The Enchanted Tapestry: A Chinese Folktale,* in *Publishers Weekly,* Vol. 231, No. 8, March 13, 1987, p. 82.

This is a perfect marriage of tale and art. Skillful and immediate, the text retells a Chinese story of a poor weaver woman with three sons, two selfish and one loving. When her most precious handmade tapestry is blown away on a magical wind, two sons grieve over the lost sale value, and the third grieves with her simply because it was hers. One by one, she sends her sons to retrieve it, but a sorceress waylays the first two with gold. The third son succeeds, despite icy rivers and walls of fire. The tapestry then becomes real, and mother and son enter its paradise-like world, while the two greedy sons return as beggars in the end. Here are elements of so many tales, Western and Chinese: the magical quest, sheer visual poetry and the contrast of love and greed. The pace and clarity of the narrative support the length, and Gal's art will sustain even a very young child's interest. A beautiful book.

Susan H. Patron

SOURCE: A review of *The Enchanted Tapestry: A Chinese Folktale,* in *School Library Journal,* Vol. 33, No. 10, June-July, 1987, p. 89.

Traditional themes of punishing greed and rewarding filial duty are used in this blending of several versions of a Chinese folktale. The widowed mother of three grown sons makes her living by weaving beautiful silk tapestries. After she labors over a tapestry which embodies her dreams for prosperity, her sons are put to a test of courage and daring. Only the youngest loves his mother enough to prevail—and he wins a beautiful fairy to boot. The illustrations, combining watercolor, colored pencils, and gouache, call to mind the faded, washed-out appearance of a very old silk tapestry. Unfortunately these soft tones do not support the text, which describes "brilliant red flowers" and "rich green meadows." The characters are illustrated in the same style as the tapestry itself, creating some confusion between the world of the larger or outer story and the scenes depicted on the woman's loom.

📖 *IDUNA AND THE MAGIC APPLES* (retold by Marianna Mayer, 1988)

Publishers Weekly

SOURCE: A review of *Iduna and the Magic Apples,* in *Publishers Weekly,* Vol. 234, No. 7, August 12, 1988, p. 459.

Iduna is a fair-haired goddess from ancient Norse mythology who tends a magic garden in the kingdom of Asgard. In her verdant domain, flowers grow alongside clear streams, sweet grass and abundant fruit trees, but the greatest treasure of all is a chest of golden apples that give everlasting youth and vitality to the gods. In this vivid retelling of a haunting tale, disaster strikes when Thiassi, hateful enemy of the gods, succeeds in abducting Iduna and the apples from her paradise. With Iduna imprisoned in a fortress of stone, death haunts the once-invincible gods and the magic garden withers into a perpetual doom. An ominous black raven looks on from the border on each page, lending a spooky touch, but the artwork—for all its careful touches and ornate landscapes—is occasionally uneven. Most distressing are the portrayals of Iduna; her image is inconsistent throughout the book.

Ronald Jobe

SOURCE: A review of *Iduna and the Magic Apples,* in *School Library Journal,* Vol. 35, No. 8, April, 1989, p. 114.

A stirring picture-book rendition of the Norse myth of how Iduna's apples kept Odin and the other gods from growing old, until Thiassi, a monstrous giant in hideous bird shape, plotted to kidnap her and gain the power of the apples. After evil black insects, evolved from Thiassi's cast-off feathers, sting Iduna with their poisonous venom, she becomes alarmingly weak. This provides the opportunity for the god Loki, succumbing to treachery as a condition for saving his own life, to deliver her to Thiassi. The Everlasting Garden begins to die as winds, rain, and snow battle it. The gods themselves begin to age and decline, until they coerce Loki to rescue Iduna. The text is a delight. Mayer's poetic style of writing echoes the beauty and tranquility of the Everlasting Garden. Lyrical descriptive passages will evoke vivid scenes in readers' imaginations. Superbly crafted, the retelling is made more compelling by Mayer's astute use of engrossing dialogue as well as embedded phrases and short sentences and implied pauses. Gal's sweeping compositions dramatically evoke the myth's ever-changing mood. Strikingly framed by identical side panels (albeit in the same muted sepia tones), the double-page spreads offer a visual interpretation in a majestic classical style. Gal uses a resin-color wash with egg tempera on paper technique highlighted by cross hatchings and colored pencil to add detail and texture. The action is perceived as frozen-in-time vignettes, each poignant moment enhancing the narrative. This book will be a valuable addition to mythology collections.

📖 *A FLASK OF SEAWATER* (written by P. K. Page, 1989)

Ellen Fader

SOURCE: A review of *A Flask of Sea Water,* in *The Horn Book Magazine,* Vol. LXVI, No. 1, January-February, 1990, p. 60.

The goat herd, deeply in love with the princess after only a brief glance at her face, becomes a competitor for her hand in marriage, along with two others who are eager to reign with her when the old king dies. Whoever returns first with a flask of sea water will be declared the winner—no easy feat for residents of this landlocked kingdom where only members of the royal family have seen the ocean. Unbeknownst to the goat herd, the princess and her fairy godmother have conspired to ensure that he is the winner; he survives his long and perilous journey and its attendant trials with aplomb, grace, and wisdom, proving himself a worthy husband for the princess. While Page breaks no new ground in her story, she exhibits a great facility for combining the well-known, standard elements of the traditional fairy tale— love at first sight, a contest to win a spouse, a quest, and the supernatural—into an original fairy tale that will entrance children, especially the great majority who so rarely encounter this genre of imaginative writing. Gal's illustrations, reminiscent of Persian miniatures, are appropriately dominated by rich golds and blues, drawing the reader into the otherworldliness and magic of the story. A smoothly written, attractive book.

Sarah Ellis

SOURCE: "News from the North," in *The Horn Book Magazine,* Vol. LXVI, No. 3, May-June, 1990, pp. 366-69.

Another quest for the sea forms the structure of P. K. Page's *A Flask of Sea Water.* Illustrated by Laszlo Gal, this stylish extended fairy tale is reminiscent of "The King of the Golden River," with its mountain setting and the testing of three young men. In Page's story the king of landlocked Ure offers his daughter in marriage to the man who can produce a flask of sea water. There are three contenders. Idle Stabdyl is fooled into believing that a lake is the sea and is humiliated when the water he triumphantly produces is found to be fresh. Vain Mungu arrogantly spurns all the help he is offered on the journey and finally makes a foolish wish that banishes him to a solitary island. But Galaad, the dusty goat herd, is rewarded for his kindness and tenacity with magic that enables him to conquer the many obstacles in his path and return triumphant.

The story is told antiphonally as the three threads twine together. Plot devices echo classic fairy stories—a wicked wizard who turns men into animals; a magic token to be used "'only when all else fails'"; a golden locket that marks the hero. We are on familiar ground, and the tone never falters. The telling includes some elements that bring it closer to fantasy than to fairy tale. A comic logical/illogical mouse could have come straight out of Carroll. There is a higher degree of psychological realism than in the traditional fairy tale. Mungu is a particularly interesting version of the absolutely focused despot. The limits of the wizard's power over him are telling: "Although he could assist Mungu in bringing about Mungu's own desires, he was completely unable to put ideas or wishes in Mungu's head." But while Page extends the fairy tale conventions, we never sense parody or weariness or anything but respect for the form.

P. K. Page is a poet, and she brings a poet's gifts to the story. Her words have the simplicity and weight of an oft-told tale. She uses precise images: "eyes as black as licorice"; the sea "salty as a kipper . . . salty as an anchovy." Her cadences are simple: "And every morning when the dew lay in the valley, he drove his goats up to the high meadows where the air was clear and the grass was sweet. And every evening when the sun dropped behind the topmost peaks of the westerly mountains, he drove them down to the valley again." And she makes effective use of a sensual luxuriousness matched only by Gal's Persian miniature-style illustrations: "It was a beautiful garden. Peacocks strutted across its smooth green lawns. Fountains sprinkled drops of water like glittering jewels. Lilies, lady slippers, and shooting stars grew among the blue-eyed grasses near the pool. . . . The air was heady with scents of cinnamon, clove, and apricots. Bright birds sang." In an author's note Page writes, "All my life, I have loved fairy tales." Given the loveliness of *A Flask of Sea Water,* we are not surprised.

POME AND PEEL: A VENETIAN TALE
(retold by Amy Ehrlich, 1990)

Publishers Weekly

SOURCE: A review of *Pome & Peel: A Venetian Tale,* in *Publishers Weekly,* Vol. 236, No. 25, December 22, 1989, p. 56.

Young readers will be entranced by this Venetian fairy tale, with its many classic ingredients: a couple who cannot have a child, a wizard who casts spells and the moral dilemma of an overheard conversation. In Ehrlich's stylish retelling, the wizard gives the childless couple an apple and guarantees that the wife will have a child nine months after she eats it. The woman consumes the fruit and her maid eats the peel; they both become pregnant. Their sons, Pome and Peel, are born within hours of each other and raised as brothers. Years later the boys seek out the wizard's daughter, famed for her beauty; she disobeys her father and agrees to marry Pome. The angry wizard puts three curses on his daughter; in trying to protect the girl, Peel finds himself the victim of the most terrible curse of all. Gal's elegant medieval paintings, replete with sprawling cityscapes and lavishly costumed characters, contain many imaginative details that capture the story's magic and romance.

Karen Litton

SOURCE: A review of *Pome & Peel: A Venetian Tale,* in *School Library Journal,* Vol. 36, No. 7, July, 1990, p. 76.

Tiny print on the verso of the title page cites the source of this dark Venetian tale of loss and restoration. A childless wife eats a magic apple, and her maid eats the peel; both become pregnant. The resulting sons grow up as brothers and, as young men, travel to find an unlaughing wizard's daughter. Released by the brothers, she departs with them to marry Pome. Feeling betrayed, her father curses his daughter, but after three witches intervene, Peel deflects the curse through behavior that strikes others as murderous. Condemned to death, he reveals the truth of his deeds, causing himself to turn to stone; the remorseful wizard restores the boy's life at his daughter's petition. It's a complex tale happening over a long time span and in different places, weighty with events and traditional folkloric elements. While the orderly telling manages it all comfortably, the result is more academic than lively. Gal's tempera paintings glow with near-Italianate light, and the color is much cleaner than in some of his earlier Canadian work. The highly controlled composition incorporates detail into the page design to convey place and time. But control is the organizing force here, and for all the operatic events and the visual theatricality, the mood of both words and pictures remains glacial and studied. Potentially of interest to folklore students, but its child appeal is questionable.

PRINCE IVAN AND THE FIREBIRD: A RUSSIAN FOLKTALE (retold by Gal, 1991)

Kenneth Radu

SOURCE: A review of *Prince Ivan and the Firebird: A Russian Folktale,* in *Canadian Children's Literature,* No. 67, 1992, pp. 71-3.

[I]mpressed by Russian costume and architecture, Laszlo Gal sets his illustrated retelling of *Prince Ivan and the Firebird* in the time of the Muscovy Boyars. . . .

Although Gal is faithful to the incidents of the story for the most part, there are questionable omissions in his version. The incorporation of proverbs and ritualistic formulae is part of the unique charm of Russian folklore which Gal generally avoids. "He rode near and far, high and low, along by-paths and byways—for speedily a tale is spun, but with less speed a deed is done—until he came to wide, open field, a green meadow" (Afanas'ev). In Gal's version, this special Slavic quality is absent: "For many days he travelled in the direction from which the Firebird had appeared that night in the garden. Heavy clouds were almost touching the earth when he arrived at a vast meadow."

Prince Ivan and the Firebird is a complex amalgam of pagan images and motifs and Orthodox Christian belief as influenced by the Byzantine Church. When the sleeping Ivan is murdered by his brothers, for example, having won firebird, a wonderful horse, and a beautiful princess, he lies "dead" for 30 days before the great wolf, his mentor and servant throughout the story, restores his life. In the Orthodox Church calendar, the thirtieth day after the burial of a believer is crucially important, a feast day. The number 30 is spiritually significant. Gal reduces the time to a meaningless 10 days. Moreover, the wolf requires both the waters of life and death to "resurrect" the prince, but Gal makes do with the water of life.

Perhaps these objections are mere academic quibbles, but a retelling of any symbolic story so specifically connected to a region, a religion, or a people should endeavour to preserve what is culturally unique to the tale or all stories risk sounding like the homogenized narratives so beloved of Disney productions.

The real strength and beauty of this book, of course, lie in Gal's full-page pictures. Here the artist is superior to the writer and the illustrations truer to the Russian spirit. The style of pre-Romanov aristocracy, the details of

interior decoration, the characters extravagantly costumed in Boyar robes, the mixture of pagan and Christian, are handsomely depicted in *Prince Ivan and the Firebird* by an artist-illustrator with a fine and delicate sense of colour and a remarkable sense of cultural detail. The firebird itself is especially handsome in its pinkish hues.

Marion Scott

SOURCE: A review of *Prince Ivan and the Firebird: A Russian Folktale,* in *Canadian Materials,* Vol. XX, No. 3, May, 1992, p. 158.

The classic Russian tale of Prince Ivan's quest for the elusive firebird, his triumph over his jealous brothers, and his winning of a beautiful princess is ably retold and illustrated by Laszlo Gal.

Gal is an award-winning illustrator who has successfully illustrated a wide variety of folk- and fairy-tales, most notably *The Little Mermaid, The Twelve Dancing Princesses,* and *Canadian Fairy Tales.*

As a reteller, Gal proves to be fluent and sure. He follows the original tale closely. He occasionally adds motivation for Ivan, but this is not gratuitous and serves to make the story a little more cohesive. The illustrations are generally attractive and appealing. Beautifully rendered details of architecture and costume convey both the flavour of the Russian setting and a touch of fantasy. Gal also makes effective use of orange, red and ochre tones in conveying the story's theme. Where the artwork does disappoint slightly is in its slightly static quality and rather bland faces. These, however, are minor quibbles.

All in all, this is a good version of a fascinating tale that is not widely available in quality picture-book editions. A welcome edition to core collections in both school and public libraries.

Denise Anton Wright

SOURCE: A review of *Prince Ivan and the Firebird: A Russian Folktale,* in *School Library Journal,* Vol. 38, No. 7, July, 1992, p. 68.

Accomplished illustrations and a faithful retelling bring one of Russia's best-known folk legends to life. Gal has individualized his version of the story with evocative language and flowing imagery. Using a blend of watercolor, colored pencil, and chalk pastels, he has fashioned a lush dreamlike world based in the reality of Old Russia. In this world, striking landscapes and menacing woods provide the backdrop for Prince Ivan's adventures. Gal seems to be most comfortable in his stylized depictions of architecture, interiors, and costumes; his humans and animals are often stilted and marred by inconsistencies of scale. Also, set against the textured background of the paintings, the rather lengthy text is cramped and, at times, difficult to read. But overall, the colorful and radiant paintings convey the splendor and power of traditional Russian folklore. Whether read independently or shared aloud with older audiences, this interpretation deserves a place in most collections.

📖 *EAST OF THE SUN AND WEST OF THE MOON* (retold by Gal, 1993)

Kit Pearson

SOURCE: A review of *East of the Sun and West of the Moon,* in *Quill and Quire,* Vol. 59, No. 10, October, 1993, p. 37.

Laszlo Gal, one of Canada's most talented illustrators, has chosen to retell and illustrate the beautiful Norwegian folktale *East of the Sun and West of the Moon,* the story of a brave young girl who passes all the necessary tests and, with her magic helpers, frees the prince she loves from a troll's spell. Gal's retelling gives the girl a name—Ingrid—and extends the ending in a satisfying way (the lovers travel back to the castle for an elaborate wedding celebration). This story is simpler and more child-like than the original, and some may quarrel with the portrayal of Ingrid's decision to go with the white bear as her own choice rather than as the result of her greedy father's persuasion. No doubt the author is trying to emphasize her goodness and courage, but it may make her too much of a martyr for some tastes.

Nonetheless, Gal's marvellous pictures are what make this retelling special. Never have his illustrations glowed with such inner light and rich colour, as if they were reflecting the Northern lights of the story's Scandinavian setting. There is a stunning, full-colour picture for each page of text, plus decorative drawings on the facing pages. Children ages 5-10 will love lingering over the details of castles, trolls, reindeer, winged wind-men, and illuminated skies.

Frieda Wishinsky

SOURCE: "Portraits of the Past," in *Books in Canada,* Vol. XXIII, No. 1, February, 1994, p. 49.

Though beautiful in colour and design, Laszlo Gal's *East of the Sun and West of the Moon* lacks this wondrous, haunting quality. Instead, Gal's retelling of a Norwegian tale has a static, formal style that limits this book's appeal.

A young girl named Ingrid agrees to follow a mysterious white bear who promises riches to her poor family. The bear, of course, is an enchanted prince, and he is leading Ingrid to his palace. One night, despite the bear's warning, Ingrid seeks his true identity, and the bear

disappears. Realizing her affection for him, Ingrid begins a perilous quest to find the bear. She travels through woods, up mountains, encountering such creatures as giants and trolls along the way to his stepmother's castle east of the sun and west of the moon. All these dangers are depicted in the drawings, but they're neither frightening nor startling. Faces are expressionless, while backgrounds are merely decorative and flat. The writing is lacklustre too, informative rather than dramatic or moving. This is a pretty book, but a good picture-book should be more.

Gillian Martin Noonan

SOURCE: A review of *East of the Sun and West of the Moon,* in *Canadian Materials,* Vol. XXII, No. 3, May, 1994, p. 80.

Ingrid is the youngest and most beautiful child of a poor woodcutter and his wife. So that his family will no longer have to live in poverty, the woodcutter gives Ingrid to a mysterious white bear. Ingrid's new life with the bear in a far away castle is quite wonderful. She has all that she wants and the bear is good to her, but Ingrid misses her family. A visit to her family, now surrounded by prosperity, precipitates disaster for Ingrid and the bear. To undo an evil spell, Ingrid must use all her cunning to find her way to the castle that lies east of the sun and west of the moon.

Laszlo Gal, the award-winning illustrator, has retold and illustrated this traditional Norwegian folk-tale in fine style. The full-page illustrations are filled with vivid yet soft colours and have a decidedly medieval flavour to them. Gal's illustration of the South Wind is particularly noteworthy.

The text is straightforward, allowing the illustrations to descriptively enrich the tale. Some young readers may find this story rather slow-paced and drawn out but all should find the ending quite satisfactory.

Folktales come from a markedly different era than the one in which we now live. This characteristic should always be kept in mind when they are being read. Nevertheless, this reviewer feels quite strongly that the imagery connected with a "mysterious man" lying in bed with Ingrid at night, with the bear warning Ingrid not to talk to her mother alone, and with Ingrid's mother expressing concern to her youngest daughter about who or what this "mysterious man" is may have disturbing associations for some readers. It is unfortunate that our awareness of the crassness in humanity may cause us to spurn some of the best stories in literature.

This edition of *East of the Sun and West of the Moon* is not necessarily a must have for any library. Many collections will already hold it. Gal's illustrations are quite beautiful and, for those interested in his work or that of other Canadian illustrators, this is a fine example.

Carole H. Carpenter

SOURCE: A review of *East of the Sun and West of the Moon,* in *Canadian Children's Literature,* No. 77, 1995, pp. 55-62.

In keeping with his previous works, Gal's *East of the Sun [and West of the Moon]* is an aesthetic delight. The text is a good retelling of a traditional Norwegian story and the illustrations are elegant and appropriate both to the spirit of an Old World wonder tale and to the specifics of old Norse culture. It is worth noting that the central figure, a female, is in keeping with the many powerful females to be found in traditional tales and quite unlike those reshaped by the pens of nineteenth-and twentieth-century retellers-cum-popularists. This girl has brains as well as beauty and uses both, along with the magic requisite to the fairy-tale genre, to bring about what she wants to occur—she is mistress of her own life, both good and bad.

Yet, despite these fine qualities, Gal's book would be promptly, if regrettably, eliminated from the AESOP PRIZE competition on the basis of criteria three and five. The folklore is not enhanced by being presented in this work; it is used, but is not better understood as a result. Other than through the illustrations, the tale is not placed in its context; there is no indication of how it relates to other traditional tales from Norway or anywhere else; nothing is indicated about its usual tellers or audience. More serious, though, is Gal's failure to give credit to his source(s) and to indicate how his telling differs from anyone else's, published or otherwise. Had he used a portion of Lewis's *Narnia* series, or a segment of an Andersen tale, he would have been obliged to acknowledge it or face potential copyright violation. Unfortunately, here there is only one line—on the dust jacket not in the bound contents—indicating the Norwegian connection. Little effort would be necessary to provide the requisite annotation and even a bibliography for further reading. If the reteller does not wish to undertake the task, the publisher should employ a folklore graduate student to do so. Otherwise, those who produced this otherwise excellent book are effectively guilty of misappropriation of voice. The oral tradition may be largely in the public domain; it should not be open to avoidable abuse.

📖 *MERLIN'S CASTLE* (1995)

Teya Rosenberg

SOURCE: A review of *Merlin's Castle,* in *Canadian Book Review Annual,* 1996, p. 442.

Ralphy (Raphaella) narrates her adventure with her brother Marco and his lizard Donatello. Dinosaurs fascinate Marco, and he longs for Donatello to grow large and terrible. On Christmas Eve, Ralphy, Marco, and Donatello discover a paper castle in a book; inside that castle, they meet Merlin. Since all three wish for Donatello to grow large, Merlin sends them to find the place where giant lizards live. Once there, they will be able to transform Donatello with the magic words Merlin gives them. With some trial and error, they find that place. But after becoming large and terrible, Donatello realizes that he values his friendship with Marco more, so all three return home, where Donatello is once more a small lizard, albeit somewhat transformed by their adventure.

Gal has beautifully illustrated *Merlin's Castle* with his trademark use of lovely color and tone. The story itself has something for everyone: dinosaurs, a wizard, a journey in a flying balloon, a hint of danger, the true love of a pet, male and female protagonists. All the pieces, however, do not entirely pull together. The magical elements are convoluted and convenient rather than consistent and convincing. Ralphy and Marco's father illustrates children's books; this detail plus a great variety of references and allusions makes this story seem written chiefly for the Gal family rather than being an esthetic whole in its own right. There are fun details, but those details overwhelm the story. Recommended with reservations.

Katherine Matthews

SOURCE: A review of *Merlin's Castle,* in *Canadian Children's Literature,* No. 87, 1997, pp. 85-8.

The story of *Merlin's Castle* is problematic from beginning to end. In fact, there are far too many stories going on at once here, and the attempt to place them in the form of a circular tale fails. Here, the circle is broken—Gal's ending doesn't send the reader back to the beginning, thus discouraging the reader from re-reading to appreciate the circular nature of the story. As well, the illustrations are oddly flat, creating neither emotional response nor interest. Finally, many elements of the story are highly distracting: Donatello functions as either an obscure art reference or as a confusing pop culture reference (will readers question the fact that Donatello is a lizard, when he really should be a Ninja Turtle?); and Merlin, whose archetypal presence carries great weight, is reduced to a mere plot device. All of this plot hangs on a very flimsy thread, and the thread frays quickly.

📖 *TIKTALA* (written by Margaret Shaw-MacKinnon, 1996)

Karen Hutt

SOURCE: A review of *Tiktala,* in *Booklist,* Vol. 92, No. 21, July, 1996, p. 1831.

After expressing her wish to become a great soapstone carver, Tiktala, a young Inuit girl, is sent to find her spirit helper. Transformed into a harp seal, Tiktala gains the understanding and wisdom she needs to return to her people and begin practicing her carving. Softly colored illustrations in cool blues and greens fill the double-page spreads, beautifully showing how the seals live and Tiktala's homecoming. A pleasant addition to the multicultural shelf, with somewhat more text than the traditional picture-book selection.

Elizabeth S. Watson

SOURCE: A review of *Tiktala,* in *The Horn Book Magazine,* Vol. LXXII, No. 4, July-August, 1996, p. 456.

Her desire to become a famous soapstone carver leads Tiktala on a search for spirit help; she journeys in the form of a harp seal, the animal that she wishes to carve, and is guided by another seal sent to help her. While the village scenes before and after her transformation are depicted in realistic, concrete, solid forms of houses and people, the spirit journey is cast in appropriately dreamy, flowing scenes that follow the seals through the Arctic waters among schools of fish and past mountains of ice and softly glowing sunsets. The artist's interpretation supports the fantasy and helps make the mystical story accessible to younger children. The them that art grows out of experience grows naturally out of the book.

📖 *THE PARROT: AN ITALIAN FOLKTALE*
(Retold by Gal, with Raffaella Gal, 1997)

Patricia Morley

SOURCE: A review of *The Parrot: An Italian Folktale,* in *Canadian Book Review Annual,* 1997, p. 542.

Laszlo and Raffaella Gal, a father/daughter team of illustrators, breathe new life into a retelling of an old Italian folk tale. A merchant's daughter is loved by a young prince and an evil king. The king takes advantage of the merchant's absence on a trading trip by sending his soldiers to capture the girl. Suspecting the king's intent, the prince turns himself into a parrot, flies to the girl's window, and so bewitches her with his tales that she will not turn from him to answer the door when the soldiers knock.

The parrot's tale-within-a-tale cleverly echoes the outer tale of the merchant's daughter and the king's schemes. The parrot/prince, an archetypal Scheherazade, preoccupies the girl until her father returns. Of course all ends well, with the lovers united.

The heart of the book lies in the dramatic full-page illustrations, which typically show the girl utterly absorbed in watching a scene that illustrates the parrot's tale (again, a scene-within-a-scene, which parallels the double plot). The sumptuous, richly colored paintings in pencil, oil, and egg tempera are bold and beautiful, and reinforce the gothic mood of a damsel in danger. The viewer

From Tiktala, *written by Margaret Shaw-MacKinnon. Illustrated by Laszlo Gal.*

becomes a third level in this intriguing set of visual and narrative boxes that stimulate both eye and mind.

Gwyneth Evans

SOURCE: A review of *The Parrot: An Italian Folktale,* in *Quill and Quire,* Vol. 63, No. 8, August, 1997, p. 37.

The Parrot is a retelling of an Italian folktale, adapted and gorgeously illustrated by the renowned Canadian illustrator Laszlo Gal and his daughter Raffaella. The Gals respond to the structure of the story—a tale within a tale—by imaginatively combining uncoloured pencil drawings with richly coloured egg tempera and oil paintings, thus suggesting the two different story worlds that the book takes us into. In both stories, a beautiful girl is desired by an evil king, who threatens but ultimately can't prevent her marriage to a young prince. In the framing story, the girl remains oblivious to the threat, as she is absorbed in the story being told her by a wonderful parrot. The parrot is actually the good prince, who has so transformed himself in order to gain and hold her attention. The girl keeps her door locked against the king's soldiers so as not to disrupt the storytelling. In the parrot's tale, the girl takes a more active role, by searching for her kidnapped father, fending for herself in the woods, and eventually bringing about the rescue and restoration of the lovesick prince, who lies on his bed in a Snow White-like trance until the princess intervenes. This element of the book should allay concerns about the passivity of folktale heroines.

The real star of **The Parrot,** however, is neither prince nor princess but the art of storytelling. The Gals celebrate the power of a good story to grip its hearers, to warn them of evil in the world, and to bring delight: when the girl learns that her parrot is really a prince who wants to marry her, she immediately agrees because he has proven himself such a wonderful storyteller. Many imaginative techniques are used in the illustrations and book design to enhance the sense of moving in and out of the two worlds of the stories. For example, a colour wash or plain white wash is used for the background of the text, and the brilliantly hued parrot bridges the margin and the picture on each page when he is telling his story. The changing details of the design invite the young reader's attention, and the use of colour beautifully suggests the transformative power of imagination and love.

Hazel Rochman

SOURCE: A review of *The Parrot: An Italian Folktale,* in *Booklist,* Vol. 94, No. 2, September 15, 1997, p. 237.

The power of story is the center of this picture book retelling of a classic Italian folktale. It is really a tale within a tale. A prince transforms himself into a parrot to save a beautiful princess from a wicked merchant. The parrot tells her a story that holds her spellbound and that prevents her from opening the door as the wicked merchant's soldiers bang to be let in. The story the parrot tells is very much her story, and the parallels, though deliberate, may confuse listeners, who might also wonder why the soldiers don't just bash down the door instead of knocking so politely. However, the lush, romantic illustrations help keep things clear softly shaded gray pencil for the listening princess, brilliant detailed oils for the parrot and his story. This is a tale that lends itself to being acted out as readers' theater.

Jane Doonan

SOURCE: A review of *The Parrot: An Italian Folktale,* in *School Librarian,* Vol. 46, No. 1, Spring, 1998, p. 24.

Have you ever made up a story to an enthralled listener but found yourself running out of invention? If so, you will sympathise with the eponymous hero of this classic Italian folk tale within a tale. The parrot is (of course) a prince in disguise, voluntarily transformed so that he may protect a beautiful young woman from the evil designs of a wicked king, while her merchant father is away. The parrot promises to tell the beautiful maiden the most marvellous story in the world but if anything stops him, he will leave and she will never know the ending. At regular intervals during the telling the king's soldiers come banging at the merchant's door, but the maiden will not brook interruptions. The parrot only just about manages to keep going until the merchant returns.

The visual narrative is given a double framework. The parrot and the maiden are drawn in pencil, while the parrot's love story is shown in colour. At moments of high emotional drama the colour flows into the listener as she empathises with her fictional counterpart. The merchant's daughter, in her richly embroidered Renaissance robes, is posed against backgrounds which evoke Tuscan hill towns and landscape. This is the territory where Fine Art meets the art of the picture book.

Additional coverage of Gal's life and career is contained in the following sources published by The Gale Group: *Contemporary Authors,* **Vol. 161** and *Something about the Author,* **Vols. 52, 96.**

John Mole

1941-

English author of poetry.

Major works include *Once There Were Dragons: A Book of Riddles in Words and Pictures* (1979), *Boo to a Goose* (1987), *The Mad Parrot's Countdown* (1990), *The Conjuror's Rabbit* (1992), *Copy Cat* (1997).

INTRODUCTION

Although he has published copious volumes of verse for children, Mole is not, strictly speaking, a "children's poet." Having begun his career writing for adults, Mole can instead be described simply as a poet—a poet whose work has often focused on childhood thoughts and themes in a manner that holds appeal for young and mature readers alike. With the exception of *Copy Cat*, a rhyming story appropriate for preschoolers and early primary graders, Mole's eclectic repertoire of riddles, verses, and rhyming tales for children is well suited to readers nine years old and up who are prepared for the challenge of poetry appreciation. A great deal of Mole's work may also appeal to early teenagers. "Much of my work," Mole told *Contemporary Authors,* "has been concerned with the experience of childhood—not in any blandly nostalgic sense, but in the attempt to dramatize the fascination and bewilderment of being young." Critics have debated which of the poet's works are actually for children. Yet for many, it is this blurred classification that has made Mole a popular favorite of poetry lovers spanning a wide range of age groups.

Mole has been praised by critics for his exceptional technical skill, his widely varied subject matter, and his rare talent for writing verses that charm both adults and children. With his deft use of rhyme and rhythm, his love of language, and his complex interweaving of dark and light themes, reviewers have often pointed to Mole as an ideal fit for poetry study in the classroom. Critic Dennis Hamley pointed out, "[Mole's] easy mastery of language and form means there is never a false note." Reviewer Marcus Crouch also commented that Mole's work has achieved success with young students because "like most children, he loves the sound of words, and he is good at matching sense (or nonsense) with sound."

Mole has been frequently commended by critics for his ability to shed fresh and original light on childhood thoughts and feelings without sentimentality or condescension. At times, however, Mole has been critiqued for employing language and subjects that appear to lie beyond the scope of his intended audience of junior

readers. While he has concurred that his vision of childhood experience is not always lighthearted or simple, Mole has maintained a firm commitment to creating fanciful, thought-provoking poetry without changing his style. "There's a tremendous scope for anarchic fun if you're a children's writer, but if you lose sight of your own truth, you're done for," Mole told *Something about the Author (SATA)*. True to his belief, Mole has utilized vocabulary and themes that challenge children, rather than assuming their possible limitations. For this reason, Mole has developed a reputation as a skillful, subtle poet unafraid to challenge readers of all ages.

Biographical Information

Born in England, Mole earned a bachelor of arts degree from Magdalene College at Cambridge in 1964. In 1968, he married freelance artist Mary Norman, who would later enrich several volumes of his poetry with her simple yet powerful black-and-white illustrations. Mole taught for nearly three decades before choosing to leave the classroom in 1998 to pursue writing and lecturing on a full-time basis.

Mole began publishing poetry for adults in 1973, and by 1979 had become well established as a significant contemporary English poet. As a result, he was frequently invited to classrooms to read his work. However, Mole needed a selection of children's poetry to draw from, so he began crafting riddles that would help young students learn to appreciate poetry, particularly when hearing it read aloud. He told *SATA,* "I often use [riddles] as a warm-up when I visit schools, and as a way into talking to children about magic, the power of language, and the effect of metaphor." These successful classroom experiences led to the publication of Mole's first book for children, *Once There Were Dragons: A Book of Riddles in Words and Pictures.*

Major Works

No ordinary collection of riddles, Mole's first book for children is a brain-teaser designed to challenge and entertain young people and adults simultaneously. In *Once There Were Dragons: A Book of Riddles in Words and Pictures,* thirty verses cryptically describe typical household objects, such as a table, a gate, or a typewriter. Mary Norman's illustrations provide the answers to the cleverly crafted and challenging rhymes. In order to further enhance the fun of guessing, however, the corresponding pictures are printed out of sequence, rather than on the facing page as the reader may expect. For those too curious to resist, the solutions are all available on the back page. Many critics have commented on the artistic merit of both the riddles and the illustrations. Chris Waters noted that "the writing is skilful, poised, and fairly sophisticated in tone and many of the riddles stand on their own feet as respectable poems."

Mole's second collection of poems for children, *Boo to a Goose,* also received critical acclaim for providing a selection of works well suited for reading aloud. Verse riddles, counting rhymes, and original poems are at once fanciful and slightly sinister. All, however, are rooted in the lives and expectations of children in today's world. Subjects such as having a Coke in the cafeteria and receiving unwanted Christmas gifts are presented alongside songs about an abandoned car and a cacophonous look at the chaos of the circus. Praising the collection, reviewer Gavin Ewart wrote, "[p]robably the best thing is the lack of whimsy; this is, in most respects, a common-sense, realistic poetry."

The Mad Parrot's Countdown is another children's collection showcasing Mole's keen ability to combine humor with thought-provoking seriousness in modern-day language that young people can relate to. An unusual and unpredictable roster of characters appear in the verses, including Marcel Proust, Toulouse-Lautrec, Nietzche, Kierkegaard, and Churchill's dog. The collection contains witty, imaginative poems, which present, as Pam Harwood wrote, "a varied collection of poems both in subject matter and difficulty, ranging from the roll-around-on-the-floor hilarity kind to those that provoked thought."

In *The Conjuror's Rabbit,* Mole's third collection for children, the poet again captures a wide variety of subjects and tones. Mole offers keen, often humorous observations of both people and animals in various forms that appeal to a child's imagination. Charles Causley notes, "[t]here is hope and fun, as well as sadness, in this most civilized collection: the work of a true poet."

While few of Mole's books are accessible to very young children, *Copy Cat* is one exception that is suited for both preschool and primary graders. In this rhyming story, a small boy named Oliver wakes up one morning to find a strange cat sitting on his bed, staring at him oddly. The feline follows Oliver everywhere he goes, duplicating his every move, until the boy decides to mimic the cat in return. The cat departs, but the next day an unknown dog appears on Oliver's bed. Oliver prevents a second round of mimicry by staring the dog down first. Once again playing with rhyme and repetitive sound, Mole has created a simple story ideal for reading aloud. One *Kirkus Reviews* critic noted that with *Copy Cat* "Mole deftly conveys just how vexing mimics are, with a couple of refrains that story-hour listeners will find impossible to resist."

Awards

Mole received the Eric Gregory Award from the Society of Authors in 1970 and the Signal Award for outstanding contribution to poetry for children in 1988. In 1994, Mole was again honored by The Society of Authors with the Chomondeley Award for poetry.

TITLE COMMENTARY

📖   ***ONCE THERE WERE DRAGONS: A BOOK OF RIDDLES IN WORDS AND PICTURES* (with Mary Norman, 1979)**

Chris Waters

SOURCE: "Poem Urgent as Sweets," in *The Times Educational Supplement,* No. 3311, November 23, 1979, p. 34.

Scott Fitzgerald once said that the test of a first-rate mind was in its ability to maintain, simultaneously, two contradictory ideas: it is also a very useful way of beginning with poetry, via the riddle, for in getting us to see one thing in terms of another, it is sowing the seeds of metaphor. Guessing the answers is also fun. John Mole recently spent some time as a visiting writer in primary classes and has assembled a collection of riddles he has written for children, illustrated by his wife [Mary Norman]. The illustrations answer the riddles, but out of sequence, to enhance the fun of guessing. The writing is skilful, poised, and fairly sophisticated in tone and many of the riddles stand on their own feet as respectable poems:

> Thick set, accomplice of mortality,
> I tell you secrets in a broken tongue
> About yourself, about the stony-hearted
> Riddle that my words become.
>
> (A gravestone)

Others, I find slightly too extended and reliant on general knowledge rather than perception of a central image; however, we cannot all be Anglo-Saxons, and overall this is an enjoyable and teasing collection.

Margery Fisher

SOURCE: A review of *Once There Were Dragons· A Book of Riddles in Words and Pictures,* in *Growing Point,* Vol. 18, No. 5, January, 1980, p. 3635.

Warned that the pictures do not correspond to the rhymes opposite which they are printed, children will find their patience is rewarded as they make the necessary match and 'if you end up really stuck the answer's at the back'. The black-and-white illustrations, enigmatic and beautifully shaped on the page, lead logically and not too easily to the solution of lines laconic and full of neatly phrased clues—like 'We're a kind, you might say, Of aerial raincoat' or 'My legions thicken on each window pane, A gathering of dusk, perpetual gloom'. An unusual, provocative collection of riddles, elegantly produced, for quick-witted children from ten or so, and adults as well.

E. Colwell

SOURCE: A review of *Once There Were Dragons: A Book of Riddles in Words and Pictures,* in *The Junior Bookshelf,* Vol. 44, No. 2, April, 1980, pp. 85-86.

This is no ordinary book of riddles for children, but a group of poems which happen to hide a riddle and a series of black and white drawings which happen to give the answer. The reader can look for clues to match poem and picture together if he wishes, for the two parts are never opposite to each other. Both poems and illustrations have individual merit, quite apart from any riddle that lies hidden in them.

This is not a book for young children but it might well be appreciated by older boys and girls.

Alan Brownjohn

SOURCE: "Poems and Jokes," in *The Times Literary Supplement,* No. 4034, July 18, 1980, p. 810.

Once There Were Dragons comprises thirty teasers of varying difficulty, disguising simple objects like a table,

a gate or a typewriter—and sets them along-side Mary Norman's simple yet evocative drawings in the wrong order. You guess the object, then look for the picture somewhere else. Most children will in most cases find the answers without "getting" all the small clues dropped on the way; no matter they can work out the details later, and perhaps obtain some food for thought of another kind. This is Mole's alarm clock:

> You should be glad that through the dark
> I kept awake; instead
> With something like a grunt or bark
> You bash me on the head;
> Which only goes to show, I'd say,
> As sure as I'm wound tight,
> That people often break by day
> The vows they made last night.

It has a nice metaphysical touch; and it might jump an alert child straight into the tone of poems much more serious than playful riddles: children may learn by leaps as well as by painful steps. Many of John Mole's riddles will function as excellent poems in their own right: one of the tougher ones, with an Audenesque note about it, displays a preoccupation with mortality that is the only slight fault in an immensely skilled and pleasurable little collection.

Marcus Crouch

SOURCE: A review of *Once There Were Dragons: A Book of Riddles in Words and Pictures,* in *School Librarian,* Vol. 29, No. 1, March, 1981, p. 41.

When schoolchildren, as they are untiringly fond of doing, ask one another riddles, they are sharing in a pastime which is among the oldest in the world. They were asking riddles—some of them the same ones—when the sphinx was a kitten. John Mole's riddles are in verse and, although very much belonging to our own times, they evoke something of the spirit of the Anglo-Saxon poems to which Kevin Crossley-Holland has recently given fresh life. They are serious and funny, admirable as verse, not too easy but not prohibitively difficult to solve. Mr Mole's wife, Mary Norman, helps the reader out with a set of brilliant wash drawings. These are the answers, but they are scattered haphazardly through the book, and those who approach it in a proper spirit will first work on the poem, then confirm their findings by looking at the picture, and only then—if at all—look for the answers on the back page. It is a jolly little book which will sharpen the wits while exercising the reader's feeling for words and for form.

📖 *HOMING* (1987)

John Lucas

SOURCE: "London Airs," in *New Statesman,* Vol. 113, No. 2925, April 17, 1987, p. 29.

Death has more than a walk-on part in *Homing*. There are, for example, elegies on the jazzmen Pee-Wee Russell and Ben Webster, the latter of which is particularly fine and prompts the thought that over the years Mole has written enough good poems about jazz and its exponents to suggest that an enterprising publisher ought to bring them together. There is figurative death—of love, of marriage—in **"The Doll's House"**, a typically mordant fable poem about the ritualising of words inside a relationship: 'After tonight/We shall probably find them./ If not,/They have lived with us long enough/To find their own way back.' And in **"Coming Home"**, which *New Statesman* readers will vividly remember from its first appearance in these pages, Mole has produced a poem whose technical brilliance properly serves its stark, horrifying subject-matter: a loved child who grows up to become a soldier and who in the course of duty kills a loved child. This is the nightmare of history from which it is impossible fully to awake, so that an English poet, remote from events the poem describes, nevertheless registers how they impinge on his consciousness.

> And that's the reason why this can't go on,
> And why it's almost culpable to write,
> And why I can't stop thinking of our son
> And of how easily we sleep at night,
> How in the house if anybody screams
> We joke next morning. It was only dreams.

By tearing this stanza out of the poem I've disrupted the careful logic with which Mole builds up an awareness of how we are part of a world from which evil will not go away. I haven't, I hope, falsified its extraordinary power.

Mole is a gifted comic writer, as **"From Doctor Watson's Casebook"** shows. Yet the gift does not lapse into cosiness. **"The Song of the Pie"** sings ominously about the kind of Thatcherite Britain where we are all expected to conform: 'But why should you make such a fuss/ When we promise that things will go well?/All the best eggs vote for us./They know it's the truth we tell.' I think of Gavin Ewart as an admirer of this poem, as I'm sure Graves would have admired **"The Doll's House"** and Auden seen much to praise in **"Coming Home"**. These names are not invoked out of random pretentiousness, but in order to give a sense of Mole's achievement, and in the angry knowledge that Secker & Warburg have announced their intention of dropping him from their already pitifully short poetry list. This is another way in which London can't be compared with Prague—or with any other capital city, come to that. For where else in the world would you find publishers guilty of such crass philistinism, such blatant stupidity?

Dennis Hamley

SOURCE: A review of *Homing*, in *School Librarian*, Vol. 35, No. 2, May, 1987, p. 181.

Most accessible of important contemporary poets, John Mole has a special relevance to schools because he provides an ideal model for GCSE and A-level students to explore. He is frequently called a 'technician'. He is; his easy mastery of language and form means there is never a false note. Which is why his work provides such excellent example for anyone seriously essaying the craft of poetry.

But he is so much more. This collection, like the others, provides seemingly effortless wit which conveys deep and universal feeling; the true significance of the ordinary. Look at poems like **"The Circuit"**, **"The Station Wife"**, **"Coming Home"** and **"Firstlings"** for this. Or **"Answer Phone"** or **"The Mad Parrot's Countdown"** for a disturbingly dexterous verbal humour. Every poem works. The book is a delight.

D. W. Hartnett

SOURCE: "Acute Angles," in *The Times Literary Supplement,* No. 4047, September 18-24, 1987, p. 1024.

In a brief *ars poetica* which concludes his latest collection, *Homing*, John Mole imagines "An undressed language, / A simple purpose / Like the child's tyrrannical / *Me! Me! Me!*"—only swiftly to undercut this ideal: "But that little face / Is of deprivation, / A stone, a cloud / Or a flower, autonomous . . . ". Fascinated by innocence and innocent angles of vision, Mole's poetry can also accommodate a darker, more adult world. In his best work poet and child participate in a dance of disquieted complicity. *Homing* has its share of such work.

Mole is at his most straightforward when he re-invents the landscape of childhood. Although ghosts stalk through **"Firstlings"**, their world is reassuringly impervious to adult unease: "Whose are those feathery tears that keep coming? / Somebody weeps without a sound / And leaves his grief heaped up on the ground." It's only snow. However, when *Homing* leaves behind this kingdom of muffled, perpetually immature wisdoms, problems can arise. Poems about corrupted innocence grow shrill behind the mask of social conscience. In **"Last Night"** inner-city rioters are glibly pigeon-holed as "grown children". Equally knowing are the volume's MacNeice-like exercises in parable such as **"Every Little Mouse"** and **"Toy Bricks"**.

Elsewhere adult and child meet on more equal ground. **"Adder"** invokes a childhood already unnervingly vulnerable to grown-up experience: "Victory V, / Black V for venom, / Churchill's long cigar, / The hiss of Hitler . . . ". This leads to a comic yet uneasy fusing of man and boy: "Herr Leviathan, / The Poisonous One . . . / In my dream, inside / A Chilprufe sleeping suit, / I killed him nightly / With bare hands." Stanzaic, yet structured round units of line and phrase, the poem's language pivots on a sophisticated simplicity. Several other poems use war as a catalyst for the mixing of innocence and guilt. The most intriguing of these—**"Coming Home"**—describes how a young soldier is haunted by his murder of "a child that couldn't run away". The poet's own peaceful domesticity is night-marishly implicated: "And that's the reason why this can't go on, / And why it's almost culpable to write, / And why I can't stop thinking of our son / And of how easily we sleep at night . . . ". The iambics caress the tortured emotion with eerie smoothness. This is a poetry unwilling to trust finalities, least of all its own.

📖 *BOO TO A GOOSE* (1987)

Gavin Ewart

SOURCE: "Two-Way Traffic," in *The Times Literary Supplement,* No. 1287, November 20-26, 1987, p. 1287.

John Mole has written only one book specifically for children—*Once There Were Dragons*—but in the other six books to date there have been poems likely to appeal to younger readers scattered throughout. Even in the collections of "adult" verse there are pieces that are riddles or simple nursery songs—such as, for example **"Nobody's Last Words"** in *In and Out of the Apple,* a slightly sinister riddle in a book that also contains the sequence **"Penny Toys"**, geared to the lives and expectations of children. It is hard, in fact, to separate the childlike from the childish; and this has always been one of Mole's strengths, as he exploits the two-way traffic between both. Children are as intelligent as adults, and in their chosen subjects well informed. What they lack, naturally enough, is experience of life.

Boo to a Goose is a selection from the whole *oeuvre.* The little songs can be disturbing. One describes a "cold" and carefree fish:

> Yes, we all admired him
> As we kept our distance, all
> Except one huge and hungry shadow
> Leaping from the depths
> Which ate him whole.

Death is a presence, though not named; yet all young watchers of television Nature programmes know that she is red in tooth and claw. The distance between the adult and the child is not very great, when it's a question of general menace. The riddles, likewise, and there are fourteen, are as taxing for adults as for children (but perhaps I'm not very good at riddles); the best are very well written:

> Grand and solo, polished brightly,
> Dance of practised fingers nightly,
> Claire de lunar or moonlightly.
> Presto, forte, pathetique,
> The world is mine because I speak
> A language common yet unique.

"Under the Tree" is a satire on unwanted Christmas presents, that any child would understand:

> At least it's not an oven glove
> *From Cynthia and Ron with love.*

> *Affectionate regards—Aunt Grace*
> Something she broke and must replace.

> The shop will not take this one back
> *To all of you from Uncle Jack.*

Just occasionally there are faults, where the idea of rhyme is stretched a bit (town/flown), or the throwaway line strikes a dead note at the end of a poem— "It is too late" at the conclusion of **"The Zebra"**, where his stripes are compared to prison bars, or "Pike, I wish I had your go", the last, unrhyming, line of a poem which is made of true rhymes and assonances.

In performance, such things can be overcome; and for reading aloud to groups of children these poems are obviously very suitable. They are also, in their way, sophisticated. The Knife-thrower and his bride sing together:

> Then as we grow old we'll remember
> The miraculous day we first knew
> That the thrill of cold steel
> Could teach us to feel
> Sensations so poignant and true.

Probably the best thing is the lack of whimsy; this is, in most respects, a common-sense, realistic poetry, where skinheads yell *"Sod it!"* and a girl says "Meet me for a coke in the cafeteria". The final section, **"The Big Top"** (quoted above), is described as "an entertainment for several voices" and it's not hard to imagine this series of circus poems as a successful performance piece. It's good for children, moreover, to be exposed to words like "cacophony" and "polyphonous" and the hysterical hype of the Circus Master ("that raucous, gallimaufrous razmataz").

Marcus Crouch

SOURCE: A review of *Boo to a Goose,* in *School Librarian,* Vol. 36, No. 1, February, 1988, p. 23.

John Mole, I suspect, is a poet. Peterloo Poets, to whom we are indebted for the introduction of several important new writers, have published a selection of his poems for children in an attractive and delightfully illustrated paperback. John Mole believes in rhythm and even rhyme. His verses are fairly traditional in technique. His subjects, mostly closely related to the experience of children, range over a wide field. His viewpoint is always original, his comments relaxed and humorous. Like most children, he loves the sounds of words, and he is good at matching sense (or nonsense) with sound. This selection ends with an 'entertainment for several voices' about the circus, which might be worth testing out in class or as a school project.

Charles Causley

SOURCE: "Trust the Teader," in *The Times Educational Supplement,* No. 3753, June 3, 1988, p. 45.

With **Boo to a Goose** John Mole produces that rarity a collection of verse as telling and successful with the child as with the adult. I can imagine no-one "growing out", so to speak, of these poems. Like Ted Hughes, the author refuses to patronize his audience. His approach is uncompromising and there is total trust in the capacity for response of his reader. Here, firmly organized and presented, are verse riddles, counting rhymes and original poems rooted in the world of today. John Mole's powerful and mysterious songs for an abandoned car, for example, seem to me masterpieces of their kind.

THE MAD PARROT'S COUNTDOWN (1990)

Charles Causley

SOURCE: "Parrot Fashion," in *The Times Educational Supplement,* No. 3858, June 8, 1990, p. B15.

With his brilliantly successful **Boo to a Goose** John Mole demonstrated the rare ability to write poems that appeal simultaneously to the child and the adult. If further proof were needed, it is to be found in abundance in **The Mad Parrot's Countdown,** a collection of 35 (mainly) new poems but which also includes a number of pieces rescued from earlier books. The range of form, theme and style is astonishing. At a first reading, it's impossible to predict what may be coming next. The writing is of a high order, accomplished, light of touch, firm in perception, as in **"First Snow":**

> Who am I? and where have I woken?
> It wasn't the same when I went to bed.
> I still feel me inside my head
> Though now a different language is spoken.

What might at first appear to be simple poems of place—a classroom at night, an abandoned building, a house inexplicably empty and in which "Nobody answers and even the cat/(Who doesn't like rain) is not in the hall"—reveal a numinous quality that recalls the best of de la Mare with never a hint of the fey or the antique. The delicate subject of broken relationship is handled with great tenderness and skill in **"The Call":**

> You didn't answer when I called
> Although I knew you must have heard . . .
> Had I somehow lost the knack?
> Were you really not to blame?
> Why did you never call me back
> Or let me know you'd changed the game?

There is also a fine gaggle of comic poems calculated to engage the youngest as well as the oldest. The subjects are often surprising: "Marcel Proust's my hero,/ Marcel Proust's my man./I'll tell you why/Marcel's my guy/And I'm his biggest fan." Elsewhere, we encounter Toulouse Lautrec, one of "those famous blokes/ Who're reckoned to be good at art/But never finish

what they start." At a slightly less artistically exalted level, there is the slurpily entertaining **"Pig Sings"**, and a merciless family portrait:

> Sing a song of Christmas,
> Sing a song of grub,
> Sing a song of Grandpa
> Boozing in the pub.

A set of verses on Churchill's dog derives checkily, and without acknowledgement, from Pope and there is some excellent advice to the insomniac on an alternative to counting sheep: "Think of the tomatoes in the greenhouse." And, after all the knockabout, one is stopped in one's tracks by the startling beauty of **"Moth":**

> Pity my silence pressing at your window
> Frail and motionless against the night;
> A baffled spectre framed by blackness,
> Little moonflake, prisoner of glass.
> This is my journey's end, receive me.
> Brilliant keeper, rise and let me in.

No doubt about it: this collection by John Mole, with its always apposite, sometimes whizzbang, often moving illustrations by Mary Norman, is a must.

Tony O'Sullivan

SOURCE: A review of *The Mad Parrot's Countdown,* in *School Librarian,* Vol. 38, No. 4, November, 1990, p. 156.

The Mad Parrot's Countdown deserves serious consideration for inclusion on the shelves and in the class poetry box, for these poems by John Mole are not only witty in themselves but surely a cause of wit in others. I have watched John Mole share the tricks of his mystery in book weeks and poetry workshops; he has the knack of showing how following a particular form can liberate the latent talent and the diffident muse. This collection of poems, richly and affectionately illustrated by Mary Norman, is like those exotic tins of assorted biscuits brought out at Christmas—unusual, varied and appetising. No teacher poet can escape the spell of school, as **"The Joke"**, **"The Classroom"** and **"Asking for Trouble"** testify, poems which describe with accuracy and humour classroom customs. Here is a poet who enjoys a challenge: how quickly can you find rhymes for Montaigne, Kierkegaard and Nietzsche? 'The regretful philosopher apologises to his cat' picks up this gauntlet.

Cats, bats, monkeys and musical instruments that cause more pain than pleasure are to be found in the first layer. In the second layer, my favourites were: his Alices who set out 'to vanquish the force of wonder'; the sybaritic schoolboy whose hero was Marcel Proust 'who wrote all his books in bed'; and **"Carnival Sunday"**, a celebration to be relished by those who have a love-hate relationship with garden fêtes where time is spent: 'Buying old annuals you'll never read/And guessing the weight of a bear gone to seed.'

Best of all, the bottom layer, advice by a young artist to Toulouse-Lautrec 'who couldn't paint to save his neck' and whose models were selected from: 'One of those fagged-out, scrawny dollies/That kick their legs up at the Folies.'

A choice assortment without a doubt.

Pam Harwood

SOURCE: A review of *The Mad Parrot's Countdown,* in *Books for Keeps,* No. 66, January, 1991, p. 8.

A varied collection of poems both in subject matter and difficulty, ranging from the roll-around-on-the-floor hilarity kind to those that provoked thought and were more serious. I loved **"A Painting Lesson"** where young Benjamin Mole offers a few hints to Toulouse Lautrec. The **"Pig Songs"** were more difficult with their nursery rhyme rhythm, but having 'tuned in' they were clever and funny. My favourite was **"A Ghost Story"**—a brilliantly unnerving description of coming home to an empty house. Really finger-tingling reading.

📖 *CATCHING THE SPIDER* (1990)

Gillian Clarke

SOURCE: "Speaking to the Poet in the Child," in *The Times Educational Supplement,* No. 3894, February 15, 1991, p. 29.

That child in me loved *Catching the Spider.* John Mole's memory of the haunted house of childhood is fresh, the empty swing still swinging. He tackles the nightmare the child never tells. These poems have the rhythm and rhyme, the friend-words and stranger-words—like "bestow", "universal", "muster"—that nourish the poet in the child. Here too are "discs" and "dishes" bright with their new meanings, Gran grumbling that no one sits down to a proper meal any more, absent fathers, Craig, Jamie, and Samantha with her headphones on. Such transitory "relevance" is far from shallow because this collection allows also for the big seriousness of childhood, and the sudden desperate emptinesses, as in **"The Lost Ball"**. Such poems as **"The Whisper"** make mystery of the ordinary and haunt the mind with metaphor: "Around the world the whisper goes/And everything that hears it grows."

Valerie Caless

SOURCE: A review of *Catching the Spider,* in *School Librarian,* Vol. 39, No. 2, May, 1991, p. 69.

There is a poem in this original collection for everyone. Humour, pathos, wisdom and wit are all here. There is rhyme, rhythm and free verse, easy poems and those which require more attention. Each reader will soon have

favourites. Perhaps two short poems quoted here will help to give a taste of the feast inside these pages. 'Four things to remember when writing a poem': 'A watched pot/ Never boils/ A watched phone/Never rings/ A watched clock/Never strikes/ A watched song/Never sings.'

> **Lost and found**
> In my parents' eyes I see
> The child that I was meant to be
> But who's gone missing? Them or me?
>
> And who is it owns this tangled ground
> Where each of us plays lost and found
> Until there's nobody around?

It seems churlish to mention that the page numbers on some pages are missing, which makes the index of first lines a little hard to use!

Frances Ball

SOURCE: A review of *Catching the Spider,* in *The Junior Bookshelf,* Vol. 55, No. 4, August, 1991, pp. 162-63.

John Mole has the ability to shine a light into corners of childhood life without writing-down or sentimentalising. Some of the poems in this collection look at uncomfortable subjects or reveal more pleasant ones in a new light. In **"The Shoes"**, he captures the sadness a child feels as he looks at some shoes his/her missing father has left behind:

> These are the shoes
> That dad walked out in
> When we didn't know
> Where he was going,
> When I tried to lift
> His suitcase,
> When he said goodbye
> And kissed me. . . .

A slight shift of title, and in **"Foot-Work"** he achieves a very different, lighthearted effect:

> Walking down an empty street
> Your footsteps argue with your feet. . . .

Amongst the forty-one poems, children will find many that reflect their own experiences, others that will help them gain insight into new ones. A useful collection for juniors.

📖 *THE CONJUROR'S RABBIT* (1992)

Lucinda Fox

SOURCE: A review of *The Conjuror's Rabbit,* in *School Librarian,* Vol. 40, No. 4, November, 1992, p. 156.

Children will enjoy this latest collection of poems by John Mole for the wide variety of themes and moods captured. He has the ability to portray ideas and thoughts from the whimsical to the prosaic. There is the title poem where the rabbit ponders 'What am I doing stuck in this hat?'; and **"The Library at Night"** where 'Novels tired of being read/guess each other's plots instead'. Poems with more everyday themes are **"The Prompt"** where a small girl is struck dumb with stage fright; and **"Scaling the Mountain"** which describes a boy still wanting to climb on to his father's shoulder although he is almost too big. This is a miscellany to keep and dip into. In each black and white illustration by Mary Norman she has captured the spirit of the poem.

Charles Causley

SOURCE: "Space between the Words," in *The Times Educational Supplement,* No. 3999, February 19, 1993, p. 2.

John Mole's ***The Conjuror's Rabbit*** maintains the enviably high standard he set himself with his award-winning ***Boo to a Goose.*** Here now is another set of luminous and well-judged poems, never a phrase too many, never one short, always demonstrating that there is infinitely more to the good poem than the number of words lying on the page. John Mole loves language, uses it with subtlety and skill, and is quite unafraid of making demands on his young audience. The effect, quietly engineered, is always arresting, often surprising. The pictures they paint, the sentiments they express, seem to dissolve and re-assemble before one's eyes as if by some process of magic. A single example: the haunting **"A Change of Scene"** in which "They seemed a mother and her child/Picnicking in a golden field/ And not a cloud was in the sky/ And nobody was asking why" becomes a vision of "Millions of mothers crouching there,/ Millions of children eating air." There is hope and fun, as well as sadness, in this most civilized collection: the work of a true poet.

Morag Styles

SOURCE: A review of *The Conjuror's Rabbit,* in *Books for Keeps,* No. 79, March, 1993, pp. 28-29.

The Conjuror's Rabbit by John Mole is his third collection for children. The book has attractive black-and-white line drawings by Mary Norman. Mole has an assured place in the children's canon, combining well-observed 'snapshots' of people and animals with a nice sense of humour. He uses form inventively: there's a triolet, a villanelle, riddles, of course, and a new version of a nursery rhyme. Here's an extract from one of the best poems:

> Millions of mothers crouching there,
> Millions of children eating air.
> I couldn't go, I had to stay.

> It's only dreams that go away
> And this was not a dream, I knew.
> The day had come, the night was through
> And everyone was asking why,
> And so was I. And so was I.

A collection for thoughtful readers of about nine and older.

W. Magee

SOURCE: A review of *The Conjuror's Rabbit,* in *The Junior Bookshelf,* Vol. 57, No. 4, August, 1993, p. 155.

John Mole, a long established poet for adults, brings out his third collection of poems for children. Thirty-five poems in a wide variety of forms offer the serious reader plenty of toothsome goodies. Here are poems recalling childhood experiences, poems as accurate observations, descriptive pieces, riddles, character sketches, and poems detailing moments of sadness. The tone is quiet, almost subdued yet manages a wide range of mood. John Mole uses rhyme effectively and without strain [as in **"Bully"**]—

> Face to face
> And eye to eye,
> His cold lips shape
> The easy lie.

Mary Norman's rather heavy-handed black and white illustrations are liberally scattered throughout the book. At times they make the poems inappropriately sombre. The combination of text and picture—properly serious rather than flip or throwaway—makes for a solid read. A rewarding, thought-provoking and enriching collection for good readers in the 9-12 years age range who are prepared to persevere and involve themselves with good quality work.

DEPENDING ON THE LIGHT (1993; also as *Selected Poems,* 1995)

Celia Gibbs

SOURCE: A review of *Depending on the Light,* in *School Librarian,* Vol. 41, No. 4, November, 1993, p. 163.

There are some fine poems in this new collection of John Mole's work and many readers will appreciate the quiet enjoyment of particular moments that he writes about. Mole's idiom is modern and accessible and the topics include much about the passing of life and the memories of childhood. He handles details and evokes objects precisely; readers will see the scene in front of them whether it is **"The Toybox"**, the rocking horse in **"The Present"**, or events of family disharmony. Mole received the Signal Award for his book for children ***Boo to a Goose,*** and teenagers in the secondary school and their teachers will find this volume a good addition to the collections of contemporary poets in the library. It will balance the work of poets who take more public and committed positions.

Bernard O'Donoghue

SOURCE: "Models of Perseverance," in *The Times Literary Supplement,* No. 4730, November 26, 1993, p. 15.

In "Keeping Going", a major recent poem, printed in the *New Yorker,* dedicated to his farmer brother, Seamus Heaney pays tribute to the virtue of perseverance in your given work. John Mole has the virtue praised in an earlier Heaney poem, "A Daylight Art", of practising his right art from the start and persevering in it, often without enough recognition from the market-place. Yet each of his eight volumes of grown-up poems (the distinction has to be made only because Mole is a very successful writer of sophisticated poems for children) has addressed a different subject.

His seventh volume, *Homing,* was concerned with the complicated emotions associated with the home: security, anxiety, fragility. *Depending on the Light* has an equally sustained theme, though one not so easy to infer from its title. This is taken from **"The Waking"**, where what depends on the light is which painter is best compared to the sensual smile of someone just woken up: Rembrandt, Matisse or Vermeer. The point is not laboured, but it is a matter of mood, related once again to the tensions of people's existence at close quarters. What gives these poems their edge is that Mole's world is not one of settled security threatened by breach; the serpent is always quietly inside this Eden. People are yoked together by love or circumstance, but there is always a greater or lesser degree of separateness. An extreme case is **"Travellers"**, a very tense encounter on a train in which a "pin-striped thug" is roused to fury by a girl sitting next to him relentlessly eating carrots: "click, click, click, click". When he protests aggressively, the girl says with conclusive reasonableness: *"I think there's something wrong with you."* Probably; but it's something that's wrong with all of us at close quarters.

The italics in this line are a favourite device of the book; more poems have them than not. Their function is plain and effective: they indicate the doomed attempt to communicate familiar, repeated utterance. For Mole, the hearer-speaker relationship, however well meant, is never ideal. Thus there are other, more solemn separating factors. The most important is age, implying the ultimate uncrossable divide, that which separates the living from the dead. Recurrent figures here are "the fathers / who were children" (**"A Different Dream"**), familiar from earlier Mole poems like **"The Fair"**. Relations between the male generations are everywhere, culminating in the poignant and precise last poem **"Going On"**, with its pun on going to bed, dying and persevering. The poet is thinking of his father's ageing:

And why must I recall this now
As half-way up the stairs
I hear my grown son calling
Going on, then, Dad?
An early night? Sleep well.

Separateness here is not a matter of personality; it is a lamentable fact of life in the face of which sympathy is in vain.

The family is not the only setting for Mole's contained, minatory parables. Sometimes the public world is much closer, usually in regular poetic forms (of which Mole once said that they do not hamper meaning but trap it in). The political poets of the 1930s, especially MacNeice, come to mind, as in this defamiliarized view of an army base near (too near) the seaside:

Revolving turrets'
Moony plates
Protect a world
Which waits and waits.

In the same vein, his Goethe translation, **"The Walking Bell"**, recalls the artless menace of Blake's *Songs,* as did **"The Lost Boy"** in *Homing.*

There *is* an answer of sorts to separateness and anxious questioning: patience and repose. This is beautifully expressed in the book's opening poem **"The Cherry Tree"**: the cherry is free of anxiety, being "So unequivocal"

Not you, not me, with our same
Questions,
The old stones'
Word game . . .

Of *Do you love, me*
As much as . . . ?

By now the lucid universality of Mole's poems means that the distinction between poetry for children and for adults is fading. This book adds another half-dozen or so to Mole's complement of some of the most engaging English poems of the past quarter-century.

📖 *BACK BY MIDNIGHT* (1994)

D. A. Young

SOURCE: A review of *Back by Midnight,* in *The Junior Bookshelf,* Vol. 58, No. 4, August, 1994, pp. 135-36.

John Mole's *Back by Midnight* is compiled from *Boo to a Goose* and *The Mad Parrot's Countdown.* He is a poet who writes because he must and if what he writes seems appropriate for young readers then why not make them available in a Puffin Anthology? He makes no concessions to his audience. His vocabulary is one that suits his purpose not the limited range of a possible reader. If the background knowledge to appreciate his references is not available to a particular reader then some kind adult will have to supply it. An appreciation of **"The Painting Lesson"** largely depends upon the reader's knowledge of Toulouse Lautrec, his times and his works. Without having met Marcel Proust, his books and his life style the wit of **"My Hero"** may pass the reader by **"The Regretful Philosopher Apologises to His Cat"** will tickle the fancy of those acquainted with Descartes, Wittgenstein, Kierkegaard, Nietzsche et al.

His verse riddles smack of the cryptic crossword clue and some of his shorter poems remain a haunting mystery that will not go away. The significance of such poems as **"The Family Game," "The Call"** and **"The Smile"** seems to lie between the lines and test the limits of literary understanding. This is an anthology for young readers with old heads upon their shoulders. In the hands of an enthusiastic teacher it could provide a key to the understanding and enjoyment of the mind of a poet.

HOT AIR (1996)

Catherine Byron

SOURCE: "Versed in Travelling," in *The Times Educational Supplement,* No. 4178, July 26, 1996, p. 8.

John Mole, already a Signal Award winner for his 1988 collection *Boo to a Goose,* also has a new book from Hodder: *Hot Air.* Title and jolly balloon-race cover are a bit misleading, for this book offers something very precious and almost endangered in contemporary poetry for children. Peter Bailey's half dozen pen-and-ink drawings within the text are wonderfully in tune.

There is solitariness and melancholia in these poems, words for sad times and for days of drifting, of necessary daydreaming. They offer spaces for stillness and separation, such as **"Next to Nowhere"**: "No one/ Seems to own it . . . and that's why/I like it, why it's getting better/All the time." Holidays are for days like this, as well for noise and laughter.

Vida Conway

SOURCE: A review of *Hot Air,* in *School Librarian,* Vol. 44, No. 4, November, 1996, p. 167.

This collection of around fifty poems is characterised by simple language and the rhymed, rhythmical verse that has an immediate appeal to children. Many of the subjects concern familiar experiences—cleaning the car, looking in the mirror, lining up, the generation gap— others capture less common moments of truth. As well as amusing, John Mole's verse provokes thought, compassion and reflection. Some of these poems will be enjoyed by children of 9 and upwards, but some reach out, too, to those teenagers who have hitherto found

poetry complex and unsatisfying: 'Words come out like stars sometimes and choose the darkest nights to sparkle in . . . ' The cover is attractive and colourful; the contents deserve better quality paper and presentation, but if a modest price ensures wider circulation one must be content. Recommended for the poetry shelves of both junior and secondary libraries.

COPY CAT (1997)

Kirkus Reviews

SOURCE: A review of *Copy Cat,* in *Kirkus Reviews,* Vol. LXV, No. 15, August 1, 1997, p. 1226.

The title is meant to be literal: Oliver wakes up one morning to find a strange cat at the bottom of his bed that mimics everything Oliver does—brushing his teeth, playing with blocks, watching television, having lunch. Oliver turns the tables and starts aping the cat: When the cat washes behind its ears, so does Oliver; when the cat jumps onto the dinner table, Oliver follows suit. The cat leaves, but when Oliver wakes up the next morning, a strange dog is at the foot of his bed. Mole deftly conveys just how vexing mimics are, with a couple of refrains that story-hour listeners will find impossible to resist ("the cat did too" and "Oliver did too"). [Bee] Willey's bright gouache palette is loosed upon cats in human positions and humans posturing as cats. A droll piece, and one that hits home.

Anne E. Deifendeifer

SOURCE: A review of *Copy Cat,* in *The Horn Book Guide,* Vol. IX, No. 1, July-December, 1997, p. 41.

When a strange cat appears and begins to copy everything Oliver does, from brushing his teeth to watching television, Oliver soon tires of the mimicry and decides to turn the tables. In the end, the two copycats agree to stop imitating each other. Energetic gouache artwork, rendered in bright colors, accompanies the odd and repetitive tale.

Publishers Weekly

SOURCE: A review of *Copy Cat,* in *Publishers Weekly,* Vol. 244, No. 36, September 1, 1997, p. 103.

In this neon-colored version of a well-trod tale, a strange cat appears and mimics everything young Oliver does until the boy reverses the trend and copies the cat. If the Cheshire Cat ever came down from his tree, he might look a bit like Willey's orange-striped feline, with a mischievous grin and a twinkle in his eye. The cat starts out larger than life as he floats above Oliver's building blocks or obstructs the view of the TV screen. In the illustration accompanying the text "When Oliver went into the bathroom to brush his teeth, the cat did too," the cat, whose head occupies the entire mirror (framed in toothpaste gone astray), holds toothbrush in paw, with Oliver peering around from behind. Only when Oliver turns the tables ("This just won't do! If you copy me, I'll copy you") does the colossal cat shrink down to size. By then, even cat lovers may grow weary of the text's repetition ("When the cat jumped up onto the table, Oliver did, too"). Willey's energetic gouache paintings in blacklight purple, chartreuse and flame orange lend the book an electric flair, but can't completely compensate for Molds tired, ordinary text.

Additional coverage of Mole's life and career is contained in the following sources published by The Gale Group: *Contemporary Authors*, Vol. 101; *Contemporary Authors New Revision Series*, Vols. 18, 41; *Something about the Author*, Vols. 36, 103.

Uri Shulevitz

1935-

Polish-born Israeli-American author and illustrator of picture books.

Major works include *The Fool of the World and the Flying Ship: A Russian Tale* (adapted by Arthur Ransome, 1968), *Dawn* (1974), *The Treasure* (1979), *The Golem* (written by Isaac Bashevis Singer, 1982), *Snow* (1998).

For more information on Shulevitz's career prior to 1978, see *CLR*, Vol. 5.

INTRODUCTION

Recognized by critics as an artist of wit and energy, Shulevitz successfully blends text and illustrations to produce complete and seamless picture books for elementary graders. He is known for his magical, timeless tales that unfold slowly to reveal the wonders of the natural world from a child's eye. Shulevitz has achieved success by bringing his own story ideas to life by writing with pictures, particularly in his self-illustrated work, *Snow*. In addition, he has received praise for his unique ability to interpret the works of other authors. He has illustrated delightful retellings of traditional Jewish tales, such as Isaac Bashevis Singer's *The Golem* and Sholem Aleichem's *Hanukah Money* (1978), classic folk tales such as the Grimm Brothers' *The Golden Goose* (1995), and original works by many contemporary and legendary authors, including Howard Schwartz and Robert Louis Stevenson.

Illustrating a wide variety of books over his career, Shulevitz continually changes his methods of illustration to suit the story, using techniques such as pen and ink, watercolor, Japanese reed pen, or Chinese Brush. His method of choice depends on the mood he wishes to evoke, such as the fine Oriental line of *The Silkspinners* (1967), the sprawling scenes of *The Fool of the Word and the Flying Ship: A Russian Tale*, and the Sendak-like figures of *The Fools of Chelm and Their History* (1973). Critics have enjoyed the liveliness of his characters, dream-like and cartoonish settings, and his charming, gentle humour, calling his work a "harmony of pictures and text," "evocative, timeless, and . . . irresistible," and "satisfying, with a touch of the fantastic."

After twenty years of creating, illustrating, and educating others about picture book illustration, Shulevitz wrote *Writing with Pictures: How to Write and Illustrate Children's Books* (1985), in which he details his philosophy and methodology. He recommends that the illustrator start with a story board for the purpose of organization,

but from there, he emphasizes, the artist's creativity must be allowed to take over. Shulevitz believes that the words and illustrations in a picture book should be so intimately intertwined that one cannot be understood without the other. Several of his books exemplify this, most notably *Rain Rain Rivers* (1969), *Dawn*, and *Snow*. Shulevitz summed up his philosophy of picture books in *The Illustrator's Notebook*: "A picture book is not a silly plaything. It is much more. Sometimes it can be everything to a child. A picture book can be a messenger of hope from the outside world. . . . Children are very sensitive to this, because their lives depend upon it. A destructive, lie-negating attitude will not do. Neither will a saccharine approach. A picture book does not have to be deep, but it does have to be alive."

Biographical Information

Born in Warsaw, Poland, Shulevitz remembers bombs falling on his house, buildings burning, and the streets caving in during the Nazi invasion of his hometown when he was just four years old. His family, in great danger because they were Jewish, fled Poland and wandered homeless for eight years before finally settling in Paris in 1947. In 1949 the Shulevitz family moved to the newly established country of Israel and took up residence in Tel Aviv. Shulevitz, who displayed artistic talent at an early age, was the youngest participant in a drawing exhibition at the Museum of Tel Aviv, and attended both the Teacher's Institute and the Art Institute in Tel Aviv. When the Sinai War broke out in 1956, he joined the Israeli Army and went into basic training; while serving his tour of duty he worked as an art director of a magazine for teenagers. After he left the army, Shulevitz joined a kibbutz near the Dead Sea where he designed a Haggada, the service book used for the Passover ceremony, and became a freelance artist.

In 1959, when Shulevitz was 24 years old, he moved to New York City to study painting at the Brooklyn Museum Art School, and became a citizen of the United States a few years later. He got a job illustrating Hebrew books for children, but his work was very restricted and controlled. He has said that this work proved to be good discipline for him, and helped him to improve his pen and brush techniques. It was while working at this job that he began to develop his unique illustration style. In 1963 he wrote and illustrated his first children's book, *The Moon in My Room,* which "unfolded in my head like a movie," he told *Something about the Author (SATA).* "I was the camera seeing the action conveyed by the pictures. The few words necessary to communicate the story fell into place on their own. It was all so simple and natural."

Major Works

Shulevitz's Caldecott winner, *The Fool of the World and the Flying Ship: A Russian Tale,* adapted by Arthur Ransome, tells the story of the Fool of the World—a lowly younger son of a peasant who wins the hand of the Czar's daughter as a reward for his kindness to a strange old man. "[T]he artist captures the gauche personalities of the peasant imagination and portrays the flat and ample Russian landscape. . . ," noted Paul Heins. "If the transformation of the Fool of the World suggests the final scene in a Russian Ballet based on folklore, the illustrator has not been unfaithful to the story but has simply added to it a justifiable element of visual splendor."

Dawn, another example of Shulevitz's ideal picture book, tells the story of an old man and his grandson rowing across a lake in the morning. The text is simple, sometimes just one word, and its meaning depends upon the illustrations which, in turn, require the text for a full explanation of the picture. *Dawn* is an evocation of the rising sun, showing the gradual transition of the sun during a full day—which is fully revealed in all its colorful glory on the final page. In a review for *The Horn Book Magazine* Virginia Haviland stated, "The purity of the hues, well-produced on ample spreads, the subtle graphic development from scene to scene, and the sharply focused simplicity of the few words make this a true art experience."

Drawn from the Hassidic tradition, *The Treasure* is the story of a poor man named Isaac who, compelled by a recurring dream, goes to the capital city to look for a treasure under the bridge in the royal palace. After traveling a long way, he arrives at the palace only to find it well guarded and unapproachable. When he tells his story to one of the guards the man laughs and says that if *he* believed in such things, he would have searched for treasure under the stove of a man named Isaac, whereupon Isaac returns home to find treasure under his own stove. In gratitude he builds a temple and inscribes on it the motto, "Sometimes one must travel far to discover what is near." William Jaspersohn wrote in the *Christian Science Monitor,* "[Shulevitz's] unassuming text is wonderfully enhanced by illustrations of astonishing luminosity and richness."

The Golem, written by Isaac Bashevis Singer, is based on an old Jewish tale about a clay giant brought to life to protect and bring justice to the Jewish people. In this version, a banker is falsely accused of abducting the daughter of the local Count, and the rabbi is called to create the golem and send him to defend the banker. The golem finds the girl and exonerates the banker, but the rabbi's nagging wife urges him to misuse the golem, resulting in chaos when the golem gets out of control. It is the golem's love of a servant girl that brings about his fall and allows the rabbi to lay him to rest. Betsy Hearne praised "[t]he meticulous textures and shading that give depth to Shulevitz's black-and-white drawings [and] make an intense but low-key setting for the tale."

In *Snow* a little boy hopes for snow, despite news reports predicting otherwise. The boy's wish comes true, and he watches the snow fall and drift and swirl, eventually blanketing the world. A critic for *Kirkus Reviews* called the setting "evocative, timeless, and as irresistible as the first snow," and Mary M. Burns praised the palette as "appropriately subdued, depending in the concluding pages upon the contrast between a freshly blue sky and snow-covered buildings rather than brilliant colors for effect."

Awards

Nearly all of Shulevitz's books have received awards. *The Fool of the World and the Flying Ship: A Russian Tale* won the Caldecott Medal and was included in the American Booksellers Gift to the Nation from the Library of the White House, both in 1969. Shulevitz received Caldecott Honor Book awards for *The Treasure* in 1980 and *Snow* in 1999. Additional awards for *The Treasure* included the Children's Book Award from the American Institute of Graphic Arts, a *New York Times* Best Illustrated Book of the Year, and *Horn Book* honor book, all in 1979, as well as an American Library Association Notable Book in 1980. In 1974, *Dawn* was named a notable book by the American Library Association and a *New York Times* Outstanding Book of the Year; in 1975 it won the Christopher Award; in 1976 it represented the United States on the Honor

List of the International Board on Books for Young People; and it received Brooklyn Art Books for Children citations in 1976, 1977, and 1978. In 1982 *The Golem* was named an American Library Association Notable Book, a *New York Times* Outstanding Book, and a *School Library Journal* Best Book. Besides its Caldecott Honor in 1999, *Snow* was named a Best Book in 1998 by *Publishers Weekly* and *School Library Journal*, and an Editor's Choice by *Booklist*; it also received a Blue Ribbon citation from the Center for Children's Books, an American Library Association Notable Book for Children, the Charlotte Zolotow Award, and the Golden Kite Award, all in 1999.

AUTHOR'S COMMENTARY

Uri Shulevitz

SOURCE: "Voices of the Creators," in *Children's Books and Their Creators,* edited by Anita Silvey, Houghton Mifflin Company, 1995, p. 600.

It was my good luck, when I began toting my portfolio around to publishers in 1962, that the first editor I saw was Susan Hirschman. But when she suggested I try writing my own picture book, I was horrified. Write my own story? Impossible. I was an artist, not a writer. I could imagine myself in various activities, but never in my wildest dreams had I imagined myself a writer. Writing seemed a mysterious activity, suited to those who had magical ways with words. To me, using words was like taming wild tigers.

I told Susan that I had been speaking English for less than four years. "Don't worry," she reassured me, "we'll fix your English." There was nothing to do but try. And try I did, many times. I went back to her office for months, bringing my awkward writing efforts. After many unsuccessful attempts, I finally came up with a picture book. With minor changes, it became **The Moon in My Room,** my first book. If it were not for those many unsuccessful attempts, I don't think I could have written it.

My initial fear that I could not write was based on a preconception that writing was strictly related to words and to spoken language. I had assumed that using many words skillfully was central to writing. I was overlooking what was of primary importance—*what* I had to say. I was overwhelmed by what was of secondary importance—*how* to say it.

Once I understood that *what* I had to say was of primary importance, I began to concentrate on what would happen in my story. First I visualized the action, and then I thought of how to say it in words. I realized that all I had to do was communicate the action as simply as possible. It also dawned on me that I could channel my natural inclination to visualize into my writing. That is how I wrote my first book; the story unfolded in my head, like a movie. Years later, I learned that, when writing, C. S. Lewis saw pictures, too; with Lewis, "images always come first."

The approach I used for illustrating my first book was derived from drawings I did one day while talking on the telephone. As I talked, I doodled, and I noticed that the doodles had a fresh look—the lines appeared to be moving across the page. In addition to my preconception about writing, I also had a preconceived idea of how the illustrations for that book would evolve. I had assumed they would require much effort. But instead, while my mind was busy with the phone conversation, I let the lines flow effortlessly through my hand onto the paper; they seemed to have a life and an intelligence of their own. Of course, it subsequently took considerable work and effort to develop the doodles into appropriate illustrations, but that process took place at a later stage.

When asked why they want to write children's books, many people reply, "I love children." Sentimentality, unfortunately, is no help; in fact, it is a hindrance. Sentimentality does not replace the craft that is essential in making good children's books. My first obligation is to the book, not to the audience. Only by understanding the book's structure and how it functions can I make a good book.

Rather than asking whether I am happy with a book, I ask, "Is the book happy? Are the illustrations happy?" In other words, I want to know if the story is told with clarity. Are the characters unique? Is the setting specific? Is the ending consistent with the beginning? Are the scale, size, and shape of the book suited to its content and mood? Are the parts of a book coordinated into a coherent whole?

After I consider these questions, I understand the needs of the book, and I can begin to know if the book is happy. The integrity and clarity of that book are my primary concerns.

GENERAL COMMENTARY

Zena Sutherland

SOURCE: "Uri Shulevitz," in *Children & Books, Ninth Edition,* Longman, 1997, p. 137.

Uri Shulevitz works chiefly in ink, sometimes using it in combination with wash. For the illustrations in ***Maximilian's World*** by Mary Stolz, he used a Japanese reed pen. In Isaac Bashevis Singer's ***The Fools of Chelm,*** his line drawings have a grave yet comic quality that befits the folktale style. In illustrating Arthur Ransome's **The Fool of the World and the Flying Ship,** for which Shulevitz won the 1969 Caldecott Medal, his pictures in brilliant color are faithful to the art style of the Russian background of the book. In **Hanukah Money,** his scruffy, cheerful figures echo the humor of a classic story by Shloem Aleichem. Shulevitz has illustrated with sensitivity the stories of many writers, but he has never surpassed the evocative mood and the harmony of pictures and text in his own **One Monday Morning, Rain Rain Rivers,** and **Dawn,** which was a Hans Christian Andersen Honor Book.

TITLE COMMENTARY

📖 **THE FOOL OF THE WORLD AND THE FLYING SHIP: A RUSSIAN TALE (adapted by Arthur Ransome, 1968)**

Paul Heins

SOURCE: A review of *The Fool of the World and the Flying Ship: A Russian Tale,* in *The Horn Book Magazine,* Vol. XLV, No. 1, February, 1969, p. 43.

Choosing a story from *Old Peter's Russian Tales,* the artist has faithfully depicted the action in which the scorned younger son of peasants—the Fool of the World—is rewarded for his kindness to "an ancient old man" and goes on to win the Czar's daughter. In line drawings with watercolor wash predominantly yellow and green, the artist captures the gauche personalities of the peasant imagination and portrays the flat and ample Russian landscape. The flying ship is a ship with sails, enabling the illustrator to secure movement and variety by alternating aerial with earth-bound scenes. The final two-page spread glows with color as the artist permits himself at last a greater use of blue and red. If the transformation of the Fool of the World suggests the final scene in a Russian ballet based on folklore, the illustrator has not been unfaithful to the story but has simply added to it a justifiable element of visual splendor.

Sister M. Etheldreda

SOURCE: A review of *The Fool of the World and the Flying Ship: A Russian Tale,* in *Catholic Library World,* Vol. 41, No. 5, January, 1970, p. 316.

One of the most exciting of all the Russian folk tales, retold by Arthur Ransome and illustrated by Uri Shulevitz, deservingly took the Caldecott Medal Award as the most distinguished illustrated book for 1968. No age limit should be set to this beautiful book—which because it is folk literature, belongs to people of all

times and all ages. The illustrations are a perfect complement to the tale and will rejoice the mind and heart of anyone who appreciates exceptional talent as shown by illustrators like Uri Shulevitz. Highly recommended for all school libraries.

The Times Literary Supplement

SOURCE: A review of *The Fool of the World and the Flying Ship: A Russian Tale,* in *The Times Literary Supplement,* No. 3589, December 11, 1970, p. 1448.

Arthur Ransome's retelling of **The Fool of the World and the Flying Ship** (first published in *Old Peter's Russian Tales*) is wonderfully accomplished, a primer for picture story book writers. In relating how the fool, assisted to the hilt by eight peasants invested with magical powers, outwits the Tsar and wins the hand of his daughter. Mr. Ransome creates a context in which children can come to expect the unexpected; his characterization within a small compass and his conscious but unselfconscious simplification of thought and language are a delight. Uri Shulevitz's cheerful, spacious pen and water-colour illustrations, which won the Caldecott Medal, are a little reminiscent of early Jack Yeats. The only disappointment is the Princess who is, after all, the prize. She barely drops a curtsey. The book should surely have ended with her and the fool, together at last.

📖 **HANUKAH MONEY (written by Shloem Aleichem; translated and adapted by Shulevitz and Elizabeth Shub, 1978)**

Pamela D. Pollack

SOURCE: "Christmas Books '78: a Mixed Bag," in *School Library Journal,* Vol. 25, No. 2, October, 1978, pp. 112-15.

For Jewish readers, the season's only payoff is **Hanukah Money.** Sholem Aleichem's comic sketches of a shtetl Hanukah have robust humor, as when, at Aunt Pessl's insistence, her nephews wipe their noses on her apron ("Good, good, blow real good! Don't be stingy!"). Shulevitz retains that earthiness in his translation (done with Elizabeth Shub) but refines some of it out of his spare, clean illustrations, well done as they are in the Sendakian Eastern European tradition.

Paul Heins

SOURCE: A review of *Hanukah Money,* in *The Horn Book Magazine,* Vol. LIV, No. 6, December, 1978, pp. 626-27.

A vignette of pre-World War I Eastern European Jewish life, in which the home ritual of lighting Hanukah candles and the traditional practice of frying potato pancakes becomes intertwined with the holiday custom of giving money to children as a gift for a joyous season. Told in the first person, the story not only reflects the exuberance of two young boys but by its remarkable economy of style humorously portrays the idiosyncracies of the grownups. For example, the cook Breineh is "a dark woman with a moustache," and Aunt Pessl, "a tiny woman with one black eyebrow and one white." Appropriately colored in somber tones of brown, green, mauve, and yellow, the fine-line drawings are crystal clear. Beautifully composed, filled with picturesque detail, and genially depicting the absurdness of the human comedy, the illustrations are a perfect and loving accompaniment for the classic short story.

Donnarae MacCann and Olga Richard

SOURCE: "Picture Books for Children," in *Wilson Library Bulletin,* Vol. 61, No. 4, December, 1986, pp. 48-9.

Sholem Aleichem's **Hanukah Money** is in the naturalistic mode that lets the human condition surface, "warts" and all. And Uri Shulevitz draws upon this tradition in his illustrations with vigorous, affectionate scenes of peasant life. The narrator recounts incidents from his youth in which Hanukah was celebrated with special visits from relatives, with the ritual of uncles in deep concentration over a checker game, with the complicated business of counting one's Hanukah gift money when still too young to know a zloty from a groszy.

Shulevitz ransacks a turn-of-the-century cultural past and comes up with a convincing family, and in particular, a sensitive understanding of youngsters' behaviors. Motl and his brother are alternately impish, shy, awkward, inquisitive, energetic, naive, and up to a point, patient. The artist captures these traits in two ragamuffins with large ears and hand-me-down, oversized clothes. Moreover, everything about this warm, nuclear family is made to fit together aesthetically. Shulevitz constructs his illustrations as a builder might: one object over another and blending into one another with similar colors and lines until the whole page is a complex unit of varied, overlapping shapes. The black contour lines are edged with smaller lines to build bulk as well as to accent the forms. In addition to the solid, constructed quality, there is an element of playfulness in Shulevitz's style. Objects are all slightly askew, and at times completely whimsical, as when a character floats Chagall-like into a room with a platter of rubles.

THE GOLEM (written by Isaac Bashevis Singer, 1982)

Kirkus Reviews

SOURCE: A review of *The Golem,* in *Kirkus Reviews,* Vol. L, No. 22, November 15, 1982, p. 1237.

[*The Golem*] tells of Rabbi Leib of Prague and the golem he created to save a banker and other ghetto Jews from execution for false charges. The golem accomplishes the task he's charged with, but then refuses to bend down and allow the rabbi to erase from his forehead the name of God that gives him life. Because the rabbi has given in to his wife's pleas to use the golem for an unauthorized though charitable purpose, he has lost the power over his creation. Without dramatics, Singer makes a proper mythic melodrama of the early trial, bringing out the historical and elemental reality of the climate of injustice; and his account of the golem's subsequent misdeeds and confusion is all the more effective for reading like an unadorned record. This is strong material, and Singer shrewdly recognizes the psychological and philosophical reverberations without underlining, elaborating, or deviating from the straight account. (The only explicit speculation comes in the closing suggestion that perhaps love—here the housemaid Miriam's for the golem—"has even more power than a Holy Name.") Shulevitz's black-and-white chiaroscuro illustrations, on the other hand, give the events a remote and serious look and emphasize the monumental lifelessness of the golem. One longs for a glint of life or expression somewhere—but the legend can support Shulevitz's approach.

Betsy Hearne

SOURCE: A review of *The Golem,* in *Booklist,* Vol. 79, No. 7, December 1, 1982, p. 504.

Singer has maintained a fine balance between detailing this East European Yiddish legend and keeping to its traditional simplicity. One of the leading Jews of Prague is implicated in the nefarious accusation of stealing a child for blood to make matzoth. On the instructions of a heavenly messenger, the rabbi makes a clay giant, a golem named Joseph, to protect his people, giving it life with holy letters on its brow. Joseph does save the situation; yet his strength is subject to human misuse, and he begins to question and react against his monstrous, lonely condition. The touching affection that develops between him and a housemaid makes all the more poignant his inevitable fall and return to dust. Raising the classic question of the spirit as God's creation unlimitable by man's magic or logic, this is a more subtle, less symbolic version than Beverly Brodsky's stunning Caldecott Honor Book, *The Golem,* in its graphic interpretation. The meticulous textures and shading that give depth to Shulevitz's black-and-white drawings make an intense but low-key setting for the tale, casting the golem (who in one picture looks incongruously African) as an outsized misfit who dwarfs the architectural backgrounds of arches, spires, stairs, and ceilings.

Ethel R. Twichell

SOURCE: A review of *The Golem,* in *The Horn Book Magazine,* Vol. LIX, No. 1, February, 1983, pp. 48-9.

From time to time, according to legend, a truly holy man may be empowered to fashion a golem out of clay, inscribe his forehead with the sacred name of God, and send the living effigy forth to save the Jews. When a much-respected Jewish banker is wrongfully accused of stealing Count Bratislawski's daughter, a mysterious stranger commands the pious Rabbi Lieb to do these very things. In secrecy the rabbi shapes a golem, gives him the name Joseph, and commands him to find the girl. Joseph does as he is told and with the girl in his arms, bursts into the courtroom. The banker is exonerated. But Rabbi Lieb, persuaded by a nagging wife, is tempted to use the golem for his own purpose; whereupon, it functions wildly out of control, causing fear and consternation in the city. Only through the actions of Lieb's servant girl is Joseph, in a strange and powerful conclusion, finally laid to rest. As always, the author spins his tale with a sure hand and controls the pace like a true storyteller, imbuing even the clay giant with human needs and longings. The handsome black-and-white pictures are somber in tone; scenes are lit with the chiaroscuro technique reminiscent of the Renaissance against a background of shadowy interiors and medieval towns. But the lumbering figure of the golem–half human, half clay—captures most of the attention; his grotesque antics are depicted with understated humor and underscored by the ultimate sadness of his story.

THE STRANGE AND EXCITING ADVENTURES OF JEREMIAH HUSH (1986)

Christine Behrmann

SOURCE: A review of *The Strange and Exciting Adventures of Jeremiah Hush,* in *School Library Journal,* Vol. 33, No. 6, February, 1987, pp. 84-5.

Shulevitz, best known for his beautifully designed and executed picture books, tries a longer form with mixed results. This short book contains three stories about Jeremiah Hush, a proboscis monkey existing in another world, similar to ours except that it's completely populated by animals. In the first story, Jeremiah, wondering if he is missing something, visits a sort of disco, the Shake'n'Roll Dancin' Hole: a complete letdown. It is in story number two that he discovers what is lacking: friends with whom to share his adventures. In the concluding story, he and his new friends combine forces to defeat the efforts of a foxy cheater in a pie-eating contest. The tales are held together by the lightest of constructions and are marred by an inconsistency of tone that varies from ironic to arch to genuinely appealing. The first story, in which Jeremiah is rejected by a "slim," attractive giraffe, is adult in incident and style, while the second is overlong, with too much character introduction and too little plot. The third story is by far the best, uniting all of the positive elements of the book: gentle humor, warm characterizations, offbeat plot, and evocative, lyrical descriptions. The illustrations, not surprisingly, are more consistently appealing. The line drawings are full of witty detail, extending the occasional lightness of style to a prose all too often bogged down in leaden whimsy. This gets better as it goes along and it is an interesting, imaginative effort, but it is uneven: a promise more than a fulfillment.

Ilene Cooper

SOURCE: A review of *The Strange and Exciting Adventures of Jeremiah Hush,* in *Booklist,* Vol. 83, No. 11, February 11, 1987, p. 846.

The title refers to the three vignettes as "strange adventures" and that is quite accurate. Consider: the hero of the tale, Jeremiah Hush, a proboscis monkey, is a lonely fellow who reads with envy about the opening of the Shake'n'Roll Dancin' Hole where the clientele do the wiggle-waggle with great abandon. But when Jeremiah musters his courage and spends an evening at the club, it turns out to be a disaster—overpriced drinks and uninterested females. Adults who have spent a bad night at a singles' bar can relate to Jeremiah's misery, but kids may not quite comprehend the depth of his dejection. There is more audience appeal in the final two stories, one which sees Jeremiah making friends with a canine investigator who comes to solve the case of the monkey's missing umbrella; the other describes Jeremiah's adventures at the Orangutanville fair where Jeremiah must discover whether a pie-eating champ is on the level. Even in the first segment where Shulevitz's material seems out of sync with his audience, his writing is accomplished. Amusing, devilishly insightful, and highly original, these tales will stretch readers' minds, even if they don't fully understand the escapades. Special mention must be made of Shulevitz's single-page black-and-white drawings that pepper the book. The execution is excellent, but more noteworthy is the thought and whimsy in each picture. Of these, the jazzy re-creation of the Shake'n'Roll Dancin' Hole with its deco lines and 1980s sensibilities is the most memorable.

Betsy Hearne

SOURCE: A review of *The Strange and Exciting Adventures of Jeremiah Hush,* in *Bulletin of the Center for Children's Books,* Vol. 40, No. 7, March, 1987, p. 135.

Jeremiah Hush is a middle-aged monkey inhabiting "another solar system, on a strange planet curiously resembling our own." In three stories, Jeremiah ventures from his quiet, out-of-the-way home to go to a wild disco spot in town, to search his own neighborhood for a lost umbrella, and to enter a chocolate-banana-pecan-cream pie eating contest at a country fair. His experience at the Shake'n'Roll Dancin' Hole is unsettling and lonely, but later he makes friends with a Skye terrier detective and even admits to enjoying the excitement of capturing two foxy con artists. Although the "teleblablaphone" and "autodrivemobile" are obvious word play for the entertainment of children, some of the social

From Hosni the Dreamer: An Arabian Tale, *written by Ehud Ben-Ezer. Illustrated by Uri Shulevitz.*

satire is pitched to a more adult level, as in the barflies at the disco and the service mechanic's glib bill tabulation. On the other hand, Jeremiah's true relationships are childlike and appealing, though all the characters are odd, and the tenor of the whole narrative is, despite the title, more strange than exciting. The book is, nevertheless, impressive in design and illustration, with meticulously rendered, gray, pen-and-wash drawings that cast an unearthly spell of their own.

📖 *TODDLECREEK POST OFFICE* (1990)

Publishers Weekly

SOURCE: A review of *Toddlecreek Post Office,* in *Publishers Weekly,* Vol. 237, No. 43, October 26, 1990, p. 66.

In words that are spare and to the point, the story of Toddlecreek village and its post office unfolds. Postmaster Vernon Stamps was both kind enough to allow his post office to be used as the town's social center, and

wise enough to know that even if a less than interesting person repeats the same anecdotes, perhaps there is a duty to listen. Friends were always welcome—a pair of dogs, a retired lumberman, a lonely old lady whose lamp needed fixing. Into this genial hubbub came the steely postal inspector armed with the twin virtues—accuracy and efficiency. Displeased by this communal atmosphere, she closed the post office for good. More than a gathering place was lost: a way of life disappeared, and Toddlecreek was poorer for it. Shulevitz shows himself once again to be a master of the watercolor medium—each painting glows with inner light. This message is at once age-old and timely, but the subtlety of the narrative and the stylization of the art gear this work toward an older audience.

Ilene Cooper

SOURCE: A review of *Toddlecreek Post Office,* in *Booklist,* Vol. 87, No. 6, November 15, 1990, pp. 667-68.

The small village of Toddlecreek has its own post office. It's the place where postmaster Vernon Stamps arranges money orders and takes in letters. It is also the place where Silken the dog and loner Dexter Shuffles spend their days. Vernon wants to be helpful to his patrons, so he fixes Mrs. Woolsox's lamp and sews the buttons on Albert Flex's jacket. Then, one day, the postal inspector arrives; to her expert eye, "a small village like Toddlecreek does not have enough post-office business. Therefore, this post office must be closed." Readers, who have already sat through a tedious recitation of the post office's activities, might hope at this point for a happy ending. No such luck. Vernon locks up the post office, and the patrons are left to their own devices ("Silken was never seen again. . . . Some say she went north to join the wolves. Others say she was killed by a hunter"). Then the post office is torn down. Although this looks like a traditional picture book, it is certainly not for young children. Even middle-graders who are able to read it themselves may not be much moved by this "elegy to an America that was," as the flap copy puts it. As always, Shulevitz's artwork is striking. Here he uses morning golds and midnight blue; purples express the changing mood. The geometric-looking pictures have the feel of WPA art, which works in tandem with the story's messages about life in a slower time. This will be of most use as curriculum support in units about a changing America. . . . But don't put it with the picture books.

Betsy Hearne

SOURCE: A review of *Toddlecreek Post Office,* in *Bulletin of the Center for Children's Books,* Vol. 44, No. 5, January, 1991, p. 129.

This picture-book fable about society's decline of humane concern describes a village post office that's really a social center until an inspector closes it down. Vernon Stamps, the postmaster who has been kind to strays both human and canine, must lock up his benign shelter and go to "a big city far away, where there is much post-office business but little time for a friendly hello." The strays drift or die, the post office is torn down, and "all that remains are its two flower boxes." Shulevitz's watercolor art emphasizes angular shapes and, appropriately, sunset colors. The light fades with the appearance of the militaristic postal inspector, whose gray-blue gloom throws a shadow across the floor and drains the room of warmth. Don't look for realism here: the dog that's supposed to be "part wolf and part Alaskan sled dog" looks more like a hound, and the figures have an automaton quality almost like puppets. However, it's not the stylization as much as the portentous tone that will leave preschoolers puzzled. Discuss this one with independent readers, especially as a companion to the Provensens' *Shaker Lane* and other books marking the passage of time and its erosions of tradition.

Carolyn Vang Schuler

SOURCE: A review of *Toddlecreek Post Office,* in *School Library Journal,* Vol. 37, No. 1, January, 1991, p. 80.

Dexter Shuffles, Charlie Ax, and Mrs. Woolsox–all of whose names fit them to a tee–regularly visit postmaster Vernon Stamps at the Toddlecreek post office. Here, stories are told, pleasantries are exchanged, merchandise is bartered, and the villagers are comfortable with one another. Even Silken and the Mayor, neighborhood dogs, arrive daily to take their places on the sunny spots on the floor. However, all of this ends when an inspector arrives and decrees that there is not enough official post office business, and closes the building. Shulevitz's fresh, orderly, yet angular, watercolors, which fill up the right-hand pages in complement to the text on the left, are just right for group sharing. They will also inspire "pore-over" times for one-on-one readers. The appearance of the postal inspector casts a gloom upon that unsuspecting group, and the characters magnificently become wooden in personality and expression, clearly indicating how stunned they are at the news. Both the illustrations—reminiscent of slow, quiet ways—and the original, easily told tale, create a sense of nostalgia, a celebration of simpler times. The best element is the book's absolute success in recalling "what was" and introducing today's children to America's past.

Uri Shulevitz

SOURCE: "*Toddlecreek Post Office,*" in *Booklist,* Vol. 87, No. 10, January 15, 1991, pp. 1030-31.

Since 1969 I have spent summers in a small village in upstate New York. It used to have a tiny post office. The first time I went in to buy stamps, there was a gathering of dogs in front of the building. To enter, I had to step over a large dog lying inside, taking up a sizable portion of the floor. The post office was so small that, although there were few people there, it seemed crowded and busy. But nobody seemed in a hurry to do post office business. Later, when I got to know the postmaster, I was moved by his kindness to people and animals. It was all so different from the shops in Manhattan, where owners and cash registers were at times hardly distinguishable.

Years after the post office had closed down, and wishing to tell a story about it, I talked to the now retired postmaster. He told me about the post office "regulars" who used to hang out there and about the villagers who came in with various requests, such as sharpening a saw or sewing on buttons, and how he obliged them. He related stories of the animal "regulars" like the huge, fierce-looking, but gentle dog I stepped over. And he described the woman postal inspector's unexpected appearance, which ultimately led to the post office's closing.

I worked on **Toddlecreek Post Office** for nearly two years, basing it on my personal experience as well as on what I learned from the village postmaster. Although I didn't use every incident or detail—there were too many for a picture book—nor the exact time sequence, this book is faithful to the spirit of what happened. When I began writing the story, I hoped it would have a "happy" ending. But as I worked, the story began to "write itself." I knew better than to fight the story, and I let it be what it had to be. Thus, **Toddlecreek Post Office** is about the last day of a small village post office in rural America. Its structure is similar to that of a drama, with the post office interior its stage, and the story's characters entering and exiting. Lighting is the natural light in the course of a day, beginning with the colors of dawn, and ending with the darkness of night, thus completing the cycle and setting the mood.

It has been said that, "the more specific, the more universal." Working on this story, I realized that the small post office is larger than itself, that it stands for a vanishing America, an America with a soul, and a whole way of life in danger of extinction. And by extension, the story is also about conservation and preservation of that which isn't immediately or obviously useful. It is about loss and death as well.

Is the ending appropriate for a picture book? Is anything more appropriate than the truth? Children know what loss and death mean. Grief is no stranger to them; their lives are not all fun and roses. Since the story is true, and since the truth has a cathartic, cleansing effect—because it elicits true emotions, whereas artificial, sentimental stories do not—I decided to bow to the will of the story.

THE DIAMOND TREE: JEWISH TALES FROM AROUND THE WORLD (written by Howard Schwartz and Barbara Rush, 1991)

Hanna B. Zeiger

SOURCE: A review of *The Diamond Tree: Jewish Tales from around the World,* in *The Horn Book Magazine,* Vol. LXVIII, No. 1, January-February, 1992, pp. 83-4.

A beautifully designed and produced collection comprises fifteen Jewish tales that span many centuries and come for the most part from countries of the Middle East, Africa, and eastern Europe. There are stories that readers will recognize as familiar tales, such as "The Bear and the Children," which is a variant of "The Wolf and the Seven Kids." "The Water Witch" and "The Diamond Tree" have elements of "Hansel and Gretel," and the character in "Katanya," from Turkey, is similar to Thumbelina. There are moral tales that teach lessons, such as the fifth-century story "A Tale of Two Chickens," in which the scrupulously honest rabbi receives his just reward. In "The Prince Who Thought He Was a Rooster," a nineteenth-century tale attributed to Rabbi Nachman of Bratslav, the lesson is of the genuine teacher who can descend to his student's level in order to raise him up. "Moving a Mountain" is a chance to enjoy another story about the inhabitants of Chelm, and there is even a story about a giant who went with Noah on the ark. Uri Shulevitz's watercolors, which illustrate some of the stories, add just the right touch of wit and fantasy.

Susan Giffard

SOURCE: A review of *The Diamond Tree: Jewish Tales from around the World,* in *School Library Journal,* Vol. 38, No. 3, March, 1992, p. 252.

Drawing together the threads of Jewish folk literature from places as distant as Yemen and Eastern Europe, Morocco and Germany, and ranging over 15 centuries, Schwartz and Rush weave a rich tapestry that shows the diversity of Jewish culture. In this collection of 15 stories, Elijah and King Solomon rub shoulders with witches, goblins, and the fools of the town of Chelm. This is often a benevolent universe where gentle justice reigns. Young Chusham, for example, is loved in spite of his foolishness. The story of Og, the giant who takes refuge on the ark during the great flood, illustrates the value of cooperation and repaying kindness while demonstrating the rewards of honesty. Other stories show similarities to those from other traditions. A particularly moving tale tells of how a little bird persuades King Solomon of the cruelty and stupidity of building a palace of birds' beaks. In all, the language is simple and vivid, and the narrative moves along at a good pace. The generous amount of white space makes the book accessible to younger readers. Ten tales are accompanied by Shulevitz's bright, dramatic watercolor paintings. Storytellers of varying degrees of experience and ability will find this a particularly valuable resource. An excellent collection for reading aloud or alone, with selections that are not readily available in other sources.

Anne Roiphe

SOURCE: A review of *The Diamond Tree: Jewish Tales from around the World,* in *New York Times Book Review,* April 12, 1992.

Jewish folk tales and Jewish stories belong in the library alongside the tales of other peoples, alongside Andersen and Grimm, Norse adventures and Indian myths. Every culture invents stories, shapes them to fit a communal soul, tells them to its children and passes them down through the generations. Reading these traditional stories we recognize one another's fears and triumphs; we recognize our own. A story can turn strangers into friends.

The Diamond Tree: Jewish Tales from around the World brings us tales from biblical Palestine, Iraq, Babylon, Yemen and Eastern Europe. These old stories, selected and retold by Howard Schwartz and Barbara Rush, illustrated by Uri Shulevitz, date from the 3rd to the 13th centuries and are delightful, charming inventions. Some have moral instructions hidden in their plots, some are pure entertainment reflecting ordinary people's fears of goblins and bears. Og, the biblical giant, hitches a ride on the roof of Noah's Ark and the animals join together to provide food and comfort for him (Palestine). A poor widow is given a magic date and receives a tiny daughter and a gold coin (Turkey). Children who feed crumbs to a fish are rescued by the fish when a wicked witch imprisons them under the water (Orient). In another tale, foolish men try to move a mountain in a heat wave, then believe they have succeeded (Poland).

These sometimes intricate plots are told clearly, with wit and clever timing; the oddness and the oldness of the stories lend them color and meaning. This book will give children great pleasure. Uri Shulevitz's full-page watercolor illustrations are imaginative and interesting, and the stories themselves will stimulate that place in the child's mind where magic and truth embrace. For the adult who may also read this book, or may read it aloud to children, there is an additional treat in the notes. Here the editors document the origins of the tales and point out the overlapping of events and themes with some other familiar European stories, such as "Hansel and Gretel," "Little Red Riding Hood" and "Thumbelina."

THE SECRET ROOM (1993)

Publishers Weekly

SOURCE: A review of *The Secret Room,* in *Publishers Weekly,* Vol. 240, No. 41, October 11, 1993, p. 85.

Though the exact setting is unspecified (Turkey? the Central Asian steppes? Egypt? Greece?), this tale is nonetheless imbued with very strong atmosphere. A liberal sprinkling of Mediterranean and Middle Eastern architectural elements (minarets, onion-domes, brightly tiled roofs, window moldings right out of *Aladdin*) are given a postmodern twist, enlivened by Shulevitz's stained-glass-bright watercolors and crazy-quilt graphics. Impressed with the cleverness of a simple man he meets in the desert, a king appoints him treasurer. The man quickly gains the monarch's favor—as well as the envy of the chief counselor, who plots to bring him down by accusing him of embezzlement. A search of the elderly man's home reveals a secret room, but instead of containing plunder as the wicked counselor has suggested, it's empty except for some sand and a small window—a place, the man tells the king, where he can retreat to remind himself that he's still the same simple fellow he always was. The story's message—that wealth and power don't have to corrupt, and that the measure of true wisdom is humility—carries echoes of many classic fairy tales, but the fresh delivery is Shulevitz's own.

Lauralyn Persson

SOURCE: A review of *The Secret Room,* in *School Library Journal,* Vol. 40, No. 1, January, 1994, p. 116.

A picture book of riddles, wordplay, and royal intrigue. When the king rewards a wise man's cleverness by appointing him treasurer, a villainous counselor accuses him of stealing gold and hiding it in his house. A mysterious secret room turns out to be where the treasurer goes to reflect on his good fortune and not get "too full of" himself. The writing is economical and concrete. Unfortunately, the gentle message about tempering gratitude with humility doesn't seem to fit with the rest of the tale and isn't one that will be comprehensible (or of interest) to youngsters. Shulevitz's artwork is superb. Bright, angular, stylized figures move in a timeless, dreamlike atmosphere and his use of light, shadow, and color to convey mood is extraordinary. Since this effort is unquestionably an artistic and literary success, many libraries will want to buy it. But is it a book children will like? Probably not.

Betsy Hearne

SOURCE: A review of *The Secret Room,* in *Bulletin of the Center for Children's Books,* Vol. 47, No. 6, February, 1994, p. 202.

Traveling through the desert, a king asks a stranger, "Why is your head gray and your beard black?" "Because my head is older than my beard," comes the reply. "You must not tell this to anyone until you have seen my face ninety-nine times," orders the king so he can go home and riddle his chief counselor. The stranger does tell the answer—after accepting payment of ninety-nine copper coins stamped with the king's face—and eventually replaces the jealous counselor after showing wisdom equal to his cleverness. Shulevitz has laced together folkloric motifs with an admirable simplicity that matches his clean compositions. The tempera paintings are intensely focused, with plenty of white space to offset sharply contrasting hues and angular shapes. There's an especially sly humor of expression—or expressionlessness—in the royal entourage and a certain kinship of features between the supercilious camel and the bad-tempered counselor. Despite its flaring color patterns, this is an understated book that will give young listeners solid satisfaction. The setting and costumes appear to be Russian-influenced Muslim, but there's nary a hint of the story's source.

Donnarae MacCann and Olga Richard

SOURCE: "Picture Books for Children," in *Wilson Library Bulletin,* Vol. 68, No. 7, March, 1994, pp. 122-23.

Shulevitz tells his story in such a compressed manner that it is easy to misjudge it as overly abbreviated. Actually, however, this concise lesson-story contains all that is needed to convey a sharp disparity between wise and foolish, honest and dishonest.

A hermit explains to his king why the hermit's beard is black and his hair white—namely, his head is older than his beard. The king presents this puzzle to his dull-witted counselor, who cannot answer correctly but finds the hermit and offers to purchase the answer. When the wise old man is then hauled before the royal court (having supposedly violated the command that he not explain the secret until he has seen the king's face ninety-nine times), the payment proves that he did indeed keep his promise—all ninety-nine coins contain images of the king. Plagued by further conspiracies, the hermit—now the royal treasurer—explains his innocence:

> Your Majesty, I am grateful for all the . . . riches you have given me. But I must not get too full of myself. So I come every day to this [empty] room to remind myself that I am still the same man with the gray head and the black beard whom you once met in the desert.

With this answer, the man is rewarded with the counselor post, for as the king says: "I knew you were clever. Now I know you are wise."

If all these explicit messages sound didactic, be assured that the artist's humor and resplendent court scenes are sufficient compensation. Shulevitz has a truly momentous design talent. He begins with a platoon of little Napoleons marching after their unflappable monarch. He then alternates lavishly colored interiors with unpretentious desert scenes, taking liberties with perspective and dividing space imaginatively (as, for example, when he fractures the king into approximately fifty distinct space divisions while sustaining the dominant shape). This is crisp, decorative work—Shulevitz at his best.

THE GOLDEN GOOSE (retold by Shulevitz, 1995)

Kirkus Reviews

SOURCE: A review of *The Golden Goose,* in *Kirkus Reviews,* Vol. LXIII, No. 19, October 1, 1995, p. 1428.

A drily entertaining version of the tale of the simpleton and his golden goose. Whoever touches the goose sticks to it, but the simpleton doesn't notice and wanders into a city where a king has issued a proclamation that anyone who can make his daughter laugh can marry her. The simpleton immediately heads for the palace, followed by a stuck chain of people and this parade makes the princess laugh. Then there is one more ordeal, which the simpleton easily carries out. Deadpan humor enlivens the telling, written in a style that is so elliptical as to make it read as if something were missing. The most prominent feature of the illustrations are the exaggerated and rigid outlines of angular characters and impossibly wobbly houses. Shulevitz achieves his strongest effects by putting the jagged, colored figures against white backgrounds. He deliberately creates dissonance between text and pictures, and the success of this varies from page to page: Several tableaux of trains of characters behind the oblivious simpleton are perfect in timing and delivery, but offer no clue as to why everyone comes unstuck.

Donna L. Scanlon

SOURCE: A review of *The Golden Goose,* in *School Library Journal,* Vol. 41, No. 12, December, 1995, p. 97.

The familiar Grimm tale of a simpleton who seeks his fortune gets a fresh treatment. The youngest of three sons is rewarded for his kindheartedness with a gleaming golden goose to which a chain of unwilling companions becomes attached. He makes a sad princess laugh with his silly procession and, after completing a task set by her disgruntled father, wins her hand. Shulevitz's retelling develops the part of the story involving the human chain more fully than other versions. He also incorporates an appealing repetitive rhyme that invites audience participation and adds dimension. However, two of the three tasks set by the king in most versions are omitted, resulting in an awkward, unfinished feeling to that section of the tale. The vibrant watercolor paintings, full of blocky angular characters and quirky off-kilter buildings, enhance the story. Text and illustrations mesh well, and the artist makes skillful use of both contrast and white space. The goose seems to glow within the largely warm palette of jewel-like colors with cool blue and green accents. The simpleton's face radiates innocence and goodness and, in spite of the slight awkwardness mentioned above, this is a fun version of a traditional tale.

Elizabeth Bush

SOURCE: A review of *The Golden Goose,* in *Bulletin of the Center for Children's Books,* Vol. 49, No. 5, January, 1996, p. 171.

This straightforward retelling of a simpleton's magnetic march to claim the hand of a princess should attract a new generation of listeners with its challenging chant, "Hokety, pokety, stickety, stuck, the poor peasant was down on his luck./ Wiggle and pull, he couldn't shake loose; he, too, had to follow the simpleton's goose." With eight opportunities to chime in, everyone should catch on by the time the palace guards bring up the rear. Shulevitz's pied palette and tipsy architecture set the stage for the angular, crimson-nosed characters who bumble along their journey in a droll daze. Unfortunately, a few visual glitches mar the effect: some of the spreads are confusingly composed, and the audience is never treated to a glimpse of the whole posse connected at once. Nonetheless, this title's sure to incite some giggles and provide a time-honored lesson in how to "get into a straight line."

Mary M. Burns

SOURCE: A review of *The Golden Goose,* in *The Horn Book Magazine,* Vol. LXXII, No. 1, January-February, 1996, p. 81.

Although no particular source is cited, the story of the simpleton whose kindness eventually wins him a princess bride has been commonly ascribed to the Brothers Grimm. The plot is immediately set in motion as, one by one, a peasant's three sons set forth to chop wood. Only the third, the simpleton, responds with kindness to a mysterious old man who begs for food; he is rewarded with the gift of a golden goose. The gleaming bird attracts the attention of a motley crew, including the daughters of the innkeeper in whose hostel the simpleton spends the night. Hoping only for a single feather, each finds herself stuck, the first to the goose, the others to one another—a condition that applies to everyone the simpleton encounters as he wends his way to the city, where the king has offered his daughter in marriage to the person who can make her laugh. This is a lively rendition of an appealing tale, complemented with illustrations in an angular, puppetlike style that recalls the story's folk origins. The skillful incorporation of an insistent refrain, modified for each character, begs for audience participation, as in this description of the first victim: "Hokety, pokety, stickety, stuck, poor Annabelle was down on her luck. / Wiggle and pull, she couldn't shake loose, and she had to stay with the simpleton's goose." The participants may be unlucky, but readers of this concisely told, artfully synchronized picture book will be winners.

HOSNI THE DREAMER: AN ARABIAN TALE (written by Ehud Ben-Ezer, 1997)

Publishers Weekly

SOURCE: A review of *Hosni the Dreamer: An Arabian Tale,* in *Publishers Weekly,* Vol. 244, No. 26, June 30, 1997, p. 75.

A lone dreamer in the midst of practically-minded peers may be well-trod territory in the picture book kingdom, but this jauntily illustrated retelling of an old Arabian folktale puts a fresh face on the familiar theme. Caldecott Medalist Shulevitz's color-saturated watercolors, ablaze with the fiery hues of the desert, play up the tale's exotic setting, defined not only by the broad expanses of sand and rock but also the details—bright robes, headdresses and tents, canopy-topped camels, stone stairways and minarets, and a bustling bazaar. Pivotal, more internal scenes are awash in soothing blue. Israeli author Ben-Ezer smoothly recounts the tribulations and triumphs of Hosni, a shepherd boy who longs for travel and adventure. His dreams come true when the sheik takes him to the city on a camel-trading trip. Ridiculed by his fellow travelers for spending all his earnings to buy a single verse from an elderly man, Hosni finds that his money is well spent in the end, for by heeding the man's words ("Don't cross the water until you know its depth"), he spares both himself and a young maiden from the watery death that overtakes his once-sneering companions. In good fairy-tale fashion, the pair lives happily ever after. A literary magic-carpet ride.

Cathryn M. Mercier

SOURCE: A review of *Hosni the Dreamer: An Arabian Tale,* in *The Horn Book Magazine,* Vol. LXXIII, No. 5, September-October, 1997, p. 585.

In an "Arabian story" (though one not graced by a source note) Hosni is regarded as a fool by his fellow shepherds when during his trip to the city he spends all his money on a verse. But his purchase saves his life and secures his happiness and fortune. Once again, Uri Shulevitz excels in celebrating the story of an unlikely hero. Stylized watercolor illustrations at once view the main character with quiet humor and individual dignity. The opening page finds Hosni slightly left of center, head tilted right, large oval eyes gazing left; his loose robes, substantial turban, and staff ground him. Yet, we recognize Hosni as a dreamer, one who talks to sheep by day and who, in the evenings, chooses his elders' stories over the chatter of the other shepherds. When a sick man's fate allows Hosni to join a caravan into the city, the artist shifts from portraiture to equally stylized landscape, where sand-dripped mountains dwarf the caravan of travelers. Most striking in these wide desert vistas and in the contrasted intricate, variegated market scenes is Shulevitz's command of white as color. Stark, pure white intensifies the desert heat against which the sunniest and most lustrous watercolors stand out with particular brilliance. This simply told story wins with its characterization—verbal and visual—of the charming Hosni, whose love of story brings him happiness.

Robin Tzannes

SOURCE: "Operation Desert Dream," in *New York Times Book Review,* November 16, 1997, p. 42.

What child has never been teased and left out because he had a dream or a charm that no one else could understand? *Hosni the Dreamer,* written by Ehud Ben-Ezer and based on an old Arabian folk tale, is the story of a young shepherd who, in the face of ridicule and scorn, maintains a pure and steady faith in his charm. In the end, this faith saves him from a terrible tragedy and makes him a rich and happy man.

Unlike the other shepherds, who waste their time telling jokes, Hosni loves listening to the tales of the tribal elders. At night he has vivid and beautiful dreams of the city, which he confides only to his sheep. Finally, when he joins a group of shepherds going to sell some camels, he gets his chance to see the city.

It is even more exciting than Hosni had imagined, with bustling markets selling robes and carpets and food. But Hosni shuns these temptations, and spends all his money to buy a verse from a wise man. This verse, "Don't cross the water until you know its depth," seems obscure, but Hosni accepts it as a charm without question.

From Snow, *written and illustrated by Uri Shulevitz.*

On their return journey, the shepherds have to cross a riverbed that had been dry before. Hosni, remembering the prophetic verse, warns them not to step into the water, but he is ignored. Horrified, he watches all the shepherds drown, followed by the servant of a rich young woman named Zobeide.

Hosni and Zobeide, lone survivors on the riverbank, decide to travel together. Soon they fall in love and get married. With Zobeide's riches they are able to live happily for many years.

This very charming story is beautifully illustrated by Uri Shulevitz, whose well-known books include **The Fool of the World and the Flying Ship.** One can see the influence of Persian miniatures here in his characters' highly expressive gestures and postures, and in the delightful variety of textile patterns. These colorful striped, checkered and flowered fabrics help to relieve the monotony of the endless desert, with its sand-colored rocks, sand-colored camels and sand-colored cities. These illustrations also have a rich, luminous quality that works especially well in the picture of the

golden dream reflected upon the dreamer's face, and of the moonlit desert glowing beneath a vast, starry sky.

Shulevitz's illustrations evoke a strong sense of place, which enhances the traditional flavor of Ben-Ezer's accomplished storytelling. Pictures and text work together to create a portrait of a humble and compassionate hero that young readers should love.

Ellen D. Warwick

SOURCE: A review of *Hosni the Dreamer: An Arabian Tale,* in *School Library Journal,* Vol. 43, No. 12, December, 1997, p. 81.

A "wise-fool" story set in the deserts of Arabia. Hosni, a simple shepherd, works for a sheikh. Alone much of the day, he talks to his sheep; at night, he listens to the tribal elders' tales and dreams of faraway cities. When the sheikh goes to a city to sell camels, he takes some shepherds with him, including Hosni. Each one receives a golden dinar to spend as he pleases. Dazzled, the man wanders the busy streets and crowded markets, finally exchanging his dinar for a verse, words of wisdom from an old man. Of course, the other shepherds make fun of Hosni, and, of course, the verse—a bit of homely advice—not only saves his life, but also serves to introduce him to his future wife. Basing his story on a folktale, Ben-Ezer uses crisp, vivid language throughout; he includes descriptions and phrases that suggest the tale's setting. Shulevitz's illustrations add a light, comic touch. The sheikh appears stubby and self-important; the other shepherds seem foolishly self-congratulatory. Hosni alone has a quiet dignity. The desert provides the backdrop for most of the story; its stylized landforms echo the shapes of the city towers, which in turn repeat the shapes of the shepherds' turbans and camel packs. Colors include soft greens, blues, and reds, but a desert gold predominates. The hue suggests both Hosni's good fortune and the richness of his dreams.

📖 *SNOW* (1998)

Hazel Rochman

SOURCE: A review of *Snow,* in *Booklist,* Vol. 95, No. 4, October 15, 1998, p. 418.

As he did in *Dawn* and the Caldecott Honor Book *The Treasure,* Shulevitz captures the small child's joyful vision, which can see a world in Blake's grain of sand—or in a snowflake. The innocent, small boy with his dog, uncluttered by adult experience, can see clearly what is happening around him. He counts each snowflake, one by one, until the world is white and the snow is everywhere. In contrast, the suave, sophisticated adults—the bookish authority, the cosmopolitan, the guy with a boombox, the brash announcer on TV—they are dismissive, they are certain: "No snow." But they are wrong. The setting of the clear, lovely, detailed line-and-watercolor paintings is a combination of shtetl folk art and urban contemporary, until finally the gray sky and buildings and city are totally new and white. Then the boy is free to imagine the characters of Mother Goose dancing with him and his dog in the white world of snow. Like the pictures, the rhythm of the simple, poetic words evoke the child's physical immediacy and sense of wonder as he watches snow "floating, floating through the air, falling, falling everywhere." Kids will enjoy the small child's triumph in the fact that he is right, even as they will recognize the exhilaration of a snowfall that changes what you thought you knew.

Kirkus Reviews

SOURCE: A review of *Snow,* in *Kirkus Reviews,* Vol. LXVI, No. 20, October 15, 1998, p. 1537.

Shulevitz implies that there is much to be said for youthful hope amid all the dour nay-saying from adults. Here, early flakes hold out the promise to a boy and his dog of the season's first snowfall, and prompt elders to pooh-pooh any chance of accumulation. As if by force of will, aided and abetted by the mysteries of nature—and despite radio and TV forecasts to the contrary—the flakes keep coming, swirling, dusting, covering. Finally, the town is draped in an encompassing cloak of snow; a number of storybook characters (that had been images on the facade of a children's bookstore) break into a winter dance with the young boy, giving the book a pleasantly fantastical turn. The small town European setting is the sort that Shulevitz does best: evocative, timeless, and as irresistible as the first snow.

Marianne Saccardi

SOURCE: A review of *Snow,* in *School Library Journal,* Vol. 44, No. 12, December, 1998, p. 92.

When a young boy sees a single snowflake fall, he rejoices that a major storm is on the way, despite predictions to the contrary. But it is the child who prevails as the "snowflakes keep coming and coming and coming." Shulevitz's outstanding illustrations, rendered in watercolor and pen and ink, enrich and extend the brief text. The boy and his dog appear in the lower right-hand corner of the appropriately white front endpapers, arms and legs joyfully pummeling the air, and readers can almost forecast his announcement, "It's snowing." Pictures are framed in varying amounts of white space, the largest frames engulfing the nay-saying adults. The illustrations gradually build to a two-page spread in which "the whole city is white." Shulevitz's cartoons are filled with humorous touches: buildings tilt; an oversized woman carries a tiny umbrella; a tall man wears an outrageously tall hat; a radio almost as big as the person carrying it appears to have eyes, nose, and mouth. The characters displayed in the window of "Mother Goose Books" come to life to cavort with the child among the swirling flakes. Youngsters will joyfully join the boy in his winter-welcoming dance.

Mary M. Burns

SOURCE: A review of *Snow,* in *The Horn Book Magazine,* Vol. LXXV, No. 1, January-February, 1999, p. 55.

Like most creative artists who are also critics, Shulevitz displays time and again in his own work the criteria that are the foundation of his critical theories. Snow is no exception. Through a minimalist text and carefully composed illustrations, it demonstrates his belief that the true picture book, with its inevitable melding of words and art, is a distinct genre. The premise is as simple as it is universal (at least in cold climates): the transforming power of a snowstorm. The setting is a dour, gray little town suggesting an Eastern European locale of old—except for television and radio. Neither of the latter is particularly prescient when it comes to predicting weather, for "snowflakes don't listen to radio, / snowflakes don't watch television." Only a hopeful small boy recognizes the first snowflake as a harbinger of the wonder to come. Nor is he discouraged as one adult after another tries to disabuse him. With each turn of the page, marvels occur that are presented only in the illustrations: the rooftops gradually whiten; the village becomes an enchanted landscape; nursery rhyme characters emerge from their niches in the Mother Goose bookstore, joining the small boy in a joyous winter ballet. As in Shulevitz's **Dawn,** the changes are gradual and logical-not quite as dramatic perhaps, but nonetheless satisfying, with a touch of the fantastic. The palette is appropriately subdued, depending in the concluding pages upon the contrast between a freshly blue sky and snow-covered buildings rather than brilliant colors for effect.

Additional coverage of Shulevitz's life and career is contained in the following sources published by The Gale Group: *Contemporary Authors,* **Vols. 9-12R;** *Contemporary Authors New Revision Series,* **Vol. 3;** *Dictionary of Literary Biography,* **Vol. 61;** *Major Authors and Illustrators for Children and Young Adults;* *Something about the Author,* **Vols. 3, 50, 106.**

Mildred Pitts Walter

1922-

American author of fiction, nonfiction, and picture books.

Major works include *Mariah Loves Rock* (1988), *Have a Happy . . .* (1989), *Two and Too Much* (1990), *Mississippi Challenge* (1992), *Second Daughter: The Story of a Slave Girl* (1996).

For more information on Walter's career prior to 1988, see *CLR,* Vol. 15.

INTRODUCTION

Known for her sensitive treatment of African-American history and community in works for children and young adults, Walter is noted by critics for her strong portrayals of complex and realistic African-American characters. As a writer for *Kirkus Reviews* remarked, "Walter tells her realistic story lightly, but with precision: her characters are fully realized, their relationships believable." Responsibility and family life are prominent topics in Walter's books; family relationships are represented as layered and complex, and often difficult. The role of community, especially African-American communities, is also central to Walter's books. Community relationships, too, are portrayed as complex, with communities sometimes coming together to support her young protagonists and sometimes, on the other hand, presenting obstacles to their individual goals. Walter has been commended for dealing with difficult subjects—like unemployment, divorce, and fatherless families—with sensitivity and realism. Critics have praised her for remaining true to her subjects, and filling her stories with emotion. In *Twentieth Century Children's Writers,* Carolyn Shute remarked that Walter's works are characterized by their "honesty and integrity," adding, "Walter's writing resonates with feeling and conviction of purpose."

Another central element in Walter's work is the theme of transformation. Her characters are frequently faced with a difficult situation—from family changes to slavery—to which they must respond. Through their choices Walter's characters are transformed into everyday heroes, and her readers are subtly encouraged to make such brave decisions for themselves. The author explained her motivation for writing in *Something about the Author (SATA)*: "I have tried to show the dynamics of choice, courage, and change in my books so that all readers can, through the experiences of black characters, become thoughtful; and so that black readers, through those experiences, can not only become thoughtful but aware of themselves as well." By celebrating the courage of her protagonists, Walter creates warm, rich books that reflect an understanding of children and their problems.

Biographical Information

The eighth child of a lumberman and a midwife, Walter was born in rural Louisiana and grew up facing the twin obstacles of poverty and racial prejudice. Walter drew strength from her home and community and has written of the enormous support she received from her large family and the tightly knit African-American communities in which she lived. While times were extremely tough, particularly through the years of the Depression, rural black communities in the South formed support networks for their members. Walter's sense of community, formed in her Louisiana childhood, remains with her and is present in her books for children. She was the first person in her family to go to college, and it was difficult—she sometimes worked two or three jobs to support herself and her studies. Walter told *SATA,* "Now, as I look back on those years, if the question is asked, Was it worth it? I can answer, Yes, it was, yes!" She graduated from Southern University in Louisiana in 1944, and moved to Los Angeles to become a teacher.

Once in Los Angeles, Walter was confronted with a new kind of racism: it was not the clear-cut segregation of the rural South, but a more subtle and insidious bigotry. It was in Los Angeles that Walter met and married Lloyd Walter, and both became active in the Congress on Racial Equality (CORE). CORE helped end many of the racist practices prevalent in California; for Walter, it was the beginning of a lifetime devoted to social responsibility and opposition to injustice. She was also a member of the board of directors of the American Civil Liberties Union of Southern California, and was an American delegate to the Second World Black and African Festival of the Arts and Culture in Lagos, Nigeria. Both Walter's social activism and her travels in Africa have informed her writing.

As a teacher, first in the elementary grades and then as a Head Start instructor, Walter found a serious lack of children's literature pertaining to African Americans. She complained about the dearth of materials to the owner of a local publishing company who encouraged her to write such books. "I didn't want to do it," Walter told *SATA,* "I didn't think I could become a writer." Walter's writing career began slowly; she enrolled in extension writing classes, and began writing book reviews for the *Los Angeles Times.* Eventually she gained enough confidence to write in earnest, and her first book, *Lillie of Watts: A Birthday Surprise,* was published in 1969.

Major Works

Modern American families often become complicated as divorce and remarriage create "blended" families, with stepchildren and half-siblings competing for the attention of busy parents. Walter's books about Mariah—*Mariah Loves Rock* and *Mariah Keeps Cool* (1990, now out of print)—reflect just such a complicated family. In *Mariah Loves Rock,* eleven-year-old Mariah is told that her father's daughter from a previous relationship, Denise, will be coming to live with her family. Besides fearing the loss of her father's attention, Mariah realizes that there may be material consequences to having an extra member in the household; she worries that there won't be enough money for her to see Sheik Bashara, her all-time favorite rock star, in concert. In the end, Mariah does go to the concert, but still worries over the imminent arrival of her half-sister. In this book and its sequel, *Mariah Keeps Cool,* Walter also addresses the jealousy felt by Mariah's mother for her stepdaughter and the adjustments that the family makes as they accommodate another member. In the sequel, Denise has moved in with the family, but will not obey rules and shows little respect for her extended family. Mariah deals with her fears and frustrations in a mature way, and triumphs in the big swim meet as well. Another book about the difficulties and joys of family is *Two and Too Much,* a picture book about Brandon, a young African-American boy who pitches in to help his mother by looking after his two-year-old sister, Gina. The job proves to be too big for the boy, as Gina runs wild: she gets into her mother's makeup, pours out her milk, and finally, disappears. While he and his mother search the house for his little

sister, Brandon realizes just how important his sister is to him, even though she's a big responsibility. The story of a realistic family situation, complete with frustrations as well as love, ends happily. Chris's family, too, has its ups and downs: the protagonist of *Have a Happy . . .* is upset because his father has been out of work for quite a while and Chris's birthday, which falls on Christmas Day, is coming up. The boy wants a bike so that he can take a newspaper delivery job, but is worried his family can't afford one. It is through the celebration of Kwanzaa with his Uncle Ronald that Chris learns the true importance of the seven values of the African-American holiday, and discovers the strength of his community when his extended family chips in to buy him the bike he wants. The boy's responsibility—he gets the newspaper job to help his family—is rewarded when he helps his dad find a job at the newspaper.

Mississippi Challenge is a nonfiction book for young adults chronicling the voting rights struggle experienced in the state of Mississippi through the mid-1900s. The book is unique in its focus on African Americans in leadership positions. Walter charts the movement toward equality from the beginnings of slavery in the state, through the Reconstruction period when former slave-owners controlled the government, and the era of mob lynching and the growth of the Ku Klux Klan, into the 1950s and 1960s with the actions of the Student Nonviolent Coordinating Committee and the Mississippi Freedom Democratic Party. Her account of the heroism of the black leaders and ordinary black people in the civil rights movement is meant to inspire readers while accurately depicting their struggle. A second book about the history of African Americans is *Second Daughter: The Story of a Slave Girl.* The book is the fictionalized account of the true story of Elizabeth Freeman, also known as Mum Bett. Bett was a slave in the Commonwealth of Massachusetts at the time of the Revolutionary War. In 1781 she sued for her freedom under Massachusetts law; the courts found in her favor, and she set the precedent that ended slavery in the state. *Second Daughter* is the story of Mum Bett told through Aissa, her younger sister. Because very little information about the sister exists, Walter is able to create a history for her, portraying her as more combative and outspoken than Mum Bett. Due to her quiet nature, Bett is frequently in the company of the men discussing the new Massachusetts constitution, which promotes equality for all men. This raises questions for her: if all men are equal, does that include slaves and women? These questions are pressed when Bett's owner moves to strike Aissa and Bett steps in, getting severely injured in the process. The incident encourages Bett to bring her case against her owners, citing abuse. The book culminates in a dramatic court scene, and finally, the hard-won freedom of the slaves.

Awards

In 1997 Walter won the Jane Addams Honor Book Award and the Virginia Library Association Jefferson Cup Worthy of Special Note Award for *Second Daughter: The*

Story of a Slave Girl. Mississippi Challenge received the Christopher Award in 1993. In 1987, Walter won the Coretta Scott King Award for *Justin and the Best Biscuits in the World*. She received Coretta Scott King Honorable Mentions for *Because We Are* in 1984 and *Trouble's Child* in 1986. *Because We Are* and *Brother to the Wind* both won *Parents' Choice* awards in 1984 and 1985, respectively. Walter's *Ty's One-Man Band* was the runner-up for the Irma Simonton Black Award in 1981.

AUTHOR'S COMMENTARY

Mildred Pitts Walter

SOURCE: "Social Responsibility," in *The Horn Book Magazine,* Vol. LXVII, No. 1, January-February, 1991, pp. 50-1.

When I think of social responsibility, I think of action for balance within our world. I believe that art, both visual and literary, can be useful in developing in individuals values and traits that are necessary for social responsibility. We cannot remain innocent and become socially responsible. Therefore, we must have memory. Memory is necessary for first assumptions. Memory is necessary for thoughtfulness and for self-awareness. And to be socially responsible, we must also be able to choose, have courage, and accept change.

Visual and literary images created within the experiences of a people will ring true and invoke memory. I like to think that the images I create will make all young people thoughtful and African Americans aware of themselves as well. In *Justin and the Best Biscuits in the World,* I try to show boys and girls, between the ages of eight and ten, that they are less likely to be frustrated if they know their history and accept the values that exist within their families. Consideration of others and self-knowledge are both necessary if they are to act to make their world a better place; not just for themselves, but for all living things.

The ability to choose puts human beings in control of their actions. Implied in choice is that the action taken is best, and that all other options are overruled. We cannot knowingly choose what is not good for us. The ability to pursue a course, whether it is a popular one or not, is measured in courage. The greater the courage, the greater the possibility we will act for change.

I build my characters around the dynamics of choice, courage, and change. My characters all have to make difficult choices. Martha, in *Trouble's Child,* and Sophia, in *The Girl on the Outside,* in different times and environments have to choose between remaining safely in places that provide little growth or moving outside their small worlds to full development.

Often my characters are more strong-willed than the people they symbolize. They are all, in some sense, struggling against authority—maybe someday I will find a character who struggles in accommodation with authority. I believe my characters have those values and traits which make them capable of attacking problems that require extraordinary courage. They accept the risk of putting themselves in the ranks of the few who struggle to make changes for what they believe to be the ultimate good.

I hope that young people who come in contact with these characters will find friends who will help them increase their courage to act for change; and that they, like their new-found friends, will choose their causes with care. May they understand that we are not what we say. We are what we do.

Darwin L. Henderson and Consuelo W. Harris

SOURCE: "Profile: Choice, Courage, and Change Yield Character: An Interview with Mildred Pitts Walter," in *Language Arts,* Vol. 69, No. 7, November, 1992, pp. 544-49.

Darwin L. Henderson and Consuelo W. Harris: How did you get started as a writer?

Mildred Pitts Walter: I was a kindergarten teacher, and there were few books for or about African American children. I thought it would be nice if there were more books which reflected African American experiences. I contacted a publishing company and asked why they did not publish some children's books for black children, and they replied, "Why don't you write them?" I felt I couldn't write children's books; in fact, I felt I couldn't write anything that was publishable. Finally, I wrote *Lillie of Watts Takes a Giant Step,* which Doubleday published; but after that, I was not successful and I knew I had to learn how to write.

DLH & CWH: How, then, would you describe your development as a writer?

MPW: I would describe my development as rather slow. I didn't want to write or believe I could develop that kind of art. I never felt that I had that kind of talent. Before I wrote children's books, I wrote book reviews for the *Los Angeles Times.* The book review editor for the *Times,* Robert Kursch, asked me to be guest editor when he was away. I refused because I didn't think I could do it. He insisted, citing my ability to write reviews. As a writer for the *Times,* I decided I wasn't going to be critical of other writers until I knew I could write well. I joined the Watts Writers' Group and a writers' group at a Unitarian church in Los Angeles. After that, I began to become a little more confident in my ability to write. Through the process of critiquing, I felt the other writers were helping me to hone my art. They were able to show me areas in my writing that were not clear. I would rewrite and rework a story based on other writers' comments. Being in a writers' group helped me gain more self-confidence in writing. However, the publishers thought my manuscripts were not good; and finally I went to New York and was introduced to Barbara Lalicki, an editor at Scholastic. Scholastic's Sprint Books published *The Liquid Trap* which they thought had just enough action and suspense. It was well-received, is still in print, and the photography in the book won an award. With Barbara, I found an editor who liked my work. My development as a writer has been a very long process.

DLH & CWH: Various artists and writers use differing techniques to capture the essence of the spirit of the child. Where do you get your sense of the child and childhood?

MPW: I get my sense of child and childhood from the kindergarten and elementary school children I have taught and the young adults in colleges and universities I've worked with.

DH & CH: How has your teaching experience influenced your writing? Are any of the characters in your books children or young adults you've taught?

MPW: Not really. They are all children I have taught, but not specific children. I never taught high school, but in the book *Because We Are* are the high school students with whom I worked. I worked with students at the high schools when they were suspended and were involved in demonstrations. I got a sense of their growth and development and their courage to speak out. The incident in *Because We Are* where the teacher threw the books on the floor is real. I worked with teachers and students who were facing all kinds of problems. Observing children in my kindergarten classes gave me a sense of the strength of our children. I remember a little girl who was very talkative, and I asked her why she couldn't be more like a lady. She looked at me and said, "Because I don't know no ladies." Little expressions like that made me aware that here are children who have a lot going for them if others would just listen and learn from them. She grew up to be a very fine lady. She was the queen of the Watts Parade one year. I learned from her. I didn't put her down. I never asked her that again. She didn't know any ladies, and ladies meant something altogether different to her.

DLH & CWH: In your books the protagonists all seem to learn something from their personal encounters. Cultural and adolescent lessons of life, perhaps. Mildred Pitts Walter, you are still teaching! Why? What children are you trying to teach, and what do you hope they will learn?

MPW: I want to think that my work is art, and I want to believe that I'm writing fiction that develops characters who appear real and bring children a sense of who they are. So, I write for all children. I hope that African American children who read my books will identify with the characters—see themselves living in the books and become aware of who they are. I hope the work will

move them beyond all of the problems they may be facing, knowing that they are worthy human beings. White children, I hope, will become aware of African American people and understand that differences can be good, can be all right. I want them to know we don't all have to be the same. Equal doesn't have to mean sameness. Differences can make for a more interesting encounter.

DLH & CWH: If you were teaching in a classroom of your own today, how would you use your books?

MPW: I would certainly use them to bring a sense of self to children. I would want to show children that they are from a people who always will have strong families, that families work together, and that even if they don't have a traditional family, they can still have a loving family relationship. If I were a teacher educator, I think I would use my books to show that African Americans are a strong and beautiful people and that we have a culture that is strong. Our families are intact even though they may not seem to be typical American families.

The problems that we face are those which grow out of lack of opportunities, lack of respect, and sometimes because of how we accept what others believe us to be. I would use *Have a Happy . . .* to illustrate that we have always had a sense of faith and a belief in our families, although it may not appear that way from the outside. Inside, however, there is always a struggle.

DLH & CWH: As a writer, what are you trying to communicate?

MPW: As a writer, I think of my readers as people who have to make choices. I think of my characters as people who have to make choices, too, and once they have made those choices, they have to have some courage to stand by the choices they have made. If that choice is good, they have to have the courage to say that; but if the choice is not good, then they take another route. If they stand by their choice with courage, then they are more likely to change. I see young people needing to have characters who have courage, who stand by their choices and make the changes necessary to lead productive lives. This is always the process in which I am writing, that is, working with choice, courage, and change in my characters.

DLH & CWH: You are widely traveled. What do you bring from your journeys to Africa, China, Great Britain, and Haiti that you share with children through your books?

MPW: *Brother to the Wind* very definitely came from Africa. When I was in Africa, I spoke to people who talked about the snake being the sacred animal and how at one time people believed that animals and mankind were equal in the sense of oneness with the universe. I believe that the book is about that very thing. *Because We Are* comes from the African proverb, "Because we are, I am." I tried to show that when we are all together, we are all one; and if one is not safe, then we are all not safe. The young people in the book were discriminated against, and all of them were victims. They could only solve the problem by banding together and solving it themselves. So, the theme from the African proverb is that together we are much stronger than we are separate.

DLH & CWH: Many teachers have stated that they cannot find appropriate titles reflecting African American and other parallel American cultures. What would you say to editors and publishers about seeking and developing writers whose works explore these cultures?

MPW: I've always said to publishers that there is a market for this kind of literature, that there are writers who, if given an opportunity, can develop and publish good work. Teachers, editors, and publishers have to understand that they have to take us (African Americans) from where we are. They have to respect the kind of writing we do and the kind of illustrations we do. I would like the publishers to hire black editors who can read manuscripts from an African American perspective to determine whether they are good books. The bottom line for publishers is profit. I respect that, but there is a market for these books now. There needs to be a willingness to accept books that reflect a positive image of the African American culture and other cultures as well. African American life is not all ghetto and drugs. Good fiction can reflect the true African American mind and spirit. We can have this reflection if young writers are given a chance to be published.

DLH & CWH: One element in some books that presents a barrier for many readers is the language patterns, that is, dialect. What can you recommend to readers who have difficulty with the language patterns of the characters in **Trouble's Child***?*

MPW: Most people think that there is good language and bad language. No such thing. If one can communicate in a language, that's all that is necessary. Dialect and accents would not become so painful if we understood what we were saying to one another. If we are communicating all that's been demanded and can get that across, then there is no problem. I notice that when I read from **Trouble's Child,** the audience understands very well what I'm saying, and they get the power of the words. There are some things you just can't say powerfully unless you say them in dialect. We need to prepare American people to believe that standard English is not the only language that is beautiful. I would recommend that readers or teachers who are having difficulty with the dialect encourage people who are familiar with the dialect to read to them. Then listen to the dialect to hear its beauty and rhythm and then proceed to understand it. If people would take the time to look at the word, they could read that word; and if they practice, they could learn to sound it the same way it's meant to be and see how beautiful it is.

DLH & CWH: How much of **Trouble's Child** *came from your Louisiana background? Are the characters drawn from real people and their life experiences?*

MPW: The characters are drawn from many people I have known, but not specific people. I tried very hard not to draw from specific people, but to create new characters. I do get ideas from specific people or situations, however. **My Mama Needs Me** is definitely based on my neighbor having a baby, but the story is very different. Her son never did any of the things that Jason did in the story. The characters in **Trouble's Child** have been isolated and have a culture all their own. You will notice that there are no Caucasian characters. There are some mulattos, but no Caucasians because I wanted this to be symbolic of black people isolated on an island, doing the things we usually do in terms of disciplining each other—harshly sometimes, yet loving and allowing growth in spite of ourselves. We really do what we have to do in spite of the obstacles we face, and that's what **Trouble's Child** is about.

DLH & CWH: Why did you choose to include the superstition and ritual aspects of **Trouble's Child** *when some might consider its outmoded practices symbolic of a more primitive, isolated culture?*

MPW: These are not outmoded things; these are aspects of culture which have been disrespected because they have been considered primitive. Now science is looking to Africa, the Native American cultures, and China for healing techniques and practices—these so-called primitive ways of healing. I want children to know that the spirit is as powerful as the mind, and if you combine the two, whatever you need is there. The healing power is there.

DLH & CWH: In **Justin and the Best Biscuits in the World,** *you write about a special relationship between a 10-year-old boy and his grandfather. Many books feature grandparents as key figures in children's stories; however, Justin's grandfather is a formative person in Justin's life. Why did you choose this combination?*

MPW: I think we need to respect the idea that our elders have a lot to teach us. We should respect and love them. I wanted to show the love and the bonding that Justin had with his grandfather that so many children have had with their own grandmothers and grandfathers. Grandparents play a great role in the lives of children in every culture. In this society we have forgotten the importance of the bonding. For example, I taught my grandson how to work, how to make his bed; and we have a terrific bond. I felt that a boy should see this in a grandfather. Those characters really did achieve that special bond in **Justin and the Best Biscuits in the World.** There was one section that was very personal—when Grandpa said to Justin, "When you were born, I cried." That happened to me when I first saw my grandson. I couldn't help but cry because I knew my husband, if he were alive, would have been so proud of this baby. I hadn't intended to put that in the book, but it just happened.

DLH & CWH: **Ty's One Man Band** *is so evocative of a special time and place, full of rhythm and lyricism. Was it difficult to capture so much action and music in this relatively brief story?*

MPW: Yes, it was very difficult and almost impossible to do. I wrote that story thinking of Ty as a hero. He was pretty brave to go out into that swamp and see that strange man with that strange leg and talk to him and bring him back into the community. I was criticized for that. Some critics said you don't encourage children to talk to strangers. Ty is a hero and human, and Andro is human. That was the main point of *Ty's One Man Band*—the trusting relationship. The rhythm and movement of the book was another part, but I wanted to show what African American people were about. That is, even when we don't know one another, we can have faith and trust in each other. I expect that black people still realize this aspect of the book because they know it as their experience. I hope that others will recognize it and understand that it can be their experience, too. That is to say, develop a trusting relationship with another for whatever the purpose, just as Ty did with Andro.

DLH & CWH: What in your background compels you to develop the theme of self-pride in the variety of ways found throughout your work?

MPW: In the small town where I grew up, it was instilled in me that it's not how one looks, necessarily, but how one acts that is important. My mother taught me to be proud of myself. Although she always told me I was beautiful, I didn't believe it a lot of times. I thought there were people far more beautiful than myself. So, because of that, I knew that I was as big as the biggest person in my race, that I must build myself on those big shoulders and be free. For me, that's what freedom is— it's acting as though you are free. I wasn't taught that in those words; but by the way my mother walked, I knew she was a free woman. She instilled in me that I was a good person. I want my work to reflect characters who have come from a long line of people who have worked hard to do for their own what has to be done as they strive to become good people. I also want to reflect the care and support I remember having as I grew up in that small town.

DLH & CWH: Do you conscientiously choose a particular style to convey a message, or is the style a natural component of the story?

MPW: I've set out to show characters solving problems and telling stories. I think style is a very natural component of the way the characters tell their stories. I don't want to convey a message; but if there is one, I hope it's subtle, and the reader isn't offended. If there is a message, I prefer the reader to comprehend it through the characters, rather than my telling.

DLH & CWH: Your books include fantasy, historical fiction, picture books, and contemporary realistic fiction. These varied styles are quite accessible to children. Have you considered poetry?

MPW: I think poetry is the hardest form of writing there is. Every word is so important, and I just don't have

that kind of discipline to insure that every word has specific meaning to that line. I think writing poetry is the most difficult, then the writing of plays, then the writing of picture books. Poetry is the hardest because it is the shortest, and you are required to say so much. Writing plays is difficult because you have to capture moments. Often you have to enhance that moment—tell the whole background of that moment, and that's difficult. The picture book is very similar to that. In a picture book you're in the present. You can't always portray yesterday and tomorrow. Writing fiction is very different. I can write descriptions and dialogue together, and that's easier for me.

DLH & CWH: Mrs. Walter, your work is characterized by readability, accessibility, a sense of warmth, and positive regard for young people—evidenced by the fact that your books have been awarded so many honors. Has such recognition helped to increase their availability?

MPW: The publishers don't make my books as available as they should. People call me to say that they have a hard time getting my books because they are always out of print or out of stock. *Brother to the Wind* is only in a library edition now, and it's a very popular book. I have gone to schools and found that they couldn't get any of my books from the publishers. I don't know why that is or if it's true for other writers.

DLH & CWH: Have any of your books been translated into other languages?

MPW: Yes, just one. *My Mama Needs Me* has been translated into French and appears in a magazine in France. *Two and Too Much* is being published in England. However, publishers felt that Gina looked too old for 2 years old in the original illustrations. They felt there were certain things that a 2-year-old wouldn't do physically, and I agreed with them. They want to change the title, but we haven't settled that.

DLH & CWH: What about your latest book?

MPW: It's titled *The Mississippi Challenge* and is about the Mississippi Democratic Freedom Party. I'd like the junior high audience to know that the Mississippi Democratic Freedom Party didn't just happen. It was an outgrowth of slave revolts and the refusal of the American people to make the 14th and 15th amendments to the Constitution active. Because those laws were not obeyed, we had to make more laws. The growth of the Mississippi Democratic Freedom Party was also caused by fear of John Brown. I want them to know that John Brown was not alone. There were five black men with him on the raid. Lincoln didn't really free the African American people. African Americans have always been part of that history. This audience doesn't know about the participation of blacks before 1960. I want them to know that this history is not a lie, that it's people, those amendments to the constitution, and the people's unwillingness to obey the laws that causes history to keep repeating itself.

TITLE COMMENTARY

📖 *JUSTIN AND THE BEST BISCUITS IN THE WORLD* (1986)

Heather Vogel Frederick

SOURCE: A review of *Justin and the Best Biscuits in the World,* in *Christian Science Monitor,* February 21, 1990, p. 13.

Children who have graduated to chapter books ("and boys especially," says [children's librarian Annie Lee] Carroll), will enjoy Mildred Pitts Walter's *Justin and the Best Biscuits in the World,* a 1987 Coretta Scott King award-winner about a young boy who's feeling resentful about being asked to pitch in around the house. A visit to the family homestead, a Missouri ranch where his grandfather lives alone and fends for himself, soon cures that. Walter has included intriguing background on black cowboys, as well as the black migration West after emancipation.

📖 *MARIAH LOVES ROCK* (1988)

Kirkus Reviews

SOURCE: A review of *Mariah Loves Rock,* in *Kirkus Reviews,* Vol. LVI, No. 13, July 1, 1988, pp. 979-80.

From a Coretta Scott King Award winner, a portrait of a warm, close-knit family during the weeks before Denise, Dad's daughter from his first marriage, comes to live with them.

Concerned because she senses a problem that her parents are reluctant to discuss, 11-year-old Mariah dislikes the idea of any change in her happy family; she worries about the financial pressure of an added person (at first her parents suggest this as a reason not to go to the concert given by Mariah's favorite rock star, but in the end she chooses to give up a promised birthday present and is able to go); and she worries about making room for Denise either in her precious bedroom (cluttered with rock memorabilia) or in older sister Lynn's (tasteful and tidy). But even though she and Lynn squabble, Mariah begins to realize how kind and supportive Lynn really is; when Denise arrives (on the next to last page), she seems to be a lot like Lynn.

Walter tells her realistic story lightly, but with precision: her characters are fully realized, their relationships believable. This is a family in which kids are allowed to speak their minds, but the parents' ultimate authority is gracefully accepted. The veiled problem—Mom's jealousy, of which she is not proud—is sensitively handled.

Publishers Weekly

SOURCE: A review of *Mariah Loves Rock,* in *Publishers Weekly,* Vol. 234, No. 5, July 29, 1988, p. 234.

Mariah, 11, has always felt close to her family. She loves her tall, handsome father, her energetic mother and slightly weird sister Lynn. Her number-one love, however, is Sheik Bashara, a dazzling rock star. So when Mariah learns that Sheik Bashara will be performing in her town, she is ecstatic. The problem? Mariah's stepsister Denise, whom she refers to as "Daddy's daughter," instead of "my sister," is coming to live with them and money is a little tight. But Mariah is upset not only because of the concert, but also because she doesn't want to share her father with her stepsister. Walter (*Justin and the Best Biscuits in the World*) has taken an unusual approach in this sensitive novel. She deals with the tensions created within Mariah's family before the arrival of Denise, rather than focusing on the adjustments that will take place after she has arrived. A warm, thought-provoking book.

Robert Strang

SOURCE: A review of *Mariah Loves Rock,* in *Bulletin of the Center for Children's Books,* Vol. 42, No. 2, October, 1988, p. 57.

Mariah loves Sheik, anyway, adorning her bedroom and person with images of her favorite pop star. Sophisticated older sister Lynn prefers reggae, and, much to Mariah's embarrassment, shops in thrift stores for her new-wave outfits. The two girls also disagree on something more essential: their father's daughter by a previous relationship is coming to live with them, and while Lynn thinks it might be fun to have an older sister, Mariah is jealous. "'She's not our sister,' Mariah said with quiet force. 'She's Daddy's daughter.'" The up-and-down sibling tensions are convincingly portrayed, as is Mariah's mother's own ambivalence towards her husband's daughter. The writing is sometimes awkward and choppy, but the story of a young black girl's celebrity crush (yes, she meets him) has enough appeal to carry readers through some abrupt transitions.

Elaine Fort Weischedel

SOURCE: A review of *Mariah Loves Rock,* in *School Library Journal,* Vol. 35, No. 4, December, 1988, p. 113.

There's a lot going on in eleven-year-old Mariah's life. She's graduating from elementary school, worshipping rock star Sheik Bashara, coping with a "weird" older sister, worrying about the arrival of an older half-sister, dealing with some shifting loyalties among her friends, and trying to get to a rock concert. The plot moves along so quickly, with descriptive passages kept brief, and so many things are going on simultaneously that it is often hard to keep track of what's happening. Individual incidents often seem unfinished, and characters who are arguing in one scene are being supportive in the next, and at odds again a sentence later. While the writing is superficially similar to Walter's style in her award-winning *Justin and the Best Biscuits in the World,* this lacks the continuity and focus of that earlier work, and as a result it fails to satisfy.

📖 *HAVE A HAPPY . . .*   (1989)

Kirkus Reviews

SOURCE: A review of *Have a Happy . . . ,* in *Kirkus Reviews,* Vol. LVII, No. 14, August 1, 1989, p. 1170.

From a favorite author (Coretta Scott King Award for *Justin and the Best Biscuits in the World,* 1986), a much-needed story centering on the celebration of Kwanzaa, the seven-day celebration of the African-American heritage that extends from December 26 to New Year's.

Chris Dodd's 11th birthday is overshadowed not only by falling on Christmas Day but by his family's concern over his father's lengthy unemployment (after being laid off by an electronics firm). At this difficult time, the extended family is a source of comfort—especially Uncle Ronald, a high school teacher; his infectious enthusiasm for celebrating Kwanzaa sustains Chris—and eventually helps the whole family work toward solutions of their problems.

Plot is less important here than spirit, atmosphere, and characterization: Walter realistically portrays the Dodds' responses to their troubles, and neatly integrates the seven values of Kwanzaa into the way Chris learns to cope more constructively with their help—thus combining the values' relevance to daily living with an entertaining, uplifting story. A Swahili glossary listing the principles and symbols of Kwanzaa is included. A fine, useful book.

Julie Corsaro

SOURCE: A review of *Have a Happy . . . ,* in *Booklist,* Vol. 86, No. 1, September 1, 1989, p. 82.

Kwanzaa, an Afro-American cultural holiday celebrated the week after Christmas, is the backdrop for an appealing story that challenges some of the negative stereotypes often associated with struggling black families. Despite his father's lengthy unemployment and mounting family tensions, Chris, who is about to turn 11 on December 25, desperately wants a bicycle. In order to grant his wish, his supportive, extended clan joins forces. Chris uses his bike for a newspaper route, a situation that also leads to a job for his dad. Walter's writing is uneven, and she doesn't prepare the reader for the sudden emergence of racism. On the other hand, her portrayal of a child's concerns and emotions is strong, and this will be a welcome addition to books on the other December holidays.

Lois F. Anderson

SOURCE: A review of *Have a Happy . . . ,* in *The Horn Book Magazine,* Vol. LXV, No. 6, November-December, 1989, p. 754.

Because his father is out of work, eleven-year-old Chris wonders what he has to celebrate on his birthday, which falls on Christmas day. But on December 26th he and his family begin to celebrate with his uncle the African-American holiday of Kwanzaa. Chris and his family are able to find comfort and meaning in the seven principles of Kwanzaa: faith, self-determination, creativity, purpose, cooperative economics, collective work and responsibility, and unity. There is a positive outcome for both father and son, for they both find jobs with a newspaper delivery service. The author has presented a realistic picture of a warm, nurturing family situation and has made an excellent contribution to our understanding of Kwanzaa. This book, which should take its place on the shelf with other December holiday books, has been enhanced by a useful glossary that clarifies Swahili words appearing in the text.

Zena Sutherland

SOURCE: A review of *Have a Happy . . . ,* in *Bulletin of the Center for Children's Books,* Vol. 43, No. 4, December, 1989, p. 99.

In a pleasant story about a black family, Chris hopes to get a bicycle for his eleventh Christmas/birthday, but there seems little hope, since his father has been out of work for over a year. Because of a large and supportive extended family, the help of friends, and his own industry, Chris has a happy birthday, a merry Christmas, and a wonderful Kwanzaa. This is a book that has warmth, strong ethical concepts, and a satisfying ending, but it is weakened by stilted writing (due in part to a variance in depicting speech patterns) and in part to the obtrusively informative dialogue and exposition about Kwanzaa, which is like a lesson inserted in the narrative.

📖 *TWO AND TOO MUCH* (1990)

Denise Wilms

SOURCE: A review of *Two and Too Much,* in *Booklist,* Vol. 86, No. 14, March 15, 1990, p. 1460.

While she cleans house, Mama asks Brandon to look after his two-year-old sister, Gina—a difficult job. No matter what Brandon does to amuse her, it seems like only a short while before Gina is busy with something else, usually trouble. Inevitably, there are tears, but Brandon perseveres and things calm down—until suddenly Gina disappears. A frantic Brandon calls his mother, and the two search everywhere, finally discovering Gina asleep on the floor between her bed and the wall. Brandon is relieved, not to mention happy, that his job is finished for the time being. "She's only two, but she is too much," he says. Walter and [Pat] Cummings, who collaborated on *My Mama Needs Me* (about another black family) provide this slice-of-life vignette that will strike a sympathetic chord with kids in the same boat as Brandon. But there's no mistaking the fondness blended in with the frustrations; it's that emotional mix that makes the story appealing and credible.

Christine Behrmann

SOURCE: A review of *Two and Too Much*, in *School Library Journal*, Vol. 36, No. 4, April, 1990, p. 100.

Walter and Cummings use precise characterization and sharp attention to detail to bring freshness to the familiar situation of a young black boy who has to deal with a younger sister in the throes of the terrible twos. Brandon agrees to help his mother by watching Gina, although he'd rather do anything else—even vacuum. It's truly a tough job—she runs off to try on her mother's make-up, knocks over his toy garage, and spills her milk. After lunch, he can't find her. His anger dissipates into fear as he and his mother search the house and, when they find her napping on the floor beside her bed, his relief helps him to put his problems with Gina into perspective. What lifts this depiction of an everyday situation out of the commonplace is the immediacy with which Walter and Cummings convey Brandon's many conflicting emotions—pride, selfishness, reluctant amusement, anger, worry, love—in both language and image. Walter allows Brandon's feelings to flow out of each situation, expressing them with concrete accuracy. . . . It's a conventional predicament, one that many children will recognize, and Cummings and Walter skillfully portray its many dimensions.

Robert Strang

SOURCE: A review of *Two and Too Much*, in *Bulletin of the Center for Children's Books*, Vol. 43, No. 9, May, 1990, p. 229.

Seven-year-old Brandon rapidly regrets his generous offer to look after two-year-old Gina so that their mother can prepare for a party. Gina, whose favorite word is "no," gets into Mama's makeup ("I pretty?"), knocks down Brandon's toy garage, and pours milk into the jelly. All this appealing mayhem is brightly captured in Cummings' day-glowing, firmly lined illustrations that give graphic weight to the fuzz exploding from the vacuum cleaner, pink powder liberally scattered, and other assorted solids and liquids that fly through the air. Both pictures and

text capture family devotion as well as disaster. Although this isn't a new story, it's an ever-appealing one, and kids will find this black family a pleasure to know.

📖 *MARIAH KEEPS COOL* (1990)

Denise Wilms

SOURCE: A review of *Mariah Keeps Cool*, in *Booklist*, Vol. 86, No. 16, April 15, 1990, p. 1636.

In this sequel to *Mariah Loves Rock*, Mariah's half sister, Denise, has moved in, and though everyone welcomes her, she seems determined to be uncooperative and distant. But though Denise is a thorn in her side, Mariah has other, more positive things on her mind, namely the swim meet she and her friends are training hard for and a surprise party she wants to throw for her older sister, Lynn. The story plays out comfortably. Little by little, Mariah gains some understanding of Denise and begins to iron out the problems between them, Lynn's party is a smash, and in the long-awaited swim meet Mariah beats out her chief opponent. The strong portrayal of a warm, close-knit family is a real virtue, and Mariah's character will have broad appeal. A worthy follow-up that will please fans of the first Mariah story.

Marie Orlando

SOURCE: A review of *Mariah Keeps Cool*, in *School Library Journal*, Vol. 36, No. 6, June, 1990, p. 127.

In this sequel to *Mariah Loves Rock*, the 11-year-old black heroine begins her summer facing several challenges. First, she plans to enter an all-city swim meet never before attempted by children from their local recreation center. Then, her beloved older sister Lynn is acting mysteriously, and Mariah wants to know why. Finally, her 16-year-old half-sister Denise has come to live with the Metcalfs, and her disdain of rules and order is disrupting the family harmony. Hard work yields swim team success in the face of prejudice by some of the other participants, and Mariah discovers that Lynn is secretly volunteering at a homeless shelter. Overcoming her third challenge, handling her jealousy of her father's attention to Denise and coming to an understanding of her half-sister's behavior, requires all the maturity Mariah can muster. While the characters, setting, and dialogue ring true, the simplistic handling of a shuffled-around half-sister who feels courtesy and discipline cramp her style is less than satisfying. At the very least, one would expect the assimilation of a troubled teenager into a family would require tremendous parental effort, and none is in evidence. The father travels a lot and, when home, is not particularly sensitive to the family dynamics; the stepmother's resentment of the intruder is below the surface but still there. Young readers, however, will probably not tune into these nuances.

Frances Bradburn

SOURCE: A review of *Mariah Keeps Cool,* in *Wilson Library Bulletin,* Vol. 64, No. 10, June, 1990, pp. 116-17.

[The] need for acceptance and a real home is particularly well crafted in **Mariah Keeps Cool** by Mildred Pitts Walter. Mariah is the youngest in a family of four: her mother, father, older sister, Lynn—and then of five, when stepsister Denise arrives. In this and an earlier work, **Mariah Loves Rock,** the reader sees Mariah and the rest of the family deal with Denise's anticipated arrival and subsequent integration into the family. The strong bonds that the family of four has developed over the years are threatened as Denise fights the resentment she feels in being shuffled from one house to another because her mother can no longer control her. While Walter honestly portrays the problems of blended families, she is careful to do so with respect and understanding for all involved. The understanding and support the family gives each other and especially Denise are at the core of these light-hearted books. Young middle readers will truly like Mariah and her family.

📖 *MISSISSIPPI CHALLENGE* (1992)

Publishers Weekly

SOURCE: A review of *Mississippi Challenge,* in *Publishers Weekly,* Vol. 239, No. 41, September 14, 1992, p. 127.

Walter here painstakingly documents the courageous struggle of African Americans in Mississippi to overcome pervasive racism and to win their economic and political rights. The author notes that the influx of white cotton farmers into the state in the early 19th century led to the enslavement of four million African Americans by 1860. After the Civil War, former slaveholders' rise to power in Congress "created a new kind of bondage for African-American citizens." Walter describes the bleak era of Reconstruction and the shocking, widespread mob lynchings that occurred during the first half of this century. She then focuses on a number of groups—chief among them the Student Nonviolent Coordinating Committee and the Mississippi Freedom Democratic Party—that worked to end the violence and overturn the state's racist voting practices. Packed with statistics and quotes from historians, politicians and other observers, Walter's heavily footnoted text may prove somewhat slow going for the general reader, but she has uncovered much eye-opening material.

Kirkus Reviews

SOURCE: A review of *Mississippi Challenge,* in *Kirkus Reviews,* Vol. LX, No. 19, October 1, 1992, p. 1262.

A compelling account of the voting-rights struggles of the African-Americans of Mississippi, presenting comprehensive information (including "Freedom Summer") and ending somewhat abruptly in the mid-60's. Unlike most histories of civil-rights movements, this clearly brings forth the importance of African-Americans in leadership roles: resisting slavery, holding political office during Reconstruction, leading civil-rights projects of the 60's. Emphasizing the economic side of oppression, Walter carefully characterizes the state as "not a monolith . . . gentleness and violence stand side by side." She effectively portrays the electric atmosphere as young people were galvanized to stand up against centuries of social pressure to demand their rights. Unfortunately (like the movement?), the story peters out after the Freedom Democratic Party's stand at the 1964 Democratic Convention and the subsequent challenge to a white congressman; Walter says their victory consisted of proving the power of protest based on morals. A sobering message about the real cost of democracy.

Betsy Hearne

SOURCE: A review of *Mississippi Challenge,* in *Bulletin of the Center for Children's Books,* Vol. 46, No. 5, January, 1993, p. 159.

Because Walter's focus on the role that African-Americans have played in Mississippi is sharp and unremitting, and because the subject itself is dramatic and moving, this becomes a history book that will make readers think carefully about the democratic process as a whole. From the 1860s to the 1960s, Mississippi—of all the southern states—was the scene of the cruelest economic, political, and physical oppression of African-Americans, who had technically been freed from slavery but were in fact maintained almost inescapably in servitude. Walter describes the development of that situation, letting carefully footnoted facts speak for themselves without sensationalizing or overstating them. Her attention to detail may bog down some readers, but the action is, sadly, nonstop and violent; the black cast, though often anonymous, is just as often heroic. This is not easy to read and was probably not easy to write, but it represents a stern and important synthesis.

Sylvia V. Meisner

SOURCE: A review of *Mississippi Challenge,* in *School Library Journal,* Vol. 39, No. 1, January, 1993, pp. 140-41.

Walter outlines the history of blacks in Mississippi from prior to the Civil War through the formation of the Mississippi Freedom Democratic Party and the Mississippi Challenge in the mid-1960s. And a dire history it is. Treatment of slaves in Mississippi, according to the author, was so cruel that owners in other states controlled their bondmen and women by threatening to send them there. In unbiased language, the author indicates how the struggle for the ballot was adversely affected by such factors as sharecropping, the Understanding Clause, poll taxes, and the fear generated by the rise of the Klan and other hate groups. Well organized and clearly and interestingly written, this book documents the struggle of blacks in just one state.

Dorothy M. Broderick

SOURCE: A review of *Mississippi Challenge,* in *Voice of Youth Advocates,* Vol. 16, No. 1, April, 1993, p. 60.

Mississippi Challenge ought to have been an important book. The history of the treatment of slaves prior to the Civil War, the confusion that was rampant by both North and South during the war, and the heartbreaking betrayal of the freedmen in the name of political expediency following the war are all topics today's citizen should be aware of in order to understand the current tension in race relations in the United States.

Most of all, citizens, young and old alike, need to understand the significance of the 1964 Mississippi Freedom Democratic Party challenge to the national Democratic Party at its nominating convention. While the MFDP lost that fight, it eventually won the war, and nothing in U. S. politics has been quite the same since.

There are so many problems with Walter's attempt to tell this story that it is difficult to know where to begin. First, the book's structure does not lend itself to clarity. It bounces around from topic to topic, assuming too much in some places, such as skipping entirely the assassination of Abraham Lincoln. It assumes we *know* why Andrew Johnson was such a problem.

There are factual problems with the book. It is difficult to know how many of these are the result of sloppy proofreading and how many are the result of inadequate research. While none of the quotations are seriously distorted by omissions or the changing of the words, the lack of accuracy is a defect.

However, the real problem with the book is its pedestrian writing style. From beginning to end, the topics covered cry out for outrage. The plodding prose does an injustice to topics that demand writing that soars "on the wings of eagles." The result is a sad execution of a wonderful idea.

Herb Boyd

SOURCE: A review of *Mississippi Challenge,* in *Black Enterprise,* Vol. 23, No. 11, June, 1993, p. 29

No state exemplified the brutal sanctions of racism and discrimination like Mississippi. The deaths of Emmett Till, Medgar Evers and Schwerner, Chaney and Goodman are reminders of just how far bigots would go to protect segregation.

From a brighter point of view there were also such heroes as Bob Moses, James Forman and Fannie Lou Hamer. Both sides of this drama are accurately and poignantly evoked by Mildred Pitts Walter in *Mississippi Challenge.* Walter distills episodes peculiar to Mississippi, capturing the terrorism that threatened black life at every turn.

Walter's multi-voiced narrative flows and builds steadily to a climax with the Mississippi Freedom Democratic Party (MFDP). Chapters on the MFDP are insightful, but the need for a more studied look at the party is clear. Future scholars will use Walter's research as a launch pad to a more thorough survey of Mississippi's backwater.

KWANZAA: A FAMILY AFFAIR (1995)

Denia Hester

SOURCE: A review of *Kwanzaa: A Family Affair,* in *Booklist,* Vol. 92, No. 2, September 15, 1995, p. 173.

Walter has created a family-oriented guide to preparing for and celebrating Kwanzaa that encourages early planning and the sharing of family histories. The principles and symbols are clearly explained, and the directions for making simple gifts are accompanied by adequate line drawings. Walter's enthusiasm for her subject brightens this modest effort.

Jane Marino

SOURCE: A review of *Kwanzaa: A Family Affair,* in *School Library Journal,* Vol. 41, No. 10, October, 1995, p. 43.

The title is descriptive as this is a handbook for parents and children about celebrating the African American harvest festival. The first two chapters define the holiday: its principles, vocabulary, etc. The third chapter takes readers through the seven days, describing what to do and sometimes how to do it. There is also a chapter with crafts; all of them are fairly complex, even though each step is clearly written. A plaster *kinara* (candle holder), woven place mats made from ribbon strips, a book, a flag, and even a quilt can be family projects that will yield products that will last for years to come. Another chapter offers ideas for gifts and recipes. Walter uses the tone of a personal reminiscence to great effect here. She describes the holiday as having been *her* family's experience and invites readers to join her. In the still small but growing genre of books, this one is a worthwhile purchase.

DARKNESS (1995)

Kirkus Reviews

SOURCE: A review of *Darkness*, in *Kirkus Reviews*, Vol. LXIII, No. 20, October 15, 1995, p. 1503.

Walter teams up with newcomer [Marcia] Jameson in a meditation on the positive gifts of the dark. Seeking to counter some of the entrenched negative associations of images of darkness, Walter says, "Some wonderful things happen when there is no light." Over a series of expressive spreads the text and illustrations combine to celebrate the beginnings of life in the womb, the germination of seeds beneath the soil, the discovery of diamonds and other gems in earth's darkest recesses, and more. There are few surprises; all the images are familiar and become opportunities for reassurance. Jameson's strongly gestural brushstrokes in acrylic reinforce the brief text's consciously affirmative tone; the gentle appeal behind the words and art far outweighs the actual presentation.

Ruth K. MacDonald

SOURCE: A review of *Darkness*, in *School Library Journal*, Vol. 41, No. 11, November, 1995, p. 83.

Darkness is not an easy concept to talk about or illustrate, yet this book succeeds in doing both. The prose approaches poetry—blank verse—in its rich evocativeness. The text is descriptive as well as laudatory of darkness, as a condition of the womb and of underground, where living things start; as a condition inside the head, as the source of creativity; as a variation of the weather; and as a normal diurnal pattern. For a book about darkness, this one is unusually light—there are many degrees and varieties of it, and black and deep blue do not predominate. As Walter notes, even shadows have their different depths and shades. The paintings are done in acrylic on canvas, sometimes piled on thick, sometimes streaked so that the texture of the canvas shows through, giving another dimension to darkness, a depth echoed in the text. There is a certain abstract quality to the subject, to the illustration, to the narration, all of which become surprisingly vivid and realistic under the careful hands of author and illustrator.

SECOND DAUGHTER: THE STORY OF A SLAVE GIRL (1996)

Kirkus Reviews

SOURCE: A review of *Second Daughter: The Story of a Slave Girl*, in *Kirkus Reviews*, Vol. LXIII, No. 24, December 15, 1995, p. 1778.

Slavery in the years of the American Revolution, an era of unexpected freedoms against the backdrop of war, by the author of **Darkness.**

Narrator Aissa, whose name means "second daughter," doesn't remember her mother, who died after she was born. She is raised by her older sister, Bett, who is sold when Aissa is five to a new master and his bride. Patient, kindly Bett is trusted to serve the master and his friends as they meet to discuss their work on the new Massachusetts Constitution, which clarifies and strengthens the idea, expressed in the recently formulated Declaration of Independence, that "all men are created equal." Aissa wonders why, if that is so, certain people remain slaves, but Bett stills her questions, afraid to disrupt the status quo. When the mistress, enraged by Aissa's defiance, attempts to strike the younger woman with a heavy, blazing hot shovel, Bett takes the blow and is severely injured. Embittered, Bett decides to sue her owners for freedom with the new constitution as her rationale; the strong courtroom scene will have readers cheering. Based on a real case, this admirable historical novel is unique for the perspective it lends to the Revolution and its profound impact on the lives of all Americans.

Publishers Weekly

SOURCE: A review of *Second Daughter: The Story of a Slave Girl*, in *Publishers Weekly*, Vol. 243, No. 3, January 15, 1996, p. 463.

Walter treats fiction as the handmaiden of history and politics in this fact-based story, drawing from research about Mum Bett, a Massachusetts slave who successfully sued for her freedom shortly after the Revolutionary War. For a narrator Walter chooses Mum Bett's sister, whose name and life story have gone unrecorded. The author gives her the African name Aissa, which means "Second Daughter"; a self-satisfied, capricious mistress; a strong temperament; and an indomitable will to be free. Aissa charts the injustices as she watches her more accommodating older sister, Bett, serve men who spout Revolutionary rhetoric about liberty with no thought to the humans they treat as property. Bett's husband, a free man, is killed fighting in the Revolution, but the pension Bett receives is nowhere near enough to buy their child's freedom. In common with many other heroines reclaimed from oblivion, Bett is also a skilled folk healer. It's a story of perfect political rectitude, but the agenda here is stronger than the narrative—judging from the intriguing historical note at the end of the book, its lessons might have been even more clearly delivered as nonfiction.

Bruce Anne Shook

SOURCE: A review of *Second Daughter: The Story of a Slave Girl*, in *School Library Journal*, Vol. 42, No. 2, February, 1996, p. 115.

In 1781, a slave named Elizabeth Freeman, also known as Mum Bett, successfully sued the Commonwealth of Massachusetts. This historical novel, narrated by her fictional sister Aissa, details their lives and describes eloquently their unquenchable desire for freedom. The slave owner's wife dislikes Aissa intensely; however, Bett is a household favorite. As such, she is often present when visitors talk of events in the colonies and, using the knowledge she has accumulated, she decides to sue for her freedom, charging her owners with cruel treatment. In comparison to the treatment of their counterparts in the South, Bett, Aissa, and their kin are not badly abused. Nonetheless, the narrative includes incidents of beatings, killings, and other atrocities. Walter skillfully depicts major events of the time from a slave's perspective. She clearly shows the American Revolution as a rebellion by white male property owners to protect their own interests. When Bett triumphs in a court of law, her victory is truly an astonishing one. Occasionally, the historical descriptions slow the action somewhat, but Bett and Aissa are three-dimensional characters who should hold readers' interest. Without being sensationalized, the narrative succeeds in exposing the horrors of slavery in this country. A fine piece of historical fiction about a little-known but important woman.

Hazel Rochman

SOURCE: A review of *Second Daughter: The Story of a Slave Girl,* in *Booklist,* Vol. 92, No. 12, February 15, 1996, p. 1009.

The history is dramatic: in 1781 a slave woman, Mum Bett, took her owner to court and won her freedom under the Massachusetts Constitution. Her story is told in the voice of her fictional younger sister, Aissa, who describes the events leading up to that historic trial—what it was like to be a slave, to be sold away from home, to work for someone who saw you only as property, to hide your true self. The plot meanders, and the characterization is thin: through Aissa's eyes, people are pretty much saints or villains, though the author does show that Bett holds on to a strong sense of her inner worth. What readers will respond to are the facts of Bett's life and the bitter truth of the young slave's commentary. For the powerful leaders who are fighting the Revolutionary War and hammering out the Constitution, the sisters are invisible. As the action builds to the climax of the trial, Aissa raises the elemental question: if the great new Constitution says that all men are created equal, does "men" include black men and all women?

Elizabeth Bush

SOURCE: A review of *Second Daughter: The Story of a Slave Girl,* in *Bulletin of the Center for Children's Books,* Vol. 49, No. 9, May, 1996, p. 319.

Elizabeth, or Bett, Freeman, a colonial slave who in 1781 successfully sued for her freedom under Massachusetts law, is provided here with a fictional younger sister Aissa who recounts her own and her famous sister's life in two successive households. Readers gain a tantalizing

glimpse of a slave community still closely bound to African cultures; however, this mingling of cultures and the community's manipulation by white masters is suggested rather than developed. Walter frequently employs stilted dialogues to provide historical background ("When [Bett's father] was not readily sold, the slave merchant used him to translate the languages of the slaves to determine from where the slaves had come," Bett explains to her sister). Likewise, Aissa's melodramatic musings tend to supply more drama than substance ("[They] say I took my time coming and when I finally arrived I screamed loud and long. Did I know that I was being born a slave?"). History and chronology are confusingly handled: it's difficult to fix the ages of the two sisters, and historical characters whom Walter concedes probably never met one another interact here.

Helen Turner

SOURCE: A review of *Second Daughter: The Story of a Slave Girl,* in *Voice of Youth Advocates,* Vol. 19, No. 3, August, 1996, p. 164.

Orphan sisters Elizabeth and Lizzie, and Brom, a slave who is like their older brother, were sold to John Ashley of Massachusetts about 1750. Lizzie tells this story of the degradation and cruelty they experienced and witnessed as slaves in the Ashley household. Lizzie works mainly in the kitchen; and Elizabeth (Bett) serves the hot-tempered Mrs. Ashley, cleans the house and attends to the needs of the frequent visitors. The sisters long for liberty, and try to preserve memories of their family and their African culture.

Lizzie's headstrong temperament and rebellion against the condition of slavery bring her into frequent conflict with Mrs. Ashley. Bett is a buffer and tries to convince Lizzie that freedom can be achieved if they are patient and obedient, attributes which Lizzie views as demeaning and a waste of time. As they go about their errands, the sisters meet other slaves and also blacks who are free. One of the freemen, Josiah Freeman, courts and marries Bett although she must still live at the Ashley estate. Bett's duties enable her to learn of the efforts of Ashley and his friends to write a constitution for Massachusetts. Of particular interest to her are the discussions leading to the statement that "we . . . are equal, free and independent of each other." As the American Revolution begins, the slaves and black freemen are recruited by both sides. Josiah joins the Continental Army even though it means separation from his wife and their infant daughter, Little Bett. It is the last time they will see Josiah and the sad news of his death in battle is devastating to the sisters.

A particularly brutal attack on Lizzie by Mrs. Ashley is prevented when Bett places herself between the two. As a result, Bett is badly burned by the hot coals their mistress intended for Lizzie. This strengthens Bett's resolve to sue for her freedom. She contacts two of the lawyers involved in the Massachusetts Constitution, which is approved by voters in 1780. Joining her in the suit is Brom, who has been working as a herdsman for the Ashleys. Lawyers Sedgwick and Reeve agree to take the case which is heard in August of 1781. Bett's lawyers base their case on the "equal, free and independent" wording in the constitution, but the telling argument is Bett's injured arm, proof of abuse. Brom, Bett and Little Bett win their freedom, and Ashley must pay the cost of the suit plus thirty shillings each to Bett and Brom. Lizzie's freedom and the freedom of all slaves in Massachusetts is now assured because this and other similar suits proved that slavery in Massachusetts is illegal. Bett begins working for Lawyer Sedgwick's family where she is treated well and is much respected for her knowledge of healing. Lizzie reclaims her African name, Aissa, and moves to Boston where she finds work as a housekeeper, content at last now that she is free.

This is a fiction plus fact account of the life of Elizabeth Freeman (1742?-1829). Little is known about her sister, Lizzie, except that she was a slave in the Ashley household. The account of the trial is authentic. The misery and horror of slavery are graphically presented, as is the dilemma facing the framers of the Massachusetts Constitution: who is entitled to enjoy the rights they seek for themselves? References are made to many historical people and events, and the description of the daily lives of the slaves and their owners is vivid. Since little fiction is written about slavery in the northern colonies, this is a welcome book; but it is of special value because it is a well written and engrossing story.

📖 SUITCASE (1999)

Paul Kelsey

SOURCE: A review of *Suitcase*, in *School Library Journal*, Vol. 45, No. 9 September, 1999, p. 230.

An 11-year-old African-American boy struggles to gain self-esteem and to earn his father's love and respect. Xander is tall for his age and his dad expects him to excel at basketball, but the boy's passion in life is for art. Xander's peers, and even his sister, ridicule him because of his height and his clumsiness on the basketball court. However, he works hard to gain mastery over his awkward body, and finally achieves a degree of success as an athlete. In the process, he discovers that his father loves him and supports his artistic endeavors as well. Walter does a splendid job of drawing readers into Xander's mind and heart, and of creating characterization and setting. The plot moves well, and the sports action and the child's personal struggles should sustain the interest of even reluctant readers. The prose success-

fully brings the emotions of the young protagonist to life. The author develops the novel's theme with skill and subtlety, showing that persistence and being true to oneself ultimately brings success.

Kirkus Reviews

SOURCE: A review of *Suitcase*, in *Kirkus Reviews*, Vol. LXVII, No. 20, October 15, 1999, p. 1653.

With feet so large that he's earned the nickname "Suitcase," sixth-grader Alexander—Xander to family and friends—appears unable to play basketball. He doesn't enjoy it as much as he enjoys drawing, and he can't control his body and the ball. Trying hard to please his father, he practices daily, jumping rope and drilling, but the coach, Jeff, recognizes that Xander's talents lay elsewhere. During a routine baseball practice, Xander shows himself to be a superior pitcher; later, by drawing the winning entry in an art contest, Xander impresses his father, who is beginning to recognize his son has talent. Walter has created a story that let's readers see and appreciate Xander's progress; the lesson that everyone has at least one special purpose is familiar, but worth repeating. Those who have been teased will relish Xander's ability to disregard labels and prove the bullies wrong.

Publishers Weekly

A review of *Suitcase*, in *Publishers Weekly*, Vol. 246, No. 48, November 29, 1999, pp. 71-2.

Xander's fellow sixth-graders and his perfect older sister Brandy taunt the artistic 11-year-old by calling him "Suitcase" and "Seemore" because he is a gangly six feet two inches tall and wears a size 13 shoe. But his father's disappointment in a son who loves to draw and is always picked last at basketball stings more than his peers' jabs. With the exception of the likable Xander, the adult characters prove more compelling than the roundup of usual suspects in the elementary school cast. Into this mix, Walter injects two powerful mentors: Mrs. Cloud, the fine arts teacher, and Jeff, the insightful coach who ultimately helps him find his own game. Although Walter maintains a buoyant tone, she also delivers some painful family truths in an authentically offhand way, such as when Xander's mother jokingly tells him that his father "thinks you're lazy and don't want to ruin your long, slender artist's fingers." [Teresa] Flavin's black-and-white drawings softly chronicle Xander's transformation into confidence and ease. Readers will cheer for Xander as he develops his talents, manages to please both his father and himself, and sends his self-doubt packing.

Additional coverage of Walter's life and career is contained in the following sources published by The Gale Group: *Black Writers*, Vol. 2; *Contemporary Authors*, Vol. 138; *Junior DISCovering Authors*; *Major Authors and Illustrators for Children and Young Adults*; and *Something about the Author*, Vol. 69.

CUMULATIVE INDEXES

How to Use This Index

The main reference

Baum, L(yman) Frank 1856–
1919 .... **15**

lists all author entries in this and previous volumes of *Children's Literature Review:*

The cross-references

See also CA 103; 108; DLB 22; JRDA
MAICYA; MTCW; SATA 18; TCLC 7

list all author entries in the following Gale biographical and literary sources:

AAYA = *Authors & Artists for Young Adults*
AITN = *Authors in the News*
BLC = *Black Literature Criticism*
BLCS = *Black Literature Criticism Supplement*
BW = *Black Writers*
CA = *Contemporary Authors*
CAAS = *Contemporary Authors Autobiography Series*
CABS = *Contemporary Authors Bibliographical Series*
CANR = *Contemporary Authors New Revision Series*
CAP = *Contemporary Authors Permanent Series*
CDALB = *Concise Dictionary of American Literary Biography*
CDBLB = *Concise Dictionary of British Literary Biography*
CLC = *Contemporary Literary Criticism*
CMLC = *Classical and Medieval Literature Criticism*
DAB = *DISCovering Authors: British*
DAC = *DISCovering Authors: Canadian*
DAM = *DISCovering Authors: Modules*
      DRAM: *Dramatists Module*; *MST*: *Most-Studied Authors Module*;
      MULT: *Multicultural Authors Module*; *NOV*: *Novelists Module*;
      POET: *Poets Module*; *POP*: *Popular Fiction and Genre Authors Module*
DC = *Drama Criticism*
DLB = *Dictionary of Literary Biography*
DLBD = *Dictionary of Literary Biography Documentary Series*
DLBY = *Dictionary of Literary Biography Yearbook*
HLC = *Hispanic Literature Criticism*
HW = *Hispanic Writers*
JRDA = *Junior DISCovering Authors*
LC = *Literature Criticism from 1400 to 1800*
MAICYA = *Major Authors and Illustrators for Children and Young Adults*
MTCW = *Major 20th-Century Writers*
NCLC = *Nineteenth-Century Literature Criticism*
NNAL = *Native North American Literature*
PC = *Poetry Criticism*
SAAS = *Something about the Author Autobiography Series*
SATA = *Something about the Author*
SSC = *Short Story Criticism*
TCLC = *Twentieth-Century Literary Criticism*
WLC = *World Literature Criticism, 1500 to the Present*
WLCS = *World Literature Criticism Supplement*
YABC = *Yesterday's Authors of Books for Children*

CUMULATIVE INDEX TO AUTHORS

CUMULATIVE INDEX TO NATIONALITIES

Nationality Index

CUMULATIVE INDEX TO TITLES

Title Index

Title Index

Title Index

Title Index

Title Index

Title Index

Title Index

Title Index

Title Index

Title Index

Title Index

Title Index

Title Index

ISBN 0-7876-3226-0

9 780787 632267

90000